THE RAINBOW

A COLLECTION OF STUDIES
IN THE SCIENCE OF RELIGION

STUDIES

IN THE HISTORY OF RELIGIONS

(SUPPLEMENTS TO *NUMEN*)

XXX

THE RAINBOW

A COLLECTION OF STUDIES
IN THE SCIENCE OF RELIGION

LEIDEN
E. J. BRILL
1975

THE RAINBOW

A COLLECTION OF STUDIES
IN THE SCIENCE OF RELIGION

BY

C. J. BLEEKER

Emeritus Professor of the History and the
Phenomenology of Religions
Amsterdam

LEIDEN
E. J. BRILL
1975

ISBN   90 04   04222 9

TO THE MEMORY

OF

MY DEAR WIFE

CONTENTS

PREFACE

Voltaire has said: "Tous les genres sont bons, hors le genre ennuyeux". That is the golden rule not only for works of art, but also for the results of scholarly research. It happens that scientific works, though being granaries of learning, are simply boring.

The present author hopes that this verdict will not be passed on his volume. He himself has never got tired of his religio-historical studies, which he has pursued for half a century. On the contrary, he has constantly had the experience that there is no occupation which kindles the mind and the imagination so much as such investigations.

I hope that this volume will be a witness to my endeavours to penetrate into the secret of true religion and that at the same time it will capture the interest of the reader so that he discovers new religious perspectives and has pleasant reading.

The volume contains articles of various content: treatises on methodology, studies on subjects taken from the Ancient Egyptian religion —the author's special field of research—, sketches of a phenomenological nature and three articles on persons who each in their own way represent striking aspects of religious life. History of religion is often prevented by lack of evidence from describing the religious experiences of the individual. It is hoped that these last studies will remind the reader that in the last analysis personal faith is the subject of religio-historical study.

The author has given all articles the form of a torso, of "das Unvollendete", on purpose. He fully agrees with what his compatriot Prof. dr. L. J. van Holk once wrote on "the value of the incomplete". It surpasses human acuity and mental energy to create work which totally covers the relevant religio-historical facts. Moreover such an undertaking would be pretentious: no scholar is all-knowing. And lastly books which pretend to be exhaustive kill the desire to make inquiries on one's own initiative. A scholarly author should leave room for the thoughts of the reader and should say just enough to kindle his curiosity.

The title of the volume expresses the unshakable conviction of the author that religion in whatever all too human forms it may appear, can ultimately only be understood as a rainbow: it is the connection between heaven and earth, between a superhuman reality and mortal man.

Finally I may extend a word of cordial thanks to my colleagues Alessandro Bausani, Walter H. Caps and Eva Schwarz-Hirschmann who graciously helped me by correcting or translating some articles.

METHODOLOGY AND THE SCIENCE OF RELIGION *

Young people sometimes are under the delusion that world history
starts with their birth. They think that nobody ever has been in love,
has suffered, or has searched for the truth as they have. It is dubious
whether our generation realizes, that it is entering a new epoch and
that the decades of the middle of the twentieth century, which we are
passing, may mean a decisive turn in the history of mankind. For the
mood of a great many of our contemporaries has a pessimistic tinge,
and that not without reason. Everyone, who daily reads his news-
paper, must get the impression that we live in a world in which
morality is rapidly vanishing. After the first World War, O. Spengler
wrote, in German, a voluminous and stirring book, predicting the
decline and the downfall of the western civilization. The atrocities,
committed during the second World War, gave new food to the
pessimism of people who were convinced that humanity is on its
decline. They looked at the future with uneasiness and distress. For in
their fearful expectations they saw the sword of Damocles of a third
World War, fought out by atomic weapons, hanging on a silk thread
above the head of the present generation.

And yet hope has not left the earth. Everybody who is young in
spirit should foster the hope that a new era will dawn. Fortunately he
can do so not only on the strength of his confidence in mankind, but
primarily because there are many signs indicating that the world is
entering a new period of its existence. This will be the epoch in
which the world community becomes a reality. This time is near at
hand. We need the full power of our imagination to realize what
this fact implies. In the past, courageous and adventurous men went
out to discover unknown parts of the earth. The continents were far
away from one another. Idealists dreamt of a future in which the
nations of the earth would harmoniously live together. Today there is
theoretically no longer any *terra incognita.* Thanks to faster and more
modern means of communication the citizens of Russia, of Congo,
of South Vietnam, of China and of many other distant countries have
so to say, become our neighbours, whom we know a bit better and
with whose interests we have to reckon.

---

* Published in Edward J. Jurji, "Religious Pluralism and World Community"
(*Supplements to Numen* XV, 1969).

I

The earth has become smaller and, at the same time, wider. I may feel myself released from the duty of analyzing and describing the forces which unevitably transform the world into a unity, in different respects, economically, politically, culturally. This work has been done ably by several experts in recent publications. Suffice it to state, that, if at present the world community is not an established fact, it will be such a reality in the near future. And not only a reality, but even more, the sole condition of the wellbeing of humanity. There is an austere truth in the well-known slogan: One world or none world.

However, this does not mean, that the art of thinking of the nations will be streamlined. At the moment there are all kind of misunderstandings among the peoples of the five continents. Some of them look at each other with suspicion and hatred. It would be unrealistic not to notice that in the hearts of many people there is a deep-seated ressentiment on account of what they suffered through the brutality of nations that dominated them. One has even to admit that there have been periods in history, i.e. the Middle Ages and in certain decades of the eighteenth and the nineteenth century, in which there prevailed a greater unanimity than is present today. It sometimes looks as if the differences and the antipathies between the ideals and the world conceptions of the nations have, of late, been heightened rather than reduced. However one may expect, that these forms of disharmony will die out, though it will take time before they have totally disappeared.

But even when the various reasons for distrust and ressentiment are removed, there will still remain a great variety of persuasions primarily in the field of religion. This means that within the growing world community we have to reckon with the existence of an extensive religious pluralism, not only at present, but also for the future. The reasons behind this paradoxical fact are twofold: In the first place, all believers are very keen on keeping their special type of faith as their dearest treasure by which they safeguard their personality, their spiritual identity and their religious independency against all tendencies toward the merging of individual man in the masses. Secondly the world religions are still fully alive. Each of them claims to possess absolute truth. They are propagating their ideas and show missionary zeal in a higher degree than in the last century. It is not to be expected that they are willing to give up their independence.

Thus the surmise is that, whether we like it or not, we have to reckon both at present and in the future with the existence of a religious pluralism. This statement implies that, within the framework of this article, two questions can be discarded, though they as such are important and of current interest. These are, first, the question of whether we have to look out for a coming world religion, and, secondly, the problem of the significance of the religious pluralism. Let me restrict myself to a few remarks on both points.

There are people who expect that the world community in the making will be accompanied by the fading out of the differences between the religions and the gradual arising of a world religion. I earnestly doubt whether they are right. I can not imagine how Buddhism, Judaism, Islam and Christianity—only to mention but four religions—could ever be forged into a unity. Secondly, as to the problem of the philosophical or theological significance of religious pluralism, I would advice, that we leave this intricate question untouched. It is easy to state that there occur three well-known shades of opinion: All religions are false; all religions are true; or only one's own religion has the truth, and all others are in error. In discussing this issue, we would transgress the border-line of our discipline and we would be in danger of getting entangled into all kinds of intricate theological problems.

The problem at stake is that, whereas religious pluralism is an undeniable fact in the growing world community, we have to ponder the means and methods to increase the mutual understanding between the adherents of the different religions and forms of belief, and to accept their actual coexistence. Referring to the remark which I made at the beginning of this article, namely that humanity now apparently enters a relatively new period, I can now proceed to say that we never before have been confronted so intensely with the problem of the relationship between the religions of the world as at this juncture. In my opinion this also implies that we have to seek for new and better methods of tackling these difficult problems.

In the course of my life I have participated in many meetings dealing with this matter. Though papers were delivered by able and right-minded scholars, the resultats were at most meagre. I must confess that I have little confidence in discussion even between brilliant and highspirited people, when it is not conducted under strict scientific rules. We are living in the age of science. Natural science has won dazzling victories, thanks to the fact that its students submit to a strict scientific discipline and apply a great accuracy in their terminology and in their research. In the field of humanistic studies, we should clearly realize, that it is a requirement of the times that we introduce the right methodology into the science of religion.

II

This leads to the core and kernel of the subject of this article: Methodology and the science of religion. Mutual understanding within the range of the existing religious pluralism can only be brought about, if we scientifically require into the conditions of such a religious harmony. They are twofold: first, the willingness to take an interest in forms of foreign religion and to make an attempt at understanding their value and essence; and, secondly a clear insight into the necessity of availing oneself of all the knowledge which the science of religion puts at one's disposal.

The indispensable presupposition of mutual understanding among adherents of different religions is that they are prepared to listen to one another, to put aside their preconceptions about the religious standpoints of people belonging to other religions than their own, and to take their fellow believers of another type absolutely seriously, when these earnestly testify to their faith, even when their behavior and their utterances look queer and unintelligible. Let us be aware of the fact that understanding foreign religions is a difficult art which some people have received by nature as by grace, while others learn it slowly and imperfectly. In the latter case not only might loving interest be lacking, but also the psychological capacity of broadening one's spiritual horizon to embrace all types of religion. In my opinion we should have a realistic look at man's nature. That means that, notwithstanding the fact that we are living in the age of psychology and that the knowledge of psychological notions is widespread, the range of interest of the average man is bafflingly narrow. Therefore, we should not too soon condemn the narrow-mindedness of other people, knowing that we ourselves often fail in this respect. We should have much patience, because we clearly realize that only an education during many generations can lift people up to a level that enables them by virtue of their spiritual outlook to embrace the whole world.

The second condition of creating mutual understanding is that one make use of the method and of the insights which the science of religion puts at the disposal of everyone who is desirous of penetrating into the hidden depth of foreign religions. Uncritical admiration of exotic religious life and well-meant, but unsystematic, deliberations about the topic in question are of no avail. Clarification can be reached only by applying the typical principle of the science of religion, i.e. the phenomenological method. This thesis requires explanation. This can best be done by presenting a short description of the nature and the aim of the phenomenology of religion.

III

It is to the credit of the Leyden historian of religion P. D. Chantepie de la Saussaye, that he has presented the first sketch of a phenomenology of religion. It is part of his "Lehrbuch der Religionsgeschichte" in its edition of 1887. It is quite clear what Chantepie meant by introducing this new science. He must have realized that the study of religions leads with logical necessity to phenomenological investigations. For the history of religions not only studies the separate religions *in toto* or in parts, but also involuntarily compares the different religions of the world. Thus the so called "Algemeine, vergleichende Religionsgeschichte" or comparative religion arose.

However the phenomenology of religion takes a further step, as its name indicates, which means: the theory of the (religious) phenomena. In the process of research this science pays attention not so much to the historical surroundings of the phenomena, but rather to the ideological connections. This means that the facts are severed from their historical contexts and that they are combined in such a way that the meaning of certain phenomena such as sacrifice, magic or prayer become transparent. In this sense Chantepie wrote a first draft of the phenomenology of religion.

Since 1887 the phenomenology of religion has succesfully developed. Gradually it evolved into an independent branch of the science of religion. In order to avoid misunderstandings, it should be clearly realized that the term, phenomenology of religion, can be used in a double sense. It means both a scientific method and an independent science, creating monographs and more or less extensive handbooks. In this article I should like to focus the attention on the value and the implications of the phenomenological method. Then one should know that many phenomenologists have been influenced by the philosophical phenomenology of which E. Husserl is the chief exponent. We can skip an exposition of this type of philosophy. Suffice it to know, that several phenomenologists make use of two of the principals of Husserl, i.e. the epoché and the eidetic vision.

The first principle means the suspension of judgement. In using the epoché one puts oneself into the position of the listener, who does not judge according to preconceived notions. Applied to the science of religion, this means that it cannot concern itself with the question of the truth of religion, neither drawing a distinction between true and false religion, nor pronouncing a judgment on the question of whether religion has a metaphysical background. Phenomenology of religion must begin by accepting as proper objects of study all phenomena that are professed to be religious. Subsequently the attempt can come to distinguish what is genuinely religious from what is spurious. The second principle, that of the eidetic vision, can easily be understood. It has as its aim the search of the eidos, that is the essentials of religious phenomena.

For clarity's sake, it should be added that the phenomenology of religion uses the Husserlian principles in a figurative sense, without further philosophical implications. It is also good to know that there exist students of the science of religion—certainly not the less prominent scholars—who never use the Husserlian terminology, though they actually apply these principles. Be that as it may, it is essential that in studying foreign religions one tries to creep, so to say, out of the skin of one own's thought forms and to investigate the religious facts unbiasedly.

This attitude was admirably sketched by the late Professor W. B. Kristensen in Leyden when he wrote: "Let us not forget that there is no other religious reality than the faith of the believers. If we want to make the acquaintance with true religion, we are exclusively thrown on the pronouncements of the believers. What we think, from our standpoint, about the essence and value of foreign religions surely testifies to our own faith or to our own conception of religious belief. But if our opinion of a foreign religion differs from the meaning and the evaluation of the believers themselves, then we have no longer any contact with their religion. Not only our religion, but every religion is, according to the faith of the believers, an absolute entity and can only be understood under this aspect." The significance of this saying consists in that it emphasizes the demand for an unbiased attitude in the study of the history of religions. Actually the problem is more complicate than it appears here. There are cases in which the student of the history of religions has a better survey of a certain religion than its adherents

IV

Naturally the question arises as to the results to which the phenom-enological method leads when applied to the problem at stake. It is evident that I have to limit myself to those phenomenological insights which are relevant to the problem of clarifying the present religious pluralism. Let me draw your attention to the following points:

(1) Religion is a universal human phenomenon. Everywhere in the world and at all times since the evolution of *homo sapiens*, people both collectively and individually have worshipped superhuman force. No tribe or nation has ever been found that was wholly without a religious consciousness. Such a statement is only correct so long as it is realized that in certain cases the religious consciousness finds expression not so much in religious notions as in sacral actions. For the impartial investigator, religion, even appearing in queer, crude, and repelling forms, is recognizable, because the practised eye can discern the fear for the Holy which is characteristic of true religion. Hence religious belief is inherent in human nature. Nevertheless disbelief has been widespread since the dawn of history, and primarily in modern times. This is not the place and the time to investigate this crucial question. It might be enough to say that nobody can understand man's behaviour, neither in the past nor in the present, without taking into account religious motives prompting his religious attitudes. This holds especially true for the nations of the East, whose life is still permeated by religious notions.

(2) As Professor Kristensen stated in the words which I quoted, every religion claims to possess absolute truth. In order to understand the believer, we must take his words seriously when he declares that he has encountered God, at least when he is sincere in his confession of faith. Unfortunately hypocrisy often corrupts religion and spoils its good reputation. Everywhere human passions such as ambition, thirst for power, vanity and all kinds of sexual drives are allowed free rein under the guise of piety. No student of the science of religion should be blind to the flaws in all religions. Nevertheless religion is and remains the highest good of humanity because man in his religious belief faces the Ultimate Reality and Eternity.

(3) Religious pluralism is in itself an amorphous body of thousands of forms of religious belief and practices. In order to get a grip on this heterogenious material one needs a definition of religion by the aid of which one is able to distinguish pure religion from non-reli-

gious elements. The formulation of a definition of religion is an extremely difficult problem because it should neither be too narrow so that it excludes a part of the religious phenomena, nor too broad so that it includes some forms of pseudo-, or as Tillich calls it, quasi-religion. One of the best definitions is given by the Tillich himself. It runs like this: "Religion is the state of being grasped by an ulti-mate concern, a concern which qualifies all other concerns as preli-minary and which itself contains the answer to the question of the meaning of our life. Therefore this concern is unconditionally serious and shows a willingness to sacrifice any finite concern which is in conflict with it." It is evident that a definition like this can serve as an operative and heuristic principle.

(4) One of the generally accepted results of phenomenological inquiry is the thesis that the formal structure of religion falls into three parts. In religion there are three recurring factors, namely God, man and the relation between God and man, which is expressed in the cult and in the observance of God's laws in man's personal and social life. To put it differently, we may say that a religion is made up of a) a holy vision of the Supreme Being or of the being and the will of the Deity. b) a holy path that a man must persue in order to be freed from his sin and suffering and c) a holy action that the believer must carry out in the cult and in his personal religious life. Of this three factors the notion of God possesses a logical priority; for it is the nature of the holy vision that determines the character of the holy path and the holy action and makes them comprehensible. In this complex of ideas the inner logic of the religion is revealed.

(5) In addition to these formal characteristics phenomenologists have also drawn attention to structural relations of a more substantial nature which reveal the logical construction of the religious phenom-ena. These factors underlying the ideological structure of religion would appear to be the following:

a) the number of ways in which religious belief expresses itself is relatively limited. The same religious symbols are found throughout the world. These parallels soon attracted the attention and have been the subject of many studies in the field of comparative religion. Their real significance consists in the fact that they represent the constant forms of religion, of which the number is limited. The relation be-tween God and man is, for instance, expressed in four constantly recurring images, namely the relation between father and child, master and servant, friend and friend, and lover and beloved. Striking similarities between religions should not, however, blind the student to the fact that resemblance is usually superficial and that the idea and the intention behind identical formulations may be completely different.

b) Religion is *sui generis* and cannot be explained by non-religious factors. Every religion possesses its own individuality and can only be comprehended and described after long study. It is, however, an illusion to believe that one can ever follow a religion to which one does not personally profess. It must be remembered that the believer keeps a secret which he cannot and does not wish to reveal to non-believers and believers in other faiths. Nevertheless it is possible to obtain by factual knowledge and by religious intuition insight into what is unique in the forms of the religion one is studying.

c) Every religion has its own distinguishing factors. This is an element of truth which also occurs in other religions, though in a subordinate position, but which especially characterizes one particular religion. When describing a religion great attention should be paid to its distinguishing feature. This structural element may be illustrated by a few examples. The distinguishing feature of the religion of Zarathustra is the notion of militant piety; Judaism is pervaded by a deep fear of God's holiness, while Islam is the religion of boundless surrender and obedience.

d) The surest method of becoming acquainted with the structure of a religion is to pose the question: How do its believers receive their knowledge of God? It soon becomes evident that there are various types of "revelation". On looking at this question from the viewpoint of the historian of religions, we may say that a higher necessity has obliged various types of believers to adopt different attitudes of belief and to orientate themselves religiously in different directions in order to meet the Holy. A few examples will illustrate the principle. The religions of antiquity are founded on a cosmic vision: the universe testifies to a divine order. Indian religious thinking wrestles with the problem of transitoriness and suffering, a problem which is solved when the liberating insight is attained that the finite is but a veil and life itself an illusion. The mystic strives to release himself from all institutionalized forms of worship and to achieve the mortification of the ego in order to behold in complete emptiness and to experience in bliss the fullness of God. Adherents to the historical religions which are based upon prophetic revelation receive their knowledge of God from sacred history in which divine messengers have appeared as testimony to the way in which God has intervened on behalf of his children throughout the ages.

e) Insight into the structural elements previously mentioned leads to the conclusion that every religion is a meaningful combination of various lines of thought. This may be exemplified by applying this principle to Christianity. Obviously there are many traits of similarity between Christianity, on the one hand, and Judaism and also the Hellenistic religions, on the other. However, on closer observation one will discover that the spiritual climate behind these parallels is totally different. This means that Christianity in many respects shows a unique character. As to the way in which knowledge of God is obtained, Christianity is based on the idea of God's revelation in history. The distinguishing feature in Christianity is the idea of love. In order to grasp the essence of Christianity one should pay attention to the intertwinement of those four structural lines.

(6) In my opinion the present religious pluralism can be clarified when its different forms are studied with the aid of the principles which I developed. Then the fundamental pattern of the different religions will prove to be easily discovered. However, most religions possess a long history during which many changes in their structure have taken place. Moreover, all religions are today subjected to a number of factors which dissolve the fundamental pattern to such a degree that at times it can hardly be recognized. Religious pluralism undergoes a period of crisis. This article does not offer sufficient room to picture the transformations which the different religions undergo, apart from the fact that nobody is able to give an adequate description of what is going on in religious respect in the different corners of the world. However, the main lines can be clearly distinguished. On the one hand the original character and the inner strength of the different religions are weakened by nihilistic, humanistic and atheistic tendencies. On the other side this crisis works as a purification and often has the effect that religions pass through a renaissance. This development should be taken into account, when the components of religious pluralism are analyzed.

(7) Religious people nowadays meet each other more frequently than ever before and talk with one another on religious topics more openly than they once did. To their surprise they discover that when they approach each other humanly the points on which they agree are more numerous than they had imagined. This experience may give rise to the conception that religious pluralism could easily be

straightened out, when you look at it from the anthropological angle. To my mind this is a fallacy. It should be realized, that human life has different spiritual dimensions. In the first place man all over the world understands the typical human needs and reactions of his fellow creatures without any difficulty, whatever the color of the skin, the race or the rank in society. Because men are capable of the same emotions and the same thoughts, there exists, in the second place, a human religiosity in which religious people all over the world take part. In the religious feelings of confidence, love, and peace, in the strife for religious truth and righteousness, people of different races and corners of the world can meet each other. However, there is a third and most important dimension. This is the level of the typical pattern of each individual religion, which ultimately determines the actions and evaluations of its adherents. This pattern is unique and exceptional. It cannot be explained anthropologically. It is the task of the phenomenology of religion to make religiously understandable what is not humanly understandable.

V

Lastly I should like of point out and to stress that knowledge of the method and the insights of the science of religion is no matter for amusement or some kind of spiritual luxury, but a modern requirement. I am under the definite impression that all kinds of blunders, made on the fields of national and international politics, and of economics and in cultural and religious affairs arise from a lack of knowledge of the religious emotions and ideas of the people who are affected by certain kinds of political, economic or cultural measures. In my opinion all people, who are destined to play a leading role in the world, as politicians, economists, owners of big concerns, engineers, doctors or churchmen, should be obliged to master the principal insights of the science of religion. I am convinced that this measure would dissipate many misunderstandings and would create more harmony among the nations.

COMPARING THE RELIGIO-HISTORICAL
AND THE THEOLOGICAL METHOD *

This theme gives rise to a series of questions. For the first it is dubious whether theoretical considerations on methodology are very fruitful and attractive. Not improperly it has been said that discussing methodology is like an endlessly sharpening of a knife whilst one never gets something to eat. Such a theoretical exposition mostly is a bloodless argument which some people perhaps read with pleasure, but which is not to the taste of historians of religions. They are fascinated by the religious phenomena to such a degree, that they do not allow themselves time to reflect on the method of their study. Secondly the question arises whether one can deal with the method of history of religions and of theology without taking the object of the two disciplines into account. The method of a discipline generally results from its object. It is wellknown that each science approaches its material in its own way. Therefore one cannot compare the method of the two disciplines without taking their principles into considerations. Thirdly it is evident that there exists difference of opinion on the character and the object both of history of religions and of theology. How can the methods of the two disciplines be compared when there is no communis opinio on their principles? Fourthly it can be questioned whether it is useful to deal with the question in the abstract. It is clear that everyone who writes about the subject, starts from certain tacit presuppositions. Some decades ago objectivity was proclaimed as the sole principle of science. Nowadays scholars have come to the insight that how impartial they may try to be, everyone looks at the subject of his study from his own angle, even the students of natural science who were formerly supposed to be absolutely unbiased. This holds certainly also true for the student of history of religions. Though he is obliged to present an unprejudiced picture of the religion which he is studying, he must be conscious of the fact that he involuntarily is influenced by the attitude which he takes to the subject of his inquiry. The implications of this situation are twofold: a) the historian of religions should acknowledge that his method is coloured by his personal outlook on the material which he handles. b) he should realize that he

---

* Published in *Numen*, Vol. XVIII, Fasc. 1.

is moulded by a certain religio-historical tradition, which means that he is the follower of a certain national school. In regard to the second point it is mostly forgotten that the study of history of religions is strongly influenced by the cultural, spiritual and scholarly atmosphere in which the study takes place. One can make a further step. The character of history of religions is generally determined by the function which the discipline fulfils in the system of academical instruction of the country in question. Too little attention is paid to this background. Yet the scholarly milieu can be decisive for the manner in which the study of history of religions is conceived of. These spiritual surroundings often explain why a certain method is chosen. The present author therefore doubts whether it is of any use to treat the question of the relation of the religio-historical method to the theological method in the abstract. At any rate it will surely clarify his own standpoint when he starts by sketching the Dutch background of his study. After having described the respective problematics in Holland he can take a further step by voicing some views that have a more general and international significance.

In the Netherlands history of religions is pursued by scholars of different faculties and of different confessions. Historians of religions are to be found not only among the theologians, but also amidst the philologists, the historians, the sociologists, the psychologists, the ethnologists etc. They may be Protestants of diffent denominations, or Roman Catholics, or persons who belong to no church and do not profess any creed. This fact deserves special notice. The majority of these scholars study history of religions as an interesting subject alongside their actual professional study. They hardly come in touch with theology. They are not forced to confront their method with that of theology. They study religio-historical problems in a matter of fact way, without caring about the presuppositions of their work. There is no reason why they should puzzle their head about the problematics which is tackled in this article. Now and then their scholarly accomplishments are impressive and surprising. From this fact the conclusion can be drawn that history of religions in principle is a empirical science. It does not pronounce any value judgments, but tries to describe the course of events in an unbiased way, as the students of every segment of historical studies are bound to do. A tendentious description of history is no good. The historian of religions would disqualify himself by showing his predilection or by pronouncing his assent or dissent. Deterrent examples are those treatise on the non-

Christian religions which qualify these types of belief as the work of the devil or as the results of human sin.

There are in the Netherlands historians of religions who find themselves in another position. That are those persons who are charged to teach history of religions at the university. Remarkable enough these professorships are solely located in the faculties of theology, both Protestant and Roman Catholic. In principle it would be possible to create a professorship for the history of religions in the faculty of arts. For, history of religions is an autonomous science and is not obliged to reckon with theology or church. This step has never been taken.

There is a historical reason why history of religions is only taught in the faculty of theology. In former times the Dutch Reformed Church was the privileged national church. In the faculty of theology the dogmatics of that church was officially taught. In the nineteenth century the separation of Church and State came about. The faculty of theology became independent and accepted the principle of scholarly objectivity. The result was that by the academic statute of 1876 dogmatics were eliminated from the educational programme of the faculty of theology as a body of professors, nominated by the minister of education. This discipline was handed over to professors, appointed by the churches, who had to train the future ministers. They possessed an advisory capacity at the faculty of theology. To approach the situation from another side, one could say that the majority of the Dutch churches require that the future clergyman shall take his candidate's degree at the university. The churches themselves take care of the training for the ministry. Thus a so called "duplex ordo" was created which can be considered both as an advantage and as a drawback. In this context it is important to mention the results of this regulation. In the first place it is interesting to know that in 1876 some law makers were inclined to take the utmost consequence of the idea that the study of religion should be impartially scientific. They proposed to change the name of the faculty of theology into that of the faculty of science of religion. Fortunately this step was prevented by a certain connectedness with theology and church which still prevailed among those persons who had to take the decision in this matter. Secondly it is essential to note that instead of dogmatics philosophy of religion and later on history of religions were inserted into the system of academical instruction. In this manner history of religions got its seat in the faculty of theology. Being an independent discipline with a method of its own, history of religions was from the beginning involved in discussions with theologians, especially with those professors who teach dogmatics, about questions of the principles of its study. Some orthodox theologians refused to consider history of religions as a theological discipline. Dr. A. Kuyper, the founder of the Calvinistic "Vrije Universiteit" (Free University) treated history of religions very stepmotherly by relegating it to the appendix of his extensive, threepartite "Encyclopaedie der Heilige Godgeleerd-heid" (Encyclopaedia of the Holy Theology) (1894). In his opinion history of religions being the history of pseudo-religion, did belong to the non-theological disciplines. Since that time the tide has turned, also at the "Free University". Nevertheless those theologians who are influenced by Karl Barth are still suspicious of history of religions, because they fear that the absolute truth of the Gospel will be endangered by acknowledging the significance and the religious value of the non-Christians religions. Thus an ever recurring discussion between theologians and historians of religions is the result of the fact that they are members of the same faculty.

Unfortunately clarification in this respect is hampered by the fact that there is no communis opinio about the meaning of the notion: theology. Different denominations cherish diverging opinions. Each theologian may have his pet conception. Nevertheless two interpretations can easily be distinguished: a broader one and a narrower one. In the first place theology can be conceived of as the organic complex of disciplines in which the future minister should be trained so that he can successfully exercise his office. To these disciplines also history of religions belongs and that for obvious reasons. The theologian should both have knowledge of the "Umwelt" of the Bible so that he better understands the unique significance of the Gospel, and he should be somewhat familiar with the non-Christian worldreligions, because in a world that is rapidly becoming smaller, Christians and non-Christians daily meet and have intercourse with each other. Thus history of religions has its legitimate place in the encyclopaedia of theology. One can take a further step. There is reason to argue that the method of history of religions actually is applied to other theological disciplines. Which is this method? It is the principle of scholarly impartiality, of purely historical reseach. In the study of the Old Testament, of the New Testament, of church history, of the history of dogma—merely to mention these historical disciplines—the students apply the same critical unbiased method as the historians of religions. It is exactly this scholarly procedure which garanties the standard of theology as an academical discipline and marks its difference from theology, taught at ecclesiastical seminaries.

There is a second more strict conception of theology. This discipline can be understood in the original meaning of the word as the doctrine on God and on the salvation which He offers, as the scholarly exposition of the Gospel. The Gospel must be deduced from the Bible and is formulated by dogmatics. This last discipline cannot be studied in a disengaged way. It forces the student to take a decision in regard to the Christian truth. Thus it cannot be avoided that the question arises whether the religions, studied by history of religions, are founded on knowledge of God. If the decision might turn out in the negative, the position of history of religions in the faculty of theology is endangered. For, theology conceived in the second sense, feels itself related to the church and takes it as its duty to defend the true Christian doctrine. Actually there is a continuous tension between these two conceptions of theology, i.e. the academical-scholarly and the ecclesiastical-professing. Both have their right to exist. They balance one another. Thus, this is the place where the problem of the relation of the method of history of religions to that of theology is born. Here it is no artifical question, but an issue of current and existential interest.

However, in itself history of religions is a harmless and inoffensive business, as has already been pointed out. It studies religious facts in an empirical way, like all historians do, without bothering itself about its method. The situation becomes complicated by the fact that phenomenology of religion has a voice in the matter. In order to clarify this point it should be realized that the notion: phenomenology of religion can be used in an double sense. It means both a scholarly method and an independent science, creating monographs and more or less extensive handbooks. It is this very method which gives rise to interesting discussions. This can only be fully understood when one is familiar with the origin and the principles of the science. For this matter I may refer to the previous article and to my treatise on "The Phenomenological Method" in *The Sacred Bridge.*

Phenomenology of religion is a young science. It finds its path fumbling and it stumbles now and then. Nobody can deny that there is an element of truth in the critical remarks which are sometimes leveled at the science. For many years I have acknowledged this by writing: "Actually there is a lack of clarity in the working procedure of phenomenology of religion..." In my opinion phenomenology of religion should work out a more precise method and it should sharply delimit the field of its activity. It should keep at a clear distance from the philosophical phenomenology so that its character stands out indisputably". [1]

The attacks which are mentioned, come from the quarters of both philosophers and theologians and are directed against its right to exist, its aim and its method. It is worthwhile to pay attention to this criticism because a review thereof can cast new light on the problem at stake. In the first place the right to exist of phenomenology of religion is questioned. After my "Inleiding tot een phaenomenologie van de godsdienst" (Introduction to a phenomenology of religion) had appeared in 1934 a Dutch reviewer, Dr G. H. van Senden, wrote: "Finally we feel forced to pronounce as our opinion that also this book did not manage to convince us that phenomenology of religion bears the character of a separate part of the science of religion, having its own nature, and to be distinguished from history of religions, psychology of religion and philosophy of religion. It is possible to collect all kinds of most interesting facts under the heading: phenomenology of religion, as this book shows, but thereby its character as an indispensable and essential part of the science of religion is not sufficiently proved". He adds: "A in my opinion hybridic science as the phenomenology of religion brings about more evil than good by continuously pronouncing judgments, not justified as to their philosophical meaning and causing anything but clarification by their edifying nature and their emotional association". [2] As a consequence of his opinion the reviewer proposed that this science be divided in such a way that one part of its pretended task be allotted to history of religions and the other part to philosophy of religion. The reviewer obviously is the victim of a misconception. The origin of phenomenology of religion clearly proves that it logically developped from the history of religions and that it therefore is an autonomous discipline having its solid right to exist.

Furthermore attention should be paid to the critical remarks which Dr van Senden makes on the phenomenological method. He accuses the science for pronouncing judgments which are not philosophically justified and which by their edifying and emotional quality hamper the clarification of religion. He thereby testifies to his lack of insight

---

[1] C. J. Bleeker, *Grondlijnen eener Phaenomenlogie van den Godsdienst*, 1943, p. 21.

[2] *Barchembladen* 1943, p. 20/1.

into the nature of phenomenology of religion. It never pretended to pronounce any judgment. It even strictly refrains from this act. Neither does it intend to edify people.

In this connection the judgment of Dr Th. L. Haitjema, formerly professor of dogmatics in the University of Groningen, on the work of his colleague Dr G. van der Leeuw merits the attention. It runs like this: "The phenomenology of religion shows on three points a lack of clarity: namely (1) lack of clarity in regard to the notion "reality", (2) lack of clarity as to the concept of truth, (3) lack of clarity in its relation to theology". [3] This is the typical judgement of a theologian who makes demands on phenomenology of religion with which it by its very nature cannot comply. We refrain at the moment from a detailed refutation of the points of criticism. So much can be said that phenomenology of religion on principle abstains from a judgement on the reality and the truth of the religious phenomena and that an alleged lack of clarity in its relation to theology is not only its fault but equally of theology.

We are brief on the remarks of Dr Haitjema, because they recur in the pointed objections which Dr. J. A. Oosterbaan, professor of philosophy of religion and ethics in the university of Amsterdam, has raised, mainly in regard to the phenomenological method. [4] It can be summed up like this: (1) phenomenology of religion uses the principle of the epoché and of the eidetic vision in an illicit and unjust way, (2) it takes a certain position in regard to the question of the truth of religion, (3) it wrongly pretends to be a science of the essence of religion. This means that Dr Oosterbaan accuses phenomenology of religion of having transgressed the borders of its domain and of having infringed on the field of philosophy of religion. He should like to push back phenomenology of religion into what he considers to be its proper and original sphere of action i.e. the systematic description of the religious phenomena as part of historical studies without claiming to make statements about the essence of religion.

The critical remarks of Dr van Senden, Dr Haitjema and Dr Oosterbaan are exemplary and even up to date, because they embody the misunderstandings which are still prevailing about the relation between the method of phenomenology or history of religions and that of theology c.q. of philosophy of religion. Answering these objections I should like to emphasize the following points:

---

[3] *Vox Theologica,* Dec. 1941.
[4] *Nederlands Theologisch Tijdschrift,* Dec. 1958.

(1) since 1897, when Chantepie de la Saussaye published his first treatise on the matter, the development of both history of religions and phenomenology of religion has been such that nowadays nobody can nor will confine himself to a mere description of religious facts, like the stock-taking in an antiquated museum. The general trend is for an inquiry into the meaning and the structure of the religious phenomena. Nobody can put the clock of the historical development of a science back.

(2) when phenomenology of religion makes use of the principles of the epoché and the eidetic vision it should clearly be understood that they are handled in a figurative sense. They are void of philosophical or theological implications. They simply express the attitude of impartiality, of attentive listening which is the absolute condition for a right understanding of the import of the religious phenomena. There can be no objection against this procedure, provided that it is clearly stated in which manner this scientific technique is made use of.

(3) phenomenology of religion never pretended to be a science of the essence of religion. Its only pretension is that it may manage to detect the structure of a greater or smaller complex of religious phenomena. This is quite another business. To put it into other words: there is a striking difference between the way in which philosophy of religion and phenomenology of religion deal with this issue. The first science tries to formulate the essence of religion in a succinct definition. The second discipline aims at understanding the structure and the sence of constitutive factors of religion.

Nevertheless the question of the essence of religion plays a certain part in history of religions and phenomenology of religion. The student of both disciplines start their investigations, aided by a mostly subconscious notion of what religion is. Otherwise they would be unable to sift the chaff from the grain, i.e. the religious from the non-religious facts. Under their researches they may become conscious of the nature of true religion. This discovery can be a stimulus to articulate the implicite notion of religion. At any rate the formula, born in this way, differs from the mostly lapidary definitions of the essence of religion which philosophy of religion produces. For, what history of religions and phenomenology of religion can offer, it either is a key word, indicating the very heart of religion, [5] of it is a description of the structure of religion, according to its elements and

---

[5] C. J. Bleeker, "The Key Word of Religion" (*The Sacred Bridge*).

its composition. [6] Actually insight into the structure of religion throws a clearer light on its essence than the most carefully formulated definition can ever be able to do.

(4) it is a misunderstanding to assert that phenomenology of religion passes in any sense a judgment on the question of the truth of religion. For, it maintains the attitude of the epoché. It is equally wrong to blame this science for not pronouncing a sentence on the reality and the truth of the religious phenomena. It balances so to say on the edge of a knife. On the one hand it is loyal to the principle of epoché. On the other side it must by force of its impartiality demand that religion should be understood as what it stands for, namely as a serious testimony of religious people that they possess knowledge of God. Even an atheistic student of history of religions must accept this view-point. Otherwise he will do violence to the facts.

(5) in regard to the present argument it should above all be realized that the phenomenological principle is a method which can be and actually is applied to different branches of science. It would be easy to quote instances which show that in Holland—as surely elsewhere—this method has found application both in f. i. psychiatry and in natural science. The method possesses an universally scientific significance.

The Netherlands are one of the first countries where history of religions was studied and taught at the university. The development of the Dutch type of the discipline and its problematics may be said to possess an archetypical value. It shows that there has always been a tension between the religio-historical method and the theological method which brought about many profound discussions.

This tension is increased and at the same time put on an international level by the considerations which Dr H. Kraemer at several occasions dedicated to the study of history of religions in its relation to theology. Dr Kraemer who become famous as missionary and as advocate of the oecumenical movement, occupied during a series of years the chair of history of religions in Leiden. In this capacity he received sufficient incitement to reflect on the matter. Kraemer kept history of religions on high esteem. He did not hesitate to allot to this science its legitimate place in the faculty of theology. Nevertheless he harboured one grievance against its students, i.e. that they pretend to study the religious phenomena fully unbiased and that they deem themselves exclusively able to offer scholarly reliable knowledge of

---

[6] C. J. Bleeker, "La structure de la religon" (*The Sacred Bridge*).

religion, whereas the theologians are suspected of giving a subjective judgment, because they take a certain belief as starting-point of their studies. Kraemer rightly argued that to "understand" or to "comprehend" religion or a religion means to interpret it. Interpretation is not solely or even mainly, an intellectual but an existential activity. In regard to art this is readily acknowledged. In regard to religion this is easily forgotten, but nevertheless religion is rather the field in which man in all his activities, including his supposedly "purely" intellectual activity, can not escape his existential situation. This idea of "purely" intellectual is one of the fictions of our time. [7] In the opinion of Kraemer those historians of religion who fancy that they work purely intellectual and without any bias, do not realize that they actually build on neo-positivistic presuppositions. This attitude only gives entrance to unengaging knowledge and does not lead to a decision as, according to Kraemer, might be expected from a historian of religions, who is a member of the faculty of theology or who is in touch with theology. He concluded that "the theologian who occupies himself with the study and interpretation of Religion and Religions can and should do so with a good *philosophical* concience, provided he is ready to follow the well-founded rules of the game." The theologian who studies history of religions in his own manner does, according to Kraemer, not lag behind the official student of the discipline. Yea, he took a further step. He thought that "the rightly required impartial love of truth gets the best chance when one tries to look at the phenomena in the light of Christ, the most profound "kritikos" of all things". [8] He therefore made a plea for the creation of a "theologia religionis". This discipline could have different starting-points.

No wonder that also other scholars have proved to be supporters of this new science. Dr Oosterbaan who has already been quoted, is in favour of a theological phenomenology which he considers to be an outcome of a pneumatic theology, of a theology of the Holy Ghost. The latter discipline is explained like this: "one of its elements would be a theological phenomenology of the religious phenomena and of religion, whilst another factor would be a phenomenology of the sciences and of the philosophy in their different modes of appearance. Finally it must describe the transition of religion and philosophy in their culmination-point, where they come together (i.e. in the reli-

---

[7] H. Kraemer, *Religion and Christian Faith*, 1956, p. 51.

[8] H. Kraemer, *De plaats van godsdienstwetenschap en godsdienstfenomenologie in de Theologische faculteit.*

gious-ontological mysticism) in so far as this can be described as an immanent event." [9] The programme of the new science sounds somewhat vague and gives no clear idea of the nature of the projected theological phenomenology. One gets the impression that it will stop at *pia vota*. At any rate the programme which Dr Oosterbaan has drawn up by far exceeds the domain of history of religions and of phenomenology of religion in their traditional forms. It is dubious whether there would be many points of contact between the new science and the older ones. In the opinion of the present author this contact is a *conditio sine qua non* of the significance and of the right to exist of the new science. Without the possibility of a close cooperation a "theologia religionis" or a theological phenomenology is a still-born child.

In this connection it is interesting to know that Dr P. Tillich has devoted some words to what he calls a "theological history of religion". [10] He remarks that "the material presented by the history of religion and culture" is an important source of systematic theology. He formulates this idea as follows: "This continuous and never ending use of culture and religious contents as a source of systematic theology raises the question: How are these contents made available for us in a way parellel to the method by which the biblical theology makes biblical material available?... There is no established answer to this question, since neither a theological history of religion nor a theological history of culture has been theoretically conceived and practically established. A theological history of religion should interpret theologically the material produced by the investigation and analysis of the prereligious and religious life of mankind. It should elaborate the motives and types of religious expression, showing how they follow from the nature of the religious concern and therefore necessarily appear in all religions, including Christianity in so far as it is a religion. A theological history of religion also should point out demonic distortions and new tendencies in the religions of the world, pointing to the Christian solution and preparing the way for the acceptance of the Christian message to the adherents of non-Christian religions. One could say that a theological history of religion should be carried through in the light of the missionary principle that the New Being in Jesus as the Christ is the answer to the question asked

---

[9] J. A. Oosterbaan. "De fenomenologie der godsdienstfenomenologie" (*Nederlands Theologisch Tijdschrift*, 1958/9, p. 97 sq.

[10] P. Tillich, *Systematic Theology*, Vol. I, p. 44.

implicitly and explicitly by the religions of mankind." It was necessary to make this lengthy quotation in order to do justice to Tillich's
intention. The reaction of the present author is that Tillich failed to
prove that the theological history of religion can be an independent
discipline. Part of its task, i.e. in so far as the inquiry into types and
motives of religious beliefs is concerned, can be accomplished by phenomenology of religion, whereas the evaluation of non-Christian
religions is the concern of theology, c.q. dogmatics. This item should
be treated either in the prolegomena, or in the chapter on general
revelation, or in the paragraph on mission of the theological or dogmatic handbook in question. Moreover a theological history of religion
is strictly taken a contradiction in terminis. History of religions is a
historical study. Any attempt to give a theological appraisal of historic
facts means a transgression from historic study to theology. Naturally
theologians have the liberty to evaluate the historic course of events.
However, this is a matter of their own concern and responsibility and
is not any longer the business of historians or historians of religions.

Obviously Kraemer had a discipline in mind which works side by
side with the traditional phenomenology of religion. He formulated
its nature and task like this: "My own line is that "theologia religionis" is an attempt to clarify religion as a human phenomenon,
in the light of Jesus Christ, the true man, the normal man, the *only*
normal man in his relation to God, man and world." This means that
theology and also the faculty of theology must have the courage "to
clarify the religion on the basis of solid knowledge in the light of its
own standard and to make in this way *its specific contribution to the
science of religion*." He adds: "It is utterly astonishing that one has
still to fight with the representatives of the science of religion *in* the
faculty of theology about this right and this duty as if it was evident
and solely scientific to acknowledge without discussion the competence
of philosophy of religion to behave as the authority which has the
right and is able to produce a normative and regulative idea of religion." What Kraemer says here about philosophy of religion applies
in a sense also to history of religions and phenomenology of religion.

The last quotation raises the presumption that Kraemer's proposal
encountered resistance. So is actually the case. This goes forth from a
discussion between Dr Th. P. van Baaren, professor of the history of
religions in Groningen en Dr Kraemer in the "Nederlands Theologisch Tijdschrift" (Dutch Theological Journal) [11] Van Baaren first

---

[11] June and October 1960.

of all defends the so called "duplex orde" which in the opinion of
Kraemer, apart from its historical value, essentially is an unsound
construction. Thereafter he states: "Naturally dogmatic theology has
the full right to judge the other religions from its standpoint. "Theologia religionis" in the sense of Professor Kraemer is a beautiful and
valuable discipline, but it is totally different from the science of religion in the accepted sense of the word and one should not blame the
students of the latter science for not practising it, for, it simply is not
their concern. However, I acclaim the existence of such a discipline
without any reservation provided that it is build on solid knowledge
of science of religion in the traditional sense. My only objection is
that the results of this discipline should be in any sense normative for
the science of the "ordinary" science of religion. The opposite naturally also holds true." The present author wholeheartedly subscribes
this statement. Nobody can object to the creation of a "theologia religionis", provided that it does not claim authority over the ordinary
history of religions and provided that it does not pretend to be the
true history of religions which offers the deeper insight into the religious phenomena. It is quite conceivable that the new science would
supplement and enrich the present religio-historical knowledge and
insight. Provisionally the "theologia religionis" is a hypothetical
entity. So long there is no book of some extent available, proving its
right to exist, this new science is no serious partner in the discussion.
Moreover it is dubious whether the principal part of its task could
not be performed by dogmatics.

In another sense the question of the religio-historical method
appears in one of the writings of W. Cantwell Smith, [12] This scholar
critically discusses the concept of "religio" and the terms which are
used for the worldreligions. The scrutiny leads to the conclusion that
both the notion: religion and words as Christianity, Buddhism, Islam
should be dropped, because they thward the real religio-historical
insight. Instead thereof two notions should be introduced, i.e. "an
historical-cumulative tradition" and "the personal faith of men and
women". Elsewhere it becomes clear what has moved Smith to make
this statement. [13] He opposes to the impersonal character of a great
deal on the religio-historical studies. He puts forward the thesis: "The
study of a religion is the study of persons." This means that his con-

---

[12] W. Cantwell Smith, *The Meaning and End of Religion.*
[13] W. Cantwell Smith, "Comparative Religon: Whither-Why?" (*The History of Religions, Essays in Methodology*, 1959).

cern is the living faith of men. In his opinion one can only get to
know this by conversations with the adherents of the religion in
question. This is at the same time the only manner to find a definition
of religion which is really valuable. Therefore his conclusion runs:
"No statement about religion is valid unless it can be acknowledged
by that religion's believers... It is the business of comparative religion
to construct statements about religion that are intelligible within at
least two traditions simultaneously". This approach is by no means
ineligible. But it is not always appropriate. It can not be applied to
the study of the religions of antiquity, for the simple reason that the
adherents thereof can no longer be interviewed. These religions form
an important segment of the field of study of history of religions. In
regard to the religions of the present it is dubious whether even intelligent professors thereof have a thorough knowledge of their own
religion. The expert often knows essential peculiarities which escape
the attention of the believers. The conception of the believers must
be supplemented and verified by the expert insight of the historian of
religions. Therefore the method, advocated by Smith, has only a
limited validity. His proposal to eliminate the notion: religion and
the terms generally used for the worldreligions can not be accepted.
Nobody is blind to the problematics, involved for instance in the
term: Islam. But history of religions would be doomed to inactivity, if
it were bereft of its present apparatus of notions, how imperfect these
terms may be.

Still a third attack is made on the phenomenological method. It is
undertaken by people who believe that this discipline should serve
social, ethical or religious causes, such as the fraternization of the
nations, worldpeace or a better understanding between the followers
of the religions of the earth. Congresses for the history of religions
generally are attended by some persons who cherish these ideals and
expectations. Even lectures may voice the opinion. A noble and
learned spokesman of this standpoint was the late Dr Fr. Heiler.
Repeatedly he has with great warmth broken a lance for the idea. His
conception can best be gathered from an article, bearing the significant title: "History of Religions as a Preparation for the Co-operation
of Religions". [14] He argues therein that history of religions leads to
the insight that "there are seven principal areas of unity which the
high religions of the earth manifest" (the reality of the transcendent,

---

[14] *The History of Religions, Essays in Methodology,* 1959, p. 132 sq.

this trancendent reality immanent in human hearts, this reality the highest good, the reality of the Divine ultimate love, the way of man to God the way of sacrifice, the way to the neighbor, Love the most superior way to God) and that "a new era will dawn upon mankind when the religions will rise to true tolerance and co-operation in behalf of mankind." It is evident that peace among the nations and tolerance between the adherents of the different religions are ideals which deserve the devotion of all right thinking men. Thus organisations as "The World Congress of Faiths" and "The World Council of Churches" which respectively try to mobilize all believers and all Christians in a fight against intolerance and injustice, and insist on mutual understanding and unity, can make an appeal in wide circles. [15] Whether an historian of religions supports these movements is up to his personal decision. As a scholar he would go too far by contending that this work is part of the task of history of religions. The discipline should keep aloof from such activities. [16] In conformity with the study of history in general, history of religions is charged with the task of presenting a scholarly reliable picture of the religions of the past and of the present. It appears to me that Heiler is mistaken in double respect. Firstly it is questionable whether critical study of history of religions really can prove that there is unity between the higher religions in the seven areas which he mentions. It is to be feared that this is wishful thinking. Secondly the problem of religious tolerance which Heiler thinks will be brought about by mutual understanding of the followers of the high religions, actually is more complicated than he suggests. This has been pointed out by Dr R. J. Z. Werblowsky in a penetrating and matter of fact argument dealing with "Commitment and Indifference". [17] He rightly states that tolerance is not only a purely religious affair, but also a socio-psychological phenomenon. He further remarks that the idea of tolerance mostly results from a "philosophical mystical religiosity". Adherents of this religiosity often make the demand on certain religions, i.e. the prophetic ones, that they "should abandon some of their basic principles". It is evident that one can hardly expect that this demand is always granted. This means that it is wrong to expect that all reli-

---

[15] See: Moses Jung, Swami Nikhilananda, Herbert W. Schneider, *Relations among Religions, A Handbook of Politics and Principles*, 1963.

[16] C. J. Bleeker, "Wat beoogt de studie van de godsdienst?" (*Nederlands Theologisch Tijdschrift*, Oct. 1961, p. 1 sq.)

[17] *Robert Waley Cohen Memorial Lecture*, 1967.

gions are able and even are willing to further tolerance unconditionally. Nevertheless there is, as Werblowsky says, " "holy indifference" that stems from "an ultimate commitment"." The future task must be "to break through, beyond tolerance, exclusiveness and coexistence to the full communion of the pluralist saints".

The preceding argument leads to the following conclusions in regard to the relation of the religio-historical and the theological method:

(1) when history of religions and theology claim to be sciences, they are only permitted to use one, common method, i.e. the critical one. This means that they must treat their object according to the criteria of truth and reliability which respective are valid in both disciplines. Unfortunately offences are often committed against this general rule. In both sciences it happens that people work uncritically. They present untenable theses and they manipulate facts of doubtful value, to the detriment of the authority of their science.

(2) it has been stated that the specific method of a discipline results from its aim. Therefore a comparison between the religio-historical and the theological method is rather difficult and to a certain extent unprofitable. At any rate in transfering the method of the one science to the other one should act with great caution. However, it has been stated that the religio-historical method, the principle of the science of religion, plays a great part in some fields of the encyclopaedie of theology. This may conversively be the case with the theological method as will presently be shown.

(3) the character and also the method of theology in the strict sense of the word are determined by a) its object, i.e. the belief in God and b) its aim, namely the renewal of this belief. On account of its object theology is engaged on divine truth. Being embodied in human pronouncements this truth must be evoked by critical research. In the last resort it can not be treated in an unengaged way. It forces the theologian to assume an attitude, to make a choice, to take a decision. This act includes the task of adapting the divine truth to the present situation and of renewing the Christian faith. When a theologian does not create new theological thoughts, he merely repeats the statements of previous generations and he sticks fast in history of dogmas.

(4) history of religions studies cultural phenomena, having a religious significance, i.e. human actions and words, institutions and products of human activity which testify to the presence of religious

faiths. History of religions cannot make pronouncements about God, His existence or His nature. The word: revelation does not fit in with its terminology. At best the historian of religions can make use of the notion: hierophany, following in the steps of M. Eliade, [18] or say that some phenomena testify to an encounter of man with the Holy. It is not the duty of the historian of religions to create something new. He should respect the facts as they are. He should listen to what religious people tell. He must try to understand the faith of the believers. [19]

(5) thus there is a marked difference between history of religions and theology in the way in which they deal with religious values. The theologian ultimately assumes a personal attitude towards religious values. The historian of religions acknowledges the existence of religious values and tries to understand their significance. But his method should be completely free from any value judgment.

(6) in the context of the argument the general description of the task of history of religions presented in (4) and (5) needs further qualification. The decisive question is in which sense the discipline is taken. Is it an attempt to trace the development of great religious ideas or does it consist in a painstaking research of details, partly of a cultural, social, economic or historic nature, the results of which are published in numerous articles and monographs? In the last case this type of religio-historical work falls outside the scope of the problematics at stake. In the first instance when personal insight and phantasy of the researcher play a part, the comparison of the religio-historical and of the theological method makes good sense and is a burning and highly interesting issue.

(7) though history of religions and theology are independent disciplines, they influence one another and they can learn much from each other's method. This interaction could have the following effect: a) history of religions should never forget that religion is always centered round an absolute truth. Moreover it must search for true and pure religion which is mostly hidden among heaps of non-religious or quasi-religious facts. These are two view-points which theology would emphasize. b) theology should realize that in a great deal of its work, especially in historical studies, the only valid method is that of science of religion. For this method guarantees its scholarly character and its academic standard.

---

[18] M. Eliade, *Traité d'Histoire des Religions*, 1949.
[19] W. B. Kristensen, *Inleiding tot de godsdienstgeschiedenis*, 1955, p. 22 sq.

(8) more important than the mutual influence is perhaps the fact that the two disciplines charge one another with a certain task and that in the following way: history of religions urges theology to take the problem of the value of the non-Christian religions extremely serious. In an article on "The Significance of the History of Religions for the Systematic Theologian", [20] Tillich rightly says that "revelatory experiences are universally human". He enumerates five points, taken from the study of history of religions, which are in his opinion systematic presuppositions. These remarks show the way. Theologians who are expected to be forerunners in spiritual matters, should have the courage of definitely solve the age-long problem of the relation between Christianity and the non-Christian religions, and that by inserting in one way or another the knowledge of God, present in these religions, into its doctrine on revelation. This is what the modern world expects and hopes for. [21] On the other hand the historian of religions cannot fully keep aloof from the religious crisis of our age. Many people are spiritually uprooted. The relationship between the followers of different religions is often poisoned by hate, distrust and misunderstanding. Dr Werblowsky rightly remarks: "The students of religion cannot preach mutual understanding, but they are expected to foster strictly by their work a spirit of sympathy and tolerant understanding". [22] I myself have once written on this issue: "It is our duty to spread our light to people who do not know properly what religion is. But our task is not conversion to faith whatsoever, but simply enlightening". [23]

---

[20] *The History of Religions, Essays on the Problem of Understanding*, 1967, p. 242 sq.

[21] C. J. Bleeker, *Christ in Modern Athens, the Confrontation of Christianity with Modern Culture and the non-Christian Religions*, 1965.

[22] *Hibbert Journal*, Vol. 58, 1959.

[23] *Numen*, Vol. VIII, Fasc. 2-3, p. 239.

WIE STEHT ES UM DIE PHÄNOMENOLOGIE DER RELIGION? *

A. Zwei Gründe gibt es, um die im Titel dieses Aufsatzes enthaltene Frage zu stellen. Erstens kann die Religionsphänomenologie auf eine Geschichte von nahezu einem Jahrhundert zurückblicken. Denn in seinem bekannten *Lehrbuch der Religionsgeschichte* von 1887 hat Chantepie de la Saussaye den ersten Artikel über eine Phänomenologie der Religion veröffentlich. In diesem Jahrhundert hat die Religionsphänomenologie sich ihr Existenzrecht erobert und eine wachsende Popularität erworben, obgleich ihr Kritik nicht erspart worden ist. Besonders während der letzten fünfzig Jahren haben hervorragende Gelehrten ausführliche Artikel oder kleinere und grössere Handbücher über die Religionsphänomenologie geschrieben. Diese Schriften zeigen, dass man das Thema von verschiedenen Seiten anfassen kann. Die Religionsphänomenologie hat sich selbst gewissermassen kartiert: man kennt ihre Varianten und überblickt die ihr innewohnenden Entfaltungsmöglichkeiten. Unwillkürlich erhebt sich die Frage: wie wird es mit der Religionsphänomenologie weitergehen?

Der zweite Grund um unsere Frage zu stellen, ist die Publikation des grossen, von Geo Widengren unter dem Titel *Religionsphänomenologie* verfassten Werkes. [1] Die Erscheinung dieses magnum opus bedeutet einen Meilenstein in der Geschichte der Disziplin. Gewiss steht Widengren allen seinen Studien und auch diesem Handbuch kritisch gegenüber, in dem Sinne, dass er nicht wie Mohammed behaupten würde, dass er der letzte der Propheten sei, nähmlich die letzte Autorität auf diesem Gebiete der Wissenschaft. Aber es fragt sich: wer wird in der Zukunft die Kenntnisse sammeln können und die Originalität besitzen, ein Werk zu schreiben, das dem Buche von Widengren einigermassen gleichkommen kann, oder anders gesagt: wie wird sich das Fach weiter entwickeln?

B. Die Schriftleitung von BiOr hat mich gebeten, das genannte Werk zu rezensieren; eine Bitte, der ich deshalb gerne nachkomme, weil der Verfasser das Buch gewidmet hat "der theologischen Fakultät der Universität Amsterdam und ihrem Dekan 1962", d.h. in dem

---

* Veröffentlicht in *Bibliotheca Orientalis*, Jaargang XXVIII, N° 5/6, Sept. Nov. 1971.
[1] Walter de Gruyter & Co, Berlin, 1969 (8vo, XV + 684 S.).

Jahre, in dem ich meinem Kollege proximus in Schweden ein Doktorat honoris causa habe verleihen dürfen.

Die genannte Aufforderung hat mich aber in Verlegenheit gesetzt. Ich habe mich gefragt, ob es sinnreich und möglich sei über ein so umfangreiches und gediegenes Werk eine Rezension im üblichem Sinne des Wortes zu schreiben. Natürlich kann man verschiedener Meinung von Widengren sein, wie sich bald zeigen wird. Man wird ihn aber nie auf offenen Unrichtigkeiten ertappen können, ja es finden sich keine störenden Druckfehler im Texte, ein Beweis, dass Widengren sein Buch mit aller wünschenswerten Akkuratesse verfasst hat. Unter diesen Umständen hat es keinen Zweck, zu versuchen, eine Reihe Randbemerkungen zu machen. Überdies bietet das Buch eine so grosse Fülle von Daten und Betrachtungen, dass niemand alles dies in *einer* Rezension bewältigen könnte. Das Buch gelangt besser zu seinem Recht, wenn man es mit den Problemen konfrontiert, die sich aus der Natur der Religionsphänomenologie an sich ergeben. Was enthält dies?

Es ist klar, dass jeder Religionsphänomenologe sein eigenes "approach" zur Zielsetzung und Methode dieser Disziplin hat. Es besteht in dieser Hinsicht keine orthodoxe Lehre. Das Fach besitzt im Gegenteil so viele Facetten, das jeder seine eigene Interpretation geben kann. Damit vernachlässigt er wiederum Aspekte, die andere gesehen haben. Wie mächtig Widengrens Beherrschung der Materie auch sein möge, es versteht sich, dass selbst ihm gewisse Gesichtspunkte entgangen sind. Niemand wird ihn deswegen tadeln. Hierin spricht sich vielmehr seine Wahl aus, die er mit vollem Bewusstsein getroffen hat und die er mit Argumenten verteidigen kann. Deswegen scheint es mir, dass die Eigenart seines Werkes besser beurteilt werden kann, wenn man es in den Kontext verwandter Studien versetzt. Dabei habe ich nicht die Absicht, die Geschichte der Disziplin und die Diskussion über ihre Methode aufs neue aufzurollen. Dafür möchte ich auf frühere Schriften, in denen ich diese Fragen eingehend erörtert habe, verweisen. [2] Im Rahmen dieses kurzen Artikels will ich nur zum Vergleich mit Widengrens Arbeit eine Charakteristik von einigen bekannten Religionsphänomenologien geben.

C. Bevor ich diese "Phänomenologie" einer Anzahl phänomenologischen Werken beginnen kann, muss ich den Leser mit dem Inhalt

---

[2] Siehe die Liste der "Publications" in "Liber Amicorum" und "Comparing the Phenomenological and the Theological Method" in *Numen* XVII, Fasc. 1.

von Widengrens Werk vertraut machen. Es versteht sich, dass die Zusammenfassung eines Werkes von 684 Seiten nur äusserst summarisch sein kann.

Im Anfang des ersten Kapitels über "Religion und Magie" definiert Widengren die Religionsphänomenologie folgendermassen: "Die Religionsphänomenologie will die verschiedenen Erscheinungen der Religion klassifizieren, d.h. sie will die Religion so schildern wie sie in ihren wechselnden Lebensäusserungen erscheint. Die Religionsphänomenologie ist also die Wissenschaft von den verschiedenen Erscheinungsformen der Religion. Sie ist hingegen keine Wissenschaft von den historisch gegebenen verschiedenen Lebensformen der Religionen. Hier verläuft die Grenzlinie zwischen Religionsphänomenologie und Religionsgeschichte. Während die Religionsphänomenologie alle Äusserungen des religiösen Lebens behandelt, wo immer sie auch erscheinen, erforscht die Religionsgeschichte mit ihrer rein historischen Methode die Entwicklung der einzelnen Religionen. Die Religionsphänomenologie wird hierdurch zur systematischen Ergänzung der Religionsgeschichte". Dies ist eine klare Grenzscheidung zwischen den zwei genannten Wissenschaften. Die Definition der Religionsphänomenologie gibt aber keine Auskunft über ihre Methode.

Im ersten Kapitel macht Widengren sachkundig das Problem des Verhältnisses von Religion und Magie klar. Es fällt auf, dass er die Auffassung von "mana" als eine unpersönliche, übernatürliche Kraft energisch verneint. Seiner Meinung nach ist die Idee eines mehr oder minder persönlich gedachten Gottes ein Grundbegriff der Religion. Das geht aus Kapitel 3 und 4, die vom "Gottesglauben" handeln, hervor. Erst folgt noch Kapitel 2 über "Tabu und Heiligkeit", in dem der Verfasser diese oft nachlässig benutzten Begriffe kritisch betrachtet, ihre Bedeutung philologisch erklärt und, was die Heiligkeit betrifft, Rud. Otto's auf den "Urschauer" gegründete Auffassung von Heiligkeit kritisiert. Kapitel 3 zeichnet eine Figur, die in Widengrens religionshistorischer Forschung eine grosse Rolle spielt, nämlich den Hochgott: bei den schriftlosen Völkern in Afrika und Asien, bei den indogermanischen Völkern, in Ägypten und im Vordern Orient. Angehängt sind Unterabteilungen über die Muttergöttin und den Kulturbringer. Der letztere soll ein Derivat des Hochgottes sein (S. 91/2). Das Bild des Hochgottes stützt sich auf reichliche ethnologische und philologische Daten und erhält scharf umrissene Gesichtszüge in einigen Typologien (S. 47, 61). Dabei wird der Hochgott als Schicksalsmacht gewertet (S. 53). Der Gegenstand des vierten Kapitels ist:

Pantheismus, Polytheismus, Monotheismus. Widengren lässt den modernen, ästhetisch betonten und den älteren religiös-philosophischen Pantheismus ausser Betracht, fasst vielmehr diese Gestaltung des Gottesglaubens als diejenige Vorstellung auf, in der das All als Körper der Gottheit gesehen wird. Weiter ist er der Überzeugung, dass der Polytheismus aus dem Pantheismus hervorgegangen is (S. 3, 545). Der Monotheismus nimmt in diesem phänomenologischen Zusammenhang eine bescheidene Stelle ein. Kapitel 5 ist den "bösen Wesen und dem Bösen" gewidmet, wie sie in der indo-iranischen Religion und in der "iranischen" Gnosis, in den Religionen des alten vordern Orients, im Judentum, im Christentum und im Islam vertreten sind.

Die Kapitel 6, 7, 8 behandeln Themata, die Widengren, dank einigen Vorarbeiten völlig beherrscht, nämlich "Mythus, Glaube und Mythus, Ritus". Die Kapitel sind so inhaltsreich, dass ich nur die Titel der Paragraphen erwähnen kann: "Der Mythus als Ritualtext", "Verschiedene Kategorien von Mythen", "Mythus, Legende, Märchen", "Mythus und Geschichte". Interessant ist der siebente Kapitel über "Glaube und Mythus", und zwar in Israel und Islam, in den indogermanischen Religionen, im Buddhismus, mit einem Schlussparagraphen über "Das Verhältnis von Mythus und Glauben". Auch das Kapitel über den Ritus enthält reichen Stoff: "Das Wesen des Ritus", "Die verschiedenen Typen des Ritus: apotropäische und eliminatorische Riten, Geburts- und Initiationsriten", "Die verschiedenen Typen des Ritus: Einweihung und Taufe", "Taufe und Hochzeit", "Jahresriten", "Ritus und Volkssitte". Hinter diesen minuziösen Auseinandersetzungen liegt die bekannte Idee eines "mythical-ritual pattern" der älteren Kulturen, ein Gedanke, den Widengren mit den erforderlichen Nuancen anwendet, wie z.B. aus seinen Bemerkungen über "das Zusammenspiel von Mythus und Geschichte" hervorgeht. In Kapitel 9 sind "Beichte, Busse und Gebet" an der Reihe. Sie werden betrachtet unter den folgenden Gesichtspunkten: "Der Vordere Orient und das Judentum", "Die iranische Religion", "Indische Religionen", "Betrachtungen über Beichte und Busse". Dieser Abschnitt gibt Veranlassung, eine Bemerkung von allgemeiner Tragweite über das ganze Werk zu machen: Widengren legt viel Wert darauf, die phänomenologische Verwandtschaft zwischen den religiösen Strukturen von Mesopotamien, Iran, den späteren Religionen von "Asia Minor", einschliesslich des Judentums, ferner dem orthodoxen und heterodoxen (gnostischen) Christentum, dem Gnostizismus als solchen und dem Islam hervorzuheben.

Kapitel 10 und 11 sind dem Kultus gewidmet. Sie besprechen "Das Opfer", "Das Gabenopfer", "Das Sühneopfer", "Das Kommunionsopfer", "Die opferfeindliche Haltung", und, anlässlich des "Kultplatzes": "Symbolische Bedeutung des Heiligtums im alten Vorderen Orient", "Symbolische Bedeutung des Heiligtums unter den indo-germanischen Völker", "Der Tempel als wirtschaftliches und kultisches Zentrum", "Vom Tempel zur Basilika". Die Titel der Paragraphen lassen aufs neue einen Reichtum an interessanten Gesichtspunkten vermuten. Kapitel 12 enthält die Auseinandersetzung mit einem Lieblingsthema des Verfassers: "Das sakrale Königtum", dargestellt nach zwei Aspekten: "Die Königsideologie" und "Die Königskrönung". Das Thema ist zwar etwas abgedroschen, aber wie immer ist Widengren hier gut dokumentiert und konzis in seinen Formulierungen, so dass er einen eigenen "approach" zu bieten hat.

In Kapitel 13 beschäftigt der Verfasser sich mit den religiösen Vorstellungen hinsichtlich "Tod, und Begräbnis, Heiligenkult" und wohl nach ihren folgenden Facetten: "Die Einstellung zum Tode und zu den Toten", "Trauerbräuche", "Die Bestattungssitte", "Der Totenkult", "Der Heiligenkult". Was den letzten Gegenstand betrifft, konstatiert er in den Formen des Heiligenkultes in der antiken Religion, im Christentum und im Islam gewisse phänomenologische Übereinstimmungen, die auf einen historischen Zusammenhang hinweisen (S. 426). Darauf folgt ein Kapitel über "Geist und Seele", in dem er auf die Tatsache hinweist, dass sowohl auf arischem als auch auf semitischem Gebiet die Vorstellung herrscht, dass eine Korrespondenz besteht zwischen Gottes Geist, dem Wind und dem Geist des Menschen (S. 430). Kapitel 15 und 16 handeln von der "Eschatologie" und der "Apokalyptik", zwei Begriffe, die der Verfasser nicht im üblichen Sinne anwendet, nämlich einerseits als die Vorstellungen vom Leben nach dem Tode und andererseits als die Spekulationen über den Weltverlauf.

Die "Gnostische Einstellung" kommt in Kapitel 17 zur Sprache. Wer die Ansichte Widengrens über den Gnostizismus kennt, wundert sich nicht, dass er den "indo-iranischen Hintergrund" betont. Weiter folgen Paragraphen über "Die gnostischen Hauptmotive" und "Den gnostischen Zeitbegriff". Gut dokumentiert ist wiederum das Kapitel über "Die Mystik", mit der folgenden Einteilung: "Was ist Mystik?", "Die islamische Mystik", "Die christliche Mystik im Vorderen Orient", "Die christliche Mystik im Abendlande". Anregend ist auch Kapitel 19 über "Heiliges Wort und Heilige Schrift". Man lese aufmerksam die Paragraphen über den "Offenbarungsträger auf dem Thron", "Wort und Schrift". Daran schliesst sich Kapitel 20 über "Die Kanonbildung", in "Indien und Iran", dem "Judentum" und dem "Christentum", eine Studie, die von dem Abschnitt "Allgemeine Betrachtungen zur Kanonbildung" abgerundet wird. Das letzte Kapitel bietet Betrachtungen über "Das Individuum und die Gruppe", wobei die folgende Grössen betrachtet werden: "Die Gruppe", "Das Individuum", "Kosmos, Gesellschaft und Individuum". Am Schluss des Werkes findet man eine Bibliographie von den Arbeiten, deren vollständiger Name, Druckjahr u.s.w. im Text nicht angegeben sind, und ein dreifaches Register: 1) Verfasserregister, 2) Stellenverzeichnis, 3) Namen- und Sachregister.

D. Dieses all zu summarische Inhaltsverzeichnis macht es klar, dass Widengren ein Werk von enzyklopädischem Umfang geschaffen hat. Die deutsche sorgfältig ergänzte und stark erweiterte Ausgabe ist eine Übersetzung seines schwedischen Buches *Religionens Värld* (1953, 534 S.). Der Verfasser hat fünf neue Kapitel (5, 7, 9, 11 20) und vier neue Paragraphen hinzugefügt. Obendrein hat er mehr Material aus dem Buddhismus und dem Islam verarbeitet. Natürlich liegen dem Werke die vielen Monographien, die Widengren im Laufe der Zeit veröffentlicht hat, zugrunde. Dies bedeutet, dass diese Religionsphänomenologie ihre Materie nicht in erster Linie aus den Studien anderer Gelehrten bezieht, sondern fast gänzlich auf den eigenen historischen und philologischen Forschungen des Verfassers beruht. Das lässt Widengren so stark in seinen Auseinandersetzungen sein. Bis in die Noten spürt man, dass er die verschiedenen religionshistorischen Standpunkte studiert hat und sie im Griff hat.

Dennoch hat man Anlass, in verschiedener Hinsicht anderer Meinung zu sein als Widengren. Ohne Anspruch auf Vollständigkeit will ich im Vorübergehen die folgenden Punkte berühren: 1) Es ist zweifelhaft, ob man die Vorstellung einer unpersönlichen übernatürlichen Macht ohne weiteres verwerfen kann. Es gibt Daten, die zur Vorsicht mahnen. 2) Es könnte irreführend wirken, den Hochgott eine Schicksalsmacht zu nennen. Bei Schicksal denkt man an ein unentrinnbares Verhängnis. Es wäre besser von der souverän bestimmenden Macht des Hochgottes zu sprechen. 3) Die Verbindung, die Widengren zwischen Hochgott und Fruchtbarkeit sieht, hat keine allgemeine Bedeutung: es gibt hervorragende Vegetationsgötter, wie Osiris und Min in Ägypten, die keine Hochgötter sind. 4) Wer das grosse Werk

von J. van Baal über "Dema" (S. 988) kennt, wird finden, dass der
Verfasser diesem merkwürdigen Gottesbegriff zu wenig Aufmerksamkeit geschenkt hat. 5) Es mutet etwas fremd an, das wohlbekannte
"tat tvam asi" in einen pantheistischen Zusammenhang gestellt zu
sehen (S. 106), da es doch die erlösende Einsicht zum Ausdruck
bringt, dass die Welt nur Schein ist und das Selbst des Menschen
identisch mit dem Selbst der Welt. Dies ist kein Pantheismus, sondern Akosmismus. 6) Man könnte mit dem Verfasser streiten über
den Gebrauch der Termini: Eschatologie und Apokalyptik. Im üblichen Sprachgebrauch sind mit Eschatologie die Erwartungen über das
endzeitliche Los der Welt und des Menschen gemeint, und Apokalyptik deutet eine Literatur an, die Enthüllungen über das Ende der
Weltgeschichte enthält. Diese Bemerkungen verringern den Wert
des Werkes keineswegs, sondern sind nur ein Beweis dafür, dass der
Rezensent mit dem Verfasser mitgedacht hat.

E.   Der Wert eines wissenschaftlichen Werkes kann nur durch
Vergleich mit verwandten Studien ans Licht kommen. In Gedanken
stellt man Widengrens Religionsphänomenologie neben Bücher ähn-
licher Art. Deshalb will ich eine Anzahl dieser Werke kurz charakterisieren.
    Berühmt ist der Artikel, den Edv. Lehmann über "Erscheinungs-
welt der Religion" (Phänomenologie der Religion) in "Die Religion
in Geschichte und Gegenwart" von 1910 geschrieben hat. Der Aufsatz ist rein deskriptiv und folgendermassen eingeteilt: "Heilige
Bräuche", "Heilige Worte", "Heilige Menschen". Ein korrespondie-
render Artikel findet sich in "Lehrbuch der Religionsgeschichte" von
1925, jetzt genannt "Erscheinungs- und Ideenwelt der Religion" und
in einer minder systematischen Ordnung den Hauptformen des religiösen Lebens gewidmet.
    1933 erschien die ursprüngliche deutsche Ausgabe von Van der
Leeuws Religionsphänomenologie unter dem Titel *Phänomenologie
der Religion*. Das Werk ist so bekannt, dass ich mich auf eine kurze
Charakteristik beschränke. Die Einteilung ist logisch und übersichtlich.
Das phänomenologische Material wird nach drei Gesichtspunkten ge-
ordnet, nämlich: "Das Objekt der Religion", "Das Subjekt der Religion", "Objekt und Subjekt in ihrer Wirkung auf einander". Daran
schliessen sich Kapitel über "Die Welt" und über "Gestalten". Ein
Kapitel "Epilegomena", in dem der Verfasser sich unter anderem über
die Prinzipien der Religionsphänomenologie verbreitet, bildet den

Schluss des Buches. Van der Leeuw zeigt eine grosse Belesenheit, auch von Werken auf den Randgebieten der Religionsphänomenologie. Er hat das Vermogen eines Künstlers, sich in fremden religiösen Strukturen einzuleben. Offensichtlich war er beeinflusst vom Dynamismus, von der philosophischen Phänomenologie und von der Strukturpsychologie

In 1934 wurde meine holländische *Inleiding tot een phaenomenologie van de godsdienst* (S. 229) veröffentlicht, ein Werk, in dem schon die Grundprinzipien meiner Religionsphänomenologie verarbeitet sind, Richtlinien, die ich in späteren Büchern und Artikeln, unter anderem "De struktuur van de godsdienst" (ohne Jahreszahl, 95 S.) näher entfaltet habe und auf die ich später zurückkomme.

Das nächste Werk, das genannt werde muss, ist E. O. James' *Comparative Religion, An Introductory and Historical Study* (1938, S. 365). Aus der Einteilung lernt man die Tendenz und die Spannweite des Buches kennen. James behandelt nicht nur bekannte Themata wie "The Magic Art", "Myth and Ritual", "Monotheism", "Immortality", sondern schreibt auch über "The Way of Salvation", "Sin and Atonement", "Sacrifice and Sacrament". Er betont den Gedanken, dass Religion "the spiritual force holding society together" (S. 2, 350) sei.

Obgleich M. Eliade's *Traité d'histoire des religions* (1949, 405 S.) nicht als Religionsphänomenologie eingeführt worden ist, kann dieses Werk doch tatsächlich als solche gelten. Denn der Untertitel nennt es: "Morphologie du sacré". Mit Hilfe seiner reichen Kenntnisse, besonders von primitiven und orientalischen Religionen, beleuchtet Eliade die Bedeutung der verschiedenen "Hierophanien". Er zeigt ein feines Gefühl für den wechselnden Wert der religiösen Erscheinungsformen, für das, was er "les dévalorisations et les revalorisations du procès de manifestation du sacré" nennt. Das Buch ist besonders wichtig durch Eliade's Betrachtungen über die Funktion der Mythen und der Symbole.

Als posthumes Werk erschien in 1960 die Übersetzung der Vorlesungen von W. B. Kristensen über Religionsphänomenologie, mit dem Titel *The Meaning of Religion* (532 S.). Kristensen, der nicht den Ehrgeiz hegte sich im Auslande Ruhm zu erwerben, und der seine kurzen, inhaltreichen, nur von Quellenmaterial gestützten Studien immer auf holländisch schrieb, wird von allen holländischen Religionshistorikern geehrt als der beste Kenner der antiken Religionen. Auf seine tief schürfende Einsicht in diesen Religions-Typus gründet sich das genannte Werk hauptsächlich. Die Haupteinteilung ist diese: "General Introduction", I "Cosmology", II "Anthropology". III "Cultus" A. "Concrete Objectifications", B. "Cultic Acts".

In demselben Jahr gab K. Goldammer seine *Formenwelt des Religiösen, Grundriss der Systematischen Religionswissenschaft* (S. 528) heraus. Das Buch verdient Aufmerksamkeit, weil nämlich Widengren sich in einer Note auf S. 2 von Goldammers Auffassung der Religionsphänomenologie distanziert. Wie der Titel andeutet, ist Goldammer in erster Linie am Wesen der Religion interessiert. Sein Buch bietet in den Kapiteln 4, 5, 6, 7, und 8 eine systematische Beschreibung der religiösen Erscheinungsformen, unter dem Gesichtspunkt des Heiligen. Der Schwerpunkt liegt aber in der Einleitung und in den ersten drei Kapiteln, in denen der Verfasser sich über den Begriff "Religion", über den "Gegenstand der Religion", nämlich "Das Heilige" und über "Das Frommsein" verbreitet.

Schliesslich möge das grosse Werk von Fr. Heiler, "Erscheinungsformen und Wesen der Religion" genannt werden (1961, 605 S.). [3] Es zeugt von einer aussergewöhnlich grossen Belesenheit und einer ausgedehnten Kenntnis, auch von Gebieten, die andere Phänomenologen nicht beherrschen, wie die Geschichte der Dogmen, der Symbole und der Liturgien der christlichen Kirchen. Der Aufbau ist traditionell und erinnert an Lehmanns zuerst genannte Artikel: ausführlich werden heilige Gegenstände, Zeiten, Orte, Menschen, u.s.w. besprochen. Obgleich eine Auseinandersetzung mit den tonangebenden phänomenologischen Theorien leider fehlt, ist Heiler doch originell in seiner Auffassung von den "Erscheinungsformen und dem Wesen der Religion". Seine Ideen werden verdeutlicht durch ein Diagram auf Seite 20. Er behandelt nacheinander: A. "Die Erscheinungswelt der Religion" (435 S.), B. "Die Vorstellungswelt der Religion" (85 S.), C. "Die Erlebniswelt der Religion" (18 S.), D. "Die Gegenstandswelt der Religion" (2 S.), E. "Das Wesen der Religion" (5 S.). Das Werk kulminiert in diesem letzten Kapitel, in dem Heiler, mit Anerkennung der Unergründlichkeit des göttlichen Mysteriums, versucht, das Wesen der Religion zu umschreiben.

F.   Es fällt nicht schwer, einzusehen, dass die Religionsphänome-

---

[3] Wenn ich die Schriften von Kollegen, wie z.B. van Baaren, Hidding, al Faruqi, Jurji, Mensching und Oxtoby nicht nenne, so bedeutet dies nicht, dass sie meiner Meinung nach nichts wichtiges zur Frage beigesteuert haben, aber es will nur sagen, dass die gegebene Auslese meinen Zwecken am besten dient.

nologie Widengrens in dreierlei Hinsicht mit derjenigen Kristensens übereinstimmt. Erstens gründen beide Gelehrten ihre phänomenologischen Untersuchungen auf die Quellen, zu denen sie selbst Zugang haben. Aber die Grundfläche von Widengrens Religionsphänomenologie ist breiter als diejenigen von Kristensen. Mit der Ausnahme von China und Japan kann Widengren seine Belege aus fast allen Gebieten der Religionsgeschichte holen. Zweitens sind beide zurückhaltend in der Benutzung von Daten aus der primitiven Religion. Kristensen hat sich lange Zeit mit dieser Materie abgemüht, aber sie schliesslich verlassen, in der Überzeugung, dass er, auch wegen Mangel an Sprachkenntnissen, nicht in dieses Gebiet vordringen könne. Das ist noch immer eine Warnung, nicht gegen ernsthafte religionshistorische Forschung auf diesem Gebiet, wohl aber gegen eine unbesonnene Verwendung von Daten aus der Primitivreligion in einem phänomenologischen Zusammenhang. Drittens haben beide Phänomenologen sich wenig um die Methode gekümmert, im Unterschied von Van der Leeuw und Goldammer, und in gewissem Sinne auch von Eliade, besonders aber im Unterschied von zwei jüngeren Gelehrten, nähmlich von J. M. Kitagawa, der zur Erinnerung an J. Wach [4] einen Aufsatz über "Gibt es ein Verstehen fremder Religionen?" geschrieben hat, und J. D. J. Waardenburg, der am Schluss seiner Studie über *L'Islam dans le Miroir de l'Occident* (1961) eine minuziöse Analyse der "étapes de la compréhension" durchgeführt hat. Diese "Epochè" hinsichtlich der Methode der Epochè ist ein gutes Recht sowohl von Kristensen als auch von Widengren. Man hat aber das Gefühl, dass eine kurze Auseinandersetzung mit den phänomenologischen Prinzipien dem Werke Widengrens gut getan hätte.

Mit Eliade hat Widengren sein Interesse für Mythen, Riten und Symbole gemein. Jedoch ist der "approach" Widengrens rein religionswissenschaftlich, während bei Eliade ein gewisses "engagement" mitspricht, nämlich sein Streben, die Religionsgeschichte auch bei der Schöpfung eines "nouvel humanisme" mitwirken zu lassen. [5] Bei Widengren spürt man weiter den Einfluss G. Dumézils, dessen Bedeutung für die religionswissenschaftlichen Forschung er S. 632/5 betont. Manche Seite bezeugt, dass Widengren die komparative Methode Dumézils auf eigener Weise angewendet hat.

---

[4] Joachim Wach-Vorlesungen der theologischen Fakultät der Philipps-Universität Marburg/Lahn I, Leiden, E. J. Brill, 1963.
[5] M. Eliade, "La nostalgie des origines, méthodologie et histoire des religions", *Les Essais* CLVII, Gallimard, Paris, 1971.

Mit etwas gutem Willen kann man drei phänomenologischen Methoden unterscheiden: die deskriptive, die typologische und die phänomenologische im spezifischen Sinne des Wortes. Widengren geht weiter als zu einer rein deskriptiven Ordnung der religiösen Phänomene, wie man sie bei Lehmann und teilweise auch bei Heiler findet; denn er forscht nach dem Sinne der religiösen Komplexe. Er macht halt vor dem Suchen nach dem Wesen der Religion, wie es Goldammer und Heiler betrieben haben. Er bietet eine gut dokumentierte Typologie, die den Sinn von komplexen religiösen Erscheinungsformen klarlegt.

Tatsächlich behandelt Widengren eine Reihe von Typen religiösen Lebens. Unwillkürlich fragt man sich, warum er eben diejenigen gewählt hat, die in seinem Buch vertreten sind, und nicht andere. Das heisst: es wird nicht ganz so deutlich welches System hinter seiner Religionsphänomenologie liegt, wie das bei Kristensen und Van der Leeuw der Fall ist. Kristensen hat offensichtlich seine Religionsphänomenologie nach der Grundstruktur der Religion eingeteilt, nämlich: Gottesbegriff, Anthropologie, Kultus. Wenn man dieses Schema auf Widengrens Religionsphänomenologie anwendet, sieht man, in welcher Hinsicht sie ergänzt werden könnte: nämlich in der Anthropologie, die jetzt nur durch das Kapitel über "Geist und Seele" vertreten ist, und besonders in einer Erlösungslehre, der z.B. James Aufmerksamkeit geschenkt hat in seinen Kapitel über "The Way of Salvation" und "Sin and Atonement".

G. Nach einem Jahrhundert phänomenologischer Studien, nach der Publikation des voluminösen Werkes, das Widengren geschaffen hat, erhebt sich die Frage: Wie geht es weiter mit der Religionsphänomenologie? Es sei mir gestattet, darüber einige kurze Bemerkungen zu machen:

(1) Jeder Phänomenologe weiss aus eigener Erfahrung, dass er seinen Gegenstand bei weitem nicht in den Griff bekommt, wie umfangreich sein Handbuch auch anwächst. Der Horizont dieses Faches weicht immer weiter zurück, je näher man ihn kommt. Mit Recht beschliesst Van der Leeuw sein Buch mit den Schlussworten des Märchens: "Un sau hat allens en Enne und düt Bauk ok. Awerst allens, wat en Enne hat, geiht annerwärts von vorne wedder an". Jedenfalls weiss man etwas ganz sicher: niemand wird in Zukunft imstande sein, ein Werk zu schreiben, das dem Buche Widengrens gleich kommt. Denn das Spezialistentum setzt sich auch auf diesem Gebiete immer

mehr durch. Niemand wird sich den mächtigen Griff über das phänomenologische Material erobern können, den Widengren besitzt.

(2) In diesem Artikel ist die Aufmerksamkeit noch nicht darauf
gelenkt, dass Religionsphänomenologie eine doppelte Bedeutung hat:
es ist eine Wissenschaft, der man ein umfangreiches oder bescheide-
nes Handbuch widmen kann; aber es ist auch eine Methode der Forschung. Und diese Methode ist äusserst wichtig und sollte geklärt
werden. Denn man sollte bedenken, dass diese Methode auch normativ
für die Religionsgeschichte ist. Deshalb unterstütze ich gerne Eliades
Plädoyer für eine "herméneutique totale". [6] Mit Recht legt Eliade
dar, dass es nicht genügt, interessante Daten zu sammeln und zu ordnen. Wir dürfen uns nicht zufrieden geben, bevor wir den religiösen
Sinn auch von exotischen religiösen Phänomenen verstanden haben.
Kristensen sagte immer zu seinen Schülern: "Man muss Nüsse
knacken". Leider gibt es zu viele Nüsse, die man nicht geknackt hat.
Man lässt sie einfach liegen. Nun bedeutet dies nicht, dass man weitgehend über die Möglichkeiten des "Verstehens" spekuliert. Bei den
an sich verdienstvollen Reflexionen von Waardenburg z.B. droht die
Gefahr, dass man sich in Probleme verwickelt, die der Phänomenologe nicht beherrscht und die er den Philosophen überlassen sollte.
Man sollte nur einen einfachen Code des phänomenologische Betra-
gens aufstellen. Dazu gehört in erster Linie die sachliche Einsicht, dass
es ein religiöses Geheimnis gibt, das nur die Gläubigen kennen. Das
braucht kein Hindernis zu sein in einen Typus der Religion, den man
nicht bekennt, tief einzudringen, wenn man nur die scharf formulier-
ten phänomenologischen Richtlinien beobachtet. Meiner Überzeugung
nach ist es weiter sehr wichtig, dass jeder Religionshistoriker sich der
unausgesprochenen Voraussetzungen seiner Studien, mit denen er
arbeitet, bewusst is, wie z.B. der Begriffe wie Religion, Mythus, Ritus,
Magie, und die nicht selbstverständlich sind, sondern Probleme enthalten.

(3) Es tut auch Not, über die Zielsetzung der Religionsphänomenologie nachzudenken. So hat Van der Leeuw z.B. den vielleicht nicht
ganz gelungenen Versuch gemacht Typen der Religion zu definieren.
Widengren hat sich daran nicht gewagt. Persönlich habe ich immer
die These verfochten, dass das Ziel der Religionsphänomenologie
dreifach sei, nämlich 1) die Theoria der Phänomene, 2) der Logos
der Phänomene und 3) die Entelecheia der Phänomene. Die erste

---

[6] *Op. cit.*, S. 122 sq.

Aufgabe ist das Forschen nach dem Sinn der religiösen Erscheinungen, die sich ordnen lassen nach den Hauptthemen der Religion: Gottesbegriff, Anthropologie, und Dienst an der Gottheit in Kultus und praxis pietatis. Den Logos der Phänomene entdeckt man, wenn die Strukturen gewisser Hauptformen des Glaubens, die aus Unterschieden in der Gotteserkenntnis hervorgehen, zur Tage gefördert werden, wie z.B. der Unterschied zwischen der antiken kosmischen Gotteserkennnis und der historischen Gottesoffenbarung, auf der unter anderem Judentum und Christentum fussen. Die Entelecheia der Phänomene soll die Probleme der Entfaltung des religiösen Bewusstseins studieren. Sie kommt dem Bedenken R. Pettazzonis entgegen, der behauptete, dass die Religionsphänomenologie die historische Entwicklung vernachlässige. In diese Kategorie habe ich auch die Behandlung der Phänomene, die ich "die Kehrseite der Religion" nenne, hineingestellt, weil man oft zu idealistisch über die Religion redet. Ich schwöre keineswegs auf diese Formulierung der Zielsetzung der Religionsphänomenologie. Mein Anliegen ist nur, zu unterstreichen, dass man sich sachlich und genau von den Implikationen dieses Faches Rechenschaft geben soll.

(4) Meine Generation hat sich um die Religionsphänomenologie bemüht und besitzt wohl nicht mehr die Phantasie und Schaffenskraft, um nach Widengrens Religionsphänomenologie noch etwas Neues zu schaffen. Es muss ein jüngeres Geschlecht kommen, das die Arbeit weiter führt. Voraussetzung für phänomenologisches Gelingen wird erstens sein, dass man exakte Kenntnisse sammelt und dass man getrieben wird von derselben leidenschaftlichen Liebe zur religionshistorischen Wahrheit, die Männer wie Kristensen, Heiler, James, Eliade und Widengren beseelte. Zweitens wird man keine dicken Wälzer mehr schreiben können. Wie in der heutigen Literatur wird die Form die der "short story" sein. Aber dann müssen es "short stories" sein, die methodisch und inhaltlich noch sachlicher und kritischer aufgebaut sind als vorher. So wird man aufs neue das Problem der Methode erörtern müssen. Weiter lohnt es sich, bekannte Begriffe ganz aufs neu genau zu definieren, wie K. Rudolph dies neulich für den Mythus getan hat. [7] Schliesslich gibt es eine Fülle von nachverlässigten phänomenologischen Themen, die man nach dem Grundsatz der "herméneutique totale" durchleuchten könnte.

---

[7] K. Rudolph, *Der Beitrag der Religionswissenschaft zum Problem der sogenannten Entmythologisierung* (Kairos, Neue Folge, XII. Jahrgang 1970/Heft 3.)

IL CONTRIBUTO DELLA FENOMENOLOGIA DELLA RELIGIONE ALLO STUDIO DELLA STORIA DELLE RELIGIONI *

Nei suoi ben noti saggi "Sulla Storia delle Religioni" Raffaele Pettazzoni, il grande maestro dello studio della storia della religioni, ha pubblicato un trattato dal titolo "La figura mostruosa del Tempo nel Mitraismo". Egli caratterizza la figure come un mostro "che divora e consuma ogni cosa". Questa descrizione si può applicare non soltanto all'idea del tempo nel Mitraismo. Il tempo è stato, e ancora è, concepito da tutti gli uominini in tutte le età, come un mostro che tutto divora. Il tempo esercita questa sua azione distruttiva anche e non meno nel mondo dei dotti. Nessuna fama, per quanto grande, resiste contro il potere distruttivo del tempo. E' stupefacente quando presto dei dotti, che durante la loro vita erano stati incoronati dall'alloro della più grande fama, furono poi totalmente dimenticati. La generazione più giovane non ne conosce più nemmeno i nomi e le opere. E' come se la loro gloriosa carriera non abbia lasciato dietro di sè alcuna traccia. Chiunque conosca la forza distruttrice del tempo, nello stesso tempo si rende conto del significato di Pettazzoni come studioso di storia delle religioni. Questo stesso simposio ne è una testimonianza. Questa assemblea non è tanto una riunione di buoni amici del trapassato che cercano di tenerne artificialmente viva la memoria. E' prima di tutto una testimonianza della sua permanente importanza. Dieci anni dopo la sua morte le tesi storico-religiose di Pettazzoni sono sempre dello stesso interesse vivo come al tempo quando egli le formulò, nel senso che esse stimolano a una rivalutazione critica dei problemi che egli cercò di risolvere. Quali sono queste tesi? Non è mio compito oggi presentare una completa descrizione delle idee e dei meriti di Pettazzoni. Per una valutazione dell'opera di Pettazzoni ci si può riferire all'eccellente articolo di Dario Sabbatucci nel vol. X, fasc. I di *Numen*. Per il momento devo limitarmi a trattare le sue idee riguardanti i principi dello studio della scienza delle religioni e a proposito della relazione fra quella scienza e la fenomenologia della religione.

---

* "Proceedings of the Study Conference on the occasion of the tenth anniversary of the death of R. Pettazzoni. *Problems and Methods of the History of Religion* 1972.

Riguardo al primo punto, Pettazzoni ci ha reso un grande servigio dichiarando con chiarezza e precisione che i fenomeni religiosi, per la loro stessa natura, devono essere soggetto di una scienza autonoma. Nel suo articolo su "Storia e fenomenologia nella scienza delle religioni", inserito nei suoi saggi, egli dice: "La natura peculiare, il carattere stesso dei fatti religiosi come tali, dà loro il diritto di formare l'argomento di una scienza speciale. Questa scienza è la scienza della religione nel senso proprio delle parole, e il carattere essenziale dei fatti religiosi è la ragione necessaria e sufficiente della sua esistenza. Questa scienza non può essere filologica nè archeologica nè altro. E nemmeno può essere la somma totale dei fatti particolari studiati dalla filologia, dall'archeologia, dall'etnologia e così via. La sua definizione, in contrasto con queste varie scienze, non è questione di quantità, bensì di qualità, essendo connessa con la natura speciale dei dati che costituiscono il suo soggetto". Queste parole costituiscono la *Magna Charta* della scienza della religione. Con argomentazione logica esse rivendicano il carattere indipendente di quella scienza, dichiarando cioè che i fatti religiosi innegabilmente hanno una natura unica e che perciò devono essere soggetti di una scienza che possiede tutto l'apparato richiesto per una totale elucidazione dei fenomeni religiosi.

Per quanto riguarda il secondo punto, cioè la relazione della storia delle religioni con la fenomenologia della religione, Pettazzoni ha formulato la questione e anche indicato una possibile soluzione; ma non ha rielaborato nei dettagli la sua idea. Non c'è da stupirsi, perchè questo è realmente un problema complicato. Pettazzoni non ha potuto completamente dominarlo perchè non ha distinto abbastanza chiaramente la natura e i metodi delle due discipline. Parecchie volte si è occupato dell'argomento. I passi che più colpiscono a questo proposito si possono trovare in due articoli pubblicati rispettivamente nel vol. I fasc. 1 di *Numen* en nel vol. VI fasc. 2 della stessa rivista. In ambedue i casi egli tende a un confronto con le idee fenomenologiche del suo collega ed amico Van der Leeuw, sebbene il nome di quest'ultimo non sia menzionato nel secondo articolo.

Nell' "Aperçu Introductif" del Vol. I fasc. 1 di *Numen*, in cui egli, come direttore della rivista, presenta il nuovo periodico ai suoi abbonati, egli naturalmente pone anche il problema in questione. Prima di tuto egli formula il compito della storia delle religioni come segue: "L'Histoire des religions s'attache en premier lieu à établir l'histoire des différentes religions particulières... L'histoire des religions étudie les faits religieux dans leur rapports historiques, non seulement avec d'autres faits religieux, mais aussi avec des faits non religieux, qu'ils soient littéraires, ou artistiques ou sociaux etc...". Poi si domanda se non ci sia un pericolo che la storia delle religioni esca dalle sue linee precise dando troppa attenzione a fattori non religiosi in modo da perdere di vista il senso puramente religioso dei fenomeni. In seguito egli nota che la fenomenologia della religione è intesa per controbilanciare queste tendenze. Egli descrive la natura di quest'ultima scienza con le seguenti parole: "La phénoménologie religieuse ignore le développement historique de la religion (Van der Leeuw: "von einer historischen 'Entwicklung' der Religion weiss die Phänomenologie nichts"). Elle s'attache surtout à découper dans la multiplicité des phénomènes religieux les diverses structures. C'est la structure qui peut nous aider à déceler le sens des phénomènes religieux indépendamment de leur situation dans le temps et l'espace, de leur appartenance à un milieu culturel donné... La phénoménologie n'hésite pas à se poser en science *sui generis* essentiellement différente de l'histoire des religions ("Die Religionsphänomenologie ist nicht Religionsgeschichte": Van der Leeuw)". Indi Pettazzoni dice che in questo modo nasce "un dédoublement de la science des religions en deux sciences différents, l'une historique, l'autre phénoménologique". Egli rimpiange questo dualismo e pensa che il difetto della fenomenologia della religione è che essa trassura lo sviluppo storico dei fenomeni religiosi. Egli preferirebbe trattare ambedue le scienze come "deux instruments interdépendants de la même science, deux formes de la science des religions dont l'unité composite correspond à celle de son objet, c'est à dire la religion dans deux éléments distincts, l'expérience intérieure et les manifestations extérieures". E infine egli si domanda se questo sistema dualistico non prenda origine da "les débuts mêmes de la science des religions", cioè "le dualisme génetique, les deux sources, provenant l'une de la théologie, l'autre des sciences humanistes". Se questa supposizione fosse giusta, allora egli teme che molti ostacoli devono essere rimossi prima che le acque delle due scienze si fondano insieme nel "grand fleuve de l'histoire religieuse". Queste citazioni provano che Pettazzoni vide molto chiaramente i problemi importanti, ed è ancora dubbio se egli capì pienamente la natura della fenomenologia della religione. Secondo me è evidente che egli trascurò certi elementi nel sistema di Van der Leeuw. La sua supposizione sul fatto che quello che egli chiama il dualismo della scienza delle religioni sia originato da due fonti, cioè la teologia e le scienze umanistiche, è discutibile, perchè non corrisponde ai fatti storici, una tesi che, per mancanza di tempo, non posso qui pienamente sviluppare. In ogni caso Pettazzoni non mise la questione della relazione delle due scienze coinvolte in così chiara luce come si sarebbe dovuto fare. Questo è la ragione per la quale noi ora dobbiamo riaprire la discussione sull'argomento.

Ma prima dovremmo dare la dovuta attenziome all'importante articolo su "Il metodo comparativo" che Pettazzoni pubblicò nel vol. VI fasc. 1 di *Numen*. Egli parte schizzando il modo di procedere della scuola che nei paesi anglosassoni è chiamata "comparative religion". In secondo luogo egli fa una rassegna critica del metodo di comparazione così com'è usato dalla fenomenologia della religione. La sua conclusione è di nuovo che quest'ultima scienza trascura l'idea dello sviluppo storico. Secondo lui il panorama storico è indispensabile alla scienza della religione e ancor più alla storia delle religioni. Pure egli francamente riconosce il significato della fenomenologia della religioni. La sua preoccupazione è che l'antitesi fra le due scienze debba essere superata in modo che esse combinino le loro forze, e questo nel senso che la fenomenologia della religione accetti l'idea dello sviluppo storico e che lo studio puramente storico renda giustizia alla nozione fenomenologica del valore autonomo della religione. Questa attitudine di riconciliazione onora un grande uomo come Pettazzoni ma non dà la soluzione del problema di cui trattiamo. Questa richiede un'indagine esauriente del carattere delle due discipline.

E' difficile che ci possa essere divergenza di opinioni sul carattere della storia delle religioni. Il suo scope è quello che esprime il suo nome stesso, cioè lo studio dello sviluppo storico delle religioni del passato e del presente e primariamente di religioni separate o di certi segmenti delle medesime. Allo scopo di raggiungere un livello scientifico, questo studio deve essere fondato sulla conoscenza delle fonti di informazione e primariamente dei testi. Siccome gli studiosi della storia delle religioni generalmente hanno familiarità soltanto con la lingua et la letteratura di un ristretto numero di religioni, essi difficilmente si avventurano a uscire fuori del dominio delle loro conoscenze tecniche. Perciò è importante notare che il fenomenologo ha un punto di partenza più debole. Allo scopo di costruire considerazioni su tipi e strutture della religione, è costretto a usare fatti provenienti da differenti religioni, fatti che egli accetta sull'autorità degli esperti senza poter controllarli. Ha anche nello studio della storia delle religioni può succedere che si trattino materiali di seconda mano.

Questo è il caso nella cosidetta storia generale delle religioni che o tratta di problemi di relazione fra differenti religioni o compara una religione con l'altra. Con ciò è facile trasgredire i confini della specialità filologica e storica di ciascuno studioso. A questo proposito dovremmo attirare l'attenzione sul fatto che spesso non si fa nessuna distinzione fra la storia generale delle religioni e la religione comparata. D'altra parte alcuni non distinguono religione comparata e fenomenologia della religione, sebbene ovviamente quest'ultima scienza sia basata su di un principio differente da quello della religione comparata. Sono sempre stato fautore di una chiara distinzione fra le quattro scienze in questione. Il compito della storia delle religioni come tale non ha bisogno di ulteriori commenti. La religione comparata può comparare le religioni nel modo migliore; questo è un lavoro interessante, ma è dubbio se i risultati non siano stati alquanto sovrastimati. E' più fruttuoso cercare le caratteristiche uniche dei fenomeni religiosi, perchè essi ci dicono ciò che veramene significa religione. Secondo me la situazione deve essere notevolmente chiarificata se la storia generale delle religioni deve confinare la sua attività ai problemi della relazione fra le differenti religioni nell'ambito della continuità storica.

Queste note aprono la via a una considerazione del principio della fenomenologia della religione. Comunque, nascono subito certe difficoltà, sopratutto risultanti dal fatto che non c'è *communis opinio* sulla natura e lo scopo della scienza. Ne esistono diversi concetti. Si usano differenti nomi. Entro l'ambito di questa conferenza ritengo non sia mio compito quello di presentare la storia della scienza in questione, con riferimenti a tutti i nomi pertinenti di autori e di libri. Menziono soltanto che la mancanza di unità di opinioni esisteva già nel 1940, quando la Dr. Eva Hirschmann scrisse il suo studio, ancora degno di esser letto, dal titolo "*Phänomenologie der Religion. Eine historisch systematische Untersuchung von 'Religionsphänomenologie' und 'Religionsphänomenologischer Methode' in der Religionswissenschaft*". In questo libretto essa tratta di tredici autori che essa classifica in tre tipi, cioè, il tipo puramente descrittivo, il tipo filosofico-psicologico e il tipo strettamente fenomenologico. Dopo il 1940 la fenomenologia della religione è passata attraverso un ulteriore sviluppo che io, per mancanza di tempo, non posso descrivere, sebbene possa essere facilmente detto che ancora non c'è un accordo sulla natura e il compito della scienza. Anche in questo memento potrebbero distinguersi tre tipi: (1) la scuola descrittiva che si contenta di una sistematizzazione dei fenomeni religiosi, (2) la scuola tipologica che ha per scopo la ricerca dei differenti tipi di religione, (3) la scuola fenomenologica nel senso specifico della parola che indaga l'essenza, il senso e la struttura dei fenomeni religiosi.

Quest'ultima scuola merita speciale attenzione perchè i suoi seguaci hanno meditato non solo sullo scopo ma anche sul metodo della scienza. Pertanto la parola fenomenologia assume un doppio significato. Da una parte è una scienza indipendente che crea monografie e manuali più o meno estesi. Ma significa anche un metodi scientifico, cioè l'applicazione dei principi della cosidetta *epoché* e della visione eidetica. *Epoché* significa 'sospensione del giudizio, in questo caso della decisione riguardo alla questione sulla verita dei fenomeni religiosi. Il concetto indica l'atteggiamento di imparzialità, quell'attento ascoltare che è la condizione assoluta per una giusta comprensione dell'importanza dei fenomeni religiosi. La visione eidetica è la ricerca dell'*eidos*, cioè dell'essenza e della struttura dei fatti religiosi. Ambedue i concetti sono stati presi in prestito dalla fenomenologia filosofica di Husserl e della sua scuola, ma qui sono usati nel senso figurativo. A questo proposito dovrebbe essere notato e anche sottolineato che il metodo fenomenologico può essere applicato anche allo studio della storia delle religioni. Secondo me è anche indispensabile che questo metodo sia applicato, se lo storico delle religioni desidera raggiungere dei risultati valevoli. Così; in un certo senso, il desiderio di Pettazzoni potrebbe essere adempiuto: cioè una felice cooperazione può formarsi fra le due scienze, cooperazione che può essere utile ad ambedue le parti: La storia delle religioni otterrà i suoi migliori risultati applicando il metodo fenomenologico et la fenomenologia delle religioni riuscirà a fare dichiarazioni attendibili solo quando usa materiale che le sia provveduto dai migliori rappresentanti della storia delle religioni.

Tuttavia non si dovrebbe dimenticare che fin da principio sono state fatte delle obiezioni alla fenomenologia della religione. Recentemente lo stesso diritto di questa scienza all'esistenza è stato discusso. Quali sono le obiezioni? In primo luogo è stato criticato il nome stesso della scienza; e questo per una doppia ragione. Si è detto che il nome crea confusione perchè è quasi lo stesso di quello di una ben nota scuola filosofica, e per di più il nome mette in questione la popolarità della scienza perchè è poco chiaro per i profani. Più importante è l'osservazione che la natura della disciplina potrebbe essere meglio espressa col nome "scienza comparata della religione". Perchè infatti i fenomenologi applicano l'arte della comparazione allo scopo di capire il valore religioso dei fenomeni anche i più strani ed esotici. Personalmente preferisco il nome tradizionale: sono convinto che essa debba essere una scienza indipendente. Non ho paura del dualismo nello studio della religione, dualismo che Pettazzoni considerava così condannabile. Infatti non è nemmeno questione di dualismo, ma anzi di un sistema quadripartito. Perchè, chiunque voglia fare uno studio completo della religione, deve non solo fare della storia delle religioni e della fenomenologia della religione, ma dovrebbe cercare anche l'aiuto della psicologia della religione e della sociologia delle religione. Queste quattro discipline formano quattro vie che, se percorse nel modo giusto, portano lo studio della religione al suo vero fine.

Dopo che sono stati sufficientemente chiariti i principi della fenomenologia della religione, è ora tempo di definire il suo contributo alla storia delle religioni più esplicitamente. Il primo passo per raggiungere questa mèta è una descrizione del compito di questa scienza. Quest'opera può meglio esser fatta in due fasi: (1) in un modo negativo dicendo che cosa non è di sua competenza, (2) in senso positivo, presentando uno schizzo articolato del lavoro della scienza stessa.

Per quanto riguarda il primo punto, si farebbe un grande servizio alla fenomenologia della religione se il suo ambito di attivatà fosse chiaramente distinto da una parte da quello della fenomenologia filosofica, dall'altra da quello dell'antropologia. Secondo me un lato vulnerabile della fenomenologia di Van der Leeuw è che troppi elementi della fenomenologia filosofica sono stati in essa incorporati, nella forma di speculazione sul più profondo significato del concetto 'fenomeno'. Con ciò la fenomenologia della religione supera i limiti della sua competenza. Chiunque abbia avuto una seria discussione con i seguaci della scuola di Husserl o di Heidegger, sa che, per risolvere queste questioni, è necessaria una conoscenza tecnica e anche un pensiero penetrante. Lo studioso di storia delle religioni è un profano in questa materia e dovrebbe fare a meno di immischiarsi in queste questioni difficili. La fenomenologia della religione non è una filosofia della religione, ma sistematizzazione di fatti storici allo scopo di afferrarne il valore religioso.

D'altra parte la relazione con l'antropologia dovrebbe essere chiaramente definita. E questo perchè alcuni fenomenologi pensano che i fenomeni religiosi possano essere meglio capiti dal punto di vista antropologico. Secondo me questo anche è un errore. Per quanto im-

portante possa essere il fattore umano per la forma attuale dei fenomeni religiosi, la religione come tale, in qualsiasi forma possa apparire,
è sempre in relazione con Dio o col sacro. E' decisivo per la struttura
della religione una certa nozione di Dio e non la mentalità di coloro
che sono religiosi.

In terzo luogo la fenomenologia della religione dovrebbe mantenere
la sua distanza da tutti i tentativi di attualizzare la scienza, nel senso
di supporre che essa debba avere come soggetto principale la pro-
mozione della pace mondiale o la soluzione di problemi pratici di
fede. Si possono fare facilmente esempi di questa concezione. Tra
i partecipanti di ogni congresso di storia delle religioni vi sono sempre
alcuni che pensano che la storia e la fenomenologia della religioni
hanno per scopo la migliore comprensione fra le nazioni e la creazione
di una religione del futuro. In questo c'è un grande errore. Queste
scienze sono limitate a ricercare la verità storica senza preoccuparsi
dei risultati di queste ricerche. A questo proposito anche le considerazioni del Prof. Goodenough, che egli pubblicò nel vol. VI, fasc. 2
di *Numen,* potrebbero avere il loro posto preciso. Goodenough cer-
cava i mezzi per far rivivere lo studio della scienza della religione.
Secondo lui, l'essenza della religione sta nel problema di come l'uomo,
nella sua impotenza, possa vivere di fronte al grande sconosciuto, il
tremendum. Per lo più l'uomo si è isolato dal *tremendum* mediante
racconti mitologici e riti. Ovvero l'individuo ha spezzato il velo mitico
per fronteggiare il *tremendum* numinoso stesso. Secondo Goodenough
la scienza della reigione dovrebbe assumere un movo atteggiamento
verso il *tremendum,* cioè guardarlo con occhi tranquilli, stupiti, reve-
renti ma non spaventati. Questo è un punto di vista interessante e
rispettabile ma non è un modo di studiare scientificamente la religione. E' un'attuazione della scienza in questione, una specia di filosofia della religione e più adatta ad un profano.

Il secondo punto che dovrebbe essere chiarito è una descrizione
comprensiva del compito della fenomenologia della religione. Qui di
nuovo la mancanza di uniformità di opinioni si fa sentire in modo parti-
colarmente penoso. Tuttavia c'è un accordo generale sul fatto che
l'attività della fenomenologia della religione è molteplice. In questa
circostanza posso solo presentare le mie idee personali, non come
l'ultima parola della saggezza, ma come un esempio di come la scienza
potrebbe procedere. Secondo me il compito della fenomenologia della
religione è triplice, nel senso che questa scienza scopre tre dimensioni nei fenomeni religiosi. Tre dimensioni che sono in correlazione

l'una con l'altra, sebbene dovrebbero essere chiaramente distinte. La fenomenologia della religione deve indagare su: (1) la *theoria* dei fenomeni, (2) il *logos* dei fenomeni, (3) la *entelecheia* dei fenomeni. La *theoria* dei fenomeni scopre l'essenza e il significato dei fatti, per esempio il segnificato religioso del sacrificio, della magia, dell'antropologia. Il *logos* dei fenomeni penetra nella struttura delle forme differenti di vita religiosa. La religione non è mai un conglomerato arbitrario di concezioni e di riti, ma possiede una certa struttura con una logica interna. L'*entelecheia* dei fenomeni si rivela nella dinamica, nello sviluppo che è visibile nella vita religiosa dell'umanità. Su quest'ultimo punto Pettazzoni mi sembra che abbia capito male Van der Leeuw, perchè si è sentito offeso da alcune parole forti di quest'ultimo. Van der Leeuw considerava anche lo sviluppo nel mondo della religione. Questo è provato nel paragrafo nella sua "Phänomenologie" in cui egli tratta della "Dynamik der Religionen". Sotto questo titolo egli pone: Sincretismo, missione, risvegli, riforme. Questa sicuramente è una modesta parte degli argomenti impliciti nell'idea di sviluppo. Tuttavia, il paragrafo che ho citato prova che l'antitesi fra Pettazzoni e Van der Leeuw è meno forte di quanto sia generalmente ammessa.

Dal precedente argomentare si può dedurre facilmente il contributo della fenomenologia della relitgione allo studio della storia delle religioni. Riassumendolo in cinque punti, esso può essere formulato come segue: (1) la fenomenologia della religione può rendere un servizio alla storia delle religioni spingendo quest'ultima scienza a considerare i principi del suo studio. E' un fatto ben noto che gli storici delle religioni non si preoccupano troppo dei presupposti del loro lavoro. Non c'è da stupirsi perchè sono degli empirici che dànno la loro attenzione a prove filologiche, storiche o archeologiche. Tuttavia essi agirebbero come lo struzzo se negassero che nessuno può studiare la storia delle religioni senza partire da una visione nascosta del corso degli eventi che si stanno studiando. Ogni storico opera con un suo proprio presupposto di cui egli per lo più non è cosciente. E ne ha tutto il diritto. La questione è soltanto di sapere se egli ha scelto i principi giusti, nel senso che essi gli rendono possibile avvicinarsi ai fatti storici dal punto di vista giusto. Alcuni studi dànno l'impressione che l'autore o è vittima di idee preconcette o possiede solo una debole nozione dei problemi metodologici impliciti nello studio della storia. La fenomenologia della religione può assisterlo su questo punto, perchè ha sviluppato una teoria distinta sul metodo come trattare i fenomeni religiosi.

(2) La fenomenologia della religione aguzza l'occhio alla comprensione della natura specifica della religione e della sua funzione nella vita sociale e culturale. Lo storico delle religioni naturalmente studia la religione nel suo contesto, cioè, intrecciata, come essa è, in ogni specie di fatti non religiosi. Perciò egli è in continuo pericolo di perder di vista la vera natura della religione. La fenomenologia della religione deve continuamente ricordargli lo scope ultimo dei suoi studi, sottolineando che, sebbene la religione in nessun luogo si mostri come "Reinkultur", la storia delle religioni ha successo soltanto quando riesce a chiarire ciò che Pettazzoni ha chiamato "il valore autonomo della religione". Inoltre, secondo me, gli studi storio-religiosi acquistano il loro pieno sapore solo quando mostrano come i concetti e riti religiosi funzionano nel tessuto delle più svariate idee e forze non-religiose.

(3) La fenomenologia della religione illumina lo scopo della storia delle religioni anche in un altro senso. Secondo me, parecchi studi di storia delle religioni per così dire insistono in ricerche filologiche acutissime o in ben scritti trattati storici. Nessuno può negare che la filologia e lo studio storico sono aiuti indispensabili per la storia delle religioni. Anzi si può anche dire di più: che, senza sufficiente filologica e storica nessuno storico delle religioni raggiungerà risultati sorprendenti. Tuttavia c'è un altro lato del quadro: gli studi filologici e storici, per quanto siano brillanti, portano soltanto a metà strada. Lo studioso di storia delle religioni dovrebbe essere più ambizione, non dovrebbe mai riposare prima di aver chiarito il significato religioso di certi fenomeni, per quanto enigmatici essi possano sembrare. La fenomenologia della religione lo incita a non fermarsi finchè non ha raggiunto la vera mèta del suo studio, cioè la chiarificazione del significato dei fenomeni religiosi, sebbene, talvolta, con suo grande rincrescimento, egli debba pronunciare un "non liquet".

(4) La fenomenologia della religione può assistere lo studioso di storia delle religioni facendolo penetrare nell'essenza e nella struttura dei fenomeni religiosi. Il vero storico delle religioni è, dal punto di vista scientifico, un uomo coscienzioso; egli procede passo a passo per raggiungere le sue conclusioni. Spesso scopre tante incertezze e contraddizioni nel suo materiale che non osa pronunciarsi a proposito dell'idea diminante di un certo complesso di fenomeni. Un esempio significative di questo atteggiamento di eccessiva prudenza si può

trovare nel dotto libro dell'assiriologo Oppenheim, intitolato "L'antica Mesopotamia, ritratto di una civiltà morta". Nel quarto capitolo enumera le ragioni per le quali una storia della religione mesopotamica "non può essere scritta". I suoi argomenti sono i seguenti: le prove a disposizione sono troppo scarse e l'uomo moderno non riesce a capire gli uomini dell'antica Mesopotamia attraverso le barriere del condizionamento concettuale. Questo significa, secondo me, un colpo mortale alla storia delle religioni e testimonia nello stesso tempo, di una mancanza di coraggio scientifico e di forza di immaginazione. Senza queste ultime qualità nessuno scienziato mai riuscirebbe nel suo lavoro. Il vero fenomenologo possiede ambedue le qualità. Vediamo come questo può essere messo in opera praticamente. Questo significa, per esempio, che lo storico delle religioni parte dal presupposto che le divinità dell'antichità o dell'Oriente erano essenzialmente figura di una natura omogenea, per quanto possano essere stati più tardi aggiunti ad esse tratti arbitrari. Egli può procedere da questo punto di partenza, perchè è evidente che gli uomini religiosi non hanno mai adorato dèi che fossero un centone disorganico di caratteristiche eterogenee e sconnesse. Inoltre il concetto in questione ha un valore euristico perchè opera come una bacchetta magica che rintraccia la verità storica. D'altra parte è vero che le dichiarazioni talvolta troppo ardite del fenomenologo debbano continuamente essere messe alla prova e corrette dalla conoscenza di fatti dello storico delle religioni. In tal modo può nascere una fruttifera cooperazione fra le due discipline nella linea di quello che intendeva Pettazzoni.

(5) La fenomenologia della religione può indurre lo storico delle religioni a ponderare sulla definizione di religione che egli usa. Questa è una questione importante perchè ogni studioso di storia delle religioni tacitamente tratta una certa nozione di religione durante le sue ricerche. Egli semplicemente non può evitare di fare uso di questa nozione. Perchè altrimenti egli sarebbe incapace di distinguere fatti religiosi da materiale non-religiosi, se non possedesse un criterio per questa scelta. Stando così le cose, è di importanza massima che egli consideri coscientemente l'argomento e scelga la giusta definizione. E' un fatto ben noto che la formulazione di una definizione di religione è una questione cruciale. Nessun fenomenologo pretenderà che la sua concezione sia senza difetti; ma egli ha il vantaggio di aver riflesso sull'argomento e perciò può dare una guida allo storico delle religioni, rendendo possibile a quest'ultimo di rivedere eventualmente la sua definizione di religione che fosse troppo impersonale o imperfetta.

RELIGIONSGESCHICHTE UND RELIGIONS-PHÄNOMENOLOGIE INNERHALB DER GRENZEN DER RELIGIONSWISSENSCHAFTLICHEN VERNUNFT

Eine Skizze

Die wissenschaftliche Diskussion ist wie ein unterirdisches Feuer im Moor, das plötzlich bald hier, bald da aufflackert. So wird nun ein neuer Ruf vernommen im Lager der Religionswissenschaftler. Man verlangt nach Erneuerung der Methode. Dieser Ton klingt an u.a. aus der Reihe "Religion and Reason, Method and Theory in the Study of Interpretation of Religion" [1] und wurde auch in verschiedenen Tonarten gehört auf der Studienkonferenz "Methodology of the Science of Religion", die vom 27.-30. August 1973 in Turku (Finnland) abgehalten wurde.

Wie eine Frau mittleren Alters, die auf einmal entdeckt, dass man ihr das Altern ansieht, ein jugendliches Kostüm anzieht und ihr make up besonders sorgfältig pflegt, um auf's Neue gefallen zu können, so ist bei denen, die sich ernsthaft mit der Religionswissenschaft befassen, das Gefühl entstanden, dass sie altmodisch gekleidet umhergehen und mehr "Pfiff" an den Tag legen müssen, um bei ihren Zeitgenossen Eindruck machen zu können. Um nun die Bildersprache zu beenden: die Veränderungen in der Kultur, dem geistigen Leben und der Wissenschaft vollziehen sich in einem solch schnellen Tempo, dass auch die Religionswissenschaft sich dem Verlangen nach Erneuerung durch kritische Selbstbesinnung nicht entziehen kann, wenn sie in dem Kreis der verwandten Wissenschaften ihre Autorität geltend machen will.

Doch ist es zweifelhaft, ob man dadurch den richtigen Weg eingeschlagen hat, wenn man nur das Methodenproblem löst. Dass der Gedankenaustausch über diese Probleme vorläufig nur eine babylonische Sprachverwirrung zur Folge hatte, wie in Turku deutlich wurde, und dass die schriftliche Diskussion über diesen Gegenstand dann und wann auf Scharfmacherei herausläuft, weil der betreffende Schriftsteller seinen Diskussionspartner auf einige seiner Äusserungen

---

[1] R. D. Baird, *Category Formation and the History of Religion*, 1971; J. Waardenburg, *Classical Approaches to the Study of Religion*, 1973; *Religion, Culture and Methodology*, Papers of the Groningen Working Group for the Study of fundamental Problems and Methods of Science of Religion, 1973.

festnagelt, ohne den Leitgedanken von dessen Erörterungen Recht widerfahren zu lassen, will ich als vorübergehende Krankheitserscheinungen unbesprochen lassen. Wichtiger sind zwei andere Schwierigkeiten.

Wer prinzipiell über die religionswissenschaftliche Methode nachdenkt, begibt sich unwiderruflich auf philosophisches Gebiet. Auf diesem Gebiet ist der Religionsgeschichtler ein völliger Laie. Er ist nicht geschult für die Behandlung dieser Fragen. Das wird ganz deutlich, wenn die viel besprochene Frage nach dem Wesen der Religion zur Sprache gebracht wird. Da tritt Unkenntnis zutage was Religionsphilosophen wie E. Troeltsch und H. Scholz [2] dazu geschrieben haben, abgesehen von der Tatsache, dass diese Diskutierenden sicherlich nicht die diesbezüglichen Schriften von Hegel, Heidegger oder Sartre gelesen haben. Es würde absurd sein, von ihnen eine solche Belesenheit zu verlangen. Doch weil sie diese nicht besitzen, müssen sie sich an das alte Sprichwort klammern: Schuster, bleib bei deinen Leisten! Das bedeutet, dass derjenige, der sich ernsthaft mit Religionswissenschaft befasst, die Grenzen seiner Fachkenntnis und seiner Einsicht überhaupt kennen und sie achten muss, wenn er kein Pfuscher werden will. Es ist zweifellos seine Pflicht, gründlich nachzudenken über die Begriffe, mit denen er umgeht, aber auch hier kann er seine Meisterschaft nur dann zeigen, wenn er sich in seinen Erörterungen streng beschränkt auf das, was er als Fachmann beweisen kann, und trotzdem noch ein Interesse für andere Aspekte der Fragen, die ihn beschäftigen, aufweist. Ein treffliches Beispiel von "epochè" im Hinblick auf die methodische Problematik gibt Geo Widengren. Obwohl philosophisch wahrhaftig kein Analphabet begnügt er sich in seiner "Religionsphänomenologie" mit einigen summarischen einleitenden Bemerkungen über die Prinzipien dieses Faches, während nur ein e i n z i g e r kurzer Artikel über die Methode aus seiner Feder stammt. [3] Trotzdem hat er ein Werk geschaffen, um das ihn alle Fachgenossen beneiden können!

---

[2] E. Troeltsch, (*Gesammelte Schriften,* zweiter Band, Zur religiösen Lage, Religionsphilosophie und Ethik, 1913) hat in seinem Artikel: Was heisst "Wesen des Christentums" dargelegt, dass der Begriff "Wesen" dreierlei Bedeutung haben kann, nämlich "Das Wesen als Kritik", "Das Wesen als Entwicklungsbegriff", "Das Wesen als Idealbegriff"; H. Scholz behandelt in seiner "Religionsphilosophie" unter diesem Thema folgende Aspekte: "Begriff und Erfassung des Wesens der Religion; Die Religion als Erfassung des Göttlichen; Die Religion in ihrem Verhältnis zu den übrigen Erscheinungen des menschlichen Geisteslebens".

[3] G. Widengren, *Some Remarks on the Methodology of the Phenomenology of Religion* (Universitetet och forskningen, 1960, Seite 250-260).

Die zweite Schwierigkeit kann kurz zo furmuliert werden: es hat keinen Sinn, über die Methode einer Wissenschaft zu reden, wenn man nicht vorher deren Prinzipien geklärt hat. Die Methode ist nämlich nur der praktische Handgriff, der aus den Prinzipien hervorgeht. Obendrein darf man nicht vergessen, dass für alle Wissenschaften tatsächlich nur eine einzige Methode gilt, d.h. die kritische, mit deren Hilfe man die betreffenden Gegebenheiten sichtet, ordnet und nach ihrem Wert und ihrer Bedeutung zu verstehen trachtet. Wenn z.B. Religionswissenschaftler verlangen, dass man sich Kenntnis verschaffen muss z.B. von den Methoden der kulturellen Anthropologie, der Psychologie oder der Soziologie, dann drücken sie sich verkehrt aus. Was sie meinen, ist, dass man aufgeschlossen sein muss für die Einsichten und Studienergebnisse derartiger Wissenschaften.

Diese Überlegungen lassen vermuten, was mit dem Titel zu diesem Artikel gemeint ist. Dass diese Überschrift eine Variante des Titels einer bekannten Schrift Emanuel Kants ist, braucht kaum erwähnt zu werden. Obgleich ich es für zweifelhaft halte, ob die Religion zu ihrem vollen Recht kommt, wenn man den Glauben "innerhalb der Grenzen der blossen Vernunft" einfängt, so ist es meine feste Überzeugung, dass das Studium der Religionsgeschichte und Religionsphänomenologie nur dann fruchtbar sein kann, wenn es sich streng innerhalb der Grenzen ihrer eigenen, d.h. der religionswissenschaftlichen Vernunft, hält. Diese These begreift zwei Forderungen mit ein: erstens müssen sich die infrage kommenden Gelehrten nach den Normen der Religionswissenschaft richten, zweitens dürfen sie die Erscheinung Religion keinesfalls durch irgendwelche Theorie entwerten, sondern müssen sie in ihrem Vorhandensein achten. Bevor ich nun zur Besprechung dieser beiden Punkte übergehe, will ich nachdrücklich darauf hinweisen, dass ich nicht nur durch die Anlage dieses Artikels gezwungen bin, meinen Betrachtungen die Form einer Skizze zu geben, sondern dass ich diese Form auch bewusst gewählt habe. Er erscheint mir nämlich überflüssig, was andere und ich selbst schon früher auseinandergesetzt haben zu wiederholen. Ebenswenig ist es nötig, mit seiner Kenntnis der einschlägigen Literatur zu prahlen. [4] Die Beweisführung muss die Fragen direkt in Angriff nehmen, die jetzt beantwortet werden müssen.

---

[4] Diese Literatur ist leicht zu finden in den unter Anmerkung 1 genannten Werken; lesenswert ist noch immer Eva Hirschmann, "Phänomenologie der Religion, Eine historisch-systematische Untersuchung von 'Religionsphänomenologie' und 'religionsphänomenologischer Methode' in der *Religionswissenschaft*, 1940; s. ferner C. J. Bleeker, *The Sacred Bridge*, 1963 und die ersten Artikel in diesem Band.

Der erste Punkt gibt Veranlassung dazu, vor allem den allgemein anerkannten Unterschied zwischen Theologie und Religionswissenschaft zu betonen. Theologie im strengen Sinn des Wortes ist eine Besinnung auf den Glauben — auf den christlichen, moslimischen, oder irgend einen anderen Glauben —, trägt einen Zeugnis-Charakter und steht im Dienst einer religiösen Gemeinschaft oder Kirche, wobei man herausheben muss, dass bestimmte theologische Fächer wie das Bibelstudium oder die Kirchengeschichte in der Regel nach religionswissenschaftlichen Gesichtspunkten studiert werden. Religionswissenschaft ist die freie, vorurteilslose und kritische Erforschung der religiösen Erscheinungen. Der Grund, weshalb ich diese abgedroschene Frage wieder auf das Tapet bringe, ist folgender: man wirft heutzutage bestimmten Gelehrten, vor allem G. van der Leeuw und H. Kraemer vor, ihre Werke seien nicht frei von theologischem Einschlag. Es mag durchaus wahr sein, dass v. d. Leeuw die Grenze zwischen den beiden genannten Wissenschaften nicht immer scharf gezogen hat, obwohl er sich dieser Sache wohl bewusst war; bei ihm aber ist das eine Angelegenheit ganz am Rande und tut dem Wert seiner religionsgeschichtlichen und phänomenologischen Arbeit keinerlei Abbruch. Bei Kraemer liegt die Sache allerdings etwas anders. Ihm und einigen seiner Anhänger stand als Ideal eine *theologia religionum* vor Augen. Da aber niemals ein bedeutendes Werk erschienen ist, das die Lebensfähigkeit dieses Projektes beweisen könnte, braucht man nur wenige Worte an diese Vorstellung zu verschwenden. [5]

Das Grundprinzip der Religionswissenschaft ist also die kritische und unbefangene Bearbeitung der religiösen Erscheinungen. Diese Formulierung schliesst zwei verkehrte Auffassungen über das Ziel dieser Wissenschaft aus. Es gibt einmal Menschen, die die Ansicht vertreten, die Religionsforschung müsse in erster Linie dazu dienen, eine bessere Verständigung zwischen den Bekennern verschiedenen Glaubens zu erzielen und dabei den Weltfrieden zu fördern. Man darf wohl hoffen, dass als eine Nebenwirkung der religionswissenschaftlichen Forschung diese höheren Güter der Menschheit verstärkt werden, in diesem Zusammenhang aber ist es nötig, doppelt zu unterstreichen, dass die erwähnte Forschung von streng wissenschaftlicher Art ist, und zwar ein Suchen nach der Wahrheit um der Wahrheit willen. Zum anderen Mal erwarten andere, dass diese Wissenschaft eine Antwort geben soll auf die aktuelle und schwierige

---

[5] R. Pummer, "Religionswissenschaft or Religiology?" (*Numen,* Vol. XIX, Fasc. 2-3).

Frage nach der Religion der Zukunft. Die Voraussetzung für diesen Gedanken ist die, dass die traditionelle Theologie ihren Anspruch verloren hat, sodass nun die Religionswissenschaft an ihre Stelle treten soll. In der Tat hat hier und da die Religionswissenschaft die Theologie ersetzt. Es gibt auch Fachgenossen, die über die Art der Religion heute und in Zukunft Vermutungen anstellen. Die offizielle Religionswissenschaft aber muss den nötigen Abstand zu solchen Bemühungen wahren. Sie ist nicht befugt, über diese Angelegenheit auch nur eine einzige Aussage zu machen. Sie wird ja ausgeübt von Gelehrten, die verschiedenen Religionen, Konfessionen und Kirchen angehören, oder die ohne Bekenntnis sind. Was sie alle verbindet, ist die Forderung nach einer unvoreingenommenen Erforschung der Religion als einem Phänomen, das historische und zeitgemässe Bedeutung hat.

Das zweite Gesetz, das der religionswissenschaftlichen Vernunft entspringt, heisst: religiöse Gegebenheiten müssen in ihrer Art und ihrem Wert unangetastet bleiben. Die Gefahr, dass man die Religion verkehrt interpretiert, ist nicht nur Einbildung. Sie kommt aus zwei Richtungen, nähmlich erstens aus der "Gott-ist-tot-Theologie" und zweitens von der suggestiven Kraft, die aus der kulturellen Anthropologie und der Soziologie ausgeht.

Die "Gott-ist-tot-Theologie" ist tatsächlich eines von den Symptomen, dass viele den Blick auf die metaphysische Tiefe des Lebens und der Welt verloren haben. Diese geistige Blindheit kann Forschern die Fähigkeit nehmen zu verstehen, was der Gläubige meint, wenn er Zeugnis ablegt von seiner Begegnung mit dem Numinosen, dem Heiligen, einer höheren Wirklichkeit oder Wahrheit. Die Zahl der anzuführenden Zeugnisse dieser Art aus allen Zeiten und Völkern beträgt Legion. Die Gefahr besteht, dass man nicht mehr "glaubt" an das Bestehen einer solchen vollblütigen Religiosität und diese dann reduziert wird auf eine immanente humanistische Frömmigkeit, die noch annehmbar erscheint. Nun braucht der Forscher ja nicht persönlich daran zu glauben — die Religionswissenschaft kann und darf sich nicht über die Wahrheit der Religion äussern —, aber die wissenschaftliche Ehrlichkeit gebietet, dass man keine Tatsachen verdunkelt und solche Zeugnisse unangetastet lässt.

Die zweite Gefahr kommt aus der Richtung der kulturellen Anthropologie und Soziologie, die Beide in den letzten Jahrzehnten aus ganz erklärlichen Gründen grossen Aufschwung nahmen. Man kann zweifellos viel von diesen Disziplinen lernen, vor allem was den anthropologischen und soziologischen Kontext der religiösen Gegebenheiten angeht. Die heute oft gehörte Klage, Religionswissenschaftler hätten diese Richtung ganz unbeachtet gelassen, ist nicht berechtigt. E. O. James hat schon 1938 in seinem Buch "Comparative Religion" nachdrücklich betont, dass "religion is the spiritual force holding society together". Eine eventuelle Korrektur in der religionswissenschaftlichen Forschung unter dem Einfluss der genannten neuen Fächer darf aber nicht zur Folge haben, dass die Religion primär als eine humanistische und kulturelle Erscheinung aufgefasst wird. Wenn auch in den Kreisen der kulturellen Anthropologen das Verständnis für die Eigenart und Bedeutung der Religion erwacht ist, [6] muss man doch auf der Hut sein und darf sich nicht zur Aufgabe von erprobten religionswissenschaftlichen Prinzipien verleiten lassen. Um noch die Pünktchen auf die i's zu setzen, scheint es mir nicht überflüssig zu sein, folgende zwei Grundsätze hervorzuheben:

erstens: die religionswissenschaftliche Forschung hat nicht in erster Linie das Ziel, den religiösen Menschen als solchen zu verstehen, sondern muss ihren Ehrgeiz daran setzen zu verdeutlichen, wie der Mensch sich verhält gegenüber einer göttlichen Wirklichkeit, der er begegnet ist.

zweitens: Religion ist nicht so sehr ein Versuch des Menschen, sich in das Zusammenleben, in die Kultur einzuordnen, sondern muss als sein Streben, sein Stellung gegenüber übermächtigen, höheren Mächten zubestimmen, gewertet werden. Ich möchte noch anfügen, dass es mir nicht ratsam erscheint, bestimmte religionswissenschaftliche Begriffe wie Mythus, Ritus oder den Begriff "Religion" einseitig mit den Gegebenheiten der kulturellen Anthropologie zu untermauern, wie es bisweilen geschieht. Das ist eine viel zu schmale Basis, und obendrein sind diese Unterlagen nicht immer philologisch und historisch kontrollierbar.

Auf Grund dieser Überlegungen halte ich den ersten Teil der Definition von Religion, die Th. P. van Baaren kürzlich veröffentlichte, nämlich: "Religion is a function of culture and is connected with and interacts with other functions of culture" nicht nur für unrichtig, sondern auch für irreführend. [7] Unrichtig, weil es verschiedene Arten von Religionen gibt wie Asketismus und Prophetismus, die der Kultur völlig zuwiderlaufen. Irreführend, weil bei dieser Formulierung ver-

---

[6] Proceedings of the 1974 Annual Spring Meeting of the American Ethnological Society, Symposion on New Approaches to the Study of Religion.
[7] *Religion, Culture and Methodology* usw., S. 36.

gessen wird, dass der Sinn der Religion, die bei der religionswissenschaftlichen Untersuchung tatsächlich eine kulturelle Grösse ist, darin besteht, dass der Glaube auf eine Wahrheit und Wirklichkeit hinweist, die sich über die Kultur erhebt.

Unwillkürlich ist damit die kritische Frage nach einer allgemein annehmbaren Definition von Religion am Horizont aufgetaucht. Es ist klar, dass der Begriff "Religion" ein abstractum ist. Die Wirklichkeit lässt uns aber eine Vielgestaltigkeit von Religion sehen. Kann man denn nun eine Definition von Religion finden, die diese Vielgestaltigkeit unter eine Decke zu bringen vermag? Dazu ein paar Anmerkungen. Mancher hält es für ausgeschlossen, dass man Religionen mit einem ausgesprochen theistischen Gottesbegriff und andere Religionen, in denen der Gottesbegriff scheinbar fehlt, in e i n e r Wesensumschreibung vereinigen kann. Diesen Einwand kann man dadurch aus dem Weg räumen, indem man darauf aufmerksam macht, dass alle Religionen zu einer überweltlichen Macht tendieren, selbst der "atheistische" ursprüngliche Buddhismus, nämlich zu dem Nirvâna. Schwerer wiegt die Tatsache, dass das Suchen nach einer Definition offenbar festgefahren ist. Die Religion lässt sich nicht in einer kurzen einspurigen Formel einfangen. Um die Struktur der Religion zu bestimmen, verdient meiner Meinung nach folgende Überlegung den Vorzug: man muss als ihre konstitutiven Faktoren das erkennen, was ich genannt habe "die heilige Schau", "den heiligen Weg", "die heilige Handlung". Man kann dann leicht erkennen, dass das erste Glied dieser Trias "logisch" die Art der beiden anderen bestimmt. [8] Es freut mich, feststellen zu können, dass der kulturelle Antropologe M. E. Spiro in analoger Richtung denkt, wenn er schreibt, dass die Religion drei "subsystems" umfasst: "a belief system", "a value system" und "an action system". [9]

Eine zweite Frage ist die, ob man eine Definition von Religion haben muss, bevor man an die Arbeit geht. Die Praxis beweist, dass viele hervorragende Gelehrte vortreffliche Dienste geleistet haben, ohne sich um dieses Problem gekümmert zu haben. Sie besassen offensichtlich ein intuitives Gefühl für echte Religion, mit dem sie wie mit einer Wünschelrute arbeiten konnten. Ein solches Organ muss man wohl haben, wenn man fruchtbare Arbeit leisten will. Übrigens findet hier die Wechselwirkung statt, die W. B. Kristensen zutreffend folgendermassen umschreibt: "Research always anticipates the

[8] C. J. Bleeker, *Het Geheim van de Godsdienst*, 1973/3.
[9] Oben zitiert in Anmerkung 6, S. 102.

essence of the phenomena, which essence is nevertheless the goal of all scientific endeavour". [10]

"So far, so good", sagt der Engländer. Wie setzen die Fächer, die für gewöhnlich zu der Religionswissenschaft gerechnet werden, dieses oben beschriebene Prinzip in die Praxis um? Zunächst die Feststellung dass es die folgenden Fächer sind: Religionsgeschichte, Religionspsychologie, Religionssoziologie und Religionsphilosophie. Das letzte Fach nimmt eine besondere Stellung ein. Nicht deshalb, weil in ihm, wie zu unrecht behauptet wird, axiologische Massstäbe angelegt werden, sondern weil das Studium dieser Probleme eine Anlage zur Philosophie voraussetzt, die der Durchschnittreligionswissenschaftler nicht besitzt. Dieses Fach lasse ich aus diesem Grund unbesprochen. Auch die Religionspsychologie und die Religionssoziologie schiebe ich zur Seite, weil sie für die hier gewählte Problemstellung keine besonderen Gesichtspunkte bieten. Der Scheinwerfer für diese Untersuchung ist auf Religionsgeschichte und Religionsphänomenologie gerichtet, auf ihre Zusammengehörigkeit und auf die Art und Weise, in der in diesen Fächern gearbeitet werden muss.

Was nun die Religionsgeschichte angeht, so zerfällt dieses Fach nach allgemeinem Dafürhalten in zwei Teile, in einen besonderen und in einen allgemeinen Teil. Über die Aufgabe des besonderen Teiles der Religionsgeschichte besteht keine Unsicherheit: die spezielle Religionsgeschichte muss die einzelnen Religionen oder Teile davon bearbeiten. Die allgemeine Religionsgeschichte ist noch immer recht farblos. Sie hat noch nicht Gestalt gewonnen in einer besonderen Untersuchung. Auch fällt sie nicht zusammen mit dem, was man in den Englisch sprechenden Ländern "comparative religion" nennt. Meines Erachtens muss sie sich beschäftigen mit der wechselseitigen Beeinflussung der Religionen unter den Bedingungen von Raum und Zeit. Darüber könnte man ein interessantes Buch schreiben.

Wichtiger aber als diese formellen Bemerkungen ist die Frage, wie diese Wissenschaft ihr Material betrachtet und was sie endgültig bezweckt. Darüber will ich gern meine Meinung sagen.

Zuerst will ich aber davor warnen, dass man sich durch das Wort "Geschichte" im Namen dieses Fachs nicht irreführen lässt. Der historische Verlauf nämlich von religionsgeschichtlichen Ereignissen ist manchmal nicht mehr zu ermitteln wie etwa im Manichäismus, oder er ist nicht von wesentlicher Bedeutung, z.B. bei der Erfor-

---

[10] W. B. Kristensen, *The Meaning of Religion*, 1960, S. 8.

schung der alt-ägyptischen Religion, bei der es um die Entdeckung des Grundmodells geht. Die eigentliche Aufgabe ist deshalb nicht so sehr die Beschreibung der Entwicklung einer Religion, sondern vielmehr die, die Bedeutung einer Religion im Leben eines bestimmten Volkes zu umreissen.

Zum anderen bin ich davon überzeugt, dass man besser tut, wenn man, anstatt über Methode zu philosophieren, kritisch und sachlich den Begriffsapparat prüft, den man verwendet. Diese Erkenntnis hat mich z.B. dazu gebracht, eine Untersuchung über die religionswissenschaftliche Terminologie bei den alten Ägyptern anzustellen. [11] Ausgegangen bin ich von der Äusserung von Siegfried Morenz, dass die Begriffe: Religion, Glaube, Frömmigkeit, mit denen der Religionswissenschaftler täglich zu tun hat, in der ägyptischen Sprache nicht vorkommen. Ich schlug dann in dem Teil Deutsch-Ägyptisch des "Wörterbuches der ägyptischen Sprache" nach, welche Begriffe darin vorkämen. Dies führte zu interessanten Schlussfolgerungen: einerseits wurde klar, dass die Ägypter noch nicht das Niveau von "sophistication" erreicht hatten, auf dem wir leben, denken und über Religion sprechen, andererseits aber lernte man so die typischen Ausdrücke kennen, in denen das ägyptische religiöse Bewusstsein sich geäussert hat. Ich stelle mir manchmal ernsthaft die Frage, ob die Bekenner der Religionen, die wir studieren, ihren Glauben wiedererkennen würden in dem Bild, das wir durch unsere Fachausdrücke entwerfen.

Zum Dritten ist es nützlich, wenn wir einsehen, dass die religionswissenschaftliche Arbeit in verschiedenen Dimensionen verrichtet werden kann und auch in der Tat so stattfindet. Ohne dem Wert von philologischen oder archäologischen Detailstudien Abbruch tun zu wollen, meine ich doch, dass die eigentliche Aufgabe darin besteht, was Kristensen "to investigate what religious value the believers (Griechen, Babylonier, Ägypter usw) attached to their faith, what religion meant to them" [12] nannte.

Viertens aber schliesse ich mich gern dem vortrefflichen Hinweis van Baarens an, wenn er darauf aufmerksam macht, dass Religion in verschiedenen Stufen von Ursprünglichkeit vorkommt. [13] Diesen Gedanken möchte ich folgendermassen verdeutlichen: Seiner Zeit hat man sich sehr intensiv mit der Erscheinung "Bekehrung" beschäf-

---

[11] "Einige Bemerkungen zur religiösen Terminologie der alten Ägypter", s. diesen Band.
[12] Kristensen, oben zitiert, S. 61.
[13] *Religion, Culture and Methodology* usw., S. 42.

tigt. E. D. Starbuck schrieb darüber auf Grund einer statistischen Untersuchung ein Buch. W. James gründete seine berühmten Betrachtungen über "Varieties of Religious Experiences" auf Aufsehen erregende Fälle von Bekehrungen. Beide Methoden besitzen ihre Werte. Sozial-psychologisch liefert die Arbeitsweise Starbucks wahrscheinlich die besten Resultate. Religionswissenschaftlich gesehen erhält man zweifellos durch James' Verfahren das schärfste Bild.

Zum Schluss will ich noch ein Wort der "question célèbre" widmen, ob man zu einer Religion durchdringen kann, die man selbst nicht bekennt. Dieses Problem ist kompliziert. Jeder Gläubige hat ein Geheimnis, das der Aussenstehende nicht kennt. In jeder Religion steckt ein Kern eines Glaubenserlebnisses, zu dem der Religionswissenschaftler nicht durchdringen kann. Gläubigen lebender Religionen kann man dieses Geheimnis entlocken. Die antiken Völker haben dieses Geheimnis mit ins Grab genommen, ohne uns Erklärungen von Mythen und Riten zu hinterlassen, die sie begriffen, die für uns aber unverständlich sind. Sicherlich ist es ratsam, Anhänger der Religion, die man erforschen will, nach ihrer Überzeugung zu fragen. W. Cantwell Smith geht aber entschieden zu weit, wenn er die Gültigkeit der Beschreibung einer Religion von der Billigung durch die Bekenner dieser Religion abhängig macht. Auf Grund seiner Fachkenntnis hat der Religionswissenschaftler meistens eine bessere Übersicht und manchmal auch eine bessere Einsicht als die Gläubigen selbst. Abschliessend kann man feststellen, dass der Religionswissenschaftler trotz aller Hindernisse fähig sein wird auf Grund seiner Kenntnis der Tatsachen und seiner Liebe zu seinem Gegenstand, ein gutes Stück in den Kern einer fremden Religion einzudringen.

Die Religionsphänomenologie ist seit geraumer Zeit die Zielscheibe der Kritik. Es gibt Stimmen, die sagen, der Name sei nicht zu brauchen, weil er zu viel an Husserls Philosophie erinnere, und dass das Fach in dieser Form verschwinden müsse, weil es mit seiner zu wenig exakten Methode keine zuverlässigen Resultate erzielt habe. Diese Kritik ist nicht neu. [14] Auch in ihrer allerneuesten Form wirkt sie nicht überzeugend. Name und Fach bestanden schon, bevor die phänomenologische Philosophie auf die Bühne trat. Sie haben Beide, sogar in den Englisch sprechenden Ländern, Eingang gefunden, wo sie aber die Konkurrenz der dort so populären "Comparative Religion" überstehen mussten. Dieser Erfolg ist der imponierenden Arbeit

---

[14] C. J. Bleeker, "Comparing the religio-historical and the theological Method" (*Numen*, Vol. XVIII, Fasc. 1.).

von einer Reihe hervorragender Religionsphänomenologen zu verdanken.

Dennoch ist es selbstverständlich, dass man bei der Beschäftigung mit diesem Fach, das jetzt rund hundert Jahre als solches besteht, neue Wege einschlagen muss. Es ist aber eine Illusion, wenn man glaubt, durch einen neuen Namen eine neue Wissenschaft krëieren zu können. Es geht heute natürlich nicht nur um eine Namensänderung. Man möchte ganz neu an diese Probleme herangehen. Was einige Gelehrte als Ersatz empfehlen, vermag ich aber nicht als eine Verbesserung anzusehen. Th. P. van Baaren sieht einen gelungenen Ausweg in der Einführung dessen, was er "systematische Religionswissenschaft" nennt. [15] Es bleibt aber unklar, was er mit diesem Ausdruck meint: ein anderer Name für die Religionsphänomenologie oder eine Tautologie der Religionswissenschaft? Wenn das zuletzt Genannte gemeint sein sollte, dann muss man bedenken, dass zu dieser Wissenschaft auch die Religionsgeschichte gehört, ein Fach, das nicht in erster Linie nach systematischem Muster bearbeitet werden kann. K. Rudolph bevorzugt die Bezeichnung "vergleichende Religionswissenschaft". [16] Auch dieser Vorschlag bietet keine bessere Charakteristik des gemeinten Faches, denn man "vergleicht" zum Beispiel auch in der Religionsgeschichte und in der Religionssoziologie. Ausserdem verschleiert man und verkennt auch das eigentliche Anliegen der betreffende Wissenschaft. Das Vergleichen nämlich ist für die Religionsphänomenologie nur ein Mittel, um ihr tatsächliches Ziel zu erreichen.

Augenscheinlich hat man vergessen, was die Vorläufer in klaren Worten dazu gesagt haben. Wiederum will ich Kristensen zitieren, nicht nur, weil er sich so scharf auszudrücken vermag, sondern auch, weil er als der Gründer der niederländischen Schule von Religionsphänomenologen gelten kann. Er verfasste folgende Formulierung: "Phenomenology of Religion is the systematic treatment of the History of Religion. That is to say, its task is to classify and group the numerous divergent data in such a way that an overall view can be obtained of their religious content and the religious values they contain." [17] Ferner hat er auch deutlich die raison d'être der Religionsphänomenologie angedeutet durch den Hinweis, dass überall vorkom-

---

[15] Th. P. van Baaren, "Science of Religion as a Systematic Discipline, Some Introductory Remarks" (*Religion, Culture and Methodology* usw., S. 35 ff.)

[16] K. Rudolph, "Das Problem der Autonomie und Integrität der Religionswissenschaft" (*Nederlands Theologisch Tijdschrift,* 27. Jahrg., 2. Auflage, April 1973).

[17] Kristensen, oben zitiert, S. 61.

mende Erscheinungen wie Opfer, Gebet, Königtum zu einer phänomenologischen Behandlung zwingen. In "The Meaning of Religion",
den nach seinem Tod herausgegebenen Kollegnachschriften, findet
man auch den logisch sich ergebenden Aufbau dieses Fachs: "Cosmology; Anthropology; Cultus". Van der Leeuw hat dieses Schema
variiert in "Das Objekt der Religion; das Subjekt der Religion; Objekt
und Subjekt in ihrer Wirkung auf einander". Wie schon gesagt wurde,
habe ich als Einteilung gewählt "Die Heilige Schau; Der Heilige Weg;
Die Heilige Handlung". [18] Obendrein meine ich damit Einwänden
R. Pettazoni's, dass die Aufgabe dieser Wissenschaft ausgedehnter
ist als aus der oben beschriebenen Aufgabenbestimmung hervorgeht, begegnen zu können, wenn ich sage: der Auftrug der Religionsphänomenologie ist ein dreiteiliger: das Studium der Theōria,
des Logos und der Entelecheia der Phänomene. [19]

Gern will ich anerkennen, dass die geübte Kritik ein Symptom ist
dafür, dass das Fach einer Erneuerung bedarf. Nun bedeutet Reform
sowohl de verbis als de facto, dass man eine neue Form wählt für
bereits Bestehendes. In diesem Fall muss man auf den Fundamenten
bauen, die durch Vorgänger errichtet sind, oder, um es anders auszudrücken, man soll sich erst die Einsichten und das Denkschema
der Koryphäen des Faches zu eigen machen und dann erst etwas ganz
Neuen zu schaffen versuchen. Mit Spannung wartet man darauf, was
radikale Reformer zustandebringen. Solange noch kein Buch auf dem
Tisch liegt, das die Werke von Edv. Lehmann, W. B. Kristensen,
G. van der Leeuw, E. O. James, M. Eliade, K. Goldammer, F. Heiler,
Geo Widengren und meine eigene bescheidene Produktion in den
Schatten stellen kann, — auch wenn eine derartige neue Studie nicht
so umfangreich zu sein braucht, denn auf die Originalität kommt es
an —, kann man die geäusserte Kritik mit Gelassenheit anhören.

E i n Punkt aber, der, wie man sagt, die Methode angeht, verdient noch unsere Aufmerksamkeit. Van der Leeuw und anderen wird
vorgeworfen, sie hätten der intuitiven Methode zu viel zugestanden.
Ich will gern dafür eintreten. Nach meiner Vermutung wird dieser
kritische Einwand in Umlauf gebracht, weil bestimmte Religionswissenschaftler so beeindruckt worden sind durch die exakte Arbeitsweise der Naturwissenschaft und bestimmter Sozialwissenschaften,

---

[18] Il metodo comparativo (Numen, VI, fasc. 1).
[19] C. J. Bleeker, "The Phenomenological Method" (*Numen*, Vol. VI, fasc. 2),
"La structure de la Religion", "Some Remarks on the 'Entelecheia' of Religious
Phenomena" (*The Sacred Bridge*, 1963).

dass sie auch in ihrem Fach eine solche Exaktheit in der Forschungs-
arbeit erreichen wollen. Nach meiner festen Überzeugung gerät man
damit auf eine verkehrte Spur. Computer und Statistik werden niemals
eine tiefere Einsicht in die Bedeutung religiöser Erscheinungen bieten können. Jedes Vögelchen muss singen, wie ihm der Schnabel gewachsen ist. In den humanistischen Wissenschaften spielen Phantasie
und Schau nun einmal eine heuristische Rolle. Auch hier gilt: "Tout
sort de l'idée." Es ist der plötzliche Einfall, meist intuitiv geschenkt
mitten in mühsamer philologischer und historischer Arbeit, der die
schönsten religionswissenschaftlichen Früchte erbringt. Kristensen
erklärte: "Again and again a certain amount of intuition is indispensable". [20] Physiker denken darüber nicht anders. Einige in diesem Fach
führende Amsterdamer Kollegen haben mir erklärt, dass sie bestimmte Theorien absolut bejahten, weil ihr intuitives Gefühl für
Schönheit dadurch befriedigt würde.

---

[20] Kristensen, oben zitiert, S. 62.

HOW TO DISTINGUISH BETWEEN TRUE RELIGION
AND FALSE RELIGION? *

In his book on philosophy of religion the Danish philosopher Søren Holm tackles the difficulty of the problem how the essence of religion should be defined. In the third chapter of his book he speaks first of "the methods to define the essence" and then deals with "the relation between essence and truth". With regard to the last question, his opinion is that "one cannot theoretically and objectively state what is true and what is false Christianity".

This conclusion, which not only holds true for Christianity, but is applicable too to religion as such, is fully correct philosophically. Yet one cannot deny, that in ordinary life he is often forced to take a stand in distinguishing between true and false religion. Thus, the question arises: what is the distinction between true religion and false réligion? This is not an easy problem to solve, because truth and falsehood occur side by side in the field of religion. Sometimes the two are intertwined in a curious way and can hardly be separated. The Swedish philosopher Axel Hägerström once said: "It is contended that one can gather *edelweiss* from the snow of the Alps. In the same way the blue flower of religion buds in the darkness of superstition". This is perfectly true. The beautiful and pure flower of piety can grow up in the unhealthy mould of false religion. Thus the question arises whether there is a criterion by means of which true religion can be recognized so clearly that error and doubt are excluded.

This is a question of paramount importance, a thoroughly human problem. The desire for true religion, for fully reliable religious truth, is more wide-spread than people used to believe. For man possesses the intuitive feeling that life loses its value and is completely wasted if it might turn out that it had been built on untruth, namely not on a mistake that can be corrected, but on an absolutely false insight into the real foundation of human life. Thus is it terrible to consider that national socialism in Germany, on the authority of Hitler, its leader, sent thousands of people (mostly of the jounger generation) to death on a false belief, that is an untruth. For it is clear that the national socialistic world view, for millions of Germans, once functioned as a

* Published in swedish in *Festschrift til Søren Holm på 70-årsdagen den 4 marts 1971*.

religion, or rather a pseudo-religion. It is not necessary to believe in a real hell, in which the devil and his companions torture sinners in order to come to the insight that human life, if built on false religion, becomes a horrible joke when considered in the light of eternity. Therefore one can better understand both the passionate search for true religion and the fight for the right faith, even in its unsympathetic forms. We refer to petty intolerances, the bigotted zeal to make proselytes, and the malicious denunciation of dissenters. At the same time the salvation of the soul, together with bliss and peace in the land of eternity depend upon the possession of the true faith.

But even apart from this perspective it is of paramount importance to know whether a certain form of religion can stand the test of truth and genuineness. There are in the present chaotic culture a great number of sects and religious groups which make propaganda and try to gain adherents. If a person is not rooted in the firm soil of a personal belief, but instead is groping and wandering, seeking to find his way in the spiritual world, he is forced to develop an attitude towards all sorts of forms of religion, particularly those which present themselves in the deceptive garment of an apparent idealism. He cannot avoid the inevitable set of questions: Can I commit myself to this belief? Is it reliable and true, or shallow and false? How can I distinguish between true and false religion?

There is, or rather there was, a standpoint which tried to avoid the perpetual negotations referred to above. This was the conviction of the true believers that they possesed the entire truth — a conviction which was incorporated both in traditional Roman Catholic doctrine and in Protestant orthodoxy. The free and critical spirit of our century has severely shaken the certainty of this conviction among both Roman Catholics and Protestants, but theoretically it is still valid in certain circles. According to the official doctrine the Roman Catholic church possesses Christian truth, fully and purely. The believer can find his salvation only in the bosom of the mother church. Personal doubts regarding conviction are really not tolerated. Every one who withdraws from the obedience of the church of Rome, becomes guilty of three sins, apostasy from the church and from Christianity, heresy because he denies the truth of the dogma of the church, schism, if he breaks the unity of the church. According to Roman Catholic juridical-casuistical thinking the question has been solved once and for all and been formulated in clear statements. Some of the formulations of the *concilium romanum* (380) dealing with the function of the Holy

Ghost in the dogmas of the Trinity and of the Incarnation can be cited as examples. One finds curses repeatedly pronounced there towards all who deviate from the orthodox doctrine: *"Anathematizamus eos qui non tota libertate proclamant eum (scilicet Spiritum Sanctum) cum Patre et Filio unius potestatis esse atque substantiae"*. *"Si quis non dixerit, semper Patrum, semper Filium, et semper Spiritum Sanctum, anathema sit"*. [1] The Protestant churches have never sounded such a strong note, because they lacked the papal authority to determine what is truth and what is error. But they have constantly guarded the true doctrine and have tried to avert heresy. The famous dutch synod of Dordrecht (1618-1619) which condemned the Remonstrants, went to much trouble to clarify true belief. The so called doctrinal rules (leerregels) of Dordt within each chapter of which true doctrine is formulated, are followed by an appendix containing a repudiation of the heresies in question. These pronouncements begin with the words: "After the orthodox doctrine has been stated, the synod rejects the errors of those who teach..." Then the heresies are named. It is clear that the question about how one should distinguish true from false religion is already precluded when the matter is resolved in such an easy manner. In this setting the question arises neither openly nor formally.

But the problem really cannot be suppressed. It emerges time after time. The church has often accused the heretics with a bad conscience. At the same time the church recognized the fact that the heretics also possess a part of God's truth. St. Paul wrote in the first letter to the Corinthians: 'For there must be also heresies among you, that they which are approved may be made manifest among you" (11:19). This word gave rise to the principle: *oportet et haereses esse* = there should also be heretics. [2] Man should not try to be wiser than our Lord who, according to traditional Christian doctrine, tolerates the devil and even gives him a fair running room. Yet the question would be easy, if the devil could be recognized by the legs of the he-goat and his satanic grin. But they who were denounced and cursed proved afterwards to be bearers of the truth, while the piety of famous witnesses of God sometimes was unmasked as a cover for worldly craftiness. Oftentimes human judgment misses the mark. The trouble is that not only does unreliable human judgment play tricks on us, but that the criterion for detecting the truth is very imperfect. People

---

[1] H. Denzinger, *Enchiridion Symbolorum et Definitionum*, p. 32/3.
[2] Fr. Heiler, *Der Katholizismus*, 1923, p. 638.

generally take as criterion the fact that one belongs to the true religion or church and professes the orthodox doctrine. Unfortunately the personal religious life itself demonstrates that even if one adheres to true doctrine, there is no guarantee that he is a really pious man. In a fascinating way in his "Le Buisson Ardent" Romain Rolland describes the way of life in a little town in which his hero Jean Christoffe stayed for a while. The inhabitants of the town were intelligent, able and conscious of their true faith, at least outwardly. But behind the proud and quiet faces were passions and doubt that could suddenly break through. Rolland writes: "Tout le monde pratiquait, tout le monde croyait. Pas un n'avait un doute, ou n'en voulait convenir... Ne pas croire leur eût semblé contre nature. Ne pas croire était d'une classe inférieure, qui avait de mauvaises manières... Mais la nature reprenait sa revanche. De loin en loin, il sortait de là quelque individualité revoltée... un penseur sans frein, qui brisait brutalement ses liens... Il arrivait qu'un de leurs hôtes s'en allait, de son pas tranquille, sans autre explication, se jeter dans la fleuve".

The norm of revealed and officially approved truth apparently fails us totally when we make the attempt to sift the chaff from the wheat in a given religion. It may seem that the result of this argument leads to a relativity in our judgment and this may create an unpleasant feeling. For there is never any sure correlation between official adherence to religious truth and participation in authentic piety. Here, we are obliged to dismiss the false certainty in order to seak for a sounder one. That is, we need to find the criterium that will clarify the problem at stake. In my opinion the phenomenology of religion uses a working principle which is useful in making inquiry into the essential quality of a religion. This discipline handles two principles which give insight into the essence, the structure and the intrinsic value of the religious phenomena. The student of the phenomenology of religion first studies his material in an unbiased way and without any pronouncement about its metaphysical meaning. Secondly he tries to find the core and kernel of the numerous and sometimes strange forms of religious life. According to the saying of the late Professor Kristensen in Leiden, his ambition is to understand what religion means for religious people.

The theologian believes that God existed before men populated the earth and that he will continue to exist after the last descendend of the human race has died. Seen from this theological perspective divine truth stands firm for ever. Assessed according to phenomenological terms religion is a cultural phenomenon which does not exist *in abstracto*, but only exists when the religious idea is realized in human persons. Faith is only alive, when people profess it, live it and realize it in good works. That is its strength and its weakness. Through human beings faith can become a force which removes mountains. On the other hand, a glorious religious thought can be subverted totally through the foulness of this world and the falseness of men. Søren Holm was right when he said that there are no objective criteria for distinguishing true from false religion. Yet this is not the final word. Because man is always involved in religion, the problem gains a double significance: the concern is not simply for the truth of religion, but also for the authenticity of faith. True and authentic are related conceptions, but they are certainly not identical. The genuineness of religiosity appears from the devotion with which religious people dedicate themselves to their religious conviction. On the contrary a true belief which is not sincerely professed becomes an affair without any value. The problem has two aspects which are closely connected, but which should be distinguished because they deserve separate treatment.

The problem of the truth of religion is usually dealt with by theology and philosophy of religion. This is the way it ought to be. Then the question arises as to whether religion is an illusion or is founded in God's existence. Phenomenology of religion abstains from passing judgment on this issue. Yet in another sense phenomenology of religion is preoccupied with the question of truth, both in regard to religion as such and as concerns the different religions. This means that the phenomenology of religion rejects all theories which tend to explain religion as a result of purely psychological or social forces. There are quite a number of such theories. [3] Phenomenology of religion thinks that these conceptions "denature" religion. For religion can only be understood, in its true significance, when it is conceived of as the result of man's encounter with the Holy, with God. Phenomenology of religion can make no use of the word "revelation", because this notion originates from christian theology and presupposes the belief in a personal God (a conception which is absent from several non-christian religions). However phenomenology of religion can make use of the concept "hierophany", a term introduced by M. Eliade which means that religion derives from the appearance of the

---

[3] H. Scholz, *Religionsphilosophie*, 1921, Drittes Buch 3: *Umdeutungen der Religion*.

Holy. Though actual religiosity shows many human and sinful features—a subject which will be treated presently—yet phenomenology
of religion maintains the thesis that the believer's contentions that he
possesses religious truth must be taken seriously.

In regard to religions in the plural it should be admitted that superstition, self-deception and all kind of human passions play a great
part. This is characteristic, too, of present day Christianity. There were
and there still are people who believe that the non-christian religions
are the work of the devil. Or in a somewhat milder outlook, some
persons are convinced that these strange forms of belief are the outcome of a human pious longing, that they can be noble and beautiful,
but that they lack the proper metaphysical background. Phenomenology
of religion follows the trajectories of Nathan Söderblom who declared
that it is absurd to restrict divine revelation to Christ. In Söderbloms
view, when one recognizes that there is the belief in God in China,
Japan, India, Persia, Egypt, Babylon, Greece and Rome, he is forced
to the following dilemma: either there is real revelation outside the
Bible too, or revelation is not to be found in the Bible. The history
of religions offers no third possibility. This is perfectly right, though
the student of phenomenology of religion will prefer not to use the
word "revelation", as has been argued. The history of religions offers
many striking examples of true and pure religion. Let me quote a
single proof. Birgir Forell who accompanied the German student of
the history of religions, Rud. Otto on his voyage through the Far East,
describes Otto's departure and how he took leave of Mr Sastri, a
distinguished and highly cultured Hindu. Mr Sastri held Otto's hand
for a long time, then said: "whether we shall meet again, nobody
knows, we must leave that to Tat." Thereupon he made a gesture
in the direction of the sky, so that it became clear that "It" (sanscrit
"Tat") was a living reality to him. Out of deep respect he did not dare
to give it another name. Then he turned around hastily to hide his
emotion. It cannot be doubted that real religion is present here. [4]

The second principle question concerns the veracity of the believer.
Unfortunately religious people have in the course of the centuries
grossly sinned and brought religion in disrepute. What is even worse,
they have used religion as a cover to give free rein to their passions.
Thus the question arises: how does one distinguish sincere religiosity
from spurious and false forms. This is not easily done. For the lie
is inherent in the character of most people. For the first we find what

---

[4] Birgir Forell, *Från Ceylon till Himalaya*, 1925, p. 86-87.

in the beautiful latin name is called *pia fraus,* i.e. a white lie. One cannot always be honest. Neither is it always loving to tell the truth. One can be forced to tell untruth in some way. "Pia fraus" occurs now and then in religion. Is the white lie always pious? Where does the downright lie start? This is a thorny question.

One can smile at "pia fraus" as at a child's lie. The sensational vice starts there, where, as is contended, violent sinful passions rage under the mask of religion. The most stirring sins are undoubtedly concupiscence and appitite for power. Let us have a look at the part which these vices play in religion. The thesis is well known that religion is nothing other than beautifully disguised sexuality and erotic feelings. Since religion is a human affair, it is evident that sexuality and erotic emotions do play their part in religion. But it is grotesque to contend that religion has its origin in these passions. The question is more complicated and more interesting in a scholarly respect. We refer to the religions of the illiterate people and of the nations of antiquity, where one frequently meets sexual symbols and erotic rites. These cannot be explained by reference to the passions which are mentioned, though these do play an obvious part. The texts make clear that the people of antiquity conceived of sexuality as a great mystery, as a token of the creative power of the deity. Therefore they tried to define the nature of the deity by sexual symbols and celebrated erotic rites. Take as example the temple prostitution. There are sure proofs that this custom which is shocking for ethically minded modern man, was practiced in ancient Mesopotamia not from voluptuousness, but was considered as hard service to the goddess (e.g. to Isjtar). Thus one can easily be mistaken as to the significance of forms of religion which do not comply with our ideals. The question of true religion is complicated indeed. One must possess the power of discernment to decide what in religion is true and what is false.

Marxists often have argued that religion was used by ambitious princes and priests to control the credulous masses by deluding them into accepting the prospect of eternal bliss in heaven as a reward for their misery on earth. It is unnecessary to unmask this argument. It contradicts itself. Much more interesting is the relation between religion and magic. It has been contended often that religion is equivalent to humility. Therefore magic is sometimes decried as irreligious. For magic is suspected to coerce the gods and should therefore be irreligious. The question is not as simple as it looks. It is doubtful whether religion is identical to obedience and resignation. It is easy to quote

examples of a free attitude of the believer towards God. Let me
present a little story from the literature of the Sūfis. It is said that
God did not give rain to Israel for seven years. All prayers for rain
remained unheard. Finally God said to Moses: "I can not understand
your prayers, because your hearts are darkened by sin so that you
pray without faith. Let my servant Baruch come." At last Baruch was
found. He proved to be a poor black slave who immediately started to
pray. He began his prayer by giving the Lord a proper scolding: "Is
this the manner in which you used to art? How does this accord with
thy generosity? What possesses you? Have thine eyes become weak
or have the winds ceased to obey they will? Art thou infuriated by our
trespasses? Art thou not the God who has forgiven us long before
thou has created us sinners?" Moses was horrified by so much frankness, but God said: "This really is my servant Baruch, he makes me
laugh three times each day." And the rain poured down in a torrent
so that the people of Israel waded in the water to their knees. This
amusing story offers a curious mixture of frankness and reverence
with regard to God. 5 The same attitude is to be found in the prayer
which Luther pronounced during the illness of the elector of Saxony.
He prayed as follows: "Lieber Herr Gott, erhör doch unser Gebet
nach deiner Zusage; lasz uns doch dir die Schlüssel nicht vor die
Füsze werfen, denn so wir zuletzt zornig über dich werden und dir
deine Ehre und Zinsgüter nicht geben, wo willts du denn bleiben?
Ah, Lieber Gott, wir sind dein, mach es wie wo willst, alleine gib uns
Geduld." 6 Rud. Otto surely was correct when he remarked that religious people can have certain "religiöse Hochgefühle". Religion is not
identical with resigned submission to God's will. Faith can involve
a wrestling with God, in which man defends his rights. Religion and
magic both stem from life's emergencies and are an attempt to
define man's attitude towards the Holy, partly in submission, partly
while man exerts the small force that he possesses.

The question at stake can best be answered by referring to certain
types of so called higher religion, i.e. prophetism and mysticism. A
remarkable sensitivity to true religion has developped here. According
to the Old Testament the prophets were animated by God's spirit.
But there is also talk about a spirit of lies who offered his services to
the Lord and who spoke through the four hundred prophets who
predicted success to king Achab in his war. It was the prophet Michah

5 Tor Andrae, *I myrtenträdgården*, 1922, p. 182.
6 Luther, *Tischreden*, p. 104/5.

who unmasked those deceitful predictions. Thus in Israel people reckoned with false inspiration. Furthermore it is wellknown that mystics have sought for criteria in order to obtain certainty in the question whether their visions were a gift of God, a delusion of the devil, or perhaps an illusion of their own mind. Saint Theresa had a sharp capacity for assessing the quality of her inspirations. She writes: "When God really speaks to the soul one cannot possibly withdraw from listening to His word". To discern God's true speech St. Theresa formulated the following criteria: the absence of one's own activity; the spontaneity of the vision; its outspoken clearness; and its ethical consequences. [7]

In regard to the last criterion one is reminded of the words of St Paul in his letter to the Galatians: "But the fruit of the Spirit is love, joy, peace, longsuffering, gentleness, goodness, faith" (5:22) One knows the tree by its fruits. The good deeds prove the truth of religion. And yet it is true: the blue flower of religion buds in the darkness of superstition. This fact is a warning to be cautious in our judgment. We are not totally deprived of criteria to distinguish true religion from false religon. But such criteria should be handled with wisdom and discretion.

---

[7] Tor Andrae, *Mystikens Psykologi*, 1926, p. 278.

EINIGE BEMERKUNGEN ZUR RELIGIÖSEN TERMINOLOGIE DER ALTEN ÄGYPTER *

Zwei Aussagen von bekannten Ägyptologen haben mich inspiriert, eine Untersuchung der religiösen Terminologie der alten Ägypter anzustellen, eine Untersuchung, die keineswegs den Anspruch erhebt, erschöpfend zu sein, die jedoch meiner Meinung nach zu interessanten Ergebnissen führt. Die betreffenden Ägyptologen sind S. Morenz und H. Brugsch.

Morenz hat in der "Einleitung" zu seinem Buch über die "Ägyptische Religion" die Bemerkung gemacht, dass die ägyptische Sprache die Begriffe "Religion", "Frömmigkeit" und "Glaube" nicht kennt. [1] Dies ist zweifelsohne richtig. Er fördert damit eine bemerkungswerte Tatsache zu Tage. Denn die genannten Begriffe gehören zu der gebräuchlichsten Terminologie des modernen Glaubens und besonders der christlichen Theologie, aber auch religionshistorische Behandlung der nicht-christlichen Religionen ist kaum möglich ohne dass man sich der erwähnten Begriffen bedient.

Mit der von Morenz gemachten, rein sachlich-philologischen Bemerkung scheint die Ansicht von Brugsch in direktem Widerspruch zu stehen. Denn dieser gelehrte Ägyptologe hat behauptet, dass das alte Ägypten ein eigenes religiöses Idiom gekannt hat, in dem er sogar eine theologische, eine mystische und eine mythologische Sprache unterscheidet. [2] Die drei Paragraphen, die er in seinem Buch "Religion und Mythologie der alten Ägypter" diesem Thema gewidmet hat, zeugen zwar von seinen grossen Kenntnissen der ägyptischen Sprache, wirken jedoch nicht ganz überzeugend. Und dennoch muss man gestehen, dass er auf die richtige Spur gekommen ist.

Denn Brugsch hat geahnt, dass es im alten Ägypten eine eigene religiöse Terminologie gegeben hat. Seine Spekulationen über das dreifache religiöse Idiom stehen nur scheinbar in Widerspruch mit der philologischen Tatsache, die Morenz festgestellt hat. Denn obgleich gewisse für uns zentrale Begriffe der religiöse Terminologie in der ägyptischen Sprache fehlen, ist es kaum glaublich, dass der Ägypter überhaupt keine religiösen Ausdrücke zur Verfügung hatte. Selbstverständlich hat es eine rein religiöse Sprache gegeben. Es ist nur die

---

* Veröffentlicht in *Travels in the World of the Old Testament*, 1974.
[1] *Op. cit.*, S. 3/4.
[2] *Religion und Mythologie der alten Ägypter*, 1891, p. 51, 61, 74.

Frage, wie wir dieser religiösen Terminologie habhaft werden können und wie ihr Wortschatz aussieht. Kein Ägyptologe hat diese Problem jemals systematisch in Angriff genommen. Das heisst, es gibt noch kein Handbuch der ägyptischen religiösen Sprache. Dennoch kann man ohne Mühe in den Schriften verschiedener Ägyptologen gelegentlich Ansätze zu einer solchen Untersuchung finden. Ich habe diese dankbar benutzt. In dieser "Vorarbeit" möchte ich versuchen diese interessante Frage etwas weiter zu klären.

Meiner Ansicht nach geht die Bedeutung einer derartigen Untersuchung weit über ihren philologischen Wert hinaus. Denn sie ist eins der geeignesten Mittel, um Einsicht in das ägyptische Denken zu bekommen; im religionshistorischen Studium ist sie zweckmässiger als tiefgründige Auseinandersetzungen über die richtige religionshistorische Methode, die man heutzutage entwickelt. Wer den Glauben der alten Ägypter verstehen will, muss ägyptisch denken lernen. Und dies gelingt ihm nur, wenn er sich mit der typisch ägyptischen religiösen Terminologie vertraut macht.

Dass Morenz richtig gesehen hat, wird deutlich, wenn man "Das deutsch-ägyptische Wörterverzeichnis" im sechsten Band des "Wörterbuch der ägyptische Sprache" (W.B.) aufschlägt und darin den "Anhang" zu Rate zieht. Darin findet man "eine Zusammenstellung der Wörter in begrifflich geordneten Sachgruppen". Dieses Register gibt eine Übersicht über und eine Einsicht in den Wortschatz der alten Ägypter. Die Redakteure des W.B. haben die Wortarten in 69 Kategorien eingeteilt. Es würde den Rahmen dieses kurzen Artikels sprengen, wenn ich alle Wortarten nennen würde. Überdies ist es keine amüsante Lektüre. Dennoch gibt diese Liste der Bemerkung von Morenz erst das rechte Relief. Es zeigt sich nämlich, dass offiziell nur 5 von den 69 Kategorien religiöse Ausdrücke enthalten, das heisst 17) Götterbezeichnungen, 18) Götter(namen) 19) Kultus und Priester, 20) Totenwesen; Jenseits. Auf den ersten Blick schon fallen zwei Eigenheiten der religiösen Terminologie, wie sie vom W.B. geboten wird, deutlich auf: erstens bilden die Klassen von Begriffen, die sich ausgesprochen auf Religion beziehen, nur den vierzehnten Teil der 69 Kategorien und zweitens bezeichnen diese Wörter unverkennbar keine abstrakt-geistigen Werte, sondern sind Namen von mehr oder weniger konkreten Grössen, die hauptsächlich mit dem Kult von Göttern und Toten verknüpft sind. Im Vorübergehen darf ich wohl bemerken, dass dieser letztere Satz meine These, dass das Herz der altägyptischen Religion im Kult klopft, ungebeten bestätigt. [3] Wenn man den Inhalt der Kategorie "Kultus und Priester" näher prüft, zeigt es sich, dass darin unter anderem Wörter für Altar, Tempelgerät, Opfer und was damit zusammenhängt, Priester, Feste, Räucherung, verehren, beten, Prozession, Barke von verschiedenen Göttern vorkommen. Begriffe wie Mythus und Ritus, die der Religionshistoriker gewöhnlich — und gewiss nicht ohne Grund — verwendet, um das altägyptische religiöse Verhalten zu charakterisieren, fehlen ganz und gar. Es gibt überhaupt keine Begriffe, die von einer Reflexion über geistige Werte zeugen. Man wird sich also kaum der Schlussfolgerung entziehen können, dass es im alten Ägypten keine richtige mythologische Terminologie und keine theologische Begriffsbildung gab.

Nun wird man einwenden können, dass gewisse religiöse Ausdrücke sich vielleicht in Wortklassen mit einer profanen Überschrift versteckt haben. Das wird gelegentlich der Fall sein. Aber das beweist aufs neue wie begrenzt die Zahl der altägyptischen Begriffe tatsächlich ist, die man geschaffen hat um die Eigenart der religiösen Vorstellungen und Handlungen auszudrücken. Man könnte auch die Vermutung äussern, dass die Verfasser des W.B. nicht den richtigen Blick für die typisch religiösen Nuancen von altägyptischen Wörtern und Begriffen hatten. Das ist ein wichtiger Gesichtspunkt. Brugsch hat seine Betrachtungen über die drei Arten der religiösen Terminologie nicht ganz frei erfunden. Es muss zweifelsohne eine religiöse Terminologie geben, welche die Eigenart des altägyptischen religiösen Bewusstseins ausdrückt. Die Frage ist nur, wie man sie entdeckt.

Da will es mir scheinen, dass die beste Untersuchungsmethode wäre sich zu fragen, welche typisch religiösen Ausdrücke verwendet werden für die Hauptbegriffe der Religion, das heisst für (1) Gott (2) die Natur und das Schicksal des Menschen, (3) die kultischen Handlungen, (4) die Weltanschauung. Diese vier allgemeinen Begriffe bilden ein formelles Schema, mit welchem man die Struktur jeder Religion ausfindig machen kann. Denn gemessen an diesem Schema tritt die innere Struktur der betreffenden Religion klar zu Tage. Es wird sich zeigen, dass hier ein gewisses Glied dieses Schemas entweder schwach betont ist oder völlig abwesend ist, während ein anderes stark den Nachdruck bekommen hat, und dass dort die Verhältnisse umgekehrt liegen. In unserer Untersuchung hat man die Möglichkeit mit Hilfe dieses Schemas die typisch religiösen Ausdrücke einzufangen, die sonst durch die Maschen des philologischen

---

[3] C. J. Bleeker, *Egyptian Festivals, Enactments of religious renewal*, 1967.

Begriffsapparates schlüpfen. Es versteht sich, dass die folgende Untersuchung nur Momentaufnahmen bieten kann und auf Vollständigkeit keinen Anspruch erhebt.

Was die altägyptischen Götter betrifft, findet man nirgens eine klare, systematische, theologische Auseinandersetzung über ihr Wesen, ihre Eigenschaften und ihre Tätigkeiten. In gewissem Sinn scheint die berühmte Ptah-Theologie des Schabaka-Steines eine Ausnahme zu bilden. Wenn man jedoch den Kontext dieser theologischen Ausführungen genauer betrachtet, zeigt es sich, dass sie die Form eines Hymnus haben. Die tiefsinnigen Sätze über die Schöpfung, die zustande kam, indem der Gedanke, der im Herzen der Gottheit aufstieg, ausgesprochen wurde und über den "Logos", der den Existenzgrund alles Seienden bildet, sollen nur dazu dienen, den Ruhm Ptahs zu erhöhen. Tatsächlich muss man die Götterlieder und die "epitheta ornantia" der Götter heranziehen, um die religiösen Ausdrücke zu finden, mit denen die Ägypter das Wesen ihrer Götter ausgesagt haben.

Es gibt Ägyptologen, die davon überzeugt sind, dass man in den Texten Ideen finden kann, die mit den Eigenschaften korrespondieren die man in der Theologie der sogenannten höheren Religionen, z.B. des Judentums, des Christentums und des Islams, Gott zuschreibt. Das geht erstens deutlich hervor aus E. Ottos Studie über "Gott und Mensch, nach den ägyptischen Tempelinschriften der griechisch-römischen Zeit" (1964). In diesen spät-ägyptischen Texten, die gesprächiger sind als die älteren Texte, gibt es Umschreibungen vom Wesen der Gottheit, die Otto wiedergibt mit bekannten theologischen Begriffen, wie Einzigartigkeit, Allmacht, Allwissenheit, Gerechtigkeit, θεός σωτήρ. Zweitens hat S. Morenz in einer interessanten Erörterung die These verfochten, dass der Gedanke der Trinität schon in Ägypten vorhanden war, nämlich in der üblichen Verbindung von Ptah, Sokaris und Osiris, die eine Dreiheit und zur gleicher Zeit eine Einheit bilden sollten. [4] Er hat sogar einen Text aus dem Jahre 100 n. Chr. zitieren können, in dem seiner Meinung nach diese Idee "expressis verbis" ausgesprochen wird. [5] Weiter hat A. de Buck die sonderbaren Redewendungen, in denen das Verhältnis zwischen Shu und Atum formuliert wird, zu verdeutlichen versucht, indem er darauf hinwies, das sie eine Ähnlichkeit mit den Thesen aufweisen welche die christliche Kirche im Kampf um das "homoousios", das heisst

---

[4] S. Morenz, *Ägyptische Religion*, 1960, S. 150.
[5] Idem, S. 270 sq.

um das Verhältnis von Vater und Sohn im Gottesbegriff benutzte. [6]
Mit einigem guten Willen ist es auch möglich, Rud. Ottos berühmten
Gedanken vom "mysterium tremendum ac fascinans" der Gottheit in
den altägyptischen Texten wiederzufinden. Das habe ich in meinen
Studien über "Thoth in den altägyptischen Texten" [7] und über "Der
religiöse Gehalt einiger Hathor-Lieder" [8] zeigen können. Die Gottheit
erweist sich einerseits gnädig, ist andererseits jedoch majestätisch und
angsterregend. Von Thoth, der übrigens als der Friedenstifter und
als der Freund von den Göttern und den Menschen gilt, wird sogar
erwähnt, dass er "kommt in seinem bösen Gang" — was übrigens
auch von anderen Göttern gesagt wird. [9]

Der letzte geheimnisvolle Ausdruck lässt einen verstehen, dass die
altägyptische Terminologie durch die oben genannten Vergleiche mit
den Begriffen der christlichen Theologie ebensosehr erklärt als verschleiert wird — das letztere womöglich mehr als das erstere. Denn
die analoge Begriffe fehlen in der ägyptische Sprache. Die "Einzigartigkeit" z.B. muss man zurückfinden in Redewendungen wie "Es gibt
nicht seines (ihres) gleichen", oder "Es gibt keinen, der ihm (ihr)
ähnlich ist". Die Allmacht wird umschrieben durch Lobsprüche wie
"was aus seinem (ihrem) Mund kommt, geschieht sogleich" und "was
sein Herz denkt, geschieht sogleich". [10]

Um die typisch altägyptische religiöse Terminologie zu entdecken
und damit wahre Einsicht in den ägyptischen Glauben und das religiöse Denken zu bekommen, soll man charakterische Begriffe auf-
suchen. So verwendet der Ägypter z.B. die folgenden vielsagenden Ausdrücke um die Natur der Götter zu definieren:

(1) Das Wort *nṯr*, was die allgemein übliche Benennung der Götter ist. Bei näherem Zusehen offenbart dieses Wort die ägyptische Kon-
zeption vom Wesen der Gottheit. Die Hieroglyphe von *nṯr* ist wahrscheinlich ein Stab mit einer Fahne, der heilige Orte markierte, damit
zu einem sakralen Gegenstand wurde und in zweiter Instanz die
Gottheit bezeichnen konnte. Das Wort selbst zeigt Ähnlichkeit mit
nṯr, was sowohl Natron als reinigen bedeutet. Reinheit spielte be-
kanntlich eine hervorragende Rolle im ägyptischen Kult. *Nṯr* wurde

---

[6] A. de Buck, *Plaats en betekenis van Sjoe in de Egyptische theologie*, 1947.

[7] *Ex Orbe Religionum, Studia Geo Widengren oblata I*, 1972, S. 3 sq.

[8] "Der religiöser Gehalt einiger Hathor-Lieder" (Z.Ä.S. zu *Andenken S. Morenz*).

[9] C. J. Bleeker, *Hathor and Thoth, Two Key Figures of the Ancient Egyptian Religion*, 1973.

[10] E. Otto, *Mensch und Gott, nach den ägyptischen Tempelinschriften der grie-chisch-römischen Zeit*, 1964, S. 11, 14.

also zur Benennung von dem göttlichen Wesen, das an reinen, heiligen Orten residiert. Es ist vielsagend, dass *ntr* in den Pyramidentexten variiert mit *cnh* = Leben, *bꜣ* = "Seele" und *šhm* = Macht.[11]

(2) Das Adjektiv *nfr* and das Substantiv *nfrw*. *Nfr* ist ein merkwürdiges Wort, weil es sowohl eine ethische wie eine kosmische Bedeutungsnuance besitzt. In manchen Fällen kann *nfr* nur mit ethisch gut oder schön übersetzt werden. Aber *nfr* kann auch das kosmisch Gute bezeichnen. Der Knabe, das Fohlen, das heiratsfähige Mädchen sind *nfr*, weil sie jung sind und die ungebrochene Lebenskraft haben. *Nfr Tm* ist der junge Sonnengott, der eben aufgegangen ist. Wenn die Göttin Ma-a-t, die als Lotse im Vordersteven des Sonnenschiffes steht, das "epitheton ornans" "mit schönem Antlitz" bekommt, will das nicht sagen, das sie eine "beauty" ist — obgleich auch das zutreffen könnte —, sondern es bedeutet, dass von ihrem Gesicht der göttliche Glanz und die unwiderstehliche Macht abstrahlt. [12] Die *nfrw* ist die Schönheit, die wahre Natur, die Schöpfermacht der Gottheit. Von dem Gott Min wird gesagt, dass er "stolz ist auf seiner Schönheit". Damit wird auf seinen "phallus erectus", die zeugende Kraft besitzt, angespielt. [13]

(3) Bekannte "epitheta" der Götter, wie "der sich selber bildet", "er hat kein Vater, der seine Gestalt zeugte, er hat keine Mutter, die ihm gebar", "geheim von Geburt". [14] Dies sind charakteristische Ausdrücke, die den Gedanken wiedergeben wollen, dass die Gottheit ein ungeschaffenes Wesen ist und deshalb ihrer Natur nach ganz anders als alle Geschöpfe ist. In diesem Zusammenhang könnte man auch das "epitheton" *k3 mwt.f* = der Stier seiner Mutter nennen. Dieser sonderbare Ausdruck will sagen, dass der Gott seine eigene Mutter befruchtet und also sich selber erzeugt. [15]

(4) Daran schliesst sich gut der Gebrauch, den man von dem Verbum *hpr* = werden macht, an. Es wird benutzt zur Definition der Natur der Götter, besonders des Sonnengottes. Denn in der religiösen Terminologie wird *hpr* verstanden als: aus sich selber entstehen. Und das kann nur die Gottheit. So erklärt man den Namen des aufgehenden Sonnengottes *Hprr oder Hprj* als: "derjenige, der aus eigener

---

[11] C. J. Bleeker, The Key Word of Religion (*The Sacred Bridge*, 1963) S. 46/7.
[12] C. J. Bleeker, *De beteekenis van de Egyptische godin Ma-a-t*, 1929, S. 38 sq.
[13] C. J. Bleeker, *Die Geburt eines Gottes, eine Studie über den ägyptischen Gott Min und sein Fest*, 1956, p. 48.
[14] De Buck, *Sjoe*.
[15] H. Jacobsohn, *Die dogmatische Stellung des Königs in der Theologie der alten Ägypter*, 1939; Bleeker, *Min*.

Kraft entsteht und aufgeht". Sein Hieroglyphe ist der Skarabäus, von dem die Ägypter glaubten, dass er durch *generatio spontanea* auf der Welt kommt. Es gibt einen Text, in dem dieser Gott in einem tiefsinnigen Spiel mit dem Verbum *ḫpr* über sein eigenes Wesen spekuliert. Ich zitiere hier die englische Übersetzung von R. O. Faulkner, weil sie genauer ist und das Wortspiel besser wiedergibt als die deutsche Übertragung von G. Roeder. Die Stelle lautet folgendermassen: "When I came into being, "Being" came into being. I came into being in the form of *Ḫprj* who came into being on the first occasion. I came into being in the form of *Ḫprj* when I came into being. That is how "Being" came into being, because I was more primaeval (?) than the primaevals whom I had made". [16]

(5) Die zitierte Stelle suggeriert, dass der Ägypter seine Götter als ewige Wesen auffasste. Der Ausdruck scheint tatsächlich zu existieren. Gewisse Götter werden *nb nḥḥ ḏ.t* genannt, was man gewöhnlich übersetzt mit: Herr der Ewigkeit und der Unendlichkeit. Dennoch soll man auch hier scharf zusehen und genau horchen auf das, was das altägyptische Idiom sagt. E. Hornung bekämpft die Meinung, dass die Ägypter den Begriff der Ewigkeit im modernen Sinn haben bilden können. Er übersetzt *nb r nḥḥ ḥḳꜣ ḏ.t* mit "Herr bis an das Unabsehbare und Herrscher des Immerwährenden". [17] J. Leclant, der eine kurze Übersicht über die verschiedenen Interpretationen der genannten Begriffe gibt, meint, dass "*nḥḥ* a un caractère plus spécialement temporel et *ḏ.t* s'applique plutôt au domaine de l'espace". [18] Wie dem auch sein mag, man hört hier aufs neue die Warnung, altägyptische Ausdrücke nicht zu modernisieren. Wenn man weiss, dass, wie im Laufe dieser Darlegung klar werden wird, die Ägypter unseren Zeitbegriff nicht gekannt haben, versteht es sich, dass sie die Idee der Ewigkeit im modernen philosophischen und theologischen Sinn nicht haben konzipieren können.

(6) Eine Anzahl Götter, besonders Re, werden als Schöpfer der Welt betrachtet, dass heisst, es ist keine Rede von der Schöpfung des Kosmos, sondern von dem Entstehen der "zwei Länder", wie Ägypten damals hiess. Der geistige Horizont der Ägypter reichte anfangs nicht weiter. W. B. Kristensen hat darauf aufmerksam gemacht, dass

---

16 "The Book of Overthrowing ꜥApep" (*Bibliotheca Aegyptiaca* III, 28, 20 sq.) (Übersetzung R. O. Faulkner, J.E.A. 23. S. 166 sq.)

17 E. Hornung, "Zum ägyptischen Ewigkeitsbegriff" (*Forschungen und Fortschritte* 39, S. 334 sq.)

18 J. Leclant, "Espace et temps, ordre et chaos dans l'Egypte pharaonique" (*Revue de Synthèse*, Tome XC, série générale, juillet-décembre, 1969).

man für erschaffen das malerische Verbum "knüpfen" gebrauchte. [19] Mit diesem Bilde ist ausgesagt, dass die Teile der Erde, die im Chaos zerstreut lagen, in ihren richtigen Zusammenhang gebracht wurden. "Knüpfen" bedeutet organisieren, ein lebendiges Ganzes schaffen. Die Tod ist die Auflösung. Das Leben entsteht, die Auferstehung geschieht, indem die gesonderten Teile des Landes, die Glieder des zerstückelten Leichnams vereinigt werden. Diese Idee hat im Ritus von *sm꜄ t꜄wj* = "das Vereinigen der zwei Länder", ihren symbolischen Ausdruck bekommen. Die allen Ägyptologen wohlbekannte Handlung findet statt bei der Thronbesteigung des Pharaos und wird, der Idee und der Darstellung nach, von Horus und Seth oder Thoth vollzogen. Die zwei Götter stehen auf beiden Seiten eines grossen Hieroglyphen von *sm꜄* = vereinigen und ziehen die daran befestigten Stricke mit kräftiger Hand an. Dadurch gerät Ägypten wiederum in den Status von Leben und Harmonie. [20]

Man geht sicher nicht fehl, wenn man hinter den Begriffen "knüpfen" und "vereinigen" ein religiöses Ideal der Ägypter entdeckt. Der Ägypter war kein Zänker und hatte von Haus aus keine kriegerische Natur, wie die eroberungsüchtigen Assyrer. Er liebte den Frieden, die Harmonie, das gute ruhige Leben. Es war der Schöpfergott, der den Menschen diese Gabe mit seinem kreativen Arbeit verlieh. Denn er vereinigte nicht nur das Land, sondern er setzte auch Ma-a-t als die immerwährende und absolut gültige Weltordnung ein. Natürlich wurde diese Ordnung dann und wann zerbrochen und die Harmonie zerstört. Denn es gab Götter wie Seth, der mit Recht als "the God of Confusion" charakterisiert ist. [21] Aber dann griff ein anderer Gott ein, der den Akt des *śḥtp* volzog. Das war Thoth, der Friedenstifter. Er stellte den *ḥtp*, Frieden wieder her, indem er die kämpfenden Parteien miteinander versöhnte. Es gibt sogar einen Gott, in dem dieses Ideal personifiziert worden ist. Das ist *Ḥtp,* der Herrscher der *śḥt ḥtp,* des elysäischen Gefildes, welches im Jenseits liegt. Von ihm wird gesagt, dass "er den Kummer der älteren Generation vertreibt und die Konflikte des jüngeren Geschlechts schlichtet." [22] Nach dem ägyptischen religiösen Bewusstsein ist also der wahre Gott derjenige der ordnet, wiederherstellt, heilt, Frieden stiftet und das Leben auferstehen lässt.

Kristensens Bemerkung über "knüpfen" = schaffen ist seiner Aus-

---

[19] W. B. Kristensen, *Het leven uit de dood,* 1949, S. 77.
[20] Bleeker, *Hathor and Thoth.*
[21] H. te Velde, *Seth, God of Confusion,* 1967.
[22] Bleeker, *Hathor and Thoth,* S. 118.

einandersetzung über die Symbole der magischen Lebenskraft entnommen. Zu diesen Symbolen rechnet er z.B. das Band, das Kleid, das
Netz, also Gewebe, die von Webekunst zeugen und die deshalb, seiner
Meinung nach, von den antiken Völkern als Symbole der kosmischen
Harmonie und der magischen Schöpfungskraft aufgefasst wurden. Zu
dieser Reihe soll auch der bekannte Hieroglyphe von ᶜnḥ = Leben gehören. ²³ Ich habe diese Stellen zitiert, nicht um die Richtigkeit von
Kristensens Auslegung zu prüfen, sondern um darauf hinzuweisen,
dass man, um die typisch altägyptische Terminologie zu ermitteln, nicht
nur die Texte studieren muss, sondern auch den Symbole, in denen die
Ägypter ihre Auffasung über die Götter und das religiöse Leben ausdrückten, Aufmerksamkeit schenken sollte. E. Otto traf ins Schwarze,
als er schrieb, dass der Ägypter im Gegensatz zum griechischen begrifflichen Denken sich plastischer Bilder, lebendiger Analogien und anschaulicher Vorstellungen bediente um seine Gedanken und Gefühle zu
äussern. ²⁴ Das sind Ausdruckmittel, die zu einer religiösen Terminologie gehören, wie sie im berühmten W.B. nicht inkorporiert ist.

Das zweite Thema ist der Mensch, das heisst die religiöse Anthropologie. Es wäre nicht merkwürdig, wenn man sich im "Jahrhundert
der Psychologie" in erster Linie für die Religionspsychologie der alten
Ägypter interessieren würde. Es gibt jedoch zwei Gründe, weshalb man
dieses Kapitel überschlagen kann. Erstens sind die religiösen Gefühle
der Ägypter uns nicht genügend bekannt. Sie treten nur in einigen Texten, nämlich in den von A. Erman und B. Gun bearbeiteten Inschriften
auf Denksteinen aus der Thebanischen Necropole ²⁵ und in den
von mir studierten Hathor- und Thoth-Lieder, ²⁶ in den Vordergrund.
Zweitens machte der Ägypter keinen Unterschied zwischen Körper und
"Seele", als den materiellen und den geistigen Teil des Menschen. Aus
den Pyramidentexten z.B. geht hervor, dass der $ḏ.t$ = der Körper, eine
Kraftsubstanz bildet, die für das Fortbestehen ihres Besitzers unentbehrlich ist. ²⁷ Der "geistige" Teil des Menschen kan offenbar unter verschiedenen Aspekten gesehen werden. Denn man schreibt dem Men

²³ Kristensen, *op. cit.*, S. 47.
²⁴ E. Otto, *Ägypten, Der Weg des Pharaonenreiches*, 1955. Siehe auch: S. Schott,
Hieroglyphen, Untersuchungen zum Ursprung der Schrift, 1951.
²⁵ A. Erman, *Denksteine aus der thebanischen Gräberwelt* (Sitzungsber. der kön.
Preuss. Akad. der Wiss. 1911); B. Gun, "The Religion of the Poor in Ancient
Egypt" (*J.E.A.*, Volume III, S. 8 sq.)
²⁶ Siehe Fussnoten No 7 und 8.
²⁷ G. van der Leeuw, *Godsvoorstellingen in de oud-aegyptische pyramidentexten*,
1916, S. 32.

schen einen $k^{\jmath}$, einen $b^{\jmath}$, einen $^{\jmath}ib$ = Herz, einen $h^{\jmath}jb.t$ = Schatten und
und einen $^{\jmath}hw$ zu. Diese Grössen sind in der ägyptologischen Literatur
so wiederholt behandelt worden, dass ich auf ihr Wesen nicht näher
einzugehen brauche und die diesbezügliche Literatur unerwähnt lassen
kann. Es ist nur wichtig einzusehen, dass es sich hier um eine Plura-
lität von "Seelen" handelt, die der Mensch besitzen kann. Allerdings
muss ich das Wort "Seele" sofort wieder zurücknehmen. Neulich hat
J. Bergman in einer Studie über den $b^{\jmath}$- Begriff aufs neue vor der Ge-
wohnheit gewarnt die genannten Begriffe als "Seelen" zu bezeichnen.
Es sind Aspekte des menschlichen Wesens, das seine "numinosen"
Seiten hat, wie Rud. Otto sagen würde. Die genannte Studie von Bergman bekommt in diesem Zusammenhang besondere Bedeutung, weil
er mit vielen Zitaten klar macht, dass der $b^{\jmath}$, den nicht nur die Götter,
sondern auch die Menschen besitzen, "eine göttliche Offenbarungs-
form" ist. [28] Es kommt also darauf an einzusehen, dass alle genannten
Begriffe für die geistige Seite des Menschenwesens, letzten Endes eine
religiöse Tiefe haben. [29]

Eine religiöse Anthropologie enthält immer eine Wertschätzung des
Menschen. Das bedeutet, dass man in der Religion ein Auge hat sowohl für die Licht-, als für die Schattenseiten seiner Natur. Dies war
auch in Ägypten der Fall. Da der alte Ägypter eine scharfe Beobach-
tungsgabe hatte, wusste er sehr gut die schwachen Seiten des Menschen
zu entdecken. So gibt es eine lange Reihe von Wörtern für Sünde,
nämlich $^{\jmath}iw$, $^{\jmath}iwj.t$, $^{\jmath}isf.t$, ^{c}wt, $wh^{\jmath}$, bwt, $bt^{\jmath}$, hww, $h^{\jmath}b.t$, ^{c}b und eine
etwas kürzere Serie Wörter für Schuld, das heisst $hbr.t$, shf, $gb^{\jmath}w$, $^{c}d^{\jmath}$,
$bt^{\jmath}$. Um die Funktion dieser Wörter zu verstehen muss man bedenken,
dass der Ägypter in Gegensatz zu den Semiten keine unüberbrückbare
Kluft zwischen Gott und Mensch gähnen sah, sondern bei aller Ehrfurcht für die Götter sich ihnen verwandt fühlte, so dass er hoffen
konnte, — besonders im Tode, — Anteil an ihrer Kraft der Auferstehung zu bekommen. Sein Gefühl von Sünde und Schuld wird also
keine zerknirschende Erfahrung gewesen sein. Weiter soll man auch
hier den Ton dieser Wörter gut belauschen. Dann erfährt man, dass
die Wörter für Sünde auch verwendet werden für: Verbrechen, Torheit,
Unrecht, Leiden, Schade und dass die Wörter für Schuld die Neben-
bedeutung haben von: Versehen, Unglück, Ärgernis. Nur ausnahms-
weise stösst man in den Texten auf ein reines Gefühl von Sünde und

---

[28] J. Bergman, "B3 som gudomlig uppenbarelseform i det gamla Egypten" (*Reli-gion och Bibel*, XXIX, 1970).
[29] Rud. Otto, *Aufsätze, das Numinose betreffend*, 1923, S. 37.

Schuld, [30] Mit Recht hat Frankfort daher den Schluss gezogen: "the Egyptian viewed his misdeeds not as sin, but as aberrations... He who errs is not a sinner, but a fool, and conversion to a better way of life does not require repentance but a better understanding". [31]

Dies bedeutet, dass der Ägypter davon überzeugt war, dass sowohl seine Tugend als auch sein Glück geschützt sein würden, so lange er in Einklang mit Ma-a-t, der Weltordnung lebte. Derjenige, der diesen Lebenswandel gewählt hat, ist ein ma-a-tj = ein Gerechter. Ma-a-tj ist ein wichtiger und charakteristischer Begriff in der altägyptischen religiösen Anthropologie. In seiner profanen Bedeutung ist es der Ehrentitel des gerechten, zuverlässigen, unbestechlichen Beamten. Der religiöse Sinn geht tiefer. Der ma-a-tj ist der geistig vornehme Mann, der infolge seines Lebens in Harmonie mit Ma-a-t Milde, Weisheit und beherrschte Würde gewonnen hat. Dieses Ideal — denn das ist es selbstverständlich — kann man auch mit dem Worte: der "Schweigende" (gr) bezeichnen, dessen Gegenstück der "Hitzige" ist. Und so stehen nach dem altägyptischen Empfinden zwei Typen einander gegenüber: der Leidenschaftliche, der Habsüchtige, der Zankzüchtige, der Selbstbewuste und der Beherrschte, der Bescheidene, der Geduldige, der Fromme. [32]

Es ist allbekannt, dass die Ägypter grosse Sorgfalt auf die Mummifikation, das Begräbnis, und den Kult ihrer Toten verwendeten, in der Absicht, ihnen damit ein glückliches Fortbestehen im Jenseits zu sichern. Sie haben sich jedoch gescheut, das numinose Wort Tod auszusprechen. So nannten sie den Tod einen Schlaf [33] und umschrieben das Sterben poetisch mit den Verba *mnj* = landen und *ḫꜣꜥ* = (das Leben) verlassen. Die Unterwelt hiess bei ihnen unter anderem *ꜣigr.t* = das Reich der Ruhe. [34] Eine der Göttinnen des Jenseits ist Meresger, derer Name bedeutet: die das Schweigen liebt. [35] In diesen Begriffen spürt man das klare Bewusstsein, dass der Tod den Menschen in eine ganz andere, numinose Dimension hineinführt.

Denn man war im alten Ägypten fest davon überzeugt, dass die Verstorbenen weiter leben, ja man glaubte, dass sie eine höhere Existenz erreicht haben. Der Tote wurde in einen *ꜣḫw*, ein verklärtes Wesen, eine Lichtfigur verwandelt. Deshalb kann man die Tendenz der ganzen

---

30 C. J. Bleeker, "Guilt and Purification in Ancient Egypt" (*Numen* XIII, 2)
31 H. Frankfort, *Ancient Egyptian Religion*, 1948, S. 73/4.
32 C. J. Bleeker, *Ma-a-t*, S. 29 sq.
33 A. de Buck, "De godsdienstige opvatting van de slaap" (*JEOL*, 1939, No 4).
34 J. Zandee, *Death as an Enemy*, 1961, S. 53 sq., S. 93.
35 H. Bonnet, *Reallexikon der ägyptischen Religionsgeschichte*, 1952, 455 sq.

komplizierten Totenpflege am besten wiedergeben mit dem Verbum
$s^{ȝ}ḥ$ = dem Toten den Status eines $^{ȝ}ḥw$ geben, was praktisch bedeutet
sein Leben erneuern. [36] Obendrein durfte der Tote hoffen, dass er mit
der Hilfe von Thoth im Totengericht zu einem $m^{ȝc}$-$ḥrw$ = Gerechten,
erklärt werden sollte ($šm^{ȝc}$-$ḥrw$). $^{ȝ}ḥw$, $s^{ȝ}ḥ$, $m^{ȝc}$-$ḥrw$, $šm^{ȝc}ḥrw$ werden
regelmässig im profanen Sprachgebrauch benutzt. Hier handelt es sich
jedoch um ihre religiöse Bedeutungsnuance. Diese ist bei $m^{ȝc}$-$ḥrw$
sehr charakteristisch. $M^{ȝc}$-$ḥrw$ ist jemand dessen $ḥrw$ = Stimme als
Äusserung der Lebenspotenz $m^{ȝc}$ = in Einklang met Ma-a-t ist. Das
kann erst beim Totengericht entschieden werden, denn dort wird nicht
nur die ethische Tugend sondern auch der kosmisch-religiöse Wert
des Menschen geprüft.[37]

Drittens kommt die kultische Terminologie an der Reihe. Da die
altägyptische Religion sich an erster Stelle im Kult, in der Verehrung
von Göttern und Toten äusserte, ist es selbstredend, dass es eine reiche
kultische Terminologie gibt. Die ägyptische Sprache hat eine Anzahl
Bezeichnungen für das Heiligtum und einige wenige für das Aller-
heiligste des Tempels. Die Priester tragen ihre Namen nach ihrem
Beruf und Rangordnung. Sehr reich ist die Terminologie für alles,
was mit dem Opfer zusammenhängt — zu umfangreich um in Ein-
zelheiten zu erwähnen. Man braucht keinen besseren Beweis für die
These, dass die ägyptische Religion eine richtige Opferreligion war.

Diese Kategorien von kultischen Wörtern, die sich vermehren lies-
sen bezeichnen jedoch nur sozusagen die äussere Fassade des Kultes.
Von der geistigen Atmosphäre spürt man etwas mehr, wenn man
hört, dass es sieben Wörter für beten gibt, die sich jedoch nicht nur
auf die Bitte an die Götter, sondern auch auf die flehentliche Bitte
an den Pharao beziehen. Dasselbe gilt von neun Wörtern für verehren
und von vier Wörtern für Verehrung. Wichtig ist es, dass es verschiedene Ausdrücke für das Orakel und für die Zauberkraft gibt.
Tempel und Kult liegen in der Sphäre der Heiligkeit. Es ist deshalb
nicht verwunderlich, dass man vier Wörter antrifft, die mit "heilig"
übersetzt werden können, obgleich sie auch Nebenbedeutungen haben,
nämlich $^{ȝ}ḥ$, $šmj$, $št^{ȝ}$ und $ḏsr$. Wie gesagt, spielt die Reinheit eine
grosse Rolle im ägyptischen Kult. Es kommen vier Ausdrücke für rein,
vier für Reinheit und vierzehn für reinigen vor. Besondere Aufmerksamkeit wollen wir den zwölf Wörtern für unrein widmen: ^cb, $bt^{ȝ}$,
prt, njd, $ḥ^cḏ^{ȝ}$, $ḥḏ^{ȝ}j$, $ḥww$, $ḥȝt$, tr, trj. und $ḏw$. Die wechselnden Unter-

---

[36] Bleeker, *Festivals*, S. 139 sq.
[37] Bleeker, *Ma-a-t*, S. 70 sq.

bedeutungen sind interessant: sie reichen von Schmutz über das Verkehrte und die rituelle Unreinheit bis zu Sünde, im ethisch-religiösen
Sinn. Hier werde ich es bei dieser Übersicht bewenden lassen, in der
Überzeugung, dass man dem Geist, der im ägyptischen Kult waltete,
beträchtlich näher kommt, wenn man die folgenden Begriffe betrachtet:

(1) *št₃* = Geheimnis. Was bedeutet dieses Wort, das wiederholt
in den kultischen und funerären Texten benutzt wird? Man liest, dass
religiöse Menschen, sowohl lebendige als tote, erklären, dass sie in
gewisse Geheimnisse eingeweiht sind. Auf den ersten Blick ist man
geneigt, an die Einweihungen in griechischen und orientalischen Mysterien zu denken. In der populären Literatur über Alt Ägypten wird
denn auch viel über eine esoterische Weisheit gefabelt, die die Ägypter besessen haben sollten. Die Texte schweigen völlig darüber. Es
hat im alten Ägypten niemals geschlossene Kreise gegeben, die Geheimnisse besassen. Jedermann kannte den Inhalt der Mythologie und
die Tendenz der Riten. Das will nicht sagen, dass das grosse Publikum
Zutritt zu den Tempeln hatte. Der Tempel war keine Kirche, in der
die Gläubigen sich sammeln, sondern die Wohnung Gottes, dem der
Pharao oder der Hohepriester mit einer kleinen Gruppe Auserwähl-
ten — später wurde die Zahl sicher grösser — huldigten und dem sie
opferten. Dieser Umstand unterstrich die Wahrheit, dass es ein offenes Geheimnis gab, nämlich die Kenntnis des mysteriösen und unergründlichen Wesens der Gottheit. Davon waren die Ägypter tief
überzeugt. Deshalb sprachen sie von *št₃*. Das war eine Wahrheit, die
im Kult dramatisiert wurde, derer Heiligkeitscharakter aber so gross
war, dass sie nicht profanisiert werden durfte indem man sie abbil-
dete oder darüber redete. In den Texten rühmen Menschen sich der
Kenntnis gewisser Wahrheiten, worüber sie nicht reden dürfen. Um
Missverständnissen auszuweichen: es handelt sich hier nicht um theologische Thesen, sondern um die Einsicht in das Wesen der Gottheit,
die dem Menschen im kultischen Handeln veranschaulicht wird. [38]

(2) die *pr.t* = der Auszug. Dieses Wort bezeichnet die Prozession,
in der das Bild der Gottheit herumgetragen und dem Volke gezeigt
wurde. Die *pr.t* hatte jedoch eine tiefere Bedeutung. Es war die "epi-
phanie" der Gottheit. Um das zu verstehen, soll man bedenken, dass
das Götterbild für die Ägypter kein Stück Stein oder Holz, mit dem
Bildnis der Gottheit, war, sondern die Inkarnation der Gottheit selber.
Die Texte sagen *expressis verbis*, dass die Götter ihre Bilder in Besitz
nahmen. Deshalb ist die *pr.t* die Dramatisierung einer mythischen

[38] Bleeker, *Min*, S. 63; *Festivals*, S. 45.

Wahrheit, nämlich des Sieges des göttlichen Lebens. [39] In Bezug auf die *pr.t* von Min habe ich zu seiner Zeit zu darlegen versucht, dass es seine *msw.t* = Geburt sei, dass heisst nicht sein Hervorgehen aus einem Elternpaar, sondern seine spontane Geburt, aus sich selber, die nur ein Gott leisten kann. [40]

(3) *wts nfrw* = Emporheben der Schönheit. Kristensen hat damals mit Recht die Aufmerksamkeit auf die Bedeutung dieses Ausdruckes gelenkt. Er fungiert nämlich sowohl als Name des sakralen Schiffes als auch zur Bezeichnung des Ritus, in dem man das Boot oder das Götterbild emporhob. [41] Die Bedeutung von *nfrw* kam schon zur Sprache. *wts nfrw,* als Name des sakralen Bootes oder der genannten Ritus bringt einen Hauptgedanken der ägyptischen Religion, der im Kult in verschiedener Weise aktualisiert wurde, zum Ausdruck. Dies ist die Überzeugung, dass das göttliche Leben wiederholt triumphiert und den Sieg über Chaos und Tod davon trägt.

Schliesslich ist es der Mühe wert, sich zu fragen, wie die Weltanschauung der alten Ägypter aussah. Es ist wohlbekannt, dass sie ein geozentrisches Weltbild besassen. Sie orientierten sich nach dem Süden. Von den Himmelstrichen hatten besonders der Westen und der Osten religiöse Bedeutung, obgleich auch der Norden und der Süden in ihrer Weise in der Weltkonzeption fungierten. Der Westen, wo die Sonne untergeht, war äquivalent mit dem Totenreich, während der Osten als der Ort der Auferstehung gewertet wurde. Kristensen hat in seiner Doctorarbeit tiefschürfende Untersuchungen der religiösen Bedeutung der betreffenden Hieroglyphen und Wörter, nämlich *ʾimnt.t* und *ʾiʾb.t* durchgeführt. [42]

Man könnte noch mehr Besonderheiten des ägyptischen Weltbildes erwähnen. Sie würden jedoch nichts Wichtiges zu dieser Untersuchung beisteuern. Es ist entscheidend, dass die Weltanschauung der alten Ägypter grundverschieden von derjenigen des modernen Menschen war. Der letztere fühlt sich ergriffen von einer Dynamik, die ihn in einem fürchterlichen Tempo fortschleppt: er blickt nach der Zukunft, nach dem Jahr 2000. Der alte Ägypter besass eine statische Weltanschauung: er orientierte sich an der Vergangheit, an der Schöpfungsmythe. Diese Haltung war der Grund seiner festen Überzeugung, dass Ma-a-t, die bei der Schöpfung ein für allemal festgesetzte Welt-

---

[39] Bleeker, *Hathor and Thoth*, S. 86.
[40] Bleeker, *Min*.
[41] Kristensen, *op. cit.* S. 134 sq.,
[42] W. B. Kristensen, *Aegypternes Forestellinger om Livet efter Døden, i forbindelse med guderne Ra of Osiris*, 1896.

ordnung, sich trotz Perioden von Chaos und sozialer Auflösung immer wieder behaupten würde.

Was die daraus erfolgende Terminologie betrifft, darf ich die Betrachtungen, die J. Leclant in einem schönen Artikel über "Espace et temps, ordre et chaos dans l'Egypte pharaonique" angestellt hat, dankbar benutzen. [43] Sie bestätigen völlig die Ergebnisse meiner eigenen Forschung. Leclant macht die richtige Bemerkung, dass die ägyptische Sprache keinen Ausdruck für Raum besitzt, jedoch wohl verschiedene Wörter für Zeit, je nach deren Aspekt. In Bezug auf den Zeitbegriff stellt er fest: "il n'y a pas de véritable "progrès" des choses, ni non plus par rapport à un but vraiment final, car il n'y a pas d'entéléchie", "le temps liminaire, qui déroule sa progression du passé, du présent et du futur, n'a jamais joué un rôle essentiel dans la réflexion égyptienne", "C'est vers le passé que l'Egyptien fait face". Diese a-historische Haltung bestimmte auch die Formen des ägyptischen Verbums. Darin fehlt der Zeitbegriff: Vergangenheit, Gegenwart und Zukunft. Die Formen des Verbums geben zwei Aspekte der Handlung wieder: das vollendete und das unvollendete. Es wundert einem nicht, dass eine fortlaufende Chronologie fehlt. Denn es gab kein Geschichtsbewusstsein.

Die Ägypter haben erstaunliche Leistungen, z.B. auf dem Gebiet der Architektur, vollbracht. Und dennoch bestätigen diese Untersuchungen über die religiöse Terminologie, in der ihre naiv poetische und dennoch tiefsinnige Natur so deutlich hervorgetreten ist, völlig Leclants Schlusscharakteristik der altägyptischen Kultur. Er schreibt: "civilisation de pierre, tournée obstinément vers les résultats de ses commencements, cherchant à les répéter, sans aucun sens de ces améliorations techniques que connaissent les civilisations du métal, ouvertes aux inventions de tous ordres, éventuellement aux changements sociaux, voire même tournées vers le messianisme".

Die Zusammenfassung dieser wenigen Notizen kann kurz sein. Die religiöse Terminologie der alten Ägypter war ausgesprochen prägriechisch und typisch antik. Das heisst, sie war spontan entstanden, bildlich und frei von begrifflicher Reflexion. Dennoch zeugte diese Terminologie von einer tiefen Einsicht in das Wesen der Gottheit und von einer originellen religiösen Weisheit. Es ist meine feste Überzeugung, dass man diese merkwürdige Religion nur dann richtig sieht, wenn man die technischen Begriffe der modernen Religionswissenschaft vergisst und vorurteilslos und unbefangen die religiösen Äusserungen der alten Ägypter studiert.

[43] Leclant, *op cit.* S. 233.

RELIGIOUS TRADITION AND SACRED BOOKS IN ANCIENT EGYPT *

I

In Christian theology the question of the relation between scripture and tradition is a wellknown and much debated problem. It is a question which logically arises from the character of Christian faith and from the structure of Christian theology. It is not very hard to disclose the presuppositions of this issue. The Christian assents to the truth, which God has revealed to the patriarchs, to Moses and to the prophets of Israel, and to which Jezus Christ has given the supreme testimony by his preaching, his life and his death. The Christian faith rests on the revelation of the one God, who charged his servants to preach this message to mankind. Being a message the word of God is a living reality, transferred from mouth to mouth. It is a well-known fact that this message, at first handed down orally, soon was put down in writing. Thus two collections of holy books, containing the religious literature of Judaism and of early Christianity, came into existence. Furthermore it should be recalled, that the Christian Church made a choice from this literature, combined the two collections, called the Old and the New Testament, and invested them together with the dignity of a canon, meant to function as touchstone of orthodox belief and as defence against heresy. However, tradition did not fully die out after the scriptures, which contained the word of God, had been codified. On the contrary, continually theologicans, who appealed to it, made themselves heard. Everybody knows that the adherents of two outstanding types of theology stress the significance of respectively scripture and of tradition: Protestant theologicans underline the value of the Bible as source of Christian truth; Roman Catholic theologicans are convinced that the Christian Church can not dispense with her tradition. Though these few remarks do not exhaust the subject in question, they suffice to show that the problem of the nature and of the function of scripture and of tradition has its fixed locus in Christian theology, because it originates from the character of Christian faith itself.

---

* Published in *Holy Book & Holy Tradition Edited* by F. F. Bruce & E. G. Rupp, 1968.

II

This conference aims among others at clarifying the relation of scripture and tradition in the non-Christian religions. There are good reasons for entering upon this research. Most religions possess holy books. In some religions these books function as a canon. On the other hand tradition plays an important part in many religions. There are even religions, primarily those of illiterate peoples, which are totally based on tradition. Therefore an inquiry into the function and relation of scripture and tradition in the non-Christian religions is quite relevant.

Yet one should be cautious in transferring this issue too hastily into the field of the study of foreign religions. For the subject in question obviously is a typical Christian problem. It is dubious whether we are entitled to impose these notions on other religions. It is clear that in some religions people never reflected on the question. And even if the problem in some cases actually is present it was not thought out nor formulated in anyway. Actually we touch here on one of the key-questions of the methodology of the study of the history of religions. The historian of religions, who is Christian by birth and who is daily handling the terminology of western scholarship, must continually ask himself whether he rightly uses certain notions in order to clarify the essence and the structure of non-Christian religions.

Special cautiousness is required when one intends to apply the apparatus of western, theological conceptions to the study of one of the religions of antiquity. For, the subject of this paper is taken from that field of study. It has to deal with the relation of religious tradition to sacred books in ancient Egypt. In order to clarify the question one should sharply envisage the nature and the structure of the ancient Egyptian religion. That means, one must raise the question whether this religion contains the presuppositions that create the problem in question, as it is known in Christian theology. The answer can not be dubious. It turns out to be negative and that for reasons which will by and by be explicated. The conclusion presents itself: though the problem is by no means irrelevant, it must be reworded. This transposition is expressed in the title of this paper. My lecture does not deal with scripture and tradition in ancient Egypt, but with religious tradition and sacred books in the land of the Nile in antiquity. Which are the reasons for this formulation?

The main reason arises from the character of the ancient Egyptian religion. The Egyptian was no monotheist, but he adored many gods.

He did not derive his knowledge about these gods from the preaching of prophets, who appeared in the course of history in order to disclose the nature and the will of God, as was the case in Israel, but he believed in the existence of those gods, thanks to cosmic occurrences, which best can be called "hierophanies", when we use a term introduced by M. Eliade. These gods were surrounded by groups of worshippers. However in ancient Egypt never a spiritual community existed comparable to the Christian Church.

Thus there was no authoritative body, guarding the purity of the doctrine and the orthodoxy of the faithful. In ancient Egypt the secular and the holy community totally overlapped each other. By being a member of a family, a clan or the state, one participated at the same time in the truth and in the blessing which religion and especially the cultic rites could offer. In this connection special attention should be paid to the importance and the function of the cult. In my opinion it is generally overlooked, that the nature of the ancient Egyptian religion was cultic to a high degree, that means, the religious consciousness expressed itself not so much in a doctrine, in myth, but rather in the cult.

As no church existed in ancient Egypt, it is likewise dubious whether there really were theologians in the literal sense of the word. True theology presupposes a certain ability of thinking in a rational and unbiased way. It is doubtful whether the ancient Egyptians reached that stage of critical reflection. In my opinion one should make a clear distinction between two spheres of thinking in the ancient near East and in ancient Egypt, i.e. between antiquity in the strict sense of word on the one hand and the world of the classics on the other side. This is a thesis which I can not substantiate at this moment. Let me only point to the fact, that in classical Greece—i.e. since the appearance of the famous philosophers—a new and original art of thinking was born, namely the unprejudiced quest for the truth, the inventive and independent thought. Though the ancient Egyptians possessed a bright intellect, technical skill and organisational ability, as goes forth from their highly organised society and from their beautiful and impressive buildings, it is evident, that rational thinking, which deduces its conclusions from reasoning and experiment, was foreign to them. Their science was primitive, a mixture of practical knowledge, technical skill and magic. In none of the fields of science did they reach remarkable achievements. A well-known Egyptologist, E. Drioton, defines the level of the ancient Egyptian culture in the following way: "Elle a marqué la fin, prolongée si on le veut en apothéose, d'un stade de civilisation de l'humanité, celui de l'age de la pierre". His judgement on the so called scientific books of the Egyptians runs like this: "Ce ne sont pas des traités proprement dits, car ils ne disposent pas logiquement leur matière ni la traitent par voie de principe et de conséquence". [1] If this is right and there is no reason to question the truth of these pronouncements made by a famous Egyptologist—it is *a priori* improbable, that there were theologians, who could raise and clarify the question of the relation between scripture and tradition. It is true that many learned and pious priests lived in the valley of the Nile. However their knowledge was no real scholarship but had a bearing on the rites, which were performed in the cult and on the mythical insight on which their religion was founded.

III

The last remark gives occasion to throw light on another feature of the ancient Egyptian religion which should be taken into account. That is the modest part, which myth plays in the religious texts. It is a well-known and yet amazing fact, that none of the many Egyptian texts present a coherent description of the life, death and resurrection of Osiris. It was a Greek author, i.e. Plutarch who as the first put the myth in full down in writing. The Egyptian texts only hint to the myth. What is the function of these allusions? They are not intended to tell the myth, but to sanction certain ritual acts. This is a clear proof of the thesis, which I put forward, namely that the heart of the Egyptian religion beats in the cult. What is true of Osiris, can also be said of Re, the Sungod, who acted as Creator. It is very astonishing that in the texts no coherent description of creation is to be found. [2] And then we know, that the ancient Egyptians constantly looked back to this mythical act for their religious orientation. The best proof thereof is the hour of the ascension to the throne by a new king. This ceremony took place in the early morning after the day in which the old king passed away. This was the very hour to be chosen, because the king by his ascension to the throne should repeat the mythical act of the sungod, who by climbing the primaeval hill became the first king. Even the same verb, i.e. $ḥ^cj$ was used to indicate both the act of the sungod and his daily rise and the ascension

---

[1] E. Drioton, *Pages d'Egyptologie*, 1957, p. 29, 33, 37/8.
[2] H. Frankfort, *Ancient Egyptian Religion*, 1948, p. 131.

to the throne by the king. [3] What has been said concerning Osiris and Re, can be in a even higher degree be repeated in regard to certain other gods, as Min [4] and Sokaris. [5] They can best be characterised as non mythical figures, i.e. deities which whom hardly any myth is connected. Yet they are personifications of profound mythical ideas. These observations lead to the conclusion that the ancient Egyptian religion hardly created any doctrines, clad in a mythical garment. When there is no doctrine to be taught or preached, no authoritative holy books can come about. However, the absence of myth does not exclude original mythical conceptions. They are actually present.

To these mythical conceptions two notions belong which possess paramount importance in the framework of this argument, i.e. the idea of the divine word and the idea of the divine script. The Egyptians have thoroughly reflected on the nature and the function of the creative word. This is proved by a remarkable divine figure, called *Ḥu*. A. H. Gardiner has defined *Ḥu* as "authoritative, creative utterance". [6] *Ḥu* is no blood-warm deity. It is a kind of a numen, by Gardiner called a "personification". *Ḥu* is the divine creative word. *Ḥu* is generally accompanied by *Sia*, the wisdom, the insight into the mystery of divine life. A spell from the book of the dead tells that *Ḥu* and *Sia* originated from Re. [7] Furthermore it is told that they assisted the sungod at the creation.

The function of *Ḥu* is not restricted to his cosmogonic task. It also extents to the present. The sungod needs his help in order to conquer the dangers which threaten him in the netherworld. Thus *Ḥu* belongs to the crew of the ship of the sungod, which passed the realm of death. This creative word sounds from the mouth of the pharao, who is of divine descent and therefore is called to guard *Ma-a-t*, the order, which the sungod has instituted as creator. It is no flatery when the courtiers say to the king: "*Ḥu* is in thy mouth, *Sia* in thy heart, the place of thy tongue is a temple of *Ma-a-t*, a God sits on thy lips, so that thy orders daily are carried out". [8] The reflection on the divine word has even fostered a more profound insight.

---

[3] A. de Buck, *De Egyptische voorstellingen betreffende de oerheuvel*, 1922.

[4] C. J. Bleeker, *Die Geburt eines Gottes*, 1956.

[5] C. J. Bleeker, Egyptian Festivals, 1967 p. 51 sq.

[6] A. H. Gardiner, "Some Personifications II" (*Proceedings of the Society of Biblical Archeology*, Vol. XXXVIII, 1916); J. Zandee, *Das Schoepferwort im alten Aegypten*, (Verbum, Essays on some aspects of the religious function of words, dedicated to Dr. H. W. Obbink, 1964).

[7] 17:29/30.

[8] C. J. Bleeker, *De betekenis van de Egyptische godin Ma-a-t*, 1929, p. 33.

This appears from the famous document of the Memphite theology, to be found on the so called stone slab of Shabaka. This Pharao who belonged to the twentyfifth dynasty, of Ethiopian origin, took care that a very ancient myth on the creative word, in which the god Ptah from Memphis played the main part, was inscribed in stone, in order to prevent it from oblivion. This text is rightly supposed to contain a kind of doctrine on the Logos. This appears from the following quotation: "there arose in the heart (of Ptah), there arose on the tongue a thought... it happened that heart and tongue got control over all the members (i.e. of the deity), because they taught, that he (Ptah) was as heart in every body as tongue is every mouth, of all gods, of all men, of all cattle, of all creeping animals and of all that is alive, because he thinks as heart and because he orders all things, as he likes, by his tongue". [9] Here we find the idea of the divine, creative word, which dwells in all creatures and speaks from them. You might call this a presupposition of the conception of religious tradition.

From the text on the stone slab of Shabaka appears, that the ancient Egyptians conceived of the idea of the divine word, immanent in all living creatures and moreover in the social order and in the cult of the gods. They were also convinced, that this word had been put in writing. In their opinion the script had divine meaning. [10] This generation, which writes hastily and excessively, has lost sight of the significance of the art of writing. The ancient Egyptians knew that as the word was the audible thought so the script was the visible thought. What has been written down, is alive and exercises influence, even after the death of the writer. In the script dwells a magical, creative power. Therefore some texts in the graves, namely those which adorned the walls of hidden rooms, were not intended to be read, but served to provide the dead with the goods enumerated in them. No wonder, that creation could be conceived of as an act of writing. The texts mention the seven wise architects who wrote at the creation. In the pyramide-texts the dead king is called "the scribe of the divine book, who speaks what is and creates what not yet exists" (pyr. 1146). It is said about Thoth: "Thoth daily writes *Ma-a-t* for thee" (i.e. the sungod), [11] that means Thoth arranges the course of the sungod so to say by an act of writing. There are two

---

9 K. Sethe, *Dramatische Texte zu altaegyptischen Mysterienspielen*, 1928, p. 50, 55.
10 W. B. Kristensen, *Antieke Wetenschap*, 1940.
11 C. J. Bleeker, *De betekenis van de Egyptische godin Ma-a-t*, 1929, p. 44.

gods, who are specially connected with the art of writing, i.e. Seshat and Thoth. Seshat is the goddess of the art of writing and of reckoning. [12] Her writing has mythical significance, for, she is called "she who wrote for the first time". She fixes the number of the years of the reign of the Pharao. With her measuring rod she defines the scope of sacred buildings, to be constructed. She keeps the annals. In the last capacity she is called "she, who is the head of the house of books (or the house of life)". Thoth is still more directly connected with the actual script and with books. [13] As the wise moongod he is told to have given mankind the art of writing. Libriaries and archives are under his charge. He is particularly the author of the so called "words of God", i.e. the prescriptions for the cult, that is to say the rituals and the books of magic, as appears from the following quotation: "the scribe of the sacred books is Thoth, and it is he who will recite the ritual glorification (for the dead) in the course of every day, unseen, unheard". [14] In this connection I must refrain from a further description of the significance of the two fascinating deities.

However, it is important to mention, that Thoth is the patron of the scribes. No scribe would forget to make libation to Thoth before he started his work. For, writing was considered to be a lofty art. The office of the scribe was considered to be a desirable position. To the selfesteem and professional pride of the scribe testifies the saying: "Look, there is no occupation without a supervisor, except that of the scribe; he is supervisor himself". Significant is the admonition: "Become a scribe; he is free from work; he is not obliged to cut the earth". The ambition to become a scribe can have a deeper motive than the desire for a position, which releases a man from manual work. This appears from the exhortation which the wise Duauf gave to his son, when he—as we read—"travelled to the city in order to place him on the school of books"—. He said to him: "Might I let you love the books more than your mother, might I let you see their beauty. It is greater than any other occupation". [15]

IV

The ancient Egyptians kept the art of writing and the books in high esteem. They knew the significance of the creative word, which endures as living reality. They must have realized the significance

---

[12] H. Bonnet, Reallexikon der aegyptischen Religionsgeschichte, 1952, p. 699 seq.
[13] H. Bonnet, *op. cit.*, p. 805 seq.
[14] A. H. Gardiner, "The House of Life" (*J.E.A.*, vol. 42. p. 167/8).
[15] A. de Buck, *Egyptische verhalen*, 1938, p. 31.

of oral tradition. There are actually several indications that there existed a tradition, which was partly secular, partly sacred. As for the more secular tradition there existed a folktale tradition. [16] As all Eastern people the ancient Egyptians were great lovers of adventurous stories. They eagerly listened to the born story-tellers, who in the marketplace or in the shadow of the gate of a temple told their tales. Obviously these stories were handed down by word of mouth. The subjects of these stories were partly of a secular nature; for instance, the trials and tribulations of a shipwrecked person; the adventures of a courtier, called Sinuhe, who fled to Syria at the ascension to the throne of a new king; the tale of the doomed prince, to whom it had been predicted at his birth that he could become a victim of three hostile animals. These stories partly have the character of sagas in which old mythical ideas are elaborated in a popular way. To the last category some famous stories can be reckoned, e.g. firstly the well-kown story of the two brothers, Anubis and Bata, two persons, who obviously represent the gods Anubis and Osiris, and secondly the long text in which the course of the lawsuit between Horus and Seth is related, a story in which many droll and even scrabrous episodes, not to be found in the original myth, occur. One can conclude to the existence of this oral tradition of folk-tale from a series of stories, mostly dating from the Middle Kingdom, and written on papyri. They must be the literary fixation of the art of telling stories for many generations.

V

Beside this folk-tale tradition and loosely connected therewith a religious tradition existed which handed down mythical conceptions, magic spells and ritual prescriptions from generation to generation. We have several proofs that such a tradition existed and that it was very ancient. The old age appears e.g. from the fact, that at the close of spell 130 of the *Book of the Dead* it is told, that it dates from the time of Usaphais, a king of the first dynasty, whilst spell 64 is supposed to date back to the days of the famous king Mycerinus of the fourth dynasty. [17] At that time these spells had not yet assumed their written form. They were part of the oral tradition. One can become familiar with this tradition by paying attention to the com-

---

[16] H. Frankfort, *op. cit.*, p. 129.
[17] E. Naville, *Das aegyptische Todtenbuch der XVIIII bis XX Dynastie, Einleitung*, 1886. p. 30.

mentaries to some funeral texts. Famous and well-known instances of such commentaries are to be found in spell 17 of the Book of the Dead. A few years ago Dr. M. S. H. G. Heerma van Voss, a Dutch Egyptologist, traced the oldest version of the first part of this spell and its commentaries, namely in spell 335ᵃ of the Coffin Texts. [18] He reports that there are thirty-three versions of the spell. This fact in itself speaks for a rich variety of the religious traditions. Let me for clarity's sake make some quotations from spell 17 of the *Book of the Dead*, because this text and its commentaries are really striking.

In verse 6 the dead says: "I am the great God, who came into being of himself." The commentary, in which tradition makes itself heard, starts with the stereotyped question: "What does that mean?" The answer is: "The great God who came into being of himself, that means the water, that is Nun, the father of the gods." Then there follows: "Variant: it means Re, who created his names as lord of the Enneade." The commentary goes on "What does that mean?" The answer is: "It means Re, who created his body; thus came into being these gods who are in the train of Re."

In verse 15 the original text runs: "I am Min at his going forth. He has put his twin plumes on his head." The commentary asks: "What does that mean?" The answer is; "Min means Horus who saved his father Osiris. His going forth means his birth. As for his twin plumes on his head, Isis and Nephtys went, they put themselves on his head as two hawks. Variant: they are the great large uraei that are on the brow of his father Atum. Variant of it: they are the two eyes, which were lacking at his head."

These quotations not only present interesting instances of the mythical way of thinking of the ancient Egyptians, but they also prove, that there were great varieties in the religious tradition.

In itself the *Book of the Dead* is the illustrious example of the codification of the religious tradition. The name which Egyptologists gave to these spells suggests that it was a real book and as such comparable with the holy books of other religions. The specialist is better informed. The *Book of the Dead* contains a series of funeral spells which the Egyptologist R. Lepsius has arranged after the example of a late, (i.e. the Saitic) version of this bundle of spells. Thereby the wrong impression is created that the spells are chapters

---

[18] M. S. H. G. Heerma van Voss, *De oudste versie van Dodenboek 17ᵃ, Coffin Texts spreuk 335ᵃ*, 1963.

of a book. However the ancient Egyptians did possess sacred texts, more numerous than the number that survived. Clement of Alexandria even contends, that they had forty-two holy books. [19] One should not attach too great importance to this figure. Forty-two was a holy figure, which had symbolic value. At any rate this notice discloses that there was an extensive religious literature in ancient Egypt. Thus the question arises: which were the nature and the function of these sacred books?

In order to answer this question one should first get acquainted with the nature of Egyptian literature as such. The question arises: which literary genres did the ancient Egyptian pursue and which types are lacking? Likely to the surprise of many people the answer is, that both the epos and the drama are absent. [20] Apparently the Egyptians did not possess the sense of the epic and the dramatic. On the other hand they excelled in the narration of short stories, in the formulation of proverbs full of wisdom and in lyrics. They wrote many beautiful love-songs and sung the praise of their kings and their gods in a flowery way. When this is realized, it is not difficult to understand that the religious texts are devoid of the epic or dramatic vein. They have a novelistic or lyric character and are conspicuous by their short concise formulations. Futhermore attention should be paid to another interesting feature. Many texts, primarily the younger ones, are accompanied by pictures. So several spells of the Book of the Dead are illustrated by vignettes. Some funeral papyri mainly consist of religious representations, to which a few explanations are added. In the description of the journey of the sungod through the netherworld, generally called *Am Duat*, the main thing is the representation of the voyage of the sun-god during the twelve hours of the night. Though there is a text which links up the different scenes, the texts, written around the pictures, have no significance in themselves, but serve as explanations. This means that the illustrations of the texts are no artistic extras, but form an essential part of the texts, and sometimes even the main part. One should therewith keep in mind, that the hieroglyphs originally were a picture-writing. This can not be purely accidental. Obviously the ancient Egyptians were endowed with imagination. Their artistic taste expressed itself mainly in a

---

[19] J. Leipoldt und S. Morenz, *Heilige Schriften, Betrachtungen zur Religionsgeschichte der antiken Mittelwelt*, 1953, p. 40/1.
[20] H. Frankfort, *op. cit.*, p. 124 seq.

plastic way. They therefore expressed religious ideas in pictorial representation. Thus the illustrations form an intrinsic part of the sacred
books and hint at their nature and function.

VI

These general remarks should be followed by a description and an
assessment of the different categories of holy texts or of sacred books,
if you like. The sagas, which are popular paraphrases of mythical
ideas, have already been mentioned. It has also been told, that the
Egyptians collected wisdom-sayings. Several collections are extant.
Some examples are the teachings of Ptah-hotep, of Kagemni, of
Duauf, of king Amenemhet and the book of wisdom of Amenemope.
A special genre form the texts, which contain charms, e.g. the book
of overthrowing Apap, the snake, which tries to thwart the voyage
of the sun-god and the book with curses against Seth. Next come
the hymns, written in a lofty style and full of mythological allusions,
which praise the gods or the sacral king. To the last a number of
texts, which treat his birth and his ascension to the throne, are
dedicated. The famous texts in the temple of Queen Hatshepsut at
Deir el Bahri found the sacral kingship on the idea that the royal
child is born from the marriage of the queen with the god Amon.
Also in this case the pictures of what is going on, dominate.

A text from the Ramesseum describes the rôle of the ascension
to the throne. K. Sethe, who published this text, together with that
of Shabaka, calls them: "Dramatische Texte zu altaegyptischen Myste-
rienspiele". This title is misleading. It is highly dubious whether the
ascension to the throne can be characterized as a mystery play, in
the strict sense of the word. The ancient Egyptians had no mysteries
in the Hellenistic meaning of the word. Whether the qualification
"dramatic" is right, depends on the answer to the question whether
the theatre already existed in ancient Egypt, also on the domain of
the cult. The opinions of the Egyptologists differ. [21] I can not dwell
on this point at the moment. In my opinion it is preferable to call the
text from the Ramesseum a royal ritual. The rituals, which were
enacted in the cult of the gods, form a special category. We possess
interesting texts which have the character of a book of liturgy. Let
me mention: the order of the daily service, the ritual for the hourly

[21] E. Drioton, op. cit., p. 217 seq. G. Jéquier, Drames, mystères, rituels dans
l'ancienne Egypte (Mélanges offerts à M. Max Niedermann, 1944).

service in the cult of Osiris, the litany of the cult of Osiris, the descriptions of the festivals of Min and of Sokaris, both accompanied by pictures, which belong to the most beautiful products of Egyptian art and the texts for the cult and the festivals of Hathor and Horus, to be found in the Ptolemaic temples at Dendera, Edfu, Philae and Esne. Special attention should be paid to the texts which describe the celebration of the so called mysteries of Osiris. The principal documents are the report of Ichernofret, a courtier of king Sesostris III about the rites, fulfilled at Abydos and a text from the small temple of Osiris on the roof of the temple at Dendera.

This enumeration, which does not pretend to be exhaustive, may be closed by mentioning the funeral texts. These texts form an age-long tradition, which extends from prehistory to the last period of the Egyptian civilization. Three collections of funeral texts have become famous: the pyramid texts, published by K. Sethe, the Coffin Texts, collected and edited by A. de Buck and the funeral papyri of the new kingdom in the publication of which A. Naville, Sir E. A. Wallis Budge and lately Th. G. Allen made themselves useful. The conclusion of this survey is, that in ancient Egypt several types of sacred and authoritative texts existed, but that none of them had the character of a holy book, in the sense of a book, having a fixed shape and an unalterable wording.

VII

This thesis can best be substantiated by a further inquiry into the character and the structure of the funeral texts. For the first, the pyramid texts are collected from the tombs of six king of the Vth and the VIth dynasty, to wit Unis, Teti, Pepi, I, Meryre, Merenre and Pepi II Neferkare. Sethe has in his edition arranged these texts in a chronological and at the same time synoptic order, in the sense that starting with the spells of Unis he put together the parallel texts consecutively in horizontal series. He translated the texts, and commented on them. To this publication he added two smaller volumes containing the epigraphic and critical apparatus. In this way one gets a clear picture of the original position of the texts in the pyramids and of their function. The edition of Sethe might give the impression, that we have here a funeral book. Actually they represent complexes of texts, which apparently have arbitrarily or according to an unknown design been chosen from a richer, oral tradition. The spells of the six kings do not form closed, homogeneous wholes and in each of the six collections smaller complexes can be distinguished. Moreover after the publication of Sethe analogous spells have been discovered in other small pyramids. Meanwhile it can not be doubted that they possessed high authority, because they serve to provide the Pharao with eternal life in the hereafter and they give by their sheer presence in the tombe the guarantee thereof.

The coffin texts continue this funeral custom. They are taken from a great number of coffins, dating from the Middle Kingdom. A. de Buck has arranged these spells in the seven volumes of his impressive publication in such a way, that he first took the spells, of which the most parallel texts were present. In opposition to Sethe, de Buck has put the texts in vertical columns, which is more preferable in epigraphic and linguistic respects. These texts have not yet been thoroughly studied. A dutch Egyptologist is preparing a translation and a commentary. The quoted monograph of Heerma van Voss has shown that it is not possible to arrange the spells in a pedigree scheme and to reconstruct the oldest text. This fact confirms the conception that the coffin texts are based on an oral tradition, which has been used according to the requirements. Neither the coffin texts can really be called books; they are complexes of texts.

In this respect the *Book of the Dead* has the best claim to the title "book". For it starts with the opening words: "Here begin the spells of coming forth by day, of glorification and of coming forth from and of going into the nether world, which are to be recited on the day of the burial". This superscription pertains to the whole collection. Moreover the spells are arranged by Lepsius in the order, which in the Saitic time was more or less fixed. This does not mean that every funeral papyrus contains all and the same spells. This clearly appears from the publication of the Book of the Dead of the eighteenth to twentieth dynasty in two volumes by A. Naville. In the second volume Naville has placed one of the best papyri i.e. N° 9900 of the British Museum, which he calls Aa, in the first vertical column, to which he added the variants of other papyri. Budge and other Egyptologists have later on published other Papyri. A few years ago Th. G. Allen edited *The Egyptian Book of the Dead, Documents in the Oriental Institute Museum at the University of Chicago* in a publication of a high scholarly standard, which offers a very reliable translation of the spells. This critical edition of the funeral spells makes one stronger aware than ever before of the fact that both the text and the contents of the so called *Book of the Dead* fluctuated.

8

VIII

Next the question arises whether something is know about the way in which these sacred texts came about. Here an enigmatic term presents itself, namely "the House of Life" (*pr ʿnḥ*). Some Egyptologists have argued that "the House of Life" was a training college or even a kind of a university, solely dedicated to the composition and the study of books. This proves to be a mistake. [22] The texts mention scribes of "the House of Life". Part of their duty must have been the composition of sacred books. They also took part in the learned discussions, which were held in the "House of Life". But their office was larger than that. They were consulted in questions of medicine and magic. They could decide how royal and divine titularies were to be worded. They gave interpretation and determined the conduct of festivals. However it is dubious whether "The House of Life" had a library. On the other hand it is well-known that some temples had libraries. The room of the library in the temple of Edfu even contained a list of books. Nearly all these books are of a magico-religious nature. So also about the composition and the storage of the sacred books uncertainty prevails.

IX

The conclusion of this argument is that the problem of scripture and tradition in the usual sense of the term is not to be found in ancient Egypt. There existed an oral religious tradition, which was widely ramified. Parts of it were put down in writing. So the religious texts came into being, which can be called books in a figurative sense.

However in this process of putting down in writing some factors were active, which lastly deserve our attention, because they generally are at work in the coming in existence of holy books. They are the following. It happened in ancient Egypt that texts were put on the name of famous persons of former times in order to increase their authority. The same motive prompted the use of old-fashioned language. Furthermore, people were afraid to alter the text: apparently the text was sacrosanct. We learn that Pharaoh Shabaka, who had the document of Memphite theology written on stone, was motivated to do this by the wish to preserve a very ancient text, which he held in high respect. We know that the priests kept sacred books in the

---

[22] A. H. Gardiner, "The House of Life" (*J.E.A.*, vol. 42).

libraries of the temple. Finally it is interesting to hear that funerary texts were sometimes so holy, that they were considered to be secret. In the literal sense of the word this is a fiction, but metaphorically understood it can be true, because it is a fact that the texts often refer to secret acts, which are enacted in the cult. [23] These pecularities in the process of codification show, that though ancient Egypt knew no holy books in the ordinary sense of the word, there existed in any case a deep respect for the divine word, not only in its oral form, but also in its written shape.

---

[23] J. Leipoldt und S. Morenz, *op. cit.*, p. 16, 24, 55/6, 79, 89/90, 166.

SOME CHARACTERISTIC FEATURES OF THE ANCIENT EGYPTIAN RELIGION

History of religions is both a fascinating and a difficult discipline. It opens a wide world to the alert student which presents to his astonished eyes an endless variety of religious ideas and customs. There is hardly a science which enlarges man's spiritual horizon to such a degree as history of religions does. It gives the highest satisfaction when one manages to understand the significance of strange forms of belief. But frequently the facts show a sphinxlike nature. Sometimes evidence is scarce. In other cases texts are hardly translatable; and when you can translate the words, it is conceivable that one may not understand their meaning. Then the student of history of religions realizes that religious people possess a secret. How to elicit the hidden meaning of religious notions and rites, how to reach the core and kernel of a certain religion, of religion in general?

It is no wonder that the question of the right method of inquiry arises. And today, once again, this question is brought to the center of discussion. Two indications of this revived of interest are the symposium on "The Methodology of the Science of Religion", held 27-31 August 1973 in Turku in Finland under the patronage of the International Association for the History of Religions, and the series of publications entitled "Religion and Reason", which are devoted to "Method and Theory in the Study and Interpretation of Religion".

The present author would be the last to underestimate the importance of such methodological researches. But by experience he knows that discussions on the matter tend to become lengthy, confused and unprofitable. Unfortunately the trite saying applies here that talking about method is often like eternally sharpening your knife while you do not get anything to eat.

Therefore I am convinced that the right method of studying history of religions can best be demonstrated by showing how you actually get hold of the essence of a certain historical religion. The essence of a religion can be approached in different ways. Scholars either try to formulate a succinct definition or give a lengthy description of the religion in question. I propose to follow another procedure i.e. to pay attention to the characteristic features of the relevant religion. In this case it is the ancient Egyptian religion, which is my special field of research. This gives me the advantage of being able to refer continuously in my argument to my own studies; I can make use of previous formulations. In my opinion this example of how one tackles the problems of the study of a given religion can be enlightening for the study of the religions of Antiquity as such and *mutatis mutandis* for the study of the other religons of the world as well.

In order to visualize the characteristic features of the ancient Egyptian religion one should walk in a tripartite path. First it is necessary to consider the nature of the sources, and to inquire about the kind of information they present or do not offer. Second, the Egyptologist should make himself conscious of the picture of the Egyptian religion which he has gradually acquired. It sounds paradoxical that in order to detect the characteristic features of this religion one should first draw up a general picture of the same religion. This is only an apparent paradox. On closer and critical inspection, it is evident that the Egyptologist interprets the significance of certain gods or cultic acts against the background of what he understands to be the typical features of the religion. Usually this side of the study of the Egyptian religion is left in the dark. Methodological clarity is increased when one becomes conscious of the fact, that the general picture of a religion gives depth to the study of its specific features, and that the study of the specific characteristics enriches the general view of the religion. Thus there is a interpenetration. Third, the real task, i.e. the description of the characteristic features can be taken up. But here a question arises: is there a criterium to determine the actual characteristic features of a religion? The answer must be: nobody can prove theoretically that what he singles out as characteristic actually has this function. There is however a double guarantee: first we may trust that the experienced researcher will search diligently, sharply and without error and, second the self-evidence of the results of the study should convince even a sceptical reader that the researcher can not be far from the mark.

I. A few Methodological Considerations

A) The first question which arise, concerns the nature of the texts which supply the knowledge about the ancient Egyptian religion. It appears that there are the following categories of religious texts: (1) hymns devoted to gods and pharaohs; (2) rituals, e.g. the order of the daily cult; the litany, the texts of the hourly service and of the "mysteries" of Osiris, and the texts of the cult of Hathor and Horus; (3) the texts which express the idea of the sacral kingship, in relation to the birth and the ascension to the throne of the pharaoh; (4) funeral texts, of which category the pyramid texts, the coffin texts and the book of the dead are the principal representatives; (5) magic spells; (6) books of wisdom; and (7) legends with a mythological and religious strain.

In this connection there is no point in digressing about all the philological difficulties which the Egyptologist encounters when he tries to read the texts in order to get insight into the nature of the ancient Egyptian religion. We can skip this item. It will serve our interests better to envisage the nature, the typical traits and the function of these texts directly. Several important remarks in this matter are in order. [1]

First, the texts in question are products of a literary religious tradition. They are holy books, but they do not form a canon, i.e. a fixed list of books which are supposed to contain divine truth and which therefore possess authority. Elsewhere I have elaborated this theme at some length; I refer here to that study of mine. [2] From this inquiry the conclusion can be drawn that the Egyptians have never written books in order to develop certain religious doctrines. There was no official statement about correct belief. The religious texts served the cultic and religious needs.

Next, apart from the famous Shabaka text [3] which contains a myth of creation in the shape of a kind of Logos doctrine, meant as an eulogy on Ptah of Memphis, mythological or theological expositions are nowhere to be found. H. Frankfort has rightly pointed out that no text contains the myth of creation in extenso. [4] The only references are to what happened at the creation. The same holds true for the myth of Osiris. If Plutarch had not written his well known story about the fortunes of Osiris, it would not have been easy to get a clear picture of this myth. For the texts contain only casual references to the myth. Moreover these quotations sometimes contradict each other.

No one who is acquainted with the character of the Egyptian literature will expect to find a text with broad mythological speculations. For the Egypians never pursued the epic and the dramatic

---

[1] C. J. Bleeker, *Hathor and Thoth, Two Key Figures of the Ancient Egyptian Religion*, 1973, p. 4 sq.

[2] C. J. Bleeker, "Religious Tradition and Sacred Books in Ancient Egypt" (*Holy Book & Holy Tradition*, edited by F. F. Bruce & E. G. Rupp, 1968).

[3] K. Sethe, *Dramatische Texte zu altaegyptischen Mysterienspielen*, 1928.

[4] H. Frankfort, *Ancient Egyptian Religion*, 1948, p. 124 sq.

literary genre, but were masters in writing poetry (hymns and lyrical poems), and in telling short stories. In religious respect, they lacked the mythical imagination in which the Sumerians, the Babylonians and the Greek excelled. They are akin in this matter to the Romans whose religion is poor in myth. This fact is one of the considerations which at the time has led me to doubt whether ancient Egypt ever had theologians in the true sense of the word. This is generally accepted without any proof. [5]

The importance of the latter remark on the nature of the texts is far reaching. It places the Egyptian gods into a new light. As in the course of this argument will appear more clearly, a number of gods are a-mythical, in the sense that no myth of any scope is connected to them. Their nature must be inferred from certain attributes and symbols. This latter fact draws our attention to a source of information which is usually neglected and, with respect to which W. B. Kristensen has recognized the significance, i.e. symbolic representations. [6] In his pictorial phantasy, his visual imagination the Egyptian apparently has often interpreted his religious knowledge and insight in symbols rather than in mythological paraphrases.

It should also be realized that the texts which are generally mentioned are related to the official religion, especially to the cult of the state. Even the funeral texts which take their origin from one of the personal events of life, i.e. death, bear a somewhat impersonal character. That means that we hardly know the personal conviction and the piety of the Egyptians as individuals. Yet there are some testimonies thereof, to be found on the memorial stones of the Theban necropolis, which give a look into what has been called "the religion of the poor", [7] and in the hymns in honour of Hathor and Horus which as I pointed out testify to the religious feelings of people of a higher standing. [8] But these are exceptions. The type and the function of the bulk of the texts can be defined in no better way than by stating that they have their "Sitz im Leben" in the cult, in the strict and in the general sense of the word. It follows that the religion of

[5] C. J. Bleeker, *Egyptian Festivals, Enactments of Religious Renewal,* 1967, p. 12 sq.

[6] W. B. Kristensen, *Het leven uit de dood,* 1949; *Verzamelde Bijdragen tot de kennis van de antieke godsdiensten,* 1947.

[7] A. Erman, *Denksteine aus der thebanischen Gräberwelt* (Sitzungsberichte der Berl. Ak. der Wiss, 1911); B. Gun, "The Religion of the Poor" (*J.E.A.* III).

[8] C. J. Bleeker, "Thoth in den Altägyptischen Hymnen" (*Ex Orde Religionum, Studia Geo Widengren oblata I,* 1973); "Der religiöse Gehalt einiger Hathor-Lieder" (*Z.Ä.S.,* 9 Band, zweites Heft, 1973).

ancient Egypt is mainly of a cultic nature and that to a high extent the religious ideas can be deduced from the cultic acts and the short accompanying texts. Anyone who is not convinced of the truth of this thesis should look at the representations in the temples and in the graves. He will not fail to detect an endless series of cultic acts and especially of offering scenes.

B) The second methodological principle prescribes that close attention should be paid to ancient Egyptian religious terminology. For this matter I may refer to a study of mine on "Einige Bermerkungen zur religiösen Terminologie der alten Ägypter" which has been published elsewhere recently. [9] Therefore I can be brief. My starting point was a remark of S. Morenz that in the Egyptian language the notions "religion", "belief", "piety" do not occur, a remarkable fact, because these notions belong to the basic elements of common religious terminology. The fact suggests that the Egyptians had not yet reached the stage of religious reflection on which these notions arise. This conclusion is confirmed by the information supplied in the volume "Ägyptisch-Deutsch" of the wellknown "Wörterbuch der ägyptischen Sprache", in which the words are arranged in categories. Under the rubric "religion" one finds many words for all things that belong to the cult, but no real doctrinal terms. Yet it cannot be doubted that the Egyptians had a religious terminology. This can be detected in a number of typical religious notions and especially in religious nuances of wellknown words. The quoted study gives examples, with reference to the gods, religious anthropology, the cult, and the conception of the world. This means that in order to get hold of the typical Egyptian way of thinking one should forget one's own conceptions. That is not so easy because a dictionary of the ancient Egyptian religious terminology is still lacking.

C) The word "history of religions" suggest the idea that the main task of the discipline is to sketch the historical development of the different religions. In regard to certain religions, such as Judaism and Christianity this work can actually be done. However in the study of the ancient Egyptian religion the search for a historical perspective is irrelevant. For this religion possessed a pattern which from the beginning of historical times until the last period of the Egyptian culture has maintained its dominant position. The ancient Egyptian had no dynamic world conception in the modern sense of the world but his view of the universe and society was static. He was convinced

---

[9] Travels in the World of the Old Testament, 1974.

that Ma-a-t, the world order, which had been established at creation would eternally be valid, notwithstanding temporary chaos, lawlessness and social dissolution. [10]

This does not imply that in the course of the three thousand years of the Egyptian history no alterations took place. [11] Primarly in the cultural, social and political sector they are clearly observable. Also changes occured in religion, f.i. in the democratization of religious life—with the effect that immortality (once the prerogative of the pharaohs) was also conceded to common people—, in the queer worship of animals in the last phase of the Egyptian religion. Furthermore significant periods can be mentioned, such as the reformation of AmenophisIV-Echnation. Folkreligion led its own life as always. A special tone is stricken by the books of wisdom. Curious phenomena are the critical judgment of society and culture, uttered by the so called pseudo-prophets, and the doubts about the sense of life which is voiced in a few texts.

Yet all these phenomena do not detract from the validity of the main religious pattern. The conclusion from this fact is of paramount importance for the way in which the religio-historical facts are to be handled. Though historical nuances should not be neglected, the Egyptologist has the full right to collect his material from different periods of the Egyptian religion in order to reconstruct the image of a god, a myth or a rite. This principle helps him considerably, because the facts concerning a certain theme are generally so scarce that they only become intelligible when pieces of evidence from different periods are combined.

II. The Nature of the Ancient Egyptian Religion

A description of all the facets of the ancient Egyptian religion would exceed the scope of this article. It suffices here to pay attention to the following four typical and constitutive qualities. [12]

A) The religion of ancient Egypt belongs to the category of ancient religions. In the first place this means that it is a dead religion. Its adherents cannot be interrogated about the purport of concepts and custom which are incomprehensible to us. Secondly it means that the knowledge of the deity which the Egyptians had, was not acquired through the medium of prophetic pronunciations, but was derived

[10] C. J. Bleeker, "The Pattern of the Ancient Egyptian Culture" (*Cahiers d'histoire mondiale,* 1965).

[11] Bleeker, *Hathor and Thoth,* p. 7 sq.

[12] Idem, p. 10 sq.

from nature, from the cosmos. This does not signify that the gods were the deification of certain natural phenomena. They acted as independent, spiritual beings. It is important to note that the religious knowledge derived from nature gave rise to an image of God totally different from that of the great world religions.

In ancient Egypt thought was greatly fascinated by the dualism of life and death. The contrast between the fertile Nile valley and the arid desert as a antithesis made the Egyptians consider life and death as mutual enemies. Still they were convinced that these two powers could be reconciled, namely in the divine life which overcomes death. Hence the Egyptian gods are beings who die and thereupon demonstrate their divinity by resurrection and renewal after death.

B) In sociological respect there are two types of religion. In the first case the religious and the secular community are identical. The second type creates a religious community, a church, which now and then may come into conflict with the social order and the state. The ancient Egyptian religion belonged to the first type. It was a folk religion. This finds its expression in the fact that the pharaoh was both the ruler of the state and the highpriest. By birth people belonged to the community of the worshippers of the gods. The voice of the individual is seldom heard. The state religion prevails.

In other words, the ancient Egyptian religion was the ferment of a homogeneous culture. Different parts of life and culture, such as science, art, social life, ethics, polity were not autonomous, as is the case in modern history. Instead they formed a great homogeneous complex on which religion had put its stamp.

The divine norm of this complex was Ma-a-t, the order called into existence at the beginning of time by Re, the creator. Ma-a-t was a polyvalent notion. It signified truth, justice, order in the society and was thus a concept. But Ma-a-t also assumed the shape of a goddess and represented the cosmic order. Ma-a-t had also cultic implications: the highest offer was that of Ma-a-t. This order manifested itself in the regularity of the sunrise and sunset and in the mysterious happening in which life overcomes death and celebrates its resurrection, in the processes of nature. [13]

C) Like all other ancient religions the Egyptian religion is a polytheism, though certain monotheistic tendencies can be discerned in it. Polytheism always gives the impression of being a disorderly complex of important and insignificant gods. A first degree of order is created if

---

[13] C. J. Bleeker, *De beteekenis van de Egyptische godin Ma-a-t*, 1929.

one applies the distinction made by R. F. Spencer in contemporary
Eastern religions between "The Great Tradition" and "The Little
Tradition". In the first category he places leading mythological and
theological ideas. The second comprises the folk religion. In Egypt
innumerable *dii minores* of merely local importance and usually of
quite colourless figure, similarly occur. These have little value for
the research in the history of religions. The gods of "The Great Tradition" should form the subject of religio-historical study.

Now the Egyptian scholar-priests brought some semblance of order
into the confusion of gods by arranging them into certain systems,
in triads: a god, a goddess and a younger god as their son, or in
groups of nine or twelve gods. It would seem to me that such systems
have only formal value and do not disclose the inner structure of
Egyptian polytheism. My belief is that a functional structure can be
discovered in it. [14] I do believe that the multiplicity of Egyptian gods
falls into order when they are grouped together according to function.
Then it appears that a certain apportioning of roles has taken place
among the gods by which practically all sectors of life and world
are covered. To my mind the chief notions of the ancient Egyptian
religion were creation, maintenance of the world order, procreation and
eternal life. It is not difficult to order the prominent gods according
to the function which they fulfil in the scheme of these notions.

Obviously the ogdoad of Hermopolis and Re fulfil the function
of creation. Ma-a-t guards over the maintenance of the world order,
a task undertaken by Ptah in a different way. Also Thoth exerts this
function in his own way, by making peace between gods in conflict
and by restoring the balance of order and justice. Min of Koptos is
the typical god of procreation. Hathor also belongs in this category,
though she is a deity of a more complex nature. Osiris is the god who
bestows eternal life on the dead. Mostly he is called the god of resurrection. This is only partly true, because after being murdered by
Seth he actually becomes the monarch of the realm of the dead, the
god who presides over the judgment of the dead, giving eternal life
to those who could stand the test of the balance.

D) Man has often been called a barrel of contradictions. And yet
every strong personality possesses a character with a homogenous structure. Gods have all sorts of qualities too and engage in activities
which hardly seem compatible with one another. Nevertheless the
present author is convinced that the nature of the Egyptian gods is

[14] Bleeker, *Hathor and Thoth*, p. 18.

not a random collection of qualities brought together by incidental circumstances and events, but that each godly figure conceals a meaningful and homogeneous structure. It should be the task of the Egyptologist to detect the organic entity of the gods—and also of the cultic acts. The Egyptians were no fools. They certainly did not worship gods who should be nothing more than a peg on which to hang a number of haphazardly collected qualities.

III. Some Characteristic Features

This short article gives me the liberty to choose those features of the ancient Egyptian religion which obviously are significant. The best way to present them is to deal with them in the order of the following scheme: A) Gods, B) Anthropology, and C) Cult

A) Gods

Generally Re and Osiris are considered to be the most outstanding gods of the Egyptian pantheon. I have not the remotest intention of belittling their importance. However there are in my opinion other gods who are striking personifications of the ancient Egyptian sentiment. I have in mind the following gods: Hathor and Thoth, Min, Sokaris, and "Tefnet".

a) Hathor and Thoth seldom appear in the same mythological context or the same cultic scene. Yet they are ideologically connected with one another and they impersonate together some essential traits of the Egyptian faith. [15]

Hathor was a mighty goddess and a versatile personality. She appears in many guises. Alternately she is a cow-goddess, a tree-goddess, a patrones of love, of song and dance, and a bestower of abundance, a sky-goddess, a sun eye, a royal goddess and moreover she is concerned with foreign lands. She could pride herself in her great popularity, especially with women. The beautiful hymns dedicated to her are convincing proofs of this. These songs also reveal that Hathor could evoke sincere piety.

There can be no doubt that such a mighty goddess had a homogeneously composed character. As cow-goddess she is the personification of the primeval, creative and divine power. She is the motherly being who promotes fertility. As tree-goddess she has the same function, for the tree is the manifestation of self-renewing life. Little wonder that she was loved both by the living and the dead. The

---

[15] Idem.

deceased hoped to be of service to her so that they might attain a blessed destiny in the life hereafter. The living allowed themselves to be swept along in her whirl-wind traces, for Hathor is the goddess of enthusiasm. She loves music, song and dance and revels in happy feasts. At times her cult assumed an ecstatic character.

In addition to this élan so characteristic of her, Hathor remains faithful to the cosmic order. As sun-eye she chastises the evil-doers and the rebellious. As royal goddess she protects the king, whose duty it is to maintain order in society. In these qualities Hathor is closely akin to Ma-a-t.

Hathor presents a striking instance of an a-mythical deity. There is hardly a myth connected to her. Her nature must be deduced from the hymns, from cultic phrases and from her attributes and symbols.

In a polytheistic religion like that of ancient Egypt it is inevitable that Hathor should come into contact with many gods and goddesses. She has close relationship with Nut, Tefnet, Isis and Ma-a-t so that she is even identified with some of them. Later various husbands are ascribed to her: Shu, Harakte, Amon and especially Horus of Edfu who is incorrectly said to be her typical companion. In actual fact she guards her independence. She is too powerful a personality to be forced into any mythic context.

The polarity of her being already referred to is aptly formulated in the Egyptian expression that Hathor can be wratful as Sechmet and as gay as Bast. Sechmet is the irascible goddess of Memphis. Bast, the patroness of Bubastis mostly shows the cheerful side of her nature which made her so loved. On the one hand Hathor is a martial and grim goddess. On the other hand her favour and benevolence are highly commended. The dynamism of her divine vitality commands respect. Her wrath is much to be feared, but can be allayed. Then she reveals herself as a lovable being, as the giver of the good things of life.

Thoth is not a god of the moon, but a moon-god i.e. he manifests himself in and through the moon. In common with all moon-gods Thoth is enveloped in an atmosphere of mystery. There is even a demoniacal trait in his character. However he is mainly characterised by great wisdom and profound insight. Therefore he is the ideal god to find and maintain the order in the world of the gods, and in the regions of men. He is competent to do so, for as secretary and deputy of Re he is authorised to act as legislator. He is "the lord of the laws". The merits of Thoth for the human community can best be characterised by calling him a "cultural hero". He is the founder of the culture. He gave mankind the spoken word and created a diversity of languages. He introduced the art of writing and is therefore highly esteemed by the guild of clerks. The ritual of the cult derives from him. He is the patron of the physicians.

His significance for the gods can best be measured from the way he settles their conflicts and manages to maintain peace. He reconciled the sun-eye with Re. He separates the fighting Horus and Seth and he heals their wounds. In particular he restores intact the eye of Horus. He pacifies the savage goddess Tefnet and persuades her to come to Egypt, where she is transformed into an amiable goddess. After Osiris is murdered he helps to resuscitate Osiris. In the legal proceedings between Osiris and Seth and between Horus and Seth, he acts as advocate of Osiris and Horus and ensures their vindication. It is on this mythic example that the deceased pins his hopes to be vindicated in a like manner. The function of Thoth among the gods and the mortals can be briefly characterised by the Egyptian verbs *šḥtp* and *šmꜣꜥ-ḥrw*. He abhors disorder and restores equillibrium (*šḥtp* = *ḥtp* = *peace*). On the other hand he sees that justice is done to gods and mortals (*šmꜣꜥ-ḥrw* = *mꜣꜥ-ḥrw* = *righteous*). Finally the hyms testify by their warm tone of attachment to the affection which the Egyptian felt for Thoth.

One could say that the list of Egyptian gods is headed by Re as creator of the world system. Osiris closes it as the bestower of eternal life. The actual religious life is to a large extent governed by Hathor and Thoth, being respectively the goddess of creative élan and spiritual transport, and the god who establishes peace and continually restores world harmony. Hathor and Thoth can be compared to Dionysos who excites ecstacy and Apollo who urges obdience to meaningful order. The grandeur of both the Greeks and the Egyptians consists in their conviction that there ultimately should be an equilibrium between the forces and the ideas represented by respectively these two pairs of gods.

b) Next it is worth while to pay attention to Min, the god of Koptos. [16] Though it is not excluded that Min from southern regions has immigrated to Egypt, he was already worshipped in prehistoric times in Koptos and Achmin, and may therefore be considered as one of the oldest Egyptian gods. In several respects he is a curious god.

---

[16] C. J. Bleeker, *Die Geburt eines Gottes, Eine Studie über den ägyptischen Gott Min und sein Fest*, 1956.

Whereas many Egyptian gods are pictured as an animal or with the head of a animal, Min appears from the first in an anthropomorphic shape and never takes on another guise. His figure shows archaic features. The most conspicuous trait is that he is represented regularly as an ithyphallic mummy. It is wellknown that the worship of the phallus was wide spread in antiquity, also in Egypt. This phenomenon should not be understood as an outcome of the worship of voluptu-ousness, but must be taken as a sign of the worship of the divine creative power. As mummy Min is a dead god. The ithyphallic mummy is the mythological expression of the paradoxical truth that Min has the capacity, even as dead god, to create new life. Thereby he proves his divinity through his power to create *ex nihilo*.

Min has been identified with Horus, the sky god and with Amon, the mightly god of Thebes. Isis has been called his mother or his consort. Actually these mythological connections are of no importance and do not alter his nature. In actual fact Min is a solitary, in-dependent figure. He is the typical example of an a-mythical god.

This does not mean that he stood outside ordinary life. On the contrary, both in the court of the pharaoh and with the common people he was held in high esteem. This is proved both by the fact that he was a royal god and by the beautiful hymns sung in his honour. As royal god Min protected the king and the commonwealth. In the hymns he is praised as the bestower of fertility to man and animal. That he is a typical god of fertility is expressed in one of the oldest representations: Min is standing in his conventional shape on a pedestal; the pedestal is clearly a mond of fertile earth, while plants are luxuriantly growing behind him.

There are several gods of fertility in Egypt. The specific character of Min as god of fertility can best be understood by studying his great festival, the so called *pr.t,* — the exodus, the procession, a festival which will be described at some length later on. This festival is called the birth of Min. No mother is present at this birth. Yet Min periodically celebrates his birth. It is the spontaneous birth of the dead god who proves that he is able to renew himself.

c) One of the most intriguing gods is Sokaris. [17] He is less kown and not by far so popular as Osiris with whom he is often connected and even identified. One can define his character by comparing him with a number of gods with whom he is related. These gods are Ptah of Memphis, the creator, the artist; Osiris, a god of many qualities;

---

[17] Bleeker, *Egyptian Festivals,* p. 51 sq.

Horus, the sky god, the valiant warrior; Nefertem, the young sun-god; Khnum, who also acts as creator and pours out the fertilizing water; and Shesmu, the preparer and donor of oil and wine. Sokaris lacks the transparent rationality of Ptah, the versability of Osiris, the martial valour of Horus, the charm of youthfulness characteristic of Nefertem and the orientation towards earthly life encountered in Khnum and Shesmu. Compared with these gods he is of an inscrutable nature, striking but onesided in being, passive in appearance, a rather gloomy figure, primarily concerned with the underworld. In other words he is, in fact, more a god of death than of the dead, as Osiris was. It cannot be doubted that he is a chthonic god. The ritual of "breaking open the earth", which preceded the sowing and which was performed in the course of his festival makes it clear that he was concerned with the fertile soil. His residence was situated in the fourth and fifth hours of the netherworld. This domain is described as being hermetically sealed. The sun god, who passes through the netherworld cannot perceive Sokaris. The text declares: "Invisible and imperceptible is the secret image of the land which contains the flesh of this god (Sokaris)". This phrase expresses his ineffable character. In the fourth hour an important act takes place: Thoth hands over the wedjat-eye to Horus-Sokaris. The wedjat-eye is "the healthy eye" which symbolises the inconquerable divine life. The remarkable thing is that this eye is called Sokaris. Since the handing over takes place in the underworld, it can only mean, that, by it, Sokaris is charac-terised as a god, who potentially possesses the triumphant divine life. Osiris dies and after death manifests his spontaneous vitality. Sokaris resides in death and possesses potentally rejuvenating life.

d) Finally the goddess whom I provisionally called "Tefnet". This is a complicated story. In the preceding pages it has been told that Thoth reconciled the sun eye with Re, healed the eye of Horus, and pacified the savage goddess Tefnet. These short communications refer to myths which are nearly inextricably intertwined and in which some goddesses, notably Tefnet and Hathor are identified. In order to understand the background of these myths one should know that the Egyptians conceived of the heaven as a great face with the sun as the right eye and the moon as the left eye. To these eyes myths were connected which together with the myth about a foreign savage god-dess, formed a curious complex.

In my opinion Egyptologists have not managed to clarify this queer complex. Yet it seems to me that one can recognize three myths which are typologically different and originally independent. There was for the first the myth of the sun eye. According to one version the sun eye left Re, went astray and was brought back by Thoth. In the other conception Re sent out the sun eye in the shape of Hathor to chastise rebellious people. At its return when it found another eye in its place, it became furious and could only be pacified after it had received a raised seat at the front of Re. There is reason to presume that the first version of the myth symbolizes an extra-ordinary event, namely the eclipse of the sun. It was natural to think that the moon god Thoth went out to seek the sun eye which disappeared. The second version of this first type of the myth of the sun eye can be interpreted as presenting the scorching sun which can burn merciless in the Near East.

Secondly it is not difficult to recognize a moon myth in the famous story of the fight of Horus and Seth in which they wounded each other fiercely; notably an eye of Horus was torn out. Thoth gave the eye back to Horus and healed it. This is the wedjat eye. The myth describes the waning and the waxing of the moon.

Thirdly there is a myth of a goddess most frequently named Tefnet, who lives in far regions in the South and who by the persuasive power of Thoth is induced to come to Egypt and who was changed there into a beautiful and amiable goddess, often called Hathor. Some Egyptologists believe that this myth is identical with the story of the sun eye which went abroad. But this is another idea. Apparently this goddess does not know Egypt. She comes from "the god's land" or the other world. The significance of the myth is as follows: the savage, wrathful goddess represents the mysterium tremendum of the godhead; after having decided to leave the other world and to enter into the human sphere, she adjusts herself to the measure of man and becomes a benevolent deity. [18]

B) Anthropology

It is incorrect to ask how the ancient Egyptians thought about the relationship of body and soul. [19] The concept of an invisible soul was alien to the Egyptian. He possessed no psychology in the modern sense of the word, only a religious anthropology. In the first place, man has a body, or to use a better term: he is a body. For his person

---

[18] Bleeker, *Hathor and Thoth*, p. 119 sq., 123 sq., 127 sq.

[19] C. J. Bleeker, "The Religion of Ancient Egypt" (*Historia Religionum* I, 1969, p. 93 sq.).

and his life are highly dependent on the condition of his body, especially after death. Hence the careful embalmment of the body in order to guarantee the deceased's continued existence. Furthermore he was convinced that various spiritual potencies, in Egyptology commonly called "souls", were present in man. We find here the curious conception of a "plurality of souls". It was to these powers that man owed his wellbeing on earth and his continued existence after death.

As these "souls" have repeatedly been the object of research, [20] I can be brief in enumerating them. Of extreme importance to man is his heart (*ꜣib*), for this is the organ of physical life. But the heart is also the seat of consciousness and moral perception. In Spell 30A of the *Book of the Dead* the deceased addresses his heart and admonishes it not to testify against him in the judgment of the dead. The principal "soul" of man is his *kꜣ*. Not only man, but also gods and even buildings possess a *kꜣ*. The *kꜣ* helps and protects man and makes him powerful. Various theories have been formulated about the essence of the *kꜣ*: a "Doppelgänger", a genius, a totem sign. There are some elements of truth in all these explanations. This much is clear, that *kꜣ* was a divine being. The significance of *kꜣ* becomes manifest especially in death. The conception of the *bꜣ* places a different accent on the spiritual being of man. The *bꜣ* expresses man's desire for liberty, his will-power and also the indestructibility of his spirit which cannot be subdued by death. The last conception to be mentioned is the *ꜣḥw*. The substantive *ꜣḥw* means: splendour, spiritual power, capacity. With regard to man, the *ꜣḥw* manifests itself only after death. The *ꜣḥw* is the glorified deceased. One can say that the main object of the cult of the dead and of the festivals of the dead is to render *ꜣḥw* (*sꜣḥw*) the deceased. [21]

The conception "anthropology" has a double meaning. In the first place it indicates the view of the structure of the physical-spiritual being of man. Secondly it can also mean the evaluation of man in respect to his ethical-religious worth. As regards the last anthropological conception the Egyptians differed considerably from the Semites. The latter conceived of man as the slave of the sovereign gods, as a mortal, sinful being. The Egyptians, on the contrary, felt an affiliation with the high gods. It is surprising to read in the funeral texts how the deceased quite naturally identifies himself with the high gods. This in no way implies that he imagines himself to be the equal of

---

[20] C. J. Bleeker, *De overwinning op de dood*, 1942.
[21] Bleeker, *Egyptian Festivals*, p. 124.

the gods. For other pronouncements express deep respect, indeed an awe for the majesty of the deity. It expresses the expectation that after death the deceased will partake of the divine life.

This optimistic view on the worth of man does not imply that man is considered to be a perfect being. The Egyptian knew that man has several vices and is not always to be trusted. What about the Egyptian feelings of sin and guilt? [22] It proves that the Egyptian language has ten words to designate "sin" and six to express the concept of "guilt". Closer study reveals that the words for "sin" can, in certain circumstances be translated as: crime, injustice, calamity, suffering, damage, foolishness. The words for "guilt" also cover the following conceptions: mistake, failing, offence, damage. It is therefore questionable whether the Egyptians used these words in their purely ethical and religious sense. In this connection the testimonies of the Theban necropolis, which have already been mentioned, are highly valuable. For they contain utterances of the sense of sin and guilt and of the confidence in the mercy of the gods. On closer examination it becomes clear that these words do not originate from a feeling of unholiness, but that they are aroused by the fact that the persons in question are afflicted by calamity and illness. Only in a few cases do we meet a sincere sense of the sinful nature of man. Accordingly, H. Frankfort has spoken of "the absence of the concept of sin" in ancient Egypt. This is right, provided that one understands that according to the ancient Egyptian belief man can escape from sin by living in harmony with Ma-a-t. Both man's happiness and his virtue are guaranteed if he acts and lives in harmony with Ma-a-t. This requires wisdom. It is endangered by foolishness. Nevertheless man is considered capable of leading a virtuous and happy life.

In regard to the future of man it is well known that also here the Egyptians cherished a plurality of representations of life after death which according to our sense of logic exclude each other, while the Egyptians obviously felt no contradiction. Six conceptions can be distinguished. First, the deceased are thought to live in their graves. Second, the dead sojourn in the underworld in a dreary existence. Third, the deceased dwell in regions which can be called "islands of the blessed". Fourth, the stars are considered to be the abode of the deceased. For the fifth, the deceased is permitted to travel in the boat of Re and may thereby participate in the triumphant sun-life. Finally

---

[22] C. J. Bleeker, "Guilt and Purification in Ancient Egypt" (*Numen,* Vol. XIII, Fasc. 2).

the most impressive conception is the trial before Osiris and the bench of fourty two judges. The deceased strives to demonstrate his purity and righteousness by making a sort of "negative confession". If the act of weighing of his heart against the feather, the emblem of Ma-a-t, turns out to be favourable, Thoth declares him to be *ma-a-kheru*, this means that his voice, his life is in harmony with Ma-a-t, so that he may acquire eternal life. [23]

Attention should be paid for a moment to a personality of exceptional quality, i.e., the pharaoh. It needs hardly to be mentioned that the paraoh, as son of Re, is a sacral king. [24] One side of his dignity is sometimes forgotten. As sacral king he also is the high priest, the mediator between the world of the gods and the domain of mortal men. [25] His wife, the queen, plays a greater part than is ordinarily realized. This is why this volume contains a treatise on "The Position of the Queen in Ancient Egypt". This treatise argues that the queen is more important in a sense than the pharaoh himself, because she gives birth to the crown prince together with her divine consort, the sun god. This guarantees his divine descent and his sacral dignity.

C) Cult

This subject has two aspects: (1) the ordinary cult, and (2) the festivals. Leaving all details about the sanctuary, sacred persons, sacred objects, sacred acts and also the order of the daily cult aside, [26] we shall focus attention on the characteristic traits of the two forms of cult.

a) Ordinary cult

In the cultic formulae, especially in the offering texts, allusions to certain myths are found repeatedly. This raises the question of the function of myth in the ancient Egyptian religion and cult. This really is a complicated question. Prolonged discussion has been held about the relation between myth and ritual and about the question whether a so called "mythical-ritual pattern" is discernable in Ancient Egypt. [27] If we take the remarks about the nature of the Egyptian texts, made

---

[23] Bleeker, *Ma-a-t.*

[24] A. Moret, *Rois et Dieux d'Egypte,* 1922; H. Frankfort, *Kingship and the Gods. A Study of Ancient Near Eastern Religion as an Integration of Society and Nature,* 1948.

[25] C. J. Bleeker, "La fonction pontificale du Roi-Dieu" (*The Sacred Bridge,* 1963).

[26] *Historia Religionum* I, p. 73 sq.

[27] Bleeker, *Hathor and Thoth,* p. 14 sq.

in chapter I as a starting point, it is not difficult to state the problem in a few sentences. Certainly numerous references to myths, e.g. of Re and of Osiris occur in the cultic texts. The cultic acts are not done arbitrarily. They have a mythic sanction. Cult was no meaningless game. People worshipped the gods according to the mythical knowledge they had of these divine beings. There is thus a relation between myth and rite. But it would be overemphasizing the significance of myth, were one to conclude that we can discover a fullfledged "pattern". As has already been argued the Egyptians were no creators of myth in the form of a well balanced story. Their myths had no fixed and clear cut contours. The references may even contradict each other. That means that though cult is theoretically determined by the idea of myth the references can vary. This conclusion also holds good for the festivals.

Another question of equal importance is the magic purport of the cultic acts. [28] Here again we come upon an intricate problem. Immediately the questions arise: what is magic? is magic compatible with religion? It is neither possible nor necessary here to discuss these questions exhaustively. It suffices to state that magic can nowhere be disassociated from religion. It is evident that the Egyptians assigned a magical effect to the ceremonies of the cult. For the reason they conceived the rites as actualizations of a mythical truth which possessed creative power. The cultic acts should be accompanied by the magic word, by an incantation which actualizes the power, inherent in the mythical idea. This creative word has been embodied in two gods i.e. in *Hu*, the creative word who together with *Sia*, the wisdom, assisted at the creation of the world, and in *Heka*, the goddess of magic power, who is represented as handing over the symbol of life (*ᶜnḫ*).

There has been much talk about the mysteries which should have existed in ancient Egypt and about the esoteric wisdom which the priests possessed. In order to unravel these unfounded contentions it is useful to state the fact that the texts never mention closed societies which guarded esoteric knowledge. The mysteries proper first came into being in the Hellenistic epoch. Yet the notion of mystery (*št*) occurs frequently. People declare that they have been initiated into certain mysteries. The injunction is given that one should not reveal what has been seen in the mysteries of the temples. Certain parts of the temple were inaccessible for ordinary mortals. The principle act

---

[28] Bleeker, *Egyptian Festivals,* p. 43.

of the festival of Min of Koptos, his raising on a flight of steps or platform has not been depicted. Obviously it was a mysterious happening. These facts make us understand that the Egyptians realized the unfathomable nature of their gods and gave expression to this conviction in the cult. [29]

b) Festivals

The festivals constitute the highlights of cultic life, and therefore merit a separate treatment. From the very earliest times religious festivals have been held in Egypt. This is demonstrated by the Palermo stone which mentions a list of the principal festive events during the first five dynasties. Later on the festivals became very numerous. According to the calendar of the temple of Ramses III celebrations were held on one hunderd and sixtytwo days. It is evident that there is no point in enumerating all these festivals nor in attempting to describe the principal ones. May it suffice to remark that there were three categories of festivals: (1) festivals of the gods, (2) festivals of the king, (3) festivals of the dead. These three categories can be distinguished typologically, though in practice they were often linked together. The third category gives no reason for special remarks. Let me present some instances of the first and the second category.

A glorious festival was undoubtedly the festival of Min of Koptos, already referred to, which is depicted in the temple at Medinet Habu. The pictures show how the pharaoh in his litter and the image of Min accompanied by royal princes, priests and high dignitaries set forth in a solemn procession to celebrate the festival. Unfortunately the texts and the representations do not enable us to reconstruct the course of the festivities. However there can be no doubt about the principal acts of the festival. They are three in number: (1) the elevation of Min on his stairway as a manifestation of his "birth", (2) a harvest ritual, (3) the renewal of the pharaoh's dignity. [30]

To these three points some short explanatory comments may be given. In regard to the first point it is useful to know that *expressis verbis* this festival is called the festival of the stairway and that the text says: "how mighty is Min on his stairway". One sees clearly how servants bear the parts of this stairway in the procession. The stairway is the stylized reproduction of the hill, which is the symbol of the resurrection of divine life, since at the creation a hill rose from the

---

[29] C. J. Bleeker, "Initiation in Ancient Egypt" (*Initiation,* 1965); *Egyptian Festivals,* p. 45 sq.
[30] Bleeker, *Min.*

primeval ocean, the hill from which Re instituted the world order. The act of elevating Min on his stairway dramatizes his victory over the forces of death. It has already been mentioned that this festival was called his birth. It is curious that we find no picture of this act. Obviously it was a mystery in the sense of what has been said in the preceding paragraph. The second act, the harvest ritual, fits perfectly in with the festival of Min, who is an outspoken god of fertility. The pictures show how the pharaoh reaps the first sheaf of corn. This is a symbolic act. The pharaoh acts here as "the first harvester" who starts the harvest which Min has bestowed on men. The third act is closely linked with the second. It actualizes the renewal of the dignity of the king. There is a scene in which birds are set free. The accompanying texts tells that these birds should go to the four points of the compass in order to declare that the pharaoh has received the white crown and the red crown (respectively for South Egypt and North Egypt). This means that his royal dignity has been renewed, obviously as a reward for his cares for the harvest and, more generally, for his government of the commonwealth.

After the preceding explanation of the so called *pr.t* of Min it is quite appropriate to pay attention to the principal festival of the king, i.e. the *ḥb śd*. [31] This is an ancient festival, celebrated with archaic rites which have given rise to a series of studies without unanimity amongst Egyptologists about the meaning of this mysterious festival. One thing is pretty sure: it has wrongly been called a jubilee of the pharaoh. In that case it ought to be a repetition of the well known coronation ceremonies. One can discover no trace of these. It appears that the scarce descriptions of the festival, dating from quite different periods of the Egyptian history, show a number of variations. If we leave minor differences out of account, it is easy to recognize the constant features. The *ḥb śd* was celebrated according to a double ritual, namely one for South Egypt and one for North Egypt. The pharaoh wore an ancient garment. An important act seems to be that the king is seated in a chapel alternatively adorned with the crown of South and North Egypt. Sometimes the pharaoh performs a cultic dance. In another case the *ḏd*-pillar, connected with Osiris and symbol of resurrection, is raised, and a ritual fight takes place. In another instance the pharaoh bestowed privileges on Thebes upon decree.

In order to detect the significance of this festival one should remember that the renewal of the royal dignity took place yearly

---

[31] Bleeker, *Egyptian Festivals*, p. 91 sq.

at the Min festival. This cannot be the meaning of the ḫb śd, for it was celebrated at irregular times. In my opinion we will not be far from the truth if we assume that the word śd means garment, to wit a sacerdotal garment. It is striking that the archaic garment which the pharaoh dons, plays such an important part. The conclusion is, the ḫb śd is the festival of the garment, in the sense of a re-investiture. This means that the pharaoh at his festval was re-instituted in his office as high priest.

The famous goddess Hathor has celebrated quite a series of festivals, too many to deal with. However there is one festival which deserves closer attention: her glorious voyage to Edfu in order to visit the local Horus in the month of Epiphi. Thanks to recent research we are pretty well informed about the course of this festival which lasted fourteen days. However there is difference of opinion about its significance. There are scholars who argue that at the first meeting of Hathor and Horus a ἱερος γαμος has taken place. I have tried to prove in a painstaking argument that this explanation is absolutely out of the question. [32] Horus is not the consort *par excellence* of Hathor. Moreover she is too independent to tolerate an unique partner beside her. At an accurate reading of the texts it appears that there is no proof that the gods in question celebrated an ἱερος γαμος A comparison of this festival with well known examples of the ἱερος γαμος in Mesopotamia makes it crystal clear that in Egypt the mythical-ritual presuppositions are lacking. It is true that the festival is called "the festival of the beautiful meeting". But this includes no more than a visit out of friendship. Apparently there were different motives for the celebration of this festival: the commemoration of the victory of Horus on his enemies, the stimulation of fertility, the worship of the dead. Hathor is at home in this spiritual climate. She appears as sun eye, as goddess of fertility, as patroness of the dead.

This critical analysis of Hathor's visit to Edfu is a distinct indication of the tendency of this article. To the question of the right method of studying the ancient Egyptian religion there is only one answer: the Egyptologist should put aside the usual religio-historical apparatus of terms; he should listen unbiasedly and critically to what the Egyptians tell him. This is the kingly way to get insight into the core and kernel of this remarkable and profound religion.

Finally a question should be raised about whether there is any

---

[32] Bleeker, *Hathor and Thoth,* p. 93 sq.

logical connection between the various festivals, and whether they
can be placed in chronological order. It is evident that many local
and less important festivals were celebrated according to local traditions. Here we have only the great festivals in view. In this matter
A. H. Gardiner has paved the way by putting forward the view that
a purposeful connection must have existed between certain festivals
that were dominated by three factors: (1) seasonal activities, (2)
kingship, (3) certain mythical ideas. [33] It is possible to reconstruct this
festival scheme in part. Evidence shows that the beginning of the
Nile floods was celebrated with a festival. So, 1 Thoth was New
Year's day, and it was a great celebration. In the rhythm of the year
the festivals in Khoiak, in my opinion, dedicated to Sokaris followed
on the occasion of the preparation of the soil and the sowing of the
seed. On 1 Tybi the time of flowering began. This date marked a
new beginning. This is why it was admirably suited for the coronation, for it introduced a new period in the life of the country. The
harvest festival took place in Pachon, under the protection of Min.

In Epiphi the festive visit of Hathor to Edfu took place, as we
heard, a series of ceremonies which were of paramount importance at
least for the inhabitants of the south part of Egypt. The only pertinent
question which remains, is whether the Osiris festivals and the ḥb śd
can be fitted into this scheme. This is a difficult question. There is
no clear picture yet of the nature and the mutual relationship of the
various Osiris ceremonies, and the significance of the Osiris-festival
has been exaggerated. What makes the question the more complicated
is that various data are mentioned. Since the ḥb śd was celebrated
at irregular intervals, no starting point for study can be found in
the cycle of the seasons or in the regular course of the life of the king
or his people. The motive must have been particularly urgent. Undoubtedly Frankfort is right in saying of these state festivals: "They
marked, in fact, a critical phase in the people's relationship with the
gods and aimed at a reintegration, a readjustment or a renewal". [34]
This holds good also for the ḥb śd. We saw that the intenton was the
renewal of the sacardotical dignity of the pharaoh. The irregularity
of the festival makes us understand that there were cogent reasons for
the celebrations. As to the cause of this urgency the Egyptologist unfortunately must once again be content with a *non liquet.*

[33] A. H. Gardiner, Notice on: J. G. Frazer, "The Golden Bough, Adonis, Attis,
Osiris (*J.E.A.* 2, 1914).
[34] H. Frankfort, "State Festivals, in Egypt and Mesopotamia" (*Journal of the
Warburg and Courtoud Institute*, 1952).

THE EGYPTIAN GODDESS NEITH *

In a poem entitled "Das verschleierte Bild zu Saïs", Schiller tells of a young man who, driven by a strong desire for knowledge and insight, visited Saïs in ancient Egypt, in order to be initiated into the secret wisdom of the Egyptians. In the temple he beheld a veiled statue of huge size. In answer to his question the guide told him that the veil of the deity hid the truth, but that no mortal was allowed to lift it. Possessed as he was by a longing for the truth, he slipped into the temple at midnight and tore the veil from the statue of the deity. Nobody has ever known what he beheld. The next morning he was found senseless in the temple. Life held no more interest for him and before he died he uttered the warning that nobody should venture to disclose the truth by transgressing a divine commandment.

Obviously Schiller's direct or indirect source was the well-known passage in the ninth chapter of Plutarch's book Περὶ Ἴσιδος καὶ Ὀσίριδος in which we are told: τὸ δ'ἐν Σάει τῆς Ἀθηνᾶς, ἣν καὶ Ἴσιν νομίζουσιν, ἕδος ἐπιγραφὴν εἶχε τοιαύτην "ἐγώ εἰμι πᾶν τὸ γεγονὸς καὶ ὂν καὶ ἐσόμενον, καὶ τὸν ἐμὸν πέπλον οὐδείς πω θνητὸς ἀπεκάλυψεν".

Schiller's poem deals in particular with the second part of the inscription on the deity's statue, which is usually translated "no mortal has ever lifted my veil". Plutarch calls the goddess at Saïs Athene, adding that she is also called Isis. The Greeks, as is well known, identified the goddess Neith with Athene, and it is obvious that Plutarch's statement refers to Neith. Her veiled statue at Saïs has naturally captured people's imagination. Before the deciphering of the hieroglyphs this veiled statue had become, in a certain sense, the symbol of the ancient Egyptian religion which was thought to contain a hidden, esoteric truth. Even by the end of the nineteenth century we still see a famous Egyptologist, Heinrich Brugsch, paying attention to the famous statue in an article published in *Die Vossische Zeitung* (1892) under the title "Das verschleierte Bild zu Saïs". Unfortunately, I was unable to recover this article and Brugsch's opinion on the veiled statue remains also veiled.

One veil, however, can definitely be removed, namely the belief that

---
* Published in *Studies in Mysticism and Religion, presented to Gershom G. Scholem*, 1967.

the statue of the Saïs-deity was veiled. This conception in itself is already improbable, for, unlike Mesopotamia and Greece, [1] no veiled statues of deities occurred in ancient Egypt.

This fact should have made critical scholars suspicious of the traditional translation of the inscription as quoted by Plutarch. Actually the traditional translation of the sentence: τὸν ἐμὸν πέπλον οὐδείς πω θνητὸς ἀπεκάλυψεν raises some difficulties. πέπλος means "web", "overgarment" and can perhaps be translated by the word "veil"; ἀποκαλύπτω means "to disclose" and, in a figurative sense, "to un-riddle"; ἀποκαλύπτειν τὸν ἐμὸν πέπλον therefore can not mean, "lift my veil". It could at most mean, "uncover me by taking away my garment". However, this is a strained translation. Moreover, it calls up an idea which can hardly be right. Nobody could have thought of un-covering the goddess. Even if one might think that these words express the absolute chastity of the goddess, it is very hard to harmonize them with the preceding utterance in which the goddess says that she is that which has been, which is and which will be. In my opinion we can get into the right track only when it is realized that Neith is the patroness of the art of weaving, and that in antiquity the web was the symbol of cosmic order and of divine wisdom. [2] Thus the significance of the sentence in question would be "no mortal has ever disclosed, i.e. unriddled my web". This translation gives good sense in connection with the preceding sentence. [3] The inscription in its entirety expresses the idea that nobody has ever guessed the nature of the goddess Neith.

This warning should be enough to withhold the student of the history of religions from attempting to penetrate into the nature of Neith. On the other hand he is fascinated by her mysterious character no less than the young man in Schiller's poem. However, the historian of religions is not audacious and sacrilegious as that youngster. He knows from experience that the Egyptologist never fully understands the nature of the ancient Egyptian gods. He respects the secret in the nature of Neith which only her adherents knew. Yet he has no doubt

---

[1] Ištar wears a veil; a veiled statue of Astarte has been found (Chantepie de la Saussaye, *Lehrbuch der Religionsgeschichte*, Vol. I, Tübingen, 1925, p. 557); W. B. Kristensen, *The Meaning of Religion*, tr. J. B. Carman (The Hague 1960), p. 323, points out that goddesses of the earth like Demeter and Persephone are veiled, in token of the fact that they possess the mysterious divine life to which one should be initiated.

[2] Kristensen, *op cit.*, p. 323.

[3] My colleague, Professor J. C. Kamerbeek, the Greek scholar at the University of Amsterdam, confirmed my supposition that the sentence in question should be translated as I indicated.

of the possibility of understanding the character of Neith in its essential features. It is precisely the oracular sentence quoted by Plutarch which raises the question: Who was this enigmatic goddess?

In order to answer this question we should, in the first place, pay attention to the hieroglyphic signs by which Neith is indicated, for although hieroglyphs generally have phonetic value, they originally were a kind of ideograms. The signs which designate Neith have preserved that function. There are two of them. From time immemorial she has been rendered by two crossed arrows, often combined with a shield. They belong to the category of the sacred objects, which were worshipped as divine beings, and represent the weapons which procure victory to their bearer. [4] Apparently Neith was the patron of the victorious weapons. The same idea is rendered by the so-called determinative sign which is often added to her name, and which probably represents a case in which two bows are kept. [5]

This conception corresponds with the significance which is given to her name. The consonantal structure of her name is $N.t$. The Greeks called her Νηΐθ. In theophorous names, like Nitokris, this is abbreviated to Nit-. K. Sethe has plausibly argued that the i or the j in this name are modifications of the letter r. The original name of the goddess may therefore have been $Nr.t$, [6] which signifies "the terrifying". [7] This really is an appropriate name for a martial goddess like Neith.

Pictures of Neith are relatively few. Sometimes she appears holding two arrows and a bow in her right hand and wearing the so-called red crown on her head. [8] Her relation to the red crown will be discussed presently. Because she is considered to be the mother of the sun-god, it is natural that she now and then appears in his presence. She may be part of the crew of his boat. [9] In the pictures illustrating the famous text entitled *Am Duat* which describes the course of the sun-god through the netherworld during the twelve hours of the night, she appears in the fourth, the tenth and the eleventh hour. She is unarmed and can only be recognised by her red crown. [10] In the eleventh hour

---

[4] H. Kees, *Der Götterglaube im alten Aegypten* (Leipzig 1941), p. 102.

[5] *Wörterbuch der aegyptischen Sprache* (Leipzig 1928), 2, p. 198 (= W.B.) H. Bonnet, *Reallexikon der aegyptischen Religionsgeschichte* (Berlin 1952), p. 513.

[6] K. Sethe, *Der Name der Göttin Neith* (Z.ÄS. 43, Leipzig 1906), pp. 144-147.

[7] K. Morenz, *Ägyptische Religon* (Stuttgart 1960), p. 23.

[8] *A Guide to the Egyptian Collections in the British Museum* (London 1909), p. 126.

[9] G. Roeder, *Ägyptische Mythen und Legenden* (Zürich 1960), p. 242.

[10] M. E. Léfebure, *Le tombeau de Séti Ie, Annales du Musée Guimet* IX (Paris, 1886), I, Pl. XXIII; II, Pls. XIX, XXV, XXVI.

she appears in four forms, of which the names are translated by Jéquier as "Neith enfant, Neith reine de la Haute-Egypte, Neith reine de la Basse-Egypte et Neith fecondée". [11] The first and the second figuration of Neith wear the white crown of South Egypt. Apparently Neith is here represented as a deity, which encompasses both the two parts of Egypt and two important stages of female life: that of infancy and that of pregnancy. As Neith also acts as mother of Sebek, the crocodile-god, it is not surprising that she is represented suckling two crocodiles. [12] She also extends her care to the child of man, as is proved by a picture which shows both Neith and the *k3*, the "soul", keeping the young prince in their arms. [13] These examples may suffice.

The red crown worn by Neith shows that she is at home in North Egypt. Her name and that of the red crown even have the same consonantal scheme, i.e. *n.t.* [14] This is a surprising resemblance, though it may be conceived that the pronunciation was different. At any rate there is good reason to suppose that in prehistoric times she functioned as the patron of the delta of the Nile, of which Saïs was the capital. [15] Since then Saïs remained the centre of her cult. It cannot be doubted that Neith was a very ancient goddess: in the tombs of the kings of the first dynasties her hieroglyph occurs more than once [16] and the pyramid-texts mention her several times with some of her characteristic functions. [17] It appears that the Thinitic dynasty of South Egypt had a predilection for this goddess from North Egypt, for sixteen of the seventy stones with signs of the time of king Zer bear names composed with Neith, [18] and two consorts of king Usaphais are named after her, namely Hetepneith and Meritneith. [19] There is no real point in inquiring into her origin. Some Egyptologists suggest a Lybian origin because her hieroglyph occurred in Libya, [20] but this thesis cannot be proved. It is also possible that the Libyans borrowed this sign from the inhabitants of the delta of the Nile. At any rate speculations of

[11] G. Jéquier, *Le livre de ce qu'il y a dans l'Hadès* (Paris 1894), p. 125.

[12] R. v. Lanzone, *Dizionario* (Torino 1881-1885), tav. 175:3; Bonnet, *op. cit.*, p. 514.

[13] Roeder, *op. cit.*, p. 242.

[14] W. B. 2, p. 198.

[15] Bonnet, *op. cit.*, p. 512.

[16] W. M. Flinders Petrie, *The Royal Tombs of the Earliest Dynasties,* Vol. I (London 1900), Frontispice, I, Pls. V: 1, XXXI: 9, 11; II, Pls. XXVII, XXVIII.

[17] Pyr. 489, 510, 606, 1314, 1375, 1521, 1547.

[18] Flinders Petrie, *op cit.*, Vol. II, p. 33.

[19] Kees, *op cit.*, p. 211.

[20] Morenz, *op. cit.*, p. 245.

this kind cannot help to elucidate the nature of the goddess. She can only be understood in the light of historical evidence.

The evidence shows that the cult of Neith flourished in several periods which are far apart: in the days of the first dynasties and in the time of the pyramids; during the twenty-sixth dynasty whose residence was Saïs and which protected the patron of the city; and again in the Ptolemaic epoch, when the temple in Esna was the splendid centre of the goddess' worship. The documents of the centuries between these periods do not mention Neith. Does this silence mean that the goddess played an insignificant part or even fell into oblivion during the intermediate centuries? Should it be concluded that she was never a really popular goddess and that at best she only gained the favour of a number of kings? [21] As to the first point, an *argumentum ex silentio* is always of dubious value, especially in ancient Egypt where history shows many gaps. As a matter of fact, Neith appears from the scanty material which we possess as such a dominating personality that it is most unlikely that she let herself be eliminated for centuries. In regard to the second question, there are some proofs that Neith enjoyed the favour of ordinary people, who worshipped her piously and put their trust in her. In an interesting article on the religious content of various proverbs on scarabs, E. Drioton also mentions the saying "Le serviteur de Neith est quelqu'un qui s'assure la vie". [22] This word testifies to real piety, born from confidence in Neith. In a hymn from the temple of Esna, dedicated to Neith, one reads the following words permeated by religious enthusiasm:

> Comme il est bon de la suivre,
> comme il est doux de la prier jour et nuit
> et de s'incliner devant son nom,
> car elle est la dame de la santé,
>   et la vie est à ses ordres. [23]

These are some accidental testimonies. They prove that Neith was beloved among her adherents, even outside the royal court.

It is evident that we are ill-informed about the places of the cult of Neith. Her temples at Saïs and elsewhere are completely destroyed,

---

[21] Pauly Wissowa, *Realencyclopädie der classischen Altertumswissenschaft*, XVI (Stuttgart 1935), col. 2189.

[22] E. Drioton, *Pages d'Egyptologie* (Le Caire 1957), p. 120.

[23] S. Sauneron, *Les fêtes religieuses d'Esna aux dernières siècles du paganisme* (Le Caire 1962), p. 282. From this book several texts will be quoted in the French translation of Sauneron.

except the temple at Esna. To the north of Ṣa el-Ḥagar some insignificant ruins indicate the place where the renowned city of Saïs was situated. 24 And yet Neith possessed there an important temple, which has been rebuilt and enlarged by Psammetichus, the founder of the twenty-sixth dynasty. 25 Herodotus tells that Amasis, one of the last princes of this dynasty, erected beautiful propylaea in honour of Athene, i.e. Neith. He obtained the material for this sumptuous building from Elephantine. From there he also brought a very heavy cella cut out of one single piece of stone, whose transporation took three years. 26 The same author adds that behind the temple of Neith at Saïs there was the tomb "of him, whose name it is not permitted to pronounce", i.e. Osiris. In its neighbourhood there was a lake on which, as he says, "at night time representations of His [i.e. Osiris] passion, which the Egyptians call mysteries, are enacted". 27 Furthermore already under the Old Kingdom Neith possessed a temple in Memphis "at the north of the wall", where ladies of the nobility took care of her service. Here, as elsewhere, the goddess Hathor was her partner. 28 In general women often boast about their priesthood in the service of Neith. 29 As to the cult of Neith, it is already mentioned in the texts of the pyramids. Spell 1547 describes how the enemy of Osiris, i.e. Seth, is sacrified and which parts of his body are attributed to the different gods. Neith and her companion Selkis receive the spine. The data of the older periods tell little about festivals celebrated in honour of Neith, and Herodotus is the first to refer to this subject. He tells us that great festivals were celebrated in six cities. The third took place in Saïs, in honour of Athene, i.e. Neith. 30 Elsewhere he says that on that occasion many lamps were lighted around the houses in the open air in the night of the sacrifice. This ceremony was called the festival of the burning lamps. The reason for this festival was, as he says, a holy story, 31 presumably a part of the narrative of the search for the murdered Osiris. This communication once more points to the relation between Neith and Osiris, which will be discussed later on.

---

24 K. Baedeker, *Ägypten* (Leipzig 1928), p. 32.
25 *A Guide to the Egyptian Collections in the British Museum*, p. 258.
26 Her. II: 175.
27 Her. II: 170/1.
28 Bonnet, *op cit.*, p. 512.
29 Chantepie de la Saussaye, *op cit.*, Vol. I, p. 486.
30 Her. II: 59.
31 Her. II: 62.

These very scanty details about the cult of Neith are supplemented by the rich material yielded by the temple of Esna, situated between Luxor and Edfu, on the eastern bank of the Nile. [32] The temple was erected in the Ptolemaic era and enlarged by several Roman emperors. One naturally tends to be sceptical about the value of the information imparted by the texts in this temple, as they all date from the Hellenistic period when the influence of Greek culture and religion in Egypt was quite obvious. Yet there is no reason for scepticism. It appears that the cult of Neith at Esna was still very much alive at that time. The data suggest that the worship of Neith at that late epoch was still purely Egyptian. From these texts, which inform us about the myths and the rites at some length, conclusions can be drawn in regard to the cult of Neith in earlier centuries.

Three groups of gods were venerated in Esna: [33] (1) Khnum, together with his companions Nebtu, who was represented as a young woman and Menhyt, who had the head of a lioness like Sekhmet, and his son Heqa; (2) Neith, accompanied by her son Tutu, a god in the shape of a lion [34] and Shema Nefer (the beautiful Southern); (3) Osiris, who was buried there and Isis. Apparently Khnum and Neith were the principal gods. It was taught that they both were figurations of Tanen, the old god of Memphis, a chthonic deity who already in ancient times was linked to Ptah. [35] Neith was furthermore identified with Ermuthis or Thermuthis, [36] the Greek name of Renenutet, a goddess who functioned as nurse, educator, patron of fertility and power of destiny. [37] The significance of the identifications will be disclosed in the further course of the argument.

The texts tell us that a glorious festival was celebrated in Esna in honour of Neith. The calendar of the festivals mentions on the 13th of Epiphi—the third month of the summer-season—a great festival called: "Fête de Neith, qui sauva son fils Rê des mains de ses enfants, après l'avoir placé entre ses cornes, et qui nagea en le portant à travers les eaux; elle parvint à sa ville au moment du 13 Epiphi. Et Rê dit aux dieux: 'Faites accueil à Neith'. Faire apparaître en procession

---

[32] Baedeker, *Ägypten,* p. 347.

[33] Sauneron, *op cit.,* II/III.

[34] W.B. 5, p. 260.

[35] Bonnet, *op. cit.,* p. 769; A. de Buck, *De Egyptische voorstellingen betreffende de oerheuvel* (Leiden 1922); Maj Sandman Holmberg, *The God Ptah* (Lund 1946).

[36] Sauneron, *op. cit.,* p. 281.

[37] C. J. Bleeker, *De betekenis van de egyptische godin M-a-a-t* (Leiden 1929), p. 63; Bonnet, *op. cit.,* p. 803.

cette déesse et son collge divin; faire halte (au retour) dans la salle
d'apparition; accomplir tous les rites de la génisse noire, au moment
du soir; accomplir les rites, selon ce qui figure au rituel". [38] The
festival in question was celebrated in commemoration of the arrival
of Neith to her city. In the texts Esna and Saïs are meant alternately.
It appears that Neith arrived in her city after having saved her son,
the sun-god. Finally, the calendar briefly enumerates the rites that
should be performed.

Actually, the ritual is extant. It is called "Rituel composé pour le
temple de Neith la grande, la mère du dieu, maîtresse d'Esna, et
valable également pour le temple de Neith la grande, la mère du dieu,
maîtresse de Saïs, à l'occasion du troisième mois de l'été, le 13". [39]
The ritual is preceded by a description of the creation by Neith. This
myth did not function in the ritual, but served as a counterpart to the
creative activity of Khnum. The title of the ritual tells that it refers
both to Esna and to Saïs. The text of the ritual was perhaps of Saïtic
origin and subsequently adapted to the needs of Esna. This would
explain a number of compromises. The myth of creation of the world
by Neith will presently be dealt with. In the first place our attention
should be focussed on the ritual. It is interesting to know that the
festivals celebrated in honour of Khnum and Neith ran closely
parallel. The order of the rites was nearly the same. On a certain wall
one beholds on the southern side the boat of Khnum, carried on the
shoulders of the bearers, proceeding from the temple, while on the
northern side the boat of Neith is visible. The southern side of the
temple was dedicated to Khnum; its northern part belonged to Neith.
Neith was the equal of Khnum. [40] This is a remarkable fact, because
Khnum surely was autochthonous in Esna, while Neith was most
likely a newcomer. It proves that Neith was a powerful divine personality.

The ritual is threefold. It gives prescriptions for (1) rites which are
celebrated during the day, (2) rites which took place in the evening,
and (3) closing ceremonies. In enumerating the rites of the first category one can best follow the succinct style of the text itself. During the
day the following rites were performed: entrance into the temple of
Neith; a solemn sacrifice; recitation of the ritual of the procession of
the goddess; announcement, by the priest who conducts the ceremonies of the arrival of the goddess in the third hour of the day; ap-

[38] Sauneron, *op. cit.*, p. 26.
[39] *Ibid.*, p. 250.
[40] *Ibid.*, pp. 313 f.

pearance of Neith with her retinue; conveyance of the bow and the standard of Neith before her; "union of oneself with the sun" (a ceremony by which the statue of the goddess was placed in the light of the sun, in order that she should absorb the force of the sun-god); halt on the way back in the big hall, the retinue of the goddess taking up positions to the right and left of the statue of Neith; performance of the rites of her epiphany (the ceremony by which the deity makes her appearance to the celebrants); numerous offerings; arranging the meal of the gods; bringing the daily offering; revealing the face of the god of the city (apparently Khnum) and that of Neith, [41] recitation of the hymns of the day; adoration of the two crowns (which were considered to be divine beings); purification of the goddess' retinue with water; sanctification of the temple; the priest, who conducts the ceremonies stands with his insignia before the goddess, his face turned to the North (from which direction Neith came); recitation of the ritual of the day before the goddess; performance of the rites which pertain to the day. [42]

The course of the ritual is clear in its outline: the statue of the goddess leaves the temple together with her retinue; the procession moves to the place where the rite of the union with the sun is performed; on her way back Neith halts in the large hall (of the temple) where a series of rites are performed. Special attention should be paid to the ceremony of the epiphany. In order to grasp the significance of this rite, it should be realized that the ordinary people had no access to the innermost of the temple where the statue of the deity was standing. The cult, which took place there, was a mystery, a secret, because only a limited number of people—primarily the king and some priests—were present. [43] The epiphany of the god, the so-called *pr.t* was an event of paramount importance in the religious life of ancient Egyptians. It had a deeper meaning than his appearance outside the temple; it also meant the revelation of his nature, as a divine being, able to conquer death and to renew itself. [44] It is evident

---

[41] It is not quite clear what this rite meant. The revelation of the face of the goddess likely was her epiphany. If the wording of the text may be taken literally, in the sense that a cloth was removed from the goddess' face, this interpretation would strengthen my thesis that the usual translation of Plutarch's well-known words is wrong.

[42] Sauneron, *op. cit.*, p. 278.

[43] C. J. Bleeker, "Initiation in Ancient Egypt", in *Initiation*, Supplement to *Numen*, Vol. X (Leiden 1965).

[44] C. J. Bleeker, *Die Geburt eines Gottes, Eine Studie über den ägyptischen Gott Min und sein Fest*, tr. M. J. Freie (Leiden 1956).

that the *pr.t* caused great joy among the celebrants. This is proved
by some exclamations quoted by E. Drioton: "Puisse-je voir Amon
chaque jour!", "Heureux qui voit Amon!", "Qu'il est joyeux celui qui
voit Hathor!" [45] These utterances may serve to illuminate the significance of the epiphany of Neith during the festivals-rites which have
been described.

The celebration of the second series of rites, which dramatized
the arrival of Neith to her city, took place at nightfall. A black and
shining cow representing Neith as celestial cow, was led to the second
court of the temple. There the animal was ritually purified and adorned. Next the priest brought the cow to the landing-stage where Neith
was supposed to have landed. The priest who conducted the ceremony
recited the solemn salutation from a papyrus. Thereupon four arrows
were shot, to the South, the North, the West and the East respectively,
in order to actualize the idea that Neith conquers and annihilates her
own enemies and those of Rê and of the pharao. This act was accompanied by a recitation which puts into words the victory over all
the enemies of the goddess. [46] The texts do not mention the end of the
nightly ceremony, apparently because it was of no importance. In
this connection a detail in the account of Herodotus throws some
light on the rites in question: he saw in Saïs the statue of a kneeling
cow, wearing a purple cover and a disc of the sun between its horns.
This statue was carried around once a year, obviously during the
festival of Osiris. He heard many stories about the statue to which
he gave only partial credence. One of these stories would have it that
king Mycerinus (fifth dynasty) buried his daughter in the statue. [47]
This might mean that the girl was symbolically buried in the celestial
cow in order to bestow on her eternal life. However this may be,
Herodotus's story agrees with what we know of the rites celebrated
in Esna: the living cow represented Neith as the celestial cow, of whom
a statue stood not only in the temple in Saïs, but surely also in that
of Esna.

The closing ceremony was short, but no less significant. The procession peacefully returned to the temple. The priests sung: "Ohé,
Ohé, La voici venue dans la joie, Neith la grande vache est venue en
paix", etc. Thereafter the goddess and her retinue "appeared" on her
main seat, i.e. on her most conspicuous pedestal. Lastly a great num-

---

[45] Drioton, *op. cit.*, pp. 127-128.
[46] Sauneron, *op. cit.*, pp. 295 f.
[47] Her. II: 129-132.

ber of torches were kindled in the temple and people boisterously feasted in the city. [48] The last ceremony reminds of "the festival of the burning lamps", mentioned by Herodotus. Thus this festival rite also took place in Esna.

The preceding pages disclosed, I hope, the image of Neith; the following pages will attempt to complement this image with a description of her nature and significance. In this connection I would like to point out that my attempt to define the character of Neith was guided by the conviction that the figure of each antique deity possesses a homogenous structure and inner unity. The figure of a deity may be complicated and may exhibit many unessential features, yet we should assume that people in antiquity never worshipped gods which were a medley of qualities. If we are unable to understand these gods as homogenous figures, this is due less to the imperfect conception of people in antiquity than to a failing of our insight.

The two crossed arrows of which the hieroglyph of Neith is composed may help us to understand the goddess' nature. Neith is the patron of victorious weapons. In which sense she acts as such, remains a question. In most cases, Neith is conceived as a goddess of war. Some texts seem to support this conception. It is however equally possible to assume that originally her arrows have been the weapons of the hunter and that in prehistory she was the patron of hunting. [49] At any rate, in later times her arrows signified more than the death of the enemies. They also seemed to hold off demons. [50] The strange resemblance between the crossed arrows and the sign of the *ḥmśw.t*, the female *ka's* which are represented by two crossed arrows before a shield [51] raises the question whether Neith was not the helper in female affairs, especially childbirth. In this connection attention should further be paid to an epitheton, which she often has, namely *wp wꜣw.t* = she who opens the ways. [52] This is the name of the god of Assiut, who is akin to Anubis. As "he who opens the ways", as "scout" *Wp wꜣw.t.* discharges three functions, i.e. he leads the king during his campaign, acts as master of the ceremonies at religious festivals, primarily those of Osiris, and shows the dead the way to the hereafter. [53] It is evident that Neith does not exercise all these functions.

---

48 Sauneron, *op. cit.*, p. 302.
49 Morenz, *op. cit.*, p. 245.
50 Kees, *op. cit.*, pp. 102 f.
51 *Ibid.*
52 *Ibid.*
53 Bonnet, *op. cit.*, pp. 842 f.

When she is called *wp wȝw.t*, this does in any case mean that one would undervalue her by calling her a typical goddess of war.

This is proved by the curious fact that she also is the goddess of water, of the inundation. [54] It is tempting to assume that in her capacity of *wp wȝw.t* she made the waters of the inundation which brought fertility to the country rise in due time. In Egypt the inundation was conceived as the return of the waters of the chaos, as the waters of *Mḥt wr.t*, the great flood, the Methyer of the Greeks. [55] Between this goddess and Neith there is a close relation, in so far as Neith is represented as the primeval cow which rose from these waters. In the myth of creation, which in the texts of Esna precedes the ritual of the arrival of the goddess on the 13th of Epiphi, it is said that Neith, "l'être divine qui commenç d'être au commencement se trouvait au sein des eaux initiales... Elle se donna l'aspect d'une vache". [56] This is a very old conception. For in the pyramids texts (507-520) there is already a relation between Neith and *Mḥt wr.t*, primarily because she is the mother of Sebek, the crocodile-god. This last relation has already been mentioned. It is quite natural, because Neith is the goddess of the waters of the inundation. Spell seventy one of the Book of Dead contains an interesting reference to the relation of the two gods. Verse fifteen runs as follows: "Sebek is situated on his hill, Neith is standing on her shore". It is easy to imagine the situation: Sebek lying on a sand bank and Neith standing on the fertile shore, looking at the stream.

It appears that the connection between Neith and the primeval cow has several implications. Neith is not only a primeval deity but also a goddess of the universe. An echo of the conviction that she exercises the latter function can be heard in the inscription on her statue in Saïs, as it is quoted by Plutarch: "ἐγώ εἰμι πᾶν τὸ γεγονὸς καὶ ὂν καὶ ἐσόμενον". Her quality as primeval deity is indicated in the explanation of her name which Plutarch offers, i.e. ἦλθον ἀπ' ἐμαυτῆς [57] = "I came (into existence) out of myself". This explanation of the name of Neith probably alludes to the Egyptian verb *nᶜj* = to come. [58] It is confirmed by a line in the myth of creation of Esna, which reads: "apparue d'elle-même". [59]

---

[54] *Ibid.*, pp. 512 f.
[55] *Ibid.*, p. 459.
[56] Sauneron, *op cit.*, pp. 253-254.
[57] Plut., *op. cit.*, 62.
[58] Pauly-Wissowa, *Realencyclopädie*, col. 2189.
[59] Sauneron, *op. cit.*, p. 253.

The idea that Neith is a goddess who produces life out of herself is also expressed in the notion that she is androgynous. [60] A hymn from Esna addresses her as "la maîtresse de Saïs... dont deux tiers sont masculins et un tiers féminin; déesse initiale mystérieuse et grande, qui commença d'être au début. [61] She has no partner beside her. In Esna she is accompanied by two sons. She is the virgin goddess who procreates children without male assistance.

It is therefore not surprising that she is considered as a creator. The Esna texts give an interesting description of her creative activity. In order to appreciate this myth fully, attention should be paid to the fact that it shows both parallelism and contrast to the myth of creation of Khnum: Khnum created as an artist by using the potter's wheel, while Neith created the world in an intellectual way by pronouncing several times a word.

This myth of creation tells that in the beginning Neith found herself in the primeval waters. She assumed first the shape of a cow and thereupon that of the perch, the holy fish of Esna. She made her eyes radiant and the light came into existence. By her word she produced the primeval hill on which Esna and Saïs are situated. By speaking she also created some holy places. Next she created Egypt with joy. Thereupon, by mentioning their names, the thirty gods came into being. These gods praised her and installed themselves together with Neith on the primeval hill. On their question, who was to be born next, she answered: "Inventorions (encore) quatre propos-générateurs-d'être, donnons forme à ce qui emplit nos ventres, formulons ce qui vient sur nos lèvres, et (de la sorte) nous connaîtrons tous cela(?) aujourd'hui même". [62] After reflection Neith announced the birth of the sun-god, whose task and adventures she at once described. By a play upon a question of the gods, the ogdoade of Hermopolis arose. Then the sun-god was born: he crept out of an egg which grew out of an excretion of Neith. Mother and son joyfully embraced each other. From the tears of the sun-god men were born and from his saliva the gods. The older gods welcomed Rê. A phlegm dropped by Neith was transformed into a snake called Apap. Thereupon Thot was born in a moment of bitterness: this conception is based on a play upon the name of this god. Neith invited her son to go to Esna and

---

[60] Kees, *op. cit.*, p. 162; *A Guide to the Egyptian Collections in the British Museum*, p. 136.

[61] Sauneron, *op. cit.*, p. 110.

[62] *Ibid.*, p. 259.

to Saïs. During this process of creation Neith uttered seven creative words (*tsw*). She changed into a cow, placed Rê between her horns and swam to her city. The journey lasted four months during which she visited many cities and annihilated the enemies of Rê; on the 13th of Epiphi she arrived at Saïs. In commemoration of this event Rê instituted a festival which should be celebrated with torches. [63]

I cannot, here, comment on this interesting myth and shall confine myself to the following remarks: (1) the Egyptologist easily discovers that the myth alludes to several well-known and very old myths. It is in line with the traditonal Egyptian way of thinking and therefore makes a trustworthy impression; (2) the main tendency is to present Neith as primeval goddess and as creator; (3) creation takes place by means of the creative word, i.e. by means of seven creative utterances, the so-called *tsw*. They have been studied by W. B. Kristensen. [64] They took part in the creation, they determine man's destiny, they act as judges and they are related to the seven planets.

In her capacity of cosmogonic goddess Neith also functions as patron of the art of weaving. [65] No mortal has ever seen through her web, as the inscription of her statue in Saïs states. No wonder. For, according to a conviction common in antiquity, the cosmos is a divine web: nobody understands the mystery of the creative divine life as manifested in the universe. [66] As patron of the art of weaving Neith also procures the bandages required for mummification. This is one of the reasons why she is thought to protect the dead. As a matter of fact, she decides on life and death: "vie et mort dépendent d'un seul mot venu d'elle!" [67] For that reason she also protects magic art and medicine. As for the latter, there are indications that there existed a school of medicine in Saïs. It was likely connected with the *ḥt ꜥnḥ*, the House of Life. A text from the time of the Persian king Darius seems to say that a chief doctor who possessed the dignity of a priest of Neith was charged to restore the school in its old shape and glory. [68]

Finally, a few remarks about the relation of Neith to other gods will bring into relief some aspects of her nature and significance.

---

[63] *Ibid.*, pp. 253 f.

[64] W. B. Kristensen, *Liver efter døden* (Kristiania 1896), pp. 161 f.

[65] Bonnet, *op. cit.*, pp. 512 f.; Chantepie de la Saussaye, *op. cit.*, Vol. I, p. 482.

[66] W. B. Kristensen, *Het leven uit de dood* (Haarlem 1949), pp. 69 f.

[67] Sauneron, *op. cit.*, p. 288.

[68] H. Schäfer, *Die Wiedereinrichtung einer Ärztenschule in Saïs unter König Darius I* (Z.ÄS., Leipzig 1899), pp. 72 f.; G. Posener, *La première domination perse en Egypte* (Le Caire 1936), pp. 93 f.; A. H. Gardiner, *The House of Life* (J.E.A., London 1938), pp. 157 f.

The relation to Rê has already been treated. Neith, the primeval goddess, the heavenly cow, gave birth to Rê; she is "la mère divine de Rê, qui brille à l'horizon". [69] As goddess of the dead she also takes care of Osiris. She is then in company of Isis, Nephthys and Selkis, who stand at the four corners of his bier, [70] or as we read in pyramid-text 606, protect his throne. These four goddesses also protect the four canopic jars. When these jars are associated with the four sons of Horus, Duamutef is her partner. [71] Though Neith is no member of the court which deals with the legal case of Osiris and Horus against Seth, she is, according to the texts entitled "The contendings of Horus and Seth", consulted twice. This fact underlines her high authority. At first Rê sends a letter to her in order to consult her. In her answer Neith decidedly sides with Horus and even threatens to let the heaven fall down if her advice is not complied with. The second time Horus begs for her assistance orally. [72] It is not surprising that Neith, the heavenly cow, was already early associated with Hathor, a goddess of the heaven mostly represented in the shape of a cow. Furthermore it is significant that the Greeks identified her with Athene. Athene too is a virgin and a martial deity, though not a goddess of brutal war but of the strategy of war. [73] Her relation with Khnum is not based on affinity: here two creator-gods are standing beside each other on an equal footing. Her relation to Sebek has already been clarified.

Finally her relation to the king must be considered. Being of divine descent, the pharao is easily related to the goddess. From the fact that Neith wears the red crown the conclusion has already been drawn that she was related to the kingdom of northern Egypt. It has been pointed out that certain dynasties extremely favoured her. These princes apparently knew what one of the Esna texts says: "elle prend qui lui plaît pour être roi". [74] Her care of the king extends so far that she suckles him. By this act she not only shows herself to be a real mother, but also performs a ceremony that belongs to the coronation rites. [75]

---

[69] Sauneron, *op. cit.*, p. 110.

[70] Bonnet, *op. cit.*, pp. 512 f.

[71] *Ibid.*

[72] A. H. Gardiner, *Late-Egyptian Stories* (Bibliotheca Aegyptiaca I, Bruxelles 1932); G. Roeder, *Ägyptische Mythen und Legenden*, pp. 29, 39, 64.

[73] W. H. Roscher, *Ausführliches Lexikon der griechischen und römischen Mythologie*, Vol. III, 1 (Leipzig 1872-1902), pp. 434 f.

[74] Sauneron, *op. cit.*, p. 112.

[75] J. Leclant, "The Suckling of the Pharao as Part of the Coronation Rites in Ancient Egypt", *Proceedings of the IXth International Congress for the History of Religions* (Tokyo 1960).

THOTH IN DEN ALTÄGYPTISCHEN HYMNEN *

In einem der Sprüche des altägyptischen Totenbuches charakterisiert Thoth sich selbst folgendermassen: "Ich bin Thoth, der vortreffliche Schreiber —, der die Wahrheit schreibt, dessen Abscheu die Unwahrheit ist". [1] Das ist ein Selbstlob, das ein Gott sich erlauben kann.

Es liegt Herrn Professor Dr. Geo Widengren, dem diese Festschrift gewidmet ist, fern, sich mit seinen wissenschaftlichen Verdiensten zu brüsten. Seine Kollegen-Freunde haben aber das Recht, die Charakteristik, die Thoth von sich selbst gibt, auf ihn als Religionshistoriker und Religionsphänomenologen anzuwenden. Widengren ist tatsächlich ein hervorragender Schriftsteller, und seine ganze Produktion wird getragen von einem leidenschaftlichen Suchen nach der Wahrheit. Niemand kann dies besser bezeugen als der Autor dieses Artikels, der zwanzig Jahre mit ihm im Vorstand der "International Association for the History of Religions" zusammengearbeitet hat. Es ist hier nicht angebracht, seine Verdienste um die Religionsgeschichte eingehend zu schildern. Mir kommt es nur darauf an den Beweggrund für die Wahl des Themas dieses Beitrags zum Festschrift klarzulegen. Mir kam die zitierte Aussage des Thoth unwillkürlich in den Sinn, als ich nach dem Thema einer Studie, die im Geiste des Jubilars sein sollte, suchte. Mein Kollege-proximus und Freund Geo Widengren zeichnet sich in seiner Arbeit aus durch die Hoheit des Geistes, mit der er jedes religionshistorische Problem anfasst. Gewiss ist er ein humaner Mensch und ein treuer Freund. Wenn er zeitweise Kritik üben kann, so ist der Grund dafür, dass auch von ihm gilt, was Thoth in indirekter Weise von sich selbst sagt: "dessen Abscheu die Unwahrheit ist". In dieser Zeit der Verunreinigung, nicht nur von Wasser, Luft und Erde, sondern auch des geistigen Klimas, ist dies das beste Zeugnis, das man von einem Menschen und einem Gelehrten ablegen kann.

Es gibt noch einen zweiten Anlass zur Wahl des Themas dieser kleinen Studie. Schon einige Jahre beschäftige ich mich mit der Vorbereitung der Publikation einer Studie über Hathor und Thoth, die den Titel tragen wird: "Hathor and Thoth, two Key-Figures of the Ancient Egyptian Religion" und die hoffentlich zu gegebenen Zeit

---

* Veröffentlich in *In Orbe Religionum, Studia Geo Widengren oblata, I,* 1973.
[1] E. Naville, *Das aegyptische Todtenbuch*, 182: 2, 3.

erscheinen wird. * Selbstverständlich werde ich in diesem Buche die mythologische Bedeutung von Thoth eingehend erörtern. Meinen Schluss-sätzen kann ich hier nicht vorgreifen. Es schien mir aber lockend, den Versuch zu machen, Thoth vorläufig von einer anderen Seite zu betrachten, nämlich durch eine Untersuchung der Rolle, die er in den Hymnen spielt. Dieser "approach" hat den Vorteil, dass man Thoth so kennen lernt, wie die dichterischen Verehrer des Gottes ihn gesehen haben. Man bekommt damit einen Blick in die lebendige Frömmigkeit, die Thoth hervorgerufen hat.

Es ist wohlbekannt, dass wir den persönlichen Glauben des alten Ägypters kaum kennen. Das altägyptische Material bezieht sich hauptsächlich auf die Staatsreligion oder auf den Totenkult. In beiden Fällen werden die individuellen religiösen Erfahrungen von den offiziellen Mythen und Riten völlig verdeckt. Zwar spricht das Gemütsleben des alten Ägypters einigermassen aus den Weisheitsbüchern und aus der lyrischen Poesie, aber, weil die Ägypter in religiöser Hinsicht stark kollektiv lebten, besassen sie augenscheinlich nicht die Möglichkeit — oder fühlten nicht das Bedürfnis —, ihre persönliche religiöse Überzeugung zu äussern. Eine Ausnahme bilden die Denksteine aus der thebanischen Nekropole, die A. Erman und B. Gunn bearbeitet und veröffentlicht haben. [2] Sie werden später zur Sprache kommen. Nur indirekt kann man aus den mythologischen Daten auf das Verhältnis des Ägypters zu seinen Göttern schliessen, wie z.B. S. Morenz und E. Otto gezeigt haben. [3] In dieser Lage bedeutet es einen Gewinn für die ägyptologischen Kenntnisse, wenn man aus den Hymnen erfahren kann, wie die Menschen sich persönlich Thoth gegenüber verhielten.

Bevor die Untersuchung anfängt, scheint es mir wünschenswert, in zweierlei Hinsicht nähere Auskunft zu geben: nämlich erstens hinsichtlich der Gestalt des Thoth, und zweitens über die Beschaffenheit der poetischen Texte, welche die Unterlage dieser Studie bilden.

Was Thoth betrifft, so ist es selbstverständlich, dass im Rahmen dieses kurzen Artikels nur eine Skizze seines Wesens und seiner Bedeutung geboten werden kann. Thoth, der Beschützer von Hermopolis, ist zweifelsohne einer der Hauptgötter des alten Ägyptens. Wie manche anderen ägyptischen Götter ist er mit heiligen Tieren verbun-

---

* Inzwischen erschienen in 1973.

[2] A. Erman, *Denksteine aus der thebanischen Gräberwelt* (Sitzungsberichte der Berl. Ak. der Wiss., 1911, S. 1086 sq.); B. Gunn, The Religion of the Poor in Ancient Egypt (*J.E.A.*, Volume III, S. 8 sq.).

[3] S. Morenz, *Ägyptische Religion,* 1960; E. Otto, *Gott und Mensch,* 1966.

den und zeigt theriomorphe Züge. Er kann erscheinen in der Gestalt
eines Ibis oder eines Affen, aber meistens wird er abgebildet als
menschliche Figur mit einem Ibiskopf. Da Thoth von alters her Mondgott war, kann diese teilweise theriomorphe Gestalt nicht aus einem
archaischen Stadium der Tierverehrung herrühren, das der anthropo-
morphen Darstellung der Götter vorhergegangen sein sollte. 4 Es ist
eher Ausdruck des Gedankens, dass Götter sich mitunter in gewissen
Tieren offenbaren können. 5 Wie alle Mondgötter besitzt Thoth grosse
Weisheit, die ihn befähigt, als Gesetzgeber der Götter und der Menschen zu fungieren. In dieser Qualität spielt er eine grosse Rolle sowohl
im Licht-Mythus wie auch im Vegetationsmythus. Er gehört zu der
Schiffmanschaft des Re, dessen Schiff er "beschützt", weil er "reich an
Zauberkraft" ist. Er führt das Sonnenboot auf einer sicheren Bahn
vom Osten nach dem Westen. Denn er legt jeden Tag den Lauf des
Sonnengottes fest, oder wie es auf ägyptisch heisst: "Thoth schreibt
täglich Ma-a-t für dich (Re)". 6 Weiter schlichtete er den Streit zwischen Horus und Seth, wobei Seth dem Horus ein Auge ausriess und
Horus dem Seth seine männliche Kraft entnahm. Er schied die zwei
Kämpfer, heilte das Auge des Horus und versöhnte die zwei Streitenden. Besonders wichtig ist seine Rolle im Osiris-Mythus. In dem Prozess, den Seth gegen Horus und Osiris angestrengt hatte, trat er auf als
Rechtsanwalt für die zwei leztgenannten Götter und "rechtfertigte" sie
vor dem Gericht der Götter, was für Horus bedeutete, das er die Erbschaft seines Vaters übernehmen durfte. Der Tote gründet seine Zuversicht auf diese mythische Tat des Thoth. Er bezieht sich darauf, indem
er den Wunsch ausspricht, dass Thoth ihn gleichfalls im Totengericht
"rechtfertigen" möge. Bei dieser Skizze muss ich es bewenden lassen.
Man sollte dabei bedenken, dass dieses harmonisierende Bild des Thoth
nur die Hauptlinien seines Wesens zeichnet, also einerseits unvollständig ist und andererseits über allerhand "cruces" in der Forschung hin-
weggleitet. Die Skizze dient nur dazu, den Gott Thoth in Erinnerung
zu bringen und wird im Laufe der Auseinandersetzung ihren Wert
bekommen als Vergleichsobjekt mit dem Bilde des Thoth, das uns aus
den Hymnen entgegentritt.

  Das poetische Material, das ich benutzt habe, hat folgende Beschaffenheit: es besteht hauptsächlich aus sieben kurzen Hymnen,

4 G. Jéquier, *Considérations sur les religions égyptiennes,* 1946, unterscheidet "les
trois âges des religions égyptiennes: âge fétichiste, âge zoolatrique, âge anthropo-
morphique".

5 H. Frankfort, *Ancient Egyptian Religion,* 1948, S. 8 sq.

6 C. J. Bleeker, *De beteekenis van de Egyptische godin Ma-a-t,* 1929, S. 44.

die in Note 7 näher beschrieben werden und die ich mit den Buch-
staben A, B, C, D, E, F, und G [7] zitieren werde. Weiter hielt ich mich
für berechtigt zwei nicht-poetische Texte heranzuziehen, nämlich
einen Text aus dem Demotischen, abgekürzt als H, und ein Ostracon,
zitiert als I. [8] Ich tat das, weil beide Dokumente Zeugnis ablegen
von den Gefühlen, welche Menschen, die Unrecht erlitten haben,
in Hinsicht auf Thoth hegen. Schliesslich werde ich einige Zitate aus
den Spruchen 18,20 und 182 des Totenbuches entnehmen, um gewisse
Funktionen des Thoth schärfer beleuchten zu können. Auch dies
schien mir gestattet, weil diese Sprüche einen hymnischen Charakter
haben.

Es darf uns nicht entgehen, dass einer der Hymnen die Überschrift
trägt: "Tägliche Verehrung des Thoth". [9] Ob dieser Hymnus tatsächlich Tag für Tag gesungen wurde um Thoth zu huldigen, ist natürlich
fraglich. Das Lied war jedenfalls für den täglichen Gebrauch bestimmt.
Aus dieser Bestimmung darf man den Schluss ziehen, dass der Hymnus
für solche Menschen gedichtet war, die den Thoth als ihren Hauptgott
oder vielleicht als ihren einzigen Gott betrachteten. Diese Vermutung
wird bestärkt durch einige Zeilen aus dem Liede. Der Dichter preist
Thoth in den folgende Worten:

"Er ist der Oberste aller Götter
und aller Göttinnen,
indem er der grossen Enneade befiehlt",

und er ruft die Götter auf Thoth zu huldigen:

"O ihr Götter, die ihr im Himmel seid,
O ihr Götter, die ihr (auf Erden) seid ...
Verehret ihn, erhebet ihn, spendet ihm Lob". [10]

---

[7] A: Brit. Museum 5656, B. Turajeff, Zwei Hymnen an Thoth (*Z.Ä.S.* 33, 1895,
    S. 120 sq), A. Erman, *Die Literatur der Aegypter*, 1923, S. 186.
  B: Berliner Museum 2293, Turajeff, *op. cit.*
  C: Anast. V, 9,2 sq., Erman, *Lit.*, S. 377.
  D: Sallier I, 8,2 sq., Erman, *op. cit.*, S. 377.
  E: Anast. III, 4,12,sq., Erman, *op. cit.*, S. 378.
  F: B. Turajeff, Die naophore Statue No. 97 im Vatikan (*Z.Ä.S.* 46, S. 74 sq.).
  G: Brit. Museum 551, Ed. Meyer, Die Stele des Horemheb (*Z.Ä.S.* 15, 1877,
    S. 148 sq.).
[8] H: G. R. Hughes, A Demotic Letter to Thoth (*J.N.E.S.* 17, 1958, S. 1 sq.),
    Oriental Institute Chicago 19422.
  I: J. de Horrack. Sur un ostracon du Musée du Louvre, Lettre à Monsieur le
    Docteur Lepsius (*Z.Ä.S.* 6, 1868, S. 1 sq.).
[9] A.
[10] A.

Der Dichter eines anderen Hymnus geht noch um einen Schritt weiter. Für ihn ist Thoth ein ursprünglicher und unvergleichlicher Gott. Er bringt diesen Gedanken folgendermassen poetisch zum Ausdruck:

> "Preis dir, Thoth, Herr von Hermopolis,
> der sich selbst schafft,
> nicht ist er geboren, der einzige Gott". 11

Diese dichterischen Äusserungen geben Veranlassung, einige kurze Bemerkungen zu einem interessanten Probleme zu machen, nämlich zu der Frage nach dem Verhältnis zwischen Polytheismus und Monotheismus im alten Ägypten. Es ist klar, dass die altägyptische Religon ein durchaus polytheistisches Gepräge hatte. Man verehrte eine beschränkte Anzahl grosser Götter, die irgendwie mit kosmischen Phänomenen verbunden waren, wie Re, Osiris, Horus, Hathor, Min, Thoth und eine Unzahl *dii minores*, die meistens nur lokale Bedeutung hatten. Ein derartiger Polytheismus erklärt sich religionsphänomenologisch, wenn man bedenkt, dass die alten Ägypter offenbar in Segmenten des Kosmos und des Lebens das erfuhren, was M. Eliade "Hierophanie" nennt, ohne dass sie das Vermögen und das Bedürfnis hatten, diese Momente der Gotteserkenntnis zu einer Einheit umzuformen. 12 Trotzdem gab es monotheistische oder eher henotheistische Tendenzen. Monotheismus bedeutet in der religionshistorischen Terminologie den Glauben an einen persönlichen Gott, im Gegensatz zum Glauben an viele Götter. Mit Henotheismus ist eine Form der Religion gemeint, in der die Verehrung sich auf einen einzigen Gott richtet, obgleich man die Existenz anderer Götter voraussetzt. 13 Es erhebt sich also die Frage, ob es im alten Ägypten einen ausgeprägten Monotheismus oder vielleicht einen Henotheismus gab und was ihre Bedeutung war. Bei der Beantwortung dieser Frage gehe ich vorüber an der von H. Junker vorgebrachten These, 14 — der auch Widengren sich angeschlossen hat, 15 — dass es ursprünglich einen Gott gab, der "der grosse Gott" oder "der Grosse" genannt wurde und der die Funktion eines Himmelsgottes und eines Hochgottes hatte. Dies ist eine interessante These, die ich hier nicht näher prüfen kann, aber

---

11 G.

12 Frankfort, *op. cit.*, S. 4 sq.

13 *A Dictionary of Comparative Religion*, edited by S. G. F. Brandon, 1970, S. 450, 324.

14 H. Junker, *Pyramidenzeit*, 1949.

15 G. Widengren, *Religionsphänomenologie*, 1969, S. 75.

die mir anfechtbar zu sein scheint. [16] Auch den "Monotheismus" des
Amenophis IV-Echnaton lasse ich unbesprochen. [17] Es gibt andere
Daten, die in diesem Zusammenhang mehr Aufmerksamkeit verdienen.
Da ist erstens der Gottesbegriff, dessen sich der Verfasser des Weis-
heitsbuches von Amenomope bedient. Es wird darin von "Gott"
oder "der Gott" gesprochen, ohne dass ihm ein Namen beigelegt wird.
Dieser Gott ist offenbar der einzige, mit dem die Weisheitslehrer
rechnen. So heisst es zum Beispiel:

> "Besser ist Armut in Gottes Hand
> als Reichtum im Vorratskammer.
> Besser ist das (tägliche) Opferbrot mit einem glücklichen Herzen
> als Reichtum mit Kummer". [18]

Es handelt sich hier um den Glauben an eine namenlose Gottheit,
die als einziger Gott betrachtet wird, zu dem man Vertrauen haben
kann. Weiter geht aus gewissen Texten hervor, dass einige Götter
den Anspruch erhoben haben, "der Grosse" (wr), "der grosse Gott"
($ntr\ ^c\mathcal{3}$) oder "der grösste unter den Göttern ($^c\mathcal{3}\ imj\ ntr.w$) zu sein,
besonders Re und Osiris. [19] Was Junker für einen Urgott hält, ist
wenigstens in historischer Zeit ein Epitheton gewisser Götter, die
den höchsten Rang im Pantheon für sich in Anspruch nahmen und
die ausschliessliche Anerkennung ihrer Verehrer forderten. Im Rahmen
dieser Gedanken sollte man die gegebenen Zitate aus den Thoth-
Hymnen einordnen. Für die Dichter dieser Lieder gab es nur einen
Gott, der Verehrung beanspruchen konnte, nämlich Thoth.

Dabei vergessen die Dichter nicht, dass Thoth ursprünglich ein
Mondgott war. Das geht aus dem folgenden Anruf hervor:

> "Ich bin zu dir gekommen, du Stier unter den Sternen,
> Thoth-Mond, der am Himmel ist.
> Du bist am Himmel, deine Strahlen sind auf Erden,
> Dein Glanz erleuchtet die beiden Länder". [20]

Als Lichtgott ist Thoth eine glänzende Gestalt. Man betrachtet
seine "Schönheit" mit Freude. [21] Der Dichter ruft die Götter zu:

---

[16] J. Zandee, *De Hymnen aan Amon van Papyrus Leiden I* 350, 1948, S. 120.
[17] H. Schäfer, *Die Religion und Kunst von El-Amarna*, 1923; Zandee, *op. cit.*,
S. 116 sq.
[18] *Het boek der Wijsheid van Amen-em-ope, den zoon van Kanecht*, vertaald door
W. D. van Wijngaarden, 1930, S. 68.
[19] Zandee, *op. cit.*, S. 118 sq.
[20] B. Lied C. 2b.
[21] B. Lied C. 2a.

"Kommet und schauet den Thoth,
Wie er glänzend erscheint in seiner Krone von Oberägypten,
die ihm die beiden Herren von Hermopolis [22] aufgesetzt haben,
Damit er die Leitung der Menschen führe". [23]

Zur gleichen Zeit ehrt man ihn als Ibis und as Affe. Ein Lied
preist Thoth als den "herrlichen Ibis." [24] Der Mann, der sich über das
Unrecht beschwert, das ein Kollege im Dienste des Thoth ihm angetan
hat, spricht abwechslend von Thoth und von dem Ibis. In der von
G. R. Hughes gebotenen englischen Übersetzung seines Briefes an
Thoth erklärt er: "A communication of the humble servant N.N. unto
Thoth ... from year 11, the month of Mechir to this day I have been
doing the work of The Ibis. I left my (former) work (and) even
though I like the work for which I came to The Ibis. I (now) have no
human master." [25] Diesen Worten kann man entnehmen, dass dieser
Mann seinen menschlichen Meister verlassen hat und sich völlig in den
Dienst des Thoth, seines göttlichen Herrn, gestellt hat. Die Anklage,
die er in seinem Briefe vorbringt, klingt etwas übertrieben und sollte,
wie alle Beschwerden von Dienstpersonal im alten Orient, *cum grano
salis* genommen werden, aber an der Echtheit seiner Hingebung an
Thoth ist wohl nicht zu zweifeln.

Thoth wird also als Ibis bezeichnet. Andererseits betrachtet man
ihn auch als Affen. Es gibt ein Loblied, das ein Schreiber an eine aus
Edelsteinen hergestellte Statue des Thoth in der Gestalt eines Pavians
richtet, weil das Bildchen sein Haus schützt und ihm Glück beschert.
Der fromme Schreiber sagt:

"Preis dir, du Herr des Hauses,
du Affe mit weissem Haar und hübscher Gestalt ...
Er ist aus Sehretstein ...
Was auf seinem Haupte ist,
ist aus rotem Jaspis,
und sein Phallus ist aus Quarz". [26]

Die Dichter hegen tiefe Bewunderung für das, was Thoth zum
Wohl der Welt, der Gesellschaft und der Menschen getan hat. Ein
Dichter mahnt die Götter:

"Jauchzet in der Halle des Geb über das was er getan hat". [27]

---

[22] Horus und Seth.
[23] A.
[24] C.
[25] I. 2/3.
[26] E.
[27] A.

Ein anderer Dichter sagt:

> "Lass mich reden von deinen starken Taten, in welchem Lande ich
> auch sei.
> So wird die Menge der Menschen sagen: 'Gross ist, was Thoth tut' ". [28]

Andere Dichter verleihen diesem in allgemeinen Termini verfassten
Lob mehr Farbe, indem sie umschreiben, worin die Tätigkeit des
Thoth bestanden hat und noch besteht. So heisst Thoth

> "der Gesetzgeber im Himmel und auf Erden,
> er, der dafür sorgt, dass die Götter bleiben
> innerhalb den Grenzen ihrer Befugnisse,
> dass jede Zunft ihrer Pflicht gerecht wird,
> die Länder ihre Grenzen kennen
> und die Äcker was ihnen zugehört". [29]

Ein grosses Verdienst des Thoth ist es, dass er den Leuten die
Sprache lehrte und ihnen die Schreibkunst verlieh. So wird er gepriesen als derjenige,

> "der die Sprache und die Schrift gab". [30]

Besonders dankbar ist man für sein Bemühen um den Kultus. So
heisst es:

> "Er richtet ihre Heiligtümer (der Götter) ein, ihren Kultus in ihren
> Tempeln". [31]

Thoth ist der grosse Gesetzgeber, der Ordnung schafft in der Welt
der Götter und im Gebiet der Menschen. Er hält das kosmische Gleichgewicht aufrecht. Deshalb heisst er in den Liedern "der Herr der Wahrheit (Ma-a-t)". Dieses Epitheton hat einen besonderen Unterton. Es
bedeutet nicht nur, dass er die Wahrheit, die Gerechtigkeit und die
kosmische Ordnung wahrt, aber es drückt auch aus, dass er eine
enge Beziehung zur der Göttin Ma-a-t hat. Es ist kein Zufall, dass
Thoth und Ma-a-t zu den hervorragenden Mitgliedern der Mannschaft
des Sonnenschiffes gehören. [32] Deshalb setzt man unbedingtes Vertrauen in die Ordnung, die Thoth geschaffen hat. Ein Mann, dem
schweres Unrecht widerfahren ist, gründet seine Hoffnung auf Thoth.
Denn er weiss:

> "sein Gesetz ist ganz und gar felsenfest". [33]

---

[28] C.
[29] Bleeker, *op. cit.*, S. 65/6.
[30] B. A.
[31] A.
[32] Bleeker, *op. cit.*, S. 44.
[33] I.

Da Thoth amtiert als Sekretär des Re, versteht es sich, dass er auch Schutzherr der Schreiber ist. Die Mitglieder der im alten Ägypten hoch angesehenen Zunft der Schreiber waren die treuesten Anhänger des Thoth. Das geht auch aus den Liedern hervor. So sagt ein Dichter:

"Du Briefschreiber der Enneade, Grosser, der in Hermopolis ist,
Komm zu mir, dass du mich leitest,
dass du mich geschickt sein lässest in deinem Amt.
Dein Amt ist schöner als alle Ämter,
es macht (die Menschen) gross". [34]

Anderswo betet ein Schreiber am Hofe des Pharaos, dass Thoth ihm in seinem Amte einen Ehrenplatz verschaffen möge:

"Gib, dass N.N. Karriere mache (wachse) in der Nähe des Fürsten,
so wie du stehst im Verhältnis zum Herrn des Universums (Re)". [35]

Ein Mondgott ist immer ein weiser Gott; so auch Thoth. Seine Anhänger lassen sich führen von seiner Weisheit, wie die folgende Äusserung bezeugt:

"Du behütest meinen Mund beim Reden". [36]

Hier spricht ein Mensch, der durch die Weisheit und Besonnenheit des Thoth gelernt hat, Vorsicht beim Reden zu beobachten.

Viele Götter des Altertums waren so majestätisch mächtig, dass die Gläubigen sich ihnen mit Angst und Zittern näherten. Auch im alten Ägypten gab es solche Ehrfurcht gebietenden Götter. Obgleich Thoth höchlichst respektiert wurde, wusste er in besonderem Masse das Vertrauen und die Liebe seiner Verehrer zu wecken, weil in seinem Charakter die milden und freundlichen Züge das Übergewicht hatten. So heisst es:

"Er ist der Herr der Freundlichkeit". [37]
"Gott von einziger Güte unter den Göttern". [38]

Es gibt sogar Dichter, die in fast leidenschaftlicher Weise zeugen von ihrer Ergebenheit gegen Thoth:

"Siehe, mein Herr, der ist es, (der) mich schaft,
ja, nach ihm sehnte sich mein Herz". [39]

---

[34] C.
[35] H.
[36] A.
[37] A.
[38] B.
[39] E.

Man hat erfahren, dass Thoth Hilfe leistet und fühlt sich deshalb stark in Vertrauen auf ihn. So sagt ein Dichter:

"O Thoth, wenn du mir ein Starker sein wirst,
so fürchte ich nicht für das Auge." [40]

Ein anderer Dichter erklärt voller Stolz:

"Der Gott Thoth ist wie ein Schutz hinter mir". [41]

Der Mann, der dem Thoth einen Brief schrieb, um seine Not zu klagen über das Unrecht, das ihm angetan ist, erklärt (Übersetzung Hughes):

"If the heart be stout, one will be protected
in the presence of Thoth, twice great, Lord of Hermopolis". [42]

"Stout of heart" bedeutet, wie Hughes klar macht, dass man standhaft ist in Missgeschick. Es ist Thoth, der einem solche Standhaftigkeit schenkt.

Sehr dichterisch und zur gleichen Zeit echt fromm sagt ein anderer Dichter:

"Thoth, du süsser Brunnen für einen,
der in der Wüste durstet.
Er ist verschlossen für den, der redet,
und ist geöffnet für den, der schweigt.
Kommt der Schweigende, so findet er den Brunnen,
(Kommt) der Hitzige, so bist du (verschüttet ?)". [43]

Diesem Zitat kann man Relief verleihen, indem man es in den Kontext solcher Texten, die in demselben Ton klingen, hineinstellt. Da kommen in erster Linie die schon genannten von Erman und Gunn bearbeiteten Texte in Frage. In diesen Inschriften auf Denksteinen aus der thebanischen Gräberwelt, kommt eine persönliche Frömmigkeit zu Worte, die sonst im alten Ägypten unbekannt ist. Die Arbeiter der Nekropole bezeugen einerseits ihre Nichtigkeit und ihre Schuld gegen die Gottheit und erwähnen andererseits deren Gnade und Güte. Einige Zitate mögen genügen, um den Geist dieser merkwürdigen Texte zu kennzeichnen:

---

[40] E., es ist unsicher was mit dem "Auge" gemeint ist: handelt es sich um Furcht für das böse Auge oder hat der Dichter das Horus-Auge im Sinne?
[41] H., man schützt einem, indem man hinter ihn steht.
[42] H.
[43] D.

"Ich war ein unwissender Mensch und töricht ...
Ich sündigte gegen die Bergspitze,
und sie bestrafte mich". 44
"Ich bin ein Mann, der einen falschen Eid
bei Ptah, den Herrn der Wahrheit, ablegte,
und er liess mich Finsternis bei Tage sehen". 45
"Du, Amon, bist der Gott des Schweigenden,
der kommt auf die Stimme des Armen.
Rufe ich zu dir, wenn ich betrübt bin,
so kommst du, damit du mich rettest". 46

Diese Texte zeichnen das Ideal eines wahren Frommen, den man
"den Schweigenden" nennen kann, wie das auch in dem oben erwähnten Zitat aus den Thoth-Liedern geschieht. Dieses Ideal findet man
weiter in der Weisheitsliteratur, wo genau wie in dem Zitat aus den
Thoth-Liedern "der Schweigende" und "der Hitzige" einander gegenüber stehen. Folgendes Zitat möge dies verdeutlichen:

"Der hitzige Mensch in dem Tempel
ist wie ein Baum, der im Walde wächst:
in einem Momente verliert er seine Äste,
und er findet sein Ende auf der Schiffswerft.
Der wahre Schweigende hält sich im Hintergrunde,
er ist wie ein Baum, der in einem Garten wächst,
er wird grün und verdoppelt seine Früchte". 47

Den Kennern der Bibel ist der Symbolik dieser Zeilen wohlbekannt.
Sie werden an Psalm 1 erinnert, in dem der Mensch, der seine Lust
am Gesetzt des Herrn hat, und der Gottlose verglichen werden mit
zwei Bäumen, deren Schicksal ganz verschieden ist. Diese Neben-
bemerkung soll uns aber nicht davon abhalten die skizzierte Gedanken-
linie noch etwas weiter zu verfolgen. Dann gelangt man im alten
Ägypten zum Ideal des *"ma-a-tj"*, das heisst des Menschen, der in
Übereinstimmung mit Ma-a-t lebt. Sein Bild wird in verschiedenen
Texten gezeichnet. Er ist der Beherrschte, der Bescheidene, der Geduldige, der Fromme. Sein Gegenbild ist der Leidenschaftliche, der
Begierige, der Zanksüchtige, der Selbstgerechte. 48 Diese Bemerkungen werfen ein neues Licht auf die Bedeutung der Thoth-Lieder:
sie schenken einen Blick in eine Dimension der Frömmigkeit des
Ägypters, die uns sonst verborgen bleibt.

---

44 Die Bergspitze ist die Göttin des westlichen Berges bei Theben.
45 In diesen Texten wird Blindheit mehrmals als Strafe der Gottheit angesehen.
46 Erman, *op cit.*
47 Amenemope, S. 64.
48 Bleeker, *op. cit.*, S. 29 sq.

Es ist kein Wunder, dass man sein Wohlergehen dem Thoth zuschreibt. Denn er schenkt seinen Anhängern ein gunstiges Los. Der
Ägypter drückt das folgendermassen aus:

"*Š'j* (das Los) und *Rnnwt* (das Glück) sind bei dir". [49]

Š'j und *Rnnwt* bilden zusammen mit *Mšḥnt*, die Göttin der Geburt,
losbestimmende Mächte, die besonders bei der Geburt und im Tode,
beim Totengericht auftreten. [50]

Der Schreiber, der an das erwähnte Bild des Thoth als Pavian
ein Loblied richtet, sagt deshalb:

"Es freut sich mein Haus,
seitdem der Gott darin eintrat.
Es gedeiht und ist (reich) ausgestattet,
seitdem mein Herr es betrat". [51]

Ein anderer Dichter betet:

"Erhalte mein Haus in Ewigkeit". [52]

Um das Bild der Fürsorge, die Thoth dem Menschen schenkt,
abzurunden, sei noch erwähnt, dass aus einem nicht-poetischen Text
hervorgeht, wie stark man sich dem Thoth als einem magischen Arzt
anvertraute. Man liest dort: "Thoth kommt mit dem Zauber versehen,
um das Gift zu beschwören, damit es über kein Glied des Kranken
Macht gewinne." Und Thoth selber sagt beruhigend zum Kranken:
"Auf Befehl des Re bin ich vom Himmel gekommen, um dich Tag
und Nacht auf deinem Lager zu schützen und ebenso jeden Kranken". [53]

Es ist auffallend, dass in diesen Hymnen kaum die Rede ist von der
Rolle, die Thoth im Re-Mythus und im Osiris-Mythus spielt. Sein
Verhältnis zu Re wird nur im Vorübergehen erwähnt. In einem Hymnus findet sich vielleicht eine Anspielung auf die Funktion des Thoth
im Sonnenschiff zusammen mit Ma-a-t, wenn der Dichter alle Götter
aufruft, den Thoth zu loben,

"wenn sie ihn in dem grossen Schiff sehen, wie er Ma-a-t vor sich
hingestellt hat". [54]

---

[49] C.
[50] Bleeker, *op. cit.*, S. 62 sq.
[51] E.
[52] G. Roeder, *Urkunden zur Religion des alten Ägypten*, 1923, S. 182.
[53] G. Roeder, Urkunden zur Religion des alten Ägyptens, 1923, S. 82.
[54] B. Lied 1a.

THOTH IN DEN ALTÄGYPTISCHEN HYMNEN

Hingegen wird die Rolle, die Thoth im Prozess des Osiris und des Horus und daran anschliessend im Totenreiche, beim Totengericht, spielt, gar nicht erwähnt. Man äussert nur den Wunsch:

"Belohne meinen *k³* inmitten der vortrefflichen *k³ˢ* vor dem
                                                              Totenreich".

Dieses Stillschweigen ist umso merkwürdiger, weil der Wunsch, dass Thoth den Toten "rechtfertigen" möchte, durch das ganze Totenbuch tönt und seinen deutlichsten Ausdruck in den Sprüchen 18,20 und 182 gefunden hat. Der Grundton des Spruches 18 ist folgende Bitte:

"O Thoth, der du Osiris rechtfertigtest gegen seine Feinde, rechtfertige N.N. gegen seine Feinde vor dem Gericht in … (es werden verschiedene Orte genannt), als geschah … (es folgen Anspielungen auf mythischen Begegnisse)".

Spruch 20, der einen noch starker hymnischen Charakter hat, wiederholt dieses Thema.

In Spruch 182 zählt Thoth seine Fähigkeiten und seine Verdienste auf, unter denen seine Sorge für Osiris hervorragt. Der Wunsch des Toten, der diesen Spruch in seinen Grab mitgenommen hat, ist natürlich, dass Thoth auch ihm in derselben Weise zur Seite treten wird.

Die Thoth-Hymnen schweigen über dieses Thema. Sie sind sichtlich auf das Diesseits gerichtet. Ihre Tendenz ist das Lob des Thoth, des göttlichen Gesetzgebers, des gnädigen Gottes, der seine Anhänger, und besonders die Schreiber, mit Wohlergehen belohnt und der die feste Zuversicht bedeutet für alle Menschen, denen Unrecht widerfahren ist.

DER RELIGIÖSE GEHALT EINIGER HATHOR-LIEDER *

Die Wissenschaft erleidet immer wieder tragische Verluste. Das vorzeitige Hinscheiden von Professor Dr. S. Morenz hinterlässt eine leere Stelle, die nicht so bald ausgefüllt werden kann. Man hätte noch viele vorzügliche Studien von diesem Gelehrten erwarten können, denn er verband ausgedehnte und gediegene Kenntnisse von der Ägyptologie mit religionshistorischem Spürsinn und religiöser Intuition. Weil er selbst ein gläubiger Mensch war, spürte er immer nach dem religiösen Hintergrund der ägyptologischen Fakten und war besonders interessiert an der lebendigen Religion der alten Ägypter. Von diesem Bestreben zeugt die Einleitung seines Buches über die "Ägyptische Religion", in der er schreibt: "Es wird daher unsere Hauptaufgabe sein, die Frömmigkeit des Ägypters und seinen Glauben an die Gottheit in den dominanten Erscheinungsformen der ägyptischen Religion aufzusuchen: zunächst im Kultus selbst, dann in der Ethik, im theologischen Denken, in den Schöpfungslehren und in der Einstellung gegenüber dem Tod" (S. 4).

Deshalb glaube ich das Andenken dieses hervorragenden Gelehrten und ausgezeichneten Religionshistorikers nicht besser ehren zu können als mit einer Studie über den "religiösen Gehalt einiger Hathor-Lieder". Ich wählte dieses Thema, da ich zur Zeit mit einer Studie über Hathor und Thoth beschäftigt bin, die hoffentlich zu ihrer Zeit unter dem Titel: "Hathor and Thoth, two Key Figures of the Ancient Egyptian Religion" erscheinen wird. (Inzwischen erschienen).

Es versteht sich, dass ich meinen Schlusssätzen hinsichtlich der religionshistorischen Bedeutung Hathors nicht vorgreifen kann. Zur Einführung meiner Betrachtung des religiösen Gehaltes einiger Hathor-Lieder ist es aber unumgänglich, dass ich diese Göttin ins Gedächtnis zurückrufe, indem ich ihr Bild skizzenhaft zeichne.

Hathor war eine mächtige und uralte Göttin. Sie wird schon in den ältesten Texten erwähnt und hat im langen Laufe der ägyptischen Geschichte bis in die späten Tage der ägyptischen Religion eine vornehme Rolle gespielt, wie ihr prachtvoller Tempel zu Dendera aus der ptolemäischen Zeit beweist. Hathor zeigte sich in verschiedenen Gestalten. Sie erschien als Kuh und war dann das mütterliche, göttliche

---

* Veröffentlicht in Z.Ä.S., 99 Band, Zweites Heft, *Gedenkschrift für Siegfried Morenz*, Teil Ib, 1973.

Wesen, das das schöpferische Leben repräsentiert. Sie schenkte also Gesundheit, Überfluss, Kindersegen. Eng damit verwandt ist ihre Rolle als Schützerin der Liebe. Hathor fungierte auch als Baumgöttin, das heisst als Schenkerin des sich erneuernden Lebens, nicht nur an die Lebenden, sondern auch an die Toten. Interessant ist ihre Funktion als Göttin der Toten, die eine so tiefgehende Bedeutung hatte, dass sich Frauen mit Hathor identifizierten. In den genannten Funktionen äussert sich ihre temperamentvolle Natur, die sich auch in ihrem Kultus widerspiegelt: Er zeigte einen ekstatischen Zug, was einen nicht wundert, wenn man hört, dass Hathor Musik und Tanz überaus liebte. Ihr Wesen besass aber auch eine andere Seite. Sie war eng verbunden mit Ma-a-t, der Göttin der Weltordnung und so wurde sie Hüterin ethisch-religiöser Werte. Darauf deutet auch ihre Beziehung zu Re, dem Schöpfergott, der die Ma-a-t einsetzte, und ihr Verhältnis zum Pharao, dem göttlichen Regenten Ägyptens. Hathor war eine furchtbare Göttin, die ihre Feinde gehörig züchtigen konnte. In diesem Kontext soll man sich ihre Funktion als Himmelsgöttin denken. Denn der Himmel ist in der antiken Welt Sinnbild einer festen Ordnung. Kurz, Hathor besass als Göttin in ihrem Wesen die Polarität, die nach der Meinung Rud. Ottos charakteristisch ist für das Heilige: Sie war sowohl tremendum als fascinans. Die Ägypter gaben diesem Gedanken Ausdruck, indem sie sagten: "Sie ist grimmig wie Sechmet und fröhlich wie Bastet". Sechmet war die martiale Göttin von Memphis, die oft mit einem Löwenkopf abgebildet wird und Bastet wurde in Bubastis als Katze verehrt und galt als freundlich und fröhlich.

Aus zahlreichen Daten geht hervor, dass Hathor sehr populär war, besonders bei den Frauen. Die Personennamen, die mit Hathor gebildet sind, zeugen von der persönlichen Beziehung, die die Namenträger zu der Göttin hatten. [1] Aus den diesbezüglichen Liedern reden aufrichtige Bewunderung, innige Hingebung und tiefes Vertrauen.

Bei der Wahl seines Materials hat der Verfasser sich nicht auf die Hymnen im vollen Sinne des Wortes beschränkt. Er hat auch dankbar verwandte Texte benutzt, wie Gebete und Totensprüche. Um ein gut proportioniertes Bild der Frömmigkeit, die Hathor zu wecken wusste und die in den Liedern ihre poetische Wiedergabe gefunden hat, zu bekommen, scheint es mir ratsam, die Zeugnisse systematisch zu ordnen. Als Prinzip der Einteilung könnte man das Schema benutzen, das jeder Religion zugrunde liegt, nämlich: 1. das Gottesbild, 2. die Anthropologie, 3. der Kultus, 4. die religiöse Gemeinschaft. Deshalb

---

[1] H. te Velde, *Seth, God of Confusion*, 1967, S. 135.

werde ich versuchen, den religiösen Gehalt einiger Hathor-Lieder
nach den folgenden Gesichtspunkten darzustellen: 1. das Bild der
Göttin, 2. die Beziehung des Menschen zu Hathor, 3. Hathors Funktion im Kult, 4. ihre Rolle im Staatsleben.

A. DAS BILD DER GÖTTIN

Die Dichter der Lieder blickten in tiefer Ehrfurcht zu Hathor hin-
auf. Denn sie ist eine mächtige Göttin, die Furcht und Ehrfurcht ein-
flösst. Sie übt heftige Rache, wenn ihr Zorn gegen die Feinde ent-
brennt.

In einem Neujahrslied aus Dendera heisst es:

"Verehret Hathor, die Herrin Denderas, in allen Landen,
Denn sie ist die Herrin der Furcht.
Verehret Hathor, die Herrin Denderas, in allen Landen,
Denn sie sendet die Rachegötter gegen die Feinde". [2]

Obgleich also der Respekt vor ihrer souveränen Macht keineswegs
fehlt, überwiegen doch der Ton der Dankbarkeit für ihre Güte und
ihr Lob, weil sie die Freude liebt.

Es ist vielsagend, dass in einem Liede, das J. B. Pritchard als "A
Song of Common People" bezeichnet, ein Unbekannter aus dem Volke
rühmend sagt:

"Hathor hat die Schönheit von guten Dingen herbeigeführt". [3]

Darin äussert sich die Dankbarkeit für die Segnungen der Göttin,
die auch ganz gewöhnliche Menschen erfahren haben.

Nach der Auffassung der antiken Völker ist eine der grössten Seg-
nungen eine grosse Kinderschar. Auch dies verdankt man der Hathor.
Ein Lied aus dem Tempel von Medinet Habu enthält den folgenden
Aufruf:

"Die Ihr auf Erden lebt,
und an dieser Kapelle vorübergeht
....
Ihr feiert den grossen Gott in Medinet Habu,
Eure Frauen der Hathor, Herrin des Westens, Feste,
Damit die Göttin Eure Frauen
Euch Knaben und Mädchen gebären lasse,
Damit sie nicht unfruchtbar
Und Ihr nicht zeugungsunfähig werdet". [4]

---

[2] H. Junker, *Poesie aus der Spätzeit*, Z.Ä.S. 43, 1906.
[3] ANET S. 470.
[4] S. Schott, *Altägyptische Liebeslieder*, 1950, S. 82/83.

Hathor war beliebt, weil sie die Freude liebte und sich an Festen ergötzte. Darum sagt das Lied der sieben Hathoren:

"Wir loben dich mit herrlichen Gesängen,
Denn du bist die Herrin des Jubels, die Königin des Tanzes.
Die Herrin der Musik, die Königin des Harfenspieles,
Die Herrin der Reigen, die Königin des Kränzewindens,
Die Herrin der Myrrhen, die Königin des Tanzes, [5]
Die Herrin der Trunkenheit ohne Ende". [6]

Hathor war eine gnädige Göttin. Der Ägypter wandte sich freimütig an sie, weil er wusste, dass sie das Gebet des Menschen, der sich in Not befindet, hört und erhört. Ein Hathorpriester zeugt davon in folgender Weise:

"Ich war ein Musikant der Hathor.
Sie hört die Bitten jeder Tochter
die weint und auf Hathor baut". [7]

B. Das Verhältnis des Menschen zu Hathor

Aus dem Vorhergehenden wurde schon klar, in wie hohem Masse die Verehrer Hathors sich von ihrer Gunst abhängig fühlten. Es wundert nicht, dass man in den Liedern eine Bitte folgenden Inhalts findet:

"Ich lobe dein schönes Antlitz,
und ich befriedige jeden Tag deinen Ka.
Sei gnädig in meinem Falle,
damit ich von deiner Macht reden kann
zu allen, die mit dir unbekannt sind,
und zu allen, welche dich kennen". [8]

An einer anderen Stelle heisst es:

"Ich flehe, dass du mich erhörst, Majestät der Goldenen,
                              (Epitethon von Hathor)
Ich bete, dass du mir dein Herz zuwendest". [9]

Aus diesen Zitaten geht nicht hervor, welches der Inhalt dieser Gebete ist. Das wird klar aus der folgenden Anführung:

"Ich bete zu dir, o, Gottesmutter, Herrin von *Mfkᵌt* (Sinaï) um folgendes: Gib Lebenszeit, lass gedeihen das Begräbnis, gib eine sehr

---

[5] H. Junker, *Poesie aus der Spätzeit, Das Lied der sieben Hathoren.*
[6] Idem.
[7] S. Schott, *Altägyptische Liebeslieder,* S. 81.
[8] J. Černý, *Egyptian Stelae in the Banks Collection,* Cat. No 7; J. Vandier, *Iousâos et (Hathor) Nebet-Hétepet, Revue d'Egyptologie,* Tome 16, 1964, S. 34.
[9] A. Hermann, *Altägyptische Liebesdichtung,* 1959, S. 27/28.

lange Lebenszeit in Gesundheit und ein gutes Begräbnis nach dem
Landen (euphemistisches Wort für Sterben)''. [10]

In diesen Worten äussert der alte Ägypter seinen innigsten Wunsch,
nämlich das Verlangen nach einem langen, glücklichen Leben und
einem schönen Begräbnis, das mit allen denjenigen Riten gefeiert
wird, welche die Unsterblichkeit im Jenseits garantieren.

Aber die Sehnsucht geht auch nach geistigeren Gütern. In den
"Coffin Texts" erklärt der Tote:

"Hathor hat mich aufsteigen lassen (nämlich zum Himmel), sie
hat meine Schuld getigt." [11]

Der Ägypter wusste, dass Hathor Wahrheit und Lauterkeit forderte und dass sie die Herzen durchschaute. Deshalb sagt ein Sänger:

"Du siehst, was in seinem Herzen (des Sängers) ist,
ob auch sein Mund nicht redet.
Sein Herz ist gerade, aufrichtig sein Leib,
kein Dunkel ist in seiner Brust". [12]

Weil Hathor die Göttin der Liebe war, wandten die verliebten Leute
sich gern an sie mit der Bitte, dass sie ihr Liebesverlangen erfüllen
möge. Das ist die Tendenz der schönen Liebeslieder, die der Hathor
gewidmet sind. Die folgenden Zitate zeugen von dieser Gesinnung:

"Ich sende ein Gebet zu meiner Göttin,
Dass sie mir meine Schwester (Kosewort für Geliebte)
        als Geschenk geben möge". [13]

Und noch feuriger:

"O, Goldene, gib es in ihr Herz.
Dann werde ich zu dem Bruder (Geliebten) eilen,
und ich werde ihn küssen in der Gegenwart seiner Gefährten". [14]

Wenn zwei Liebende einander finden, erkennt man freudig in diesem glücklichen Begegnis die Fügung der Hathor. Denn eine der
Funktionen Hathors war auch, dass sie das Los des Menschen bestimmte, besonders wenn sie von den sieben Hathoren vertreten war.
So ruft eine Frau aus:

"Bruder, o, ich bin bestimmt für dich
durch die Goldene, unter den Weibern". [15]

---

[10] Boris Turajeff, "Die naophore Statue No 97 im Vatikan", Z.Ä.S. 46, S. 74 ff.
[11] C. T. V. Spell 427, 273b c.
[12] Junker, *Poesie aus der Spätzeit. Liederkranz zu Ehren der Göttin des Weines,*
Lied C 4.
[13] A. H. Gardiner, *The Chester Beatty Papyri*, No 1, 1931, S. 33.
[14] Idem.   [15] Idem S. 31.

Und zu einem Manne wird gesagt:

"Die Goldene hat sie für dich bestimmt
o, mein Freund". 16

Hathor führt also die Liebenden zueinander und dennoch haben sie das Gefühl, dass sie dem inneren Trieb ihres Herzens folgen. Davon zeugt die folgende jauchzende Aussage:

"Ich bat sie (Hathor) und sie hörte meine Bitte.
Sie bestimmte meine Herrin (Geliebte) für mich,
Und sie kam aus eigener Bewegung zu mir, um mich zu sehen.
Wie gross ist das, was mir geschieht.
Ich jauchze, ich jubele, ich bin ganz stolz,
Seit dem Moment, wo gesagt wurde: ha, hier ist sie". 17

Nicht nur während des Lebens, sondern auch nach dem Tode setzten die Verehrer Hathors ihr Vertrauen in ihre Göttin. Denn sie war eine mächtige Totengöttin. Davon zeugen eine Anzahl Sprüche, auf die E. Drioton aufmerksam gemacht hat. 18 So äussert der Tote den Wunsch:

"Möge Hathor mir ihre Hände reichen", 19

das heisst als Zeichen ihrer Gunst, indem sie den Toten zum Himmel aufsteigen lässt.

Ein dringender Wunsch des Toten war, im Gefolge Hathors sein zu dürfen. Voller Stolz erklärt ein Toter:

"Ich bin im Gefolge Hathors". 20

Dies kann bedeuten, dass der Tote in das Schiff der Göttin aufgenommen wird. Darüber handelt "Der Spruch um an Bord des Schiffes der Hathor zu gehen". Darin sagt der Tote:

"Ich wasche meine beiden Hände,
Ich laufe den Horizont hindurch,
Ich laufe das Schiff hindurch unter Aufsicht von *Iḫt wrt* 21
Ich begleite die Goldene mit den Herren des Himmels,
Ich begleite den Gott als sein Gefährte". 22

---

16 Idem S. 36.
17 Idem S. 33.
18 E. Drioton, Besprechung von A. de Buck, *The Egyptian Coffin Texts VI*, BiOr XV, No 5, Sept. 1958, S. 187 ff.
19 C. T. VI, Spell 533, 12 g^c; S. Allam, *Beiträge zum Hathorkult (bis zum Ende des Mittleren Reiches)*, S. 148.
20 C. T. VI Spell 485, 62 e.
21 W. B. I, S. 125.
22 C. T. VI, Spell 623, 239 b-f.

Die letzte Zeile erregt die Vermutung, dass es sich hier um das Schiff von Re, dem Sonnengott, handelt. Darin spielt Hathor zusammen mit Ma-a-t eine wichtige Rolle. Sie wird als "Herrin des Schiffes" bezeichnet. [23]

Weiter rühmt sich der Tote der Dienste, die er Hathor erweist, und zwar in zweierlei Hinsicht, nämlich, indem er ihr _ṯstn_ knüpft und indem er als Schreiber fungiert. Das _ṯstn_ scheint ein Brustgehänge zu sein, das Hathor als Schmuck trug. Ein Spruch aus den "Coffin Texts", mit der Überschrift: "Das Knüpfen des _ṯstn_ für Hathor" [24] beschreibt, wie Hathor als eine imposante Gestalt hervortritt, wahrscheinlich in einem grünen Gewand, dank der Sorge, die der Tote ihrer Toilette widmet:

"Meine Hände reichen ihr die _tȝjt_ [25] dar,
Das Kleid auf ihrer linken Schulter ist wie die Haut des Horus,
Ich binde ihre rechte Seite in _mfkȝt_" (Malachit, also grüne Farbe).

Der Tote macht sich besonders eine Ehre daraus, dass er Schreiber der Hathor sein darf. Das Amt des Schreibers wurde im alten Ägypten in hohen Ehren gehalten. Um so ehrenhafter war es, dies Amt bei Hathor zu bekleiden. Der Tote kann sich damit brüsten, dass er an der Spitze der Zunft der Schreiber steht:

"Ich bin befördert über alle Schreiber,
Mein Rang ist vor ihren Grossen". [26]

Er will es wohl wissen, dass er ein echter Fachmann ist:

"Ich besitze die Schreibfeder der Ma-a-t. [27]
Ich kenne den Namen der Tinte. [28]
Ich kenne den Namen des Wassernäpfchens". [29]

Aber das höchste Verlangen ist erfüllt, wenn man sagen kann, dass man wie Hathor geworden ist. So heisst es von einer Toten:

"Du erglänzt wie Hathor", [30]

---

[23] C. J. Bleeker, _De beteekenis van de egyptische godin Ma-a-t_, 1929, S. 43.
[24] C. T. VI, Spell 486, 63 k ff.
[25] W. B. V, S. 232: Stoff angefertigt von _Tȝjt_, Göttin der Webekunst.
[26] C. T. VI, Spell 540, 135 m n.
[27] Idem 135 u.
[28] C. T., Spell 545, 142 c.
[29] Idem 142 f.
[30] C. T. I, Spell 61, 261 b.

Und die Tote selber erklärt:

"Ich bin Hathor,
ich bin erschienen als Hathor,
die stammt aus der Urzeit,
die Herrin des Alls,
die von der Wahrheit lebt". [31]

Und an einer anderen Stelle:

"Ich hülle mich in das Kleid der Grossen (Hathor)
Ich bin die Grosse,
Ich bin nicht schwach, ich werde nicht vernichtet,
Mir geschieht kein Übel". [32]

Diese Äusserungen klingen blasphemisch. So sind sie aber nicht gemeint. Der Ägypter wusste genau, dass es einen Unterschied gibt zwischen Gott und Mensch. Aber er fühlte sich dermassen seinen Göttern verbunden, dass er hoffte, im Tode Anteil an ihrem Wesen zu bekommen.

C. DER KULTUS DER HATHOR

Einige Hathor-Lieder beziehen sich auf ihren Kultus und erzählen deshalb, mit welchen Gefühlen man diese Feiern beging. Auch lässt sich aus einigen nicht poetischen Texten schliessen, mit welchen Gesinnungen sowohl die Priester wie die Laien am Dienst der Hathor teilnahmen. Die Überschrift über den Türen des Horustempels in Edfu — die auch für den Hathor-Tempel in Dendera gelten darf — lautet folgendermassen: "Jedermann, der durch diese Tür eintritt, hüte sich davor, dass er in Unreinheit hineintritt, denn Gott liebt Reinheit mehr als Tausende an Reichtümern, mehr als Hunderte von Tausenden an Fein-Gold … Komme nicht in Sünde, tritt nicht hinein in Unreinheit, äussere keine Unwahrheit in seinem Hause". [33]

Was einen besonders trifft in den Liedern ist, dass man mit grosser Freude am Kultus der Hathor teilnahm und es für ein Vorrecht hielt, dass man bei ihren Festen gegenwärtig sein durfte:

Wie fröhlich kann derjenige sein, der Hathor sieht. [34]
Glücklich ist derjenige, der am Feste Hathors teilnimmt". [35]

---

[31] C. T. IV, Spell 331, 172 b h, 173 a.
[32] C. T. VI, Spell 485, 62 h-63 b.
[33] H. W. Fairman, *Worship and Festivals in an Egyptian Temple, Bulletin of the John Rylands Library,* Vol. 37, 1954/55, S. 197 ff.
[34] E. Drioton, *Pages d'Egyptologie*, 1957, S. 128.
[35] BiOr. XV No 5, S. 189.

In vielen Liedern wird Hathor in überschwenglichen Worten gepriesen. Man zählt ihre Tugenden auf und fordert die Götter auf, ihr
Lob zu singen:

"O, Neunheit des Re, preise Hathor, die Herrin Denderas,
O, ihr Götter all, verehret die Hathor, die Herrin Denderas". [36]

Einige Lieder aus Dendera beziehen sich direkt auf ihren Kult. Das
sind erstens ein Kranz von vier Liedern, am 20sten Toth zu Ehren der
Göttin des Weines (Hathor) gesungen, weiter das schon zitierte
Neujahrslied und schliesslich ein Prozessionslied, das gesungen wurde,
wenn man mit dem Bilde der Hathor in einer Prozession zum Dach
des Tempels zog, wo Hathor aufgestellt wurde, um ihren Vater Re
zu begrüssen und sich mit ihm "zu vereinigen". [37]

Aus dem zuerst genannten Liederkranz geben wir ein Zitat, weil
der Pharao darin eine Rolle spielt:

"Es kommt der Pharao zu tanzen,
Er kommt (dir) zu singen.
O, seine Herrin! sieh wie er tanzt,
O, Braut des Horus, sieh wie er hüpft". [38]

Tempeltänze sind wohlbekannt. Man weiss, dass der Pharao in gewissen Fällen die Führung hatte und zuweilen einen merkwürdigen,
altertümlichen Tanz ausführte. [39] In dem Kultus der Hathor, der
Herrin der Trunkenheit, der Musik und des Tanzes, hatte der Tanz
augenscheinlich einen begeisterten Charakter.

D. DIE ROLLE HATHORS IM STAATSLEBEN

Weil die Hathor-Lieder und -Sprüche einen lyrischen, kultischen
oder funerären Charakter tragen, ist es selbstverständlich, dass sie
kaum der Rolle, die Hathor im Staatsleben spielt, Aufmerksamkeit
schenken. Aus anderen Fakten ist aber bekannt, dass die Göttin eine
besondere Beziehung zum Pharao hatte, sogar in solchem Umfang,
dass sie eine Königsgöttin genannt werden kann. Sie säugt das Königs-
kind und später erneuert sie das Leben des Pharaos. Sie begleitet den
König, wenn er an wichtigen Festen als Hohepriester amtiert. Durch
ihre Sorge ermöglicht sie es dem König, die Ordnung in der Gesell-

---

[36] H. Junker, *Poesie aus der Spätzeit, B. Hymnus am Neujahrsfest.*
[37] A. Mariette, *Dendèrah, Description Générale*, S. 316.
[38] H. Junker, *Poesie aus der Spätzeit, Liederkranz zu Ehren der Göttin des Weines,
Lied a.*
[39] C. J. Bleeker, *Egyptian Festivals, Enactments of Religious Renewal*, 1967, S. 119.

schaft und den Wohlstand des Reiches aufrecht zu erhalten, wie es seine Aufgabe ist. Dies alles ist so wohlbekannt, dass es keine Belege dazu braucht.

Nun gibt es ein Hathor-Lied in einem Kontext, der diese Sachlage gut beleuchtet. Das ist das Lied, welches die Königskinder anstimmen, wenn Sinuhe dem Pharao seine Aufwartung macht. [40] Sinuhe floh unmittelbar nach dem Tode Amenemhet's I. aus unklaren politischen Gründen nach Syrien, wo er sich im Laufe der Zeit ein Vermögen und eine angesehene Stellung erwarb. In seinem Alter führte Heimweh ihn zurück nach Ägypten, wo der Pharao ihn empfing. Weil Sinuhe sich gewissermassen als Deserteur fühlte, fürchtete er Strafe. Es scheint, dass es im Anfang unsicher war, wie der Pharao reagieren würde. In dem Momente liess man die Königskinder hineintreten. Sie hatten sofort Mitleid mit Sinuhe, der noch asiatisch-unversorgt aussah. Die Geschichte geht also weiter: "Nun hatten sie ihre Halsketten und ihre Sistren (Attribute der Hathor) mitgebracht. Sie boten sie seiner Majestät an (mit den Worten):

"(Legt) Eure Hände auf die Schöne [41]
o, langlebender König,
(auf) den Schmuck der Herrin des Himmels.
Möge die Goldene Leben geben an Eure Nase,
Möge die Herrin der Sterne sich mit Ihnen vereinigen".

In dieser Strophe des Liedes weisen die Königskinder auf Hathor, erbitten ihren Segen für den König und appellieren indirekt an den Pharao, dass er Sinuhe gnädig sei in derselben Weise, wie Hathor ihren Verehren Gunst gewährt. Hier hat man also ein unerwartetes Beispiel von dem Einfluss, den Hathor auf politische Entscheidungen des Königs hatte.

Weil die Majorität des ägyptologischen Materials auf den Staatskultus Beziehung hat, ist uns die persönliche Frömmigkeit des alten Ägypters schlecht bekannt, obgleich man sie in indirekter Weise aus allerhand Daten teilweise ergründen kann, wie Morenz in seiner "Ägyptischen Religion" überzeugend erwiesen hat. Eine Ausnahme von der Regel bilden die Texte aus der thebanischen Nekropole, die A. Erman und B. Gunn bearbeitet haben. [42] Der letztere hat die

---

[40] ANET S. 21/22; A. de Buck, *Egyptische Verhalen*, 1928, S. 65/66.

[41] "Die Schöne" ist die Kette, die dem Pharao gereicht wird. Ketten und Sistren sind Attribute Hathors, die hier die Goldene und Herrin des Himmels und der Sterne genannt wird.

[42] A. Erman, *Denksteine aus der thebanischen Gräberwelt*, SBAW 1911, S. 1986 ff.; B. Gunn, "The Religion of the Poor in Ancient Egypt", *JEA* 3, S. 8 ff.

Frömmigkeit, die aus diesen Texten spricht, charakterisiert als "the religion of the poor".

Unter Berücksichtigung dieser Lage besteht die Bedeutung der Hathor-Lieder besonders darin, dass sie von religiösen Gefühlen, die Hathor zu wecken wusste, zeugen, auch bei Leuten von höherer Bildung, als den Arbeitern der thebanischen Nekropole. Nicht nur die Tatsache, dass der Pharao in gewissen Liedern auftritt, sondern auch der poetische Gehalt und die kunstreiche Sprache beweisen, dass sie das religiöse Sentiment von Leuten aus höheren Kreisen wiedergeben. Sie sind durchglüht von tiefer Ehrfurcht, grosser Hingebung und vollem Vertrauen auf Hathor und liefern deshalb einen Beweis der Begeisterung, die diese Göttin bei ihren Verehrern zu wecken wusste.

THE POSITION OF THE QUEEN IN ANCIENT EGYPT *

The Egyptian Pharaoh offers a clear and unequivocal instance of sacral Kingship. His divine nature can easily be inferred from his titles. He is called Horus, the golden Horus, son of Re. This means that Re, the sungod, was his father and that he was identified with Horus, the god of Heaven, who sometimes is also a sungod. The ascension to the throne of the Pharaoh was a ritual repetition of a mythical event, namely the act by which the sungod at the time of the creation of the world started to rule the universe. The Pharao thus ruled by virtue of a divine commission and with an authority higher than human power. As a sacral king he acted at the same time as a highpriest, because he was by nature the intercessor between the domain of the gods and the world of man. In all respects he is the prototype of a sacral king. No wonder that he has become the object of various penetrating studies.

It is however a curious fact that Egyptologists have never paid much attention to the wife of the Pharaoh, the Egyptian queen. Male self-complacency has perhaps prevented them from raising the question what can have been the role of the wife that sits on the throne beside this son of the gods. Yet this question is both self-evident and highly interesting. For, by marrying the Pharaoh, officially called "the good god", the princess or the lady of lower rank, who became a queen, acquired a new and very important status. She was raised to the dignity of an actress in the drama of the divine kingship and thereby placed in an influential position. It is really astonishing that Egyptologists have so long neglected the queen. This is perhaps partly due to the scarcity of data concerning her available. These are indeed not very abundant. Yet they provide us with sufficient information to construct a clear image of the position and the dignity of the Egyptian queen.

In general the significance of an office is reflected in the position which the holder of that office occupies, in other words in the degree of consideration he enjoys. This holds also good for the Egyptian queen. The first question is therefore: What position did the queen actually occupy at the court? Unfortunately we do not possess a full description of the life at the Egyptian residence, informing us about the authority which the queen exercised. However, there are some

---

* Published in La Regalità Sacra, The Sacral Kingship, 1959.

indications that she occupied a position of honour at the court and that occasionally she played an active part in the affairs of the state.

This appears in the first place from here name. She is not only called "the king's wife", "the great or principal wife of the king", but is also styled *itj.t* and *nśwj.t*, names that are feminine forms of the official titles of the king. Their literal translation is: ruler, queen. They show that the queen had a share in the dignity of her royal husband. Apparently she occupied this position since the dawn of Egyptian history, for she already appears on the reliefs of the sepulchral monument of Pharaoh Sahure, a king of the fifth dynasty. To her name is even attached an elaborate set of titles. She is called: "She, who beholds Horus and Seth, i.e. the king, great in attractiveness, great in favour, the friend of Horus, the king's wife, his beloved". [1] The occurrence of these titles, so accurately formulated, in such remote times indicates that the position of the queen had already then been fully defined. Though titles may be expression of flattery or of grandiloquence, in this case they impress us as being the exact reflection of the status of the queen, notwithstanding their poetical flavour. Apparently in the course of time the formulation of these titles underwent changes. In the New Kingdom the following titles are used: "the king's consort, the king's mother, the great wife of the king, the ruler of the two lands". [2] It sounds less poetical and is juridically formulated in a more concise manner. But the high dignity of the queen is clearer defined than in the old formula: she is the consort of the divine king, the mother of the divine prince and therefore she must have a certain power.

No wonder that ambitious queens used their influence for all kinds of intrigues. Already king Pepi II (sixth dynasty) had to encounter a palace revolution in which the queen took part. A certain Uni, a favourite of the king, narrates with justified pride that he was charged with the inquiry: "when legal procedure was instituted in private in the harem against the queen His Majesty caused me to enter, in order to hear the case alone". Many centuries later an analogous case is recorded in the report of a plot against Pharaoh Ramses III. It seems that queen Tiy had stirred up the women of the harem and had taken sides with the pretender to the throne, who intended to replace the old and grey Ramses III. [3]

[1] L. Borchardt. *Das Grabdenkmal des Königs Sa-hu-Re*, Band II, Blatt 48, Text p. 116.

[2] A. Erman-H. Ranke. *Aegypten und aegyptisches Leben in Altertum*, 1922, p. 85.

[3] BAR IV: 427.

However there were also many queens of a higher caliber. It is a remarkable fact that during the 18th dynasty several royal women came into the foreground whose personality is better known than that of any other woman of antiquity.

In the life of Ahmose, who expelled the Hyksos and founded the eighteenth dynasty, three women played an important role, viz. his grandmother Tetisheri, whom he remembers with great respect, his mother Ahhotep, the ancestress of the eighteenth dynasty, who kept her own court and wielded great influence, as is evident from various documents, and his wife Ahmose Nofretere. [4] The latter was his good counsellor. How directly and humanly the queen shared in the troubles of her royal husband appears from an inscription describing how king Ahmose and his wife conferred on the cult of their ancestors. It reads: "Now it came to pass that His Majesty sat in the audience-hall, while the great king's wife Ahmose Nofretere, who liveth, was with His Majesty. One spoke with the other, seeking benefaction for the departed dead". The king then enumerates a series of offerings. "His sister spake and answered him: Wherefore has this been remembered? And why has this word been spoken? What has come into thy heart? The king himself spake to her: I, it is, who have remembered the mother of my mother and the mother of my father, great king's wife and king's mother, Tetisheri, triumphant. Although she already has a tomb and a mortuary chapel on the soil of Thebae and Abydos, I have said that to thee in that my Majesty has desired to have made for her also a pyramid and a house in Tazeser, as a monumental donation of my Majesty". Ahmose carried out this plan. To this we owe the inscription which indirectly throws light on the position of the queen. [5]

No queen had so much influence on the affairs of the state as Tiye, the wife of Amenhotep III. Though she was not of royal descent — Yuya and Thuya are mentioned as her parents — she had managed to acquire an influential position, apparently by virtue of her strong character. Her statues show her as an active, firm personality. Amenhotep acknowledged her valour and treated her as his equal. He inscribed her name beside his own on the scarab commemorating his marriage. [6] This energetic woman after the death of her husband exchanged letters with Dushratta, king of Mitanni. Dushratta seemed

---

[4] BAR II: 52, 109.
[5] BAR II: 34-36.
[6] BAR II: 862.

to know how deeply Tiye was initiated in the secrets of government, for he wrote: "You know how your husband and I have been on friendly terms with each other. You know better than anybody else the words we have spoken with each other. Another person does not know it". He appraised her influence and her common sense very well writing later to her son, Ikhnaton: "Apply to your mother, who is completely informed". [7]

Anybody trying to assess the actual position of the queen should pay attention to the monuments from the Amarna period. They reveal the intimate life of the royal family which as a rule is hidden behind a hieratic style and conventional images. Though the beautiful face of queen Nofretete is better known than her character, it is evident that she occupied a very favourable position. Ikhnaton in his inscriptions rendered full honour to her "at the sound of whose voice there is rejoicing". He declared: "My heart is joyous over the king's wife". [8]

These facts lead to the conclusion that the Egyptian queen occupied a rather prominent position. How is this to be explained? As regards several queens of the eighteenth dynasty it is clear that they owed their position partly to the strength of their personality and partly to the progressive ideas of that period. But even where these factors are lacking the position of the queen was a favourable one. It certainly would not have been so favourable if the ancient Egyptians had not treated their wives and mothers with great respect. As a rule a man had only one legal wife, though he might have several concubines. The relation between husband and wife is described as being cordial and close. On sepulchral monuments they stand or sit beside each other. The wife is folding her arms round the neck of her husband or touches his shoulder with her hand. She accompanies him when he goes to his work and is present when he goes hunting. Special respect is paid to the mother. The Books of Wisdom teach that one should never forget the care of a good mother. Sometimes descent is reckoned in the maternal line. During the Middle Kingdom the succession in some noble families went in the same maternal lineage. [9] It is difficult to ascertain whether this is a last trace of a prehistoric matriarchate. At any rate, it testifies to the important position women generally occupied in ancient Egypt. They were not obedient slave-woman, but the equals of their husbands. This must have been true of the queen

---

[7] J. L. Pierson, *De achttiende dynastie van Oud-Egypte*, p. 87.

[8] BAR II: 959, 961.

[9] A. Erman-H. Ranke, *Aegypten* p. 175 sqq.

in an even higher degree. Nevertheless, these natural circumstances do
not fully explain her position. In fact we have not yet mentioned her
special function, viz. sacral dignity. Most scholars have sofar denied
that the Egyptian queen had a sacral function, but in my opinion this
denial is disproved by the facts.

The queen occupies a vital position in the representations and texts
describing her marriage with the god, who visits her in the shape of
her husband, and the birth of the royal child. Famous are the scenes
of the birth of queen Hatshepsut in her temple at Dêr el-Bahri and
those of the birth of Amenhotep III in the temple of Luxor. [10] These
scenes present a classic dramatization of the idea of the sacral kingship.
It has been contended that they served to legitimatize the position of
the two Pharaohs mentioned, because their royal descent was not
entirely pure. This conception is questionable, since other Pharaohs,
such as Ramses II and Ramses III are also said to have been born from
a divine marriage, though their right to the throne could not be
questioned. [11] These scenes are simply the pictorial representation of
the mythical idea of sacral kingship. In this drama the queen was a
hightly important character. She functioned as the vehicle that con-
veyed the divine substance to the royal child. It should be noted that
the god-father was an invisible figure in the background and that the
human father played no part at all. Thus the queen was the sole person
who could actually guarantee the divine nature of the crownprince.

It is true that this function of the queen is not explicitly mentioned
in the texts accompanying the scenes of the divine marriage and
birth. But it is the implicit presupposition of all that happens. This
conception is confirmed by the identification of the queen with Tefnut
and Mut, two goddesses who are her heavenly prototypes. [12] Tefnut,
who together with Shu originated from Atum, was the first and
oldest goddess. She might be called a dethroned divine queen, yet a
queen. Traces of her royal nature can be found in a wellknown story
relating that she lived as a wild lioness in Nubia and that only thanks
to the power of persuasion of Shu and Thot she could be moved to
go to Egypt. Mut was the wife of Amon, the king of the gods, and
thus a divine queen herself. The symbol of the identification of the
queen with Mut is her headdress, which consists of the skin of the
vulture, the typical headgear of Mut, who seems originally to have

[10] Naville, *Deir el-Bahri*; Gayet, *Le temple de Louxor*.
[11] A. Moret. *Du caractère religieux de la royauté pharaonique*, p. 61.
[12] C. E. Sander-Hansen, *Das Gottesweib des Amun*, 1940, p. 22, 18.

been a vulture. [13] To be more exact: this headgear is worn by some queens of the New Kingdom in their capacity as "wife of the god", namely of god Amon. This title "wife of the god" is another proof of the sacral dignity of the queen. During the eigtheenth dynasty this title was inherited by the daughter from her mother. This institution apparently served a double end: (1) it guaranteed the divine descent of the Pharao and is therefore an indication of the vital position which the queen occupied, (2) it conferred upon the queen her cultic status, which will be discussed at the end of this paper. Later on the title "wife of the god" was given to a kind of highpriestess and thereby lost its significance for the sacral kingship.

This conception of the position of the queen is confirmed by some striking facts. We learn from the texts that some kings mention their mother, but not their father. [14] The impression is gained that they were anxious to underline that their descent was pure. Secondly it should be recalled that several Pharaohs rendered much respect to the memory of their mother. [15] Thirdly it is known that general Haremhab, who founded the nineteenth dynasty, married a princess of royal blood, with the clear intention of assuring that he would have legal royal offspring. [16] Haremhab's deed was undoubtedly no exception.

The cultic function of the queen was derived from her position as it has been described. She performed certain cultic duties. Her part in the daily cult consisted in the handling of the sistrum. Ahmose-Nofretere is called: "she who holds the sistrum with beautiful hands in order to delight her father Amon". [17] She probably also conducted the singing in the temple. For Nofretete received the epitheton ornans: "who sends the Aton to rest with a sweet voice". [18] The existence is known in El Amarna of "a house of sending Aton to rest". Apparently the queen in this temple performed the vesper service, at least in theory. As a rule she will have delegated a deputy to perform her regular cultic duties. Yet we have representations of queens who sacrified. [19] A certain Huy relates that he brought Amenhotep III

---

[13] A. Erman, *Aegypten* etc., 1885, pg. 314; Sander-Hansen. *Das Gottesweib* etc., p. 18.

[14] BAR I: 755, II: 54.

[15] BAR II: 34, 798; III: 249, 505.

[16] BAR III: 28.

[17] Sander-Hansen, *Das Gottesweib* etc., p. 25.

[18] BAR II: 995.

[19] E. Naville, *The temple of Deir el-Bahri* I: XVI; BAR II: 113.

and Tiy into a temple. Thus it belonged to her duties to visit temples. [20]

Quite naturally she assisted at the great festivals. It can hardly be doubted that she was present at the ḥb-śd-festival, the so-called jubilee of the Pharao. However the older documents yield only one dubious indication of her presence at this famous festival, which was so highly important to her husband. [21] Her presence can only be proved for a later period. During the ḥb-śd-festival celebrated by Osorkon II she took part in the rites, standing together with the king on the holy platform. [22] She was also present at the erection of the ḏd-pillar, a rite which symbolised the resurrection of Osiris. Though she had a passive role, the presence of her "who fills the palace with love" was deemed indispensable. [23] Interesting is her function during the Min-festival. The queen is the sole female person in the procession, which is so beautifully portrayed in the temple at Medinet Habu. She probably bears a special title in this case, as the text mentions that the so called śmꜣj.t recites seven times certain formulas whilst she walks around the king who has just performed the harvest-rite. As the queen is the sole female person present she must be the śmꜣj.t. It is supposed that this title means: "the stranger, the nomad". The actual meaning of this title is not known. It is thought to be a remnant from pre-historic times and an indication that Min has relations with foreign countries, especially with the Southern region. [24] However this may be, it is essential to note that the queen performed an important rite at the Min-festival. By walking around the king she both expresses and realises his divine nature, since in Antiquity the circular circum-ambulation is a rite meant to dramatize the divine eternal life. It is significant of the sacral dignity of the queen that she performs here an act which is meant to renew the forces of the king. She is in this case not only his equal, but even superior to her husband as she gives him the forces, which he needs for his royal task.

---

[20] BAR II: 1016.

[21] C. G. Seligmann, *Egypt and Negro Africa*, 1934, p. 51.

[22] E. Naville, *The Festival Hall of Osorkon* II, pl. II, III, IV bis XVI.

[23] A. Erman, *Aegypten* 1885, p. 377; Ahmed Fakhry, *A note on the tomb of Kherf at Assuan* (Ann. Serv., Tom. XLII, 1943).

[24] H. Gauthier, *Les Fêtes du dieu Min*, p. 63, 97-99.

QUELQUES REFLEXIONS SUR LA SIGNIFICATION
RELIGIEUSE DE LA MER [1]

Il y a de quoi se demander quelle est la signification religieuse de la mer, puisque la mer constitue un élément de la nature si puissant que devant elle l'homme a senti depuis les temps les plus reculés son néant et son impuissance. C'est pourquoi il fut amené à lui attribuer des qualités divines. Aussi l'histoire des religions enseigne-t-elle que l'imagination mythologique des peuples habitant au bord de la mer a essayé plus d'une fois de sonder la signification profonde de l'eau et qu'il y a des dieux marins dans la religion de ces peuples à qui ils vouent un culte craintif, sachant qu'ils dépendent tout à fait de leur grâce. Or, il est curieux que les étudiants de l'histoire des religions ont prêté peu d'attention en general à ce sujet d'études. On a examiné jusque dans les moindres détails le caractère et le culte des dieux chthoniens qu'adoraient surtout les pleuples anciens. C'est là un sujet important et captivant. Car tous les peuples agriculteurs savent qu'ils dépendent de la bénédiction que donne la terre fertile au moyen d'une moisson abondante et d'une végétation luxuriante. Les conceptions mythiques considèrent la terre comme la mère qui crée la vie nouvelle et qui puis s'assimile la vie qui s'éteint pour la faire ressusciter ensuite de la mort. De l'autre côté il existe une série d'études intéressantes sur le culte du dieu céleste. Personne ne pourrait contester l'importance primordiale de ce problème religieux, puisqu'il est évident que le ciel a foudroyé depuis toujours l'humanité per suite de son caractére sublime et illimité. Pour voûter toute la terre, le ciel a suscité des sentiments numineux. Il y a même un courant nouveau dans l'histoire des religions démontrant que le dieu céleste est le dieu le plus ancien qu'on ait adoré. On a donc largement rendu justice à la signification religieuse de la terre et du ciel.

Mais il est singulier qu'on ait négligé jusqu'ici la signification religieuse de la mer. Pourtant la mer constitue —- du moins pour un certain nombre de peuples — un élément cosmique d'importance aussi primordiale que la terre et le ciel. C'est pourquoi il vaut la peine d'examiner la fonction que remplit la mer dans l'expérience et la pensée religieuses des peuples navigateurs. Un examen complet de cette matière

---

[1] Publié dans *Numen*, Vol. VI, Fasc. 3, Décembre 1959.

du point de vue de l'histoire des religions dépasserait de loin le cadre modeste de cet article. Seule une étude de grande envergure saurait rendre justice aux aspects nombreux du culte de la mer, tel que l'ont pratiqué toutes sortes de peuples au cours de l'histoire. Dans ce compte-rendu il ne peut s'agir que d'un aperçu phénomenologique.

La fonction que remplit la mer dans la vie de la population cotière ne se manifeste nettement que quand on pénètre la valeur idéale de l'eau. L'eau constitue un élément curieux. L'air et le feu le remportent sur elle en mobilité et en fugacité. L'eau a son poids énorme en commun avec la terre. Par ses masses elle peut exercer une pression irréstible. Cependant elle n'est pas aussi pesante ni aussi inerte que la terre. Elle possède une vivacité exceptionelle et une faculté d'adaptation extrême. Ce caractère multiforme ne laisse pas de captiver irrésistiblement. L'eau se laisse "toucher" comme instrument docile. A chaque instant elle montre un autre visage. Comme le jeu de masques changeant de la mer est passionnant! Tantôt le mer montre de faibles rides et un sourire avenant; tantôt elle est folâtre, juvénile et impétueuse, mais parfois elle peut être furieuse et menaçante. L'eau, c'est l'élément qui en impose à l'homme par son aspect polymorphe et mystérieux et par sa puissance énorme. L'eau est devenu le signe des vérités et des réalités les plus profondes de la vie. C'est ainsi que le poète hollandais W. Kloos a chanté la mer, qui n'arrête pas de déferler dans une houle incessante, comme le symbole de l'âme humaine insondable au possible. Voilà qui fut ressenti et dit de façon moderne.

Les peuples anciens l'ont considéré et exprimé de manière toute différente. Pour eux la mer comportait un sens tant positif que négative, un effet attractif, mais repoussant aussi. Elle constituait, comme le définit Rudolf Otto, l'auteur du livre fameux sur le problème du sacré, un mystère "tremendum ac fascinans", un mystère qui attire, mais qui n'en effraie pas moins.

La mer insondable suggère l'idée que l'eau constitue l'élément primitif, l'élément de la vie par excellence. Quiconque se rend compte de cela, ne manquera pas de comprendre pourquoi l'ancien philosophe Thales fut amené à considérer l'eau comme la matière primitive. Cet essai de définir l'essence même des choses paraît quelque peu enfantin à des gens rompus à la philosophie moderne. Pourtant cette conception est bien plus profonde qu'on ne croirait. Sans doute une cosmogonie ancienne de modèle bien connu est à la base de cette définition de la matière primitive. C'est ainsi que Apsu et Tiamat, l'eau douce et l'eau salée, sont représentés dans le récit babylonien de la genèse comme les éléments primitifs pas encore tirés du néant. La création ne pouvait avoir lieu qu'une fois ces puissances du chaos vaincues. Ea eut relativement peu de peine à maîtriser Apsu. Aucun des dieux plus âgés ne se sentit de force à combattre Tiamat, monstre redoutable. Seul le jeune dieu Marduk fut censé capable d'affronter la lutte contre Tiamat. Cependant il ne consentit à accepter cette mission périlleuse qu'à la seule condition qu'on lui conférât l'autorité royale sur l'univers des dieux et des hommes. Dès qu'il eut obtenu cette dignité, il partit en guerre contre Tiamat: le combat finit par la défaite totale de Tiamat. De son corps mort se contruisit l'univers. Ce mythe nous apprend donc de façon explicite que l'eau constitue la matière primitive dont le monde fut formé.

Le mythe égyptien de la création traite ce thème de façon analogue, mais d'un ton plus paisible. Il dit qu'à l'origine il n'y eut que l'eau primitive, appelée Noun. De cet océan primitif surgit une colline primitive. Le dieu du soleil gravit cette colline primitive, triompha des forces du chaos et ordonna le monde en instituant l'ordre cosmique, intitulé Ma-a-t. Le dieu créateur émerge donc de l'eau primitive: le principe régulateur est issu de Noun. C'est pourquoi le mort qui s'identifie avec le dieu du soleil afin d'obtenir ainsi la vie éternelle, dit: "Je suis Toum (un des noms du soleil) en existant seul en Noun, je suis Re (le nom courant désignant le dieu du soleil) à ses débuts lorsqu'il commençait à regner sur ce qu'il venait de créer". Une réminiscence de cette cosmogonie qui fait surgir le monde de l'eau, est restée dans le récit de la Genèse de la Bible — Genèse I — disant q'au commencement il y avait des ténèbres à la surface de l'abîme et que l'esprit de Dieu se mouvait au-dessus des eaux. Voici également l'eau comme élément primitif.

La fin des temps correspond aux premiers temps du monde. C'est pourquoi il n'est guère étonnant que certains peuples se représentent la fin des temps comme un retour á la situation primitive. Cette représentation se remarque dans l'Edda, notamment dans le poème célèbre Völuspà qui dépeint les évènements lors de Ragnarök, scène finale de l'histoire mondiale. Alors les dieux et les géants périssent en s'entretuant dans un combat final atroce et la terre s'anéantit. Le monde s'écroule dans l'océan. C'est ce que décrivent les vers qui suivent:

Le soleil noircit
dans la mer sombre la terre.

Le mythe égyptien de la création a emprunté ses métaphores à un événement arrivant tous les ans dans la vallée du Nil, à savoir l'inondation des régions du littoral par les eaux en cru rapide du Nil. Cela veut dire un retour périodique à l'état de chaos et donc au fond une victoire remportée par la mort. De même le déluge, dont parlent outre la Bible, nombre des mythes anciens, n'est autre chose qu'un envahissement catastrophique des eaux primitives subjugées lors de la création. Alors l'ancien Egyptien vit à la décrue des eaux que quelques endroits éminents surgissaient des flots. Cette image mit en mouvement sa phantasie créatrice de mythes. De cette façon il se représenta la création analogue aux événements lors de l'inondation annuelle, tout en raisonnant à l'inverse: pour lui l'inondation périodique fut une répétition du patron mythique de la création aux temps primitifs.

L'eau sous la forme de l'océan primitif peut constituer l'élément de la mort. Elle apporte la destruction. Le héros qui savait surmonter le désastre du déluge — dans la Bible Noah, dans le récit babylonien Utanapisjtim — devait son salut à la sagesse extraordinaire que Dieu lui avait accordée. Aussi Osiris trouva-t-il la mort dans les eaux selon une certain version de ce mythe fameux concernant la mort et la résurrection de ce dieu. Non seulement l'océan primitif, mais encore la mer actuelle fut estimée comme l'eau de la mort. On ne saurait comprendre la fonction et le rôle symbolique du bateau — aussi bien dans le culte ancien que dans l'emploi quotidien de l'antiquité — qu'en connaissant cette appréciation de la mer et de l'eau. Le bateau met en sûreté les dieux et les hommes en passant par-dessus les eaux démoniaques, comme W. B. Kristensen a démontré. Il s'ensuit que dans l'ancienne Egypte le bateau a été exalté comme un être divin et qu'il joue par conséquent un rôle prépondérant dans toutes sortes de processions de dieux.

Cependant l'eau n'apporte pas seulement la mort, elle donne aussi la vie. L'océan primitif abrite la vie en germination et l'ordre en puissance. C'est de l'océan primitif qu'émergea d'après la conception égyptienne le dieu du soleil qui crea le monde. Ea, le dieu babylonien de la sagesse, ami et protecteur des hommes, était un dieu de l'océan trônant aux abîmes des mers. Il est le mage par excellence, "l'expert parmi les dieux, qui connaît tout ce qui a un nom". C'est pourquoi il est le patron des artistes et des artisans. Ce fut Ea qui déjoua le projet d'Enlil cherchant à exterminer l'humanité, en donnant à Utanapisjtim des indications sur la maniére dont celui-ci pourrait se sauver du déluge. Il est probable qu'Ea se cache aussi sous la forme de l'homme-poisson Oannes, dont Berosus dit qu'il surgissait de la mer le matin pour instruire les hommes dans l'agriculture, la construction des villes et des temples, les métiers et les arts, et que le soir il se noyait de nouveau dans les flots. C'est donc dans la mer que s'abrite la sagesse suprême, de même que la vie véritable. Le débordement du Nil est la condition indispensable pour la fertilité de l'Egypte et fut apprécié comme tel depuis les temps les plus reculés. Cela explique pourquoi Osiris est entre autres le dieu des eaux du Nil. Plutarque raconte qu'en célébrant les mystères d'Osiris on allait en procession jusqu'au fleuve, qu'on y puisait de l'eau en qu'on s'écria alors: "Osiris a été trouvé". L'eau nouvelle, cela voulait dire la résurrection d'Osiris. Les textes parlent d'Osiris comme suit: "Il est le Nil qui réitère son rajeunissement et qui fournit aux besoins de tout le pays". Poseidon s'harmonise également avec ce cadre d'idées. Il est le frère de Hades, l'empereur redouté des enfers. Poseidon lui aussi se rattache à l'empire de la mort. Son attribut, c'est le cheval, qui dans la religion grecque constitue le symbole de l'empire de la mort. A plusieurs endroits il eut un temple et un autel en commun avec Demeter, la déesse de nature typiquement chthonienne. De l'autre côté Poseidon fut appelé phytalmios, "celui qui nourrit", parce que ses eaux surtout là où il fit jaillir des sources, apportaient la vie, voire une vie émergeant des profondeurs, c'est à dire de l'empire de la mort.

Cette vision ancienne continue à vivre dans la croyance populaire et dans la superstition, notamment chez les peules de la mer du Nord. Il y a nombre de récits d'où il ressort nettement à quel point la mer passionne par son immensité, sa profondeur, sa salinité, son flux et reflux et son jeu de vagues. La mer agitée par la tempête est un être vivant: un grand chien dévorant qui montre ses dents. Il est question autant de la vengeance que du secours de la sirène, cette Muse mysterieuse de la mer. Pourtant l'eau de la mer n'est pas seulement dangereuse, elle est aussi capable de guérir et de purifier.

La mer a exercé cet effet ambivalent sur des peuples modernes aussi. Elle repousse et effraie, mais n'en attire pas moins irrésistiblement. Elle donne la vie et la prospérité, mais elle arrache aussi la vie et cause de la misère. Chaque marin connaît ces sentiments contradictoires: sur la plaine liquide incertaine il regrette la sécurité de la terre ferme et une fois descendu à terre il est poussé par une envie irrépressible à prendre le large.

Or, il est curieux que les peuples qui vivent en majeure partie de la navigation, tels que les Hollandais, ont appris dès leur jeune âge à considérer la mer comme l'élément original, dans un sens très spécial. Ils ont réalisé dans l'appréciation de la mer une modification semble à celle apportée par Copernicus aux conceptions de l'univers. Ils se mirent à contempler le monde, non pas de la terre ferme, mais de l'eau périlleuse. La confrontation perpétuelle avec l'eau les a familiarisés avec elle à tel point qu'ils ont acquis une attitude libre du point de vue spirituel envers la vie, sans pour cela se fier jamais à la mer. Hendrik van Loon dit dans son livre intitulé: "Le livre d'or des navigateurs hollandais", que la mer comportait avant tout pour les habitants des Pays Bas un sens en ce qu'elle donnait au Hollandais la conscience de pouvoir échapper à tout moment à la tyrannie de la mesquinerie humaine du pays ou au despotisme étranger. Par là la mer répandit une atmosphère de liberté dans les petites villes hollandaises. Cette remarque est juste. L'espoir du profit et le goût d'aventures ont décidé bien des gens à se faire marins. Mais la soif de liberté était aussi de la partie. Beaucoup de réprouvés ont su se maintenir sur mer. De pareils exilés sur mer étaient pendant la révolte des Pays Bas contre l'Espagne ceux qu'on nommait "les gueux de mer", des types séditieux, amis de la liberté, qui fuyaient la terreur espagnole en prenant le large et qui de là apportaient la libération. Leurs chansons étaient empreintes d'un intense ton pathétique de liberté. L'ancien Suédois Frithiof chanté par le poète Tegner fut un exilé de ce genre. Frithiof et ses hommes constituaient à bord de leur navire Ellida la communeauté virile caractéristique des marins, qui possède ses règles de vie, son éthique, son droit et sa loi bien à elle. Ces aventuriers courant les mers — qu'aucune loi ne liait — qui prenaient en propres mains le droit, surgissant inopinément quelque part, ont donné lieu à la naissance de la légende du Vaisseau-Fantôme. C'est le récit d'un capitaine commandant un vaisseau-fantôme, qui continue à naviguer éternellement, sans jamais faire escale, parce qu'une malédiction pèse sur ce marin qui arbitrairement a pris en main son destin et sa vie. Ce personnage symbolise l'agitation sans repos du marin. Sa devise est: navigare necesse est.

Pourtant le courage du marin affrontant tous les périls sur mer n'est pas de la témérité. C'est ce qui ressort de nombreuses chansons marines. On peut y surprendre un mélange d'humeur rogue et de résignation. C'est que le marin sait qu'il risque à chaque instant de nouveau sa vie. C'est grace à des puissances supérieures qu'il vit. Il est confronté sur mer avec la mort et l'éternité, avec le fond primitif de l'existence, avec Dieu.

Nous pouvons constater en guise de conclusion que l'eau et la mer constituent des éléments de la nature si important au point de vue de l'histoire des religions, parce qu'elles se trouvent posséder un pouvoir religieux de suggestion.

CHANCE-FATE-PROVIDENCE *

Some religio-phenomenological reflections

In his famous treatise on Manicheism [1] H. Ch. Puech describes in a fascinating way, how the initial state of balance between the Kingdom of Light and the Kingdom of Darkness was upset. In the Kingdom of Evil a continuous struggle between the demons occurred. On the one hand they coupled with one another; on the other side they devoured each other. This eternal unrest was the cause, that the cosmological drama started, that the two "Natures" mixed and that "le Temps", in which mankind's salvation took place, was inaugurated. In Puech's own words: "Et c'est une accumulation fortuite de ces agitations désordonnées qui haussera le Prince des Ténèbres à la frontière supérieure de son Royaume, lui révélera brusquement la splendeur de la Lumière, fera naître en lui le désir de conquérir avec ses démons cette région étrangère et éblouissante et de se l'assimiler en l'engloutissant en lui." [2]

To use the adjective "fortuite" of the accumulation of the demoniacal forces suggests that the movement by which the Prince of Darkness was thrust towards the border of his Kingdom came about by chance. Was this event mere chance? It is hardly to be believed that Manicheism could ascribe such a far-reaching effect to an arbitrary fact. Is it not more in accordance with the pessimistic world-view of this religion to state that the said course of events was dominated by Fate? One can ask whether the defilement of "Good" by "Evil" and the tragic development which followed was not a fatal intermezzo between the paradisal situation in the beginning, when the two Kingdoms existed side by side not knowing each other, and the eternal peace which will reign in the end, when any mixture will definitely be excluded. Or must one suppose, that Manicheism considered the struggle between light and darkness, between good and evil, to be by no means utterly meaningless, because it involved man's salvation, so that the turmoil which brought the Prince of Darkness to the confine of his Kingdom was actually caused by a hidden Providence? I must leave the answer to these questions to the experts, not being suffi-

---

* Published in *Volume de Mélanges pour H. Ch. Puech*, 1974.
[1] Le Manichéisme, son fondateur, sa doctrine, 1949.
[2] p. 76.

ciently familiar myself with the matter. However, these questions prompt me to make some remarks on the role which chance, fate and providence, separately or in combination, have played in the religious life of mankind, and to do this in honour of my distinguished colleague and highly esteemed friend Prof. dr. H. Ch. Puech.

The problem of the relation between the guidance which God gives to man and the world on the one hand and chance and fate on the other hand is nowhere so sharply pictured as in Thornton Wilder's novel "The Bridge of San Luis Rey". The book deals with an old bridge which connects the two parts of a South American city. Countless generations had crossed that bridge. Suddenly the bridge collapsed. Five people of different age and social position met their death. The tragic accident roused deep emotion in San Luis Rey. However, it stimulated a priest to ponder upon the dreadful happening. He asked himself: why did these five people perish? Was the calamity chance, did fate play its cruel game or was it the result of God's providence? In order to answer these questions he went into the lives of the five persons and he followed their course up to the moment of their unexpected death. He came to the conclusion, that each of them at the moment of the accident had reached a dilemma, that they were all at a deadlock. Their sudden death could thus be considered as the sole *dénouement* which remained. Should the disaster therefore be no chance, no fate, but the outcome of God's foresight? To the priest the idea looked consoling. But he shrank from accepting it. Thus the open question remained: was it chance, did fate make itself felt, or was it God's dispensation?

It is evident that in this book the relationship between God's providence and chance and fate is conceived of as a theological problem. This version of the issue lies outside the scholarly horizon of the student of the history of religions. He may learn from the book in question that the said problem is religiously and theologically speaking an urgent one, but he takes no decision in this matter. His task is to describe the different conceptions concerning chance, fate and providence and to try to understand their religious significance. Then the question can be stated in the following way: theoretically confidence in the foresight of the gods or the deity is incompatible with chance and fate. However, quite a number of religious testimonies prove that in practice confidence in God is combined with a belief in fate, c.q. chance. No wonder, for chance and fate play such an important part in life that they cannot be ignored. This means, that people in all ages

have wrestled with the question, how belief in God could be equated
with chance and fate which they got to know as undeniable realities.
It is interesting and illuminating to investigate the solutions of the
problem which religious people of different types have found. Their
answers to the present question are not arbitrarily chosen. They are
all logical in the religious sense of the term, and they are typologically
speaking significant. The following attitudes can be distinguished
without difficulty:

1) The notion is universally accepted, that the wheel of fortune
turns in an arbitrary way. One person is born with a silver spoon in
his mouth: luck is always with him; another is an unlucky devil: he
gets all the blows. Man is generally inclined to accept, that fortune
and misfortune alternate in a whimsical way. Apparently chance plays
an important part in human life. Sometimes all goes smoothly; at other
times one gets into an awful mess. These experiences seldom take the
shape of a clear-cut conception. Chance is too vague and indeterminable
an entity ever to assume the figure of a god. Nevertheless, chance can
foster in the human heart a kind of wisdom with a tinge of religious
resignation. Man learns to think: one should resign oneself to adverse
strokes of fortune; an unexpected piece of luck is always welcome; life
is precarious by its very nature.

(2) When chance loses its ambivalent character and primarily shows
its unfavourable side, the idea of fate moves into the foreground. This
notion is often interwoven with an ancient and wide-spread popular
belief. It arises from the feeling, that there are forces which man is not
able to stand up to. Fate does in this case not appear as a sharply
defined idea, but more as a hazy figure. It certainly is not accidental,
that this belief in fate has found expression in many proverbs. Matti
Kuusi gives striking instances thereof in an article on "Fatalistic Traits
in Finnish Proverbs." [3] These proverbs testify to the conviction, that
certain events are allotted to man. Thus it is said: "Everyone has to
take his *luoto* (destiny, fate, God's dispensation)". "How could you
escape your *luoto?*". "It is fortune that steers man". "Nobody is the
smith of his own fortune". "You should not seek your fortune, if it
does not itself seek you." The last also holds true for the matrimonial
companion: one often does not get the beloved of one's choice, but the
one, who is destined thereto: "You belong to the one who is *luoto*

---

[3] *Fatalistic Belief, in Religion, Folklore, and Literature*, Papers read at the Symposium on Fatalistic Beliefs held at Åbo on the 7th-9th of September 1964, edited by H. Ringgren, 1967.

for you, granted for you, not to the one whom you have been looking
for and desiring." The proverbs express the feeling that fate hangs
like the sword of Damocles over human life.

(3) In many stories and fairy tales from antiquity and from later
ages the idea is to be found, that man's fate is linked with his birth.
Benevolent fairies come to offer the new-born child their good gifts,
or evil spirits predict a fatal future. Often the prediction comes to
fulfilment notwithstanding the precautions of solicitous parents and
then always at an unexpected hour and in an unpredictable way. At
the unguarded moment fate strikes the person in question. However,
sometimes there is mention of bad risks, which one can avoid with
courage and tact, rather than of an unavoidable fate.

In my opinion the latter is the case in an ancient Egyptian story
of a prince at whose birth the Hathors, the goddesses who presage
the future, say: "He will die either by a snake, or by a crocodile, or by
a dog." As I have dealt with the matter in detail elsewhere [4], I can
be brief here because in this connection it is sufficient to give an
instance of a prediction at birth, which has no fatal consequences.
Summarized the story runs like this: the father of the prince attempted
in vain to protect his son from the predicted calamity, by locking him
up in a house in the desert. The boy, who was not lacking in lust for
adventures, succeeded in persuading his father that he let him go out
into the world, together with his beloved dog. In Syria the prince won
a princess as his wife by his courage and his sportiveness. Thereupon
he returned to Egypt together with her. Once upon a time when he
slept, a snake made an attack upon him. His alert wife averted the
danger by killing the snake. Unfortunately the papyrus which contains
the story, breaks off at this moment. One should like to know to what
extent the crocodile and the dog threatened his life and whether he
became a victim of one of the two animals. The papyrus is so battered
at its end that the final part of the story is missing. Naturally the conceptions of the Egyptologists about the presumable ending of the story
differ: some advocate a tragical end; others fancy a happy end. Personally I am convinced that here it is a question of three dangers, from
which the prince escaped thanks to the devoted love and the vigilance
of his wife and to his own courage and his piety. For after the princess
has killed the snake she says: "Look, your god has given one of your
lots into your hand; he surely will give you also the others." Thereupon

4 C. J. Bleeker, *Die Idee des Schicksals in der alt-ägyptischen Religion* (C. J. Bleeker, *The Sacred Bridge*, 1963, p. 111 sq.).

the story tells: "Then he (the prince) sacrificed to Re, thanked him and extolled his might daily." In contradistinction to the many stories in which the fatal prediction at the birth of the person in question inavertently comes true, this tale would, if my interpretation is right, express the idea, that man can evade the unfavourable lot given to him at his birth, by the strength of his character and by his piety which procures him the assistance of his god.

(4) It is easy to make a transition from the preceding considerations to a sketch of the nature and the significance of astrology. For this curious "religion" teaches that man's fate is determined by the constellation of the stars in the hour of his birth. It is superfluous to describe the history and the tenets of astrology. It is generally known that astrology originated in ancient Mesopotamia, where people believed that there existed a correspondence between the events in heaven and those on earth, in the sense that the star-clad firmament revealed the will of the gods and thus the divine dispensations which were immutably realized. The Chaldees were the first to elaborate this lofty conception into a kind of pseudo-science which pretends to be able to scrutinize into detail the influence of the stars and of the planets on man's life. Every student of the history of religions knows that astrology, both as a world view and as a means to predict the future, conquered the whole world of antiquity. Astrological ideas and symbols are to be found in the mystery religions, in Gnosticism and in certain currents of the popular philosophy of antiquity. So strong was and is the grip of astrology on people's minds, that up to the time of the Reformation even prominent persons adhered to its teachings, and it has its devoted adepts even today.

These facts raise the question what the fascination of astrology is, and which religious needs it fulfils. In order to find an answer to this question one should consider the function and the significance of the horoscope, which is cast in the hour of birth of a person and which presents the constellation of the stars at the moment, when he came into the world. This horoscope possesses so much value, not only because it indicates how the life of the person in question will develop, but also because the peculiarities of his mental and his physical structure can be deduced from it. This means that the horoscope gives a certain knowledge about the illnesses to which this person is susceptible and about the weak and the strong sides of his character. This is what people wish to know, even if this knowledge is unfavourable. This state of affairs might give rise to the impression that astrology leads to fatalism. For the constellation of the stars at the hour of birth cannot be changed. Actually the downright fatalism which one would expect undergoes a mitigation in several respects. Firstly it is not easy to read a certain constellation of the stars with unfailing certainty. Errors are not excluded. Secondly man possesses a certain freedom of action. He is not helplessly subjected to the rule of the stars. Thirdly the guidance of the stars protects man against the caprices of the evil spirits. This was the conviction of astrologists in former times. Now that the belief in demons has died out, the believer in astrology nevertheless can feel himself safe against the many demoniacal influences active in the world and in human life. For the stars reveal the divine dispensation to which the followers of the astrological doctrine surrender in a curious *amor fati* rather than to senseless chance. Finally astrology conjures up a harmonious picture of the universe, built on the combination of holy numbers. Such a world view holds a fascination for many people, not least because it gives relief and meaning to their own tiny personality. [5]

(5) One of the characteristics of the religions of antiquity is the conviction that there exists a world order, instituted at creation and prevalent notwithstanding the permanent destructive effect of death and temporary periods of social upheaval. This world order includes the divine dispensation, to which man should subject himself. The view of the world and of man which is fostered by this conception sounds an optimistic note. Man is deemed capable of conforming to this world order. If he lives in accordance with the divine order, both his virtue and his happiness are guaranteed. On the other hand he will hopelessly go under, if he neglects this order or infringes on it.

Instances of this notion of world order are Tau in ancient China, Ṛta in Indian Vedism, Ma-a-t in ancient Egypt and Themis in ancient Greece. They are the dominating ideas of remarkable types of a homogeneous culture. This means that they encompass religion, cult, ethics, science, art, social life and the body politic. This is a grand concept which is the more fascinating because modern times merely show a complete disruption of cultural life. The nations of antiquity drew an optimistic outlook from this idea, convinced as they were, that the world order would last notwithstanding periods of social dissolution.

---

[5] F. Cumont, *Die Orientalischen Religionen im Römischen Heidentum*, 1914; F. Boll, *Sterngaube und Sterndeutung, die Geschichte und das Wesen der Astrologie*, 1918; Troels Lund, *Himmelsbild und Weltanschauung im Wandel der Zeiten*, 1924.

In their opinion every one who followed the cosmic rhythm could persue a happy life.

As this article does not pretend to offer a religio-historical inquiry, but aims at a typological description, it is superfluous to deal with all the said notions of world order. I shall confine myself to a brief treatment of Ma-a-t [6] and of Themis. [7]

Ma-a-t is both an idea and a goddess. As a notion ma-a-t signifies truth, justice, order in society. These ideals prove to be founded in a cosmic order, instituted at creation, of which Ma-a-t as goddess is the personification. Ma-a-t as world order is clearly revealed in the regular course of the sun, but also in the way in which Re each morning rises from the netherworld by conquering the forces of death. Though it is tempting to digress on the significance of Ma-a-t, this short characterization may suffice, because in the context the stress should be put on the manner in which man's lot is interwoven with Ma-a-t. This proceeds from the conviction of the ancient Egyptians that both man's happiness and his virtue are safeguarded if he lives according to Ma-at. The presupposition of this tenet is, that man is capable of living virtuously. This is the underlying principle of the books of wisdom which apparently enjoyed popularity in ancient Egypt. This literature is built on the assumption, that he who errors or commits a criminal offence, is no sinner, but a fool, who must endure the ill effects of his act. He has to blame himself for the calamity, because he did not bridle his passions and did not conform to the order of Ma-a-t.

That Ma-a-t represents the divine dispensation is apparent from the connection with Shai, Renenet and Meskhent. These are numina which each in their way determine man's fate. Shai is the lot, both in the favourable and the unfavourable sense of the word. Renenet is the midwife, the nurse and the educator, who protects and guides man from his childhood. Meskhent is the goddess of birth and the birthplace. These three numina determine the course of man's life. They appear primarily at two critical moments: at birth and after death, i.e. at the judgement of the dead. This last act is executed under the patronage of Ma-a-t. Wellknown representations from the *Book of the Dead* show how the heart of the deceased is weighed on a scale against the feather, the emblem of Ma-a-t. This means that only he can maintain himself over against the fate of death, who has lived in accordance

---

[6] C. J. Bleeker, *De beteekenis van de Egyptische godin Ma-a-t*, 1929.
[7] V. Ehrenberg, *Die Rechtsidee im frühen Griechentum, Untersuchungen zur Geschichte der werdenden Polis*, 1921.

with Ma-a-t. In that case he can be justified. His "justice" does not only consist in his ethical virtue and his cultic blamelessness, but equally in the fact that he has not infringed the cosmic order. His justification is enacted by Thoth, after the pattern of the justification of Osiris, i.e. according to a cosmic archetype, namely the victory of the divine life over death. This includes that the ancient Egyptians entertained the optimistic conviction that man is able to fulfil the divine dispensation to his benefit.

V. Ehrenberg has argued that themis can be derived from stems of verbs which mean: pile up, stand firm. Themis would have been the designation of the holy mound which was the seat of the earth goddess who gave oracles. In ancient Greece the earth goddess was the first who gave oracles. She proclaimed in the form of an oracle the order to which man should subject himself if he would escape ruin. She revealed the lot which was granted to him. Thus themis became the divine commandment and later on the norm of the ancient Greek community, i.e. the unwritten law. As goddess Themis is the daughter of Gaia, the typical earth goddess. Themis is connected with the Moirae who determine man's fate. Themis is the divine order according to which the Moirae fulfil their task, an order which is maintained by Zeus, Heimarmene, Dike, Nemesis and the Erinyes. As oracle goddess Themis speaks the wisdom which in the pregnant sense of the word is practical wisdom. She gives the good advice which one should not disregard, lest one go under.

(6) There is a sharp contrast between this conception and the pessimistic idea that man is subjected to an unavoidable fate and that, even with the best intentions, he becomes unwillingly guilty, so that he can vindicate his dignity only by an heroic downfall. This outlook is to be found on the one hand in ancient Greece, and on the other in the old Germanic religion.

Typically Greek is the fear of ὕβρις because it rouses the νέμεσις of the gods. Therefore the Delphic exhortation says: γνῶθι σεαυτόν, i.e. "know yourself", namely as a human being who is no god; do not pride yourself on your happiness and your ability, because this would stir up the φθόνος of the gods; be on your guard against ἄτη which makes man mad and seduces him to that foolishness which is bound to incur the punishment of the gods.

It is part of man's tragical position in life, that he cannot exactly define the domain inside of which he is secure from the forces which can lead him to ruin. Man's lot is that he so to speak blindfolded by the will of the gods, is led along a path upon which he by his own deeds is doomed to perdition. Simonides has said: "To be virtuous is difficult. No, it is rather impossible. It is merely the prerogative of the gods. For a man it is not possible to be not bad, when an insoluble problem gets hold of him."

This truth is dramatized in the Greek tragedies in a grand manner. The best instance of this is the tragedy of Oedipus. Immediately after his birth Oedipus was exposed, owing to an oracle. So he grew up in ignorance of his parentage. When as an adolescent he went out into the world, he killed his father Laios in a quarrel without knowing whom he had murdered. Thereupon he arrived at Thebe, his native town which he delivered from a monster, the sphinx. Naturally he was welcomed as a hero and on him the honour was bestowed to marry the queen-widow Iokaste, his own mother. Many years he reigned happily and sincerely honoured. At last, when a disaster occured, the blind seer Teiresias revealed to him that the old oracle, for which reason he had been exposed, had come true. He, the best of men, had unintentionally became entangled in severe guilt. Broken and in dispair he put out his eyes. In his madness he cursed his sons Eteokles and Polynices. Unfortunately this curse was fulfilled. [8] Thus Greek tragedy teaches that fate is inescapable.

A characteristic trait of the old Germanic religion is the belief in fate, which mostly proves to be inevitable death. No man lives longer than is decreed upon him. When he falls, it is a token that his "luck" has left him. The Valkyries who choose the heroes on the battle field for Valhalla, execute the predetermined fate. Later on fate takes the shape of the three Norns who represent past, present and future. By virtue of the belief in fate the ancient German dauntlessly met his fate. In the battle he died without self-pity, whilst he defended himself proudly to the last moment. It cannot be denied that this belief in fate of which the Icelandic sagas offer impressive instances, shows a heroic trait.

Thus in *Njál's saga*, Gunnar disregards the advice to be on his guard against two of his enemies. Proudly he answers: "Death will yet come where-ever I may be, if it is so decreed." [9] Another hero says: "There must be someone who tells what fate wishes to be said, and what is destined to happen must have its course." [10] The game of

---

[8] C. J. Bleeker, *Inleiding tot een phaenomenologie van den godsdienst*, 1934, p. 58 sq.

[9] Njáls Saga, p. 148 (*Isländska Sagor, översatta och utgivna av Hjalmar Alving*, 1943).

[10] *Gisle Surssons Saga*, p. 17/18 (Isländska Sagor etc.).

fate is also detected in the choice of the conjugal partner. When a
man of lower rank sues for the hand of the notable Astrid, her father
Vigfus declares: "This is perhaps what fate has determined for her,
though we had wished something more distinguished for a girl of our
clan." [11] The acts of the goddesses of fate are seldom represented in
a dramatic way. However, a curious passage in *Njál's saga* tells of how
a man sees twelve women ride to a women's room. He looks through
a hole in the wall and sees that they weave at a bloody weaving loom,
while they sing a song of fate. It was the Valkyries who by this act
predicted the coming battle. After the song they tore the fabric from
the loom, rent it into pieces and took each a part. Six of them rode to
the South, and six to the North. [12]

(7) All over the world and in all ages religious people have harboured ambivalent feelings towards the gods or the deity. On the one
hand they were filled with gratitude and attachment towards the divine
beings which had blessed them; on the other hand they felt a deep
awe for those higher forces, on which they as defenceless creatures
were totally dependent and to whose pleasure they were fully delivered.
The latter feeling now and then got the upper hand. In that case the
notion of fate was woven into the idea of God. This gives rise to a
conception of a deity who primarily is a being determining fate.

In this way Geo Widengren [13] presents the sky-god of some pre-
literate peoples and of certain nations of antiquity. It is not the question
here, whether the interpretation of the nature of these gods given by
Widengren is entirely correct. At any rate it contains sufficient truth
to serve as an example of this type of concept of God. It should be
added that according to Widengren it is primarily the sky-god who
fulfils the function of High God. Experts need not receive further
explanation of the implications of this thesis. They know the High
God and the discussions which have developed around this figure.

Widengren tries to prove with a wealth of facts and arguments that
the sky-god is a being which determines fate. He distinguishes three
figures: a) the sky-god is a power determining fate, who decrees both
good and evil, b) the sky-god can split himself into his two aspects
which, as the good and the evil side of his being, become more or less
independent, c) the figure of the sky-god can break up into his two

---

[11] *Viga-Glums* Saga, p. 90 (Isländska Sagor etc.).
[12] *Njáls Saga*, p. 394 sq.
[13] G. Widengren, *Hochgottglaube im alten Iran*, 1938; *Religionsphänomenologie*,
1969, Kapitel 3.

aspects which take the mythological shape of his sons. Widengren acknowledges that there is a great variety in the conceptions concerning the High God. So he also stresses that the sky-god is often the giver of rain and thus of fertility. Yet he emphasizes that this deity exercises sovereignty over man and the world. This conception can be understood, when one realizes that the sky seemingly encompasses the earth. No wonder that the highest authority was attributed to the sky-god.

With regard to the illiterate peoples Widengren has supported his thesis with facts drawn from many nations, but in a special sense from the religious life of African peoples. He has also extended this line of argument with the result that in his opinion a number of gods of ancient Iran, i.e. Mithra, Vaya, Ahura Mazda and Zervan, further Juppiter, Jahweh and Allah in a sense belong to the same category. Again it must be said that in this text it is not important whether Widengren is completely right or not. His conception of the gods in question here has an undisputed phenomenological value. It is an interesting instance of the way in which religious man tries to combine the idea of God's providence with the forces of chance and fate which assert themselves so powerfully that their reality cannot be denied.

(8) At the end of the preceding paragraph Allah was mentioned. His name prompts the reflection that, when religious man lives under the annihilating power and holiness of the only God whom he knows, the conviction must arise, that happiness or misfortune, salvation or eternal damnation, are totally dependent on the overwhelmingly powerful and holy God. A further step is taken: man's lot is already predestined before his birth. Clear instances of this belief in predestination are to be found in Islam and in orthodox Calvinism.

The Muslim belief in predestination is often wrongly considered as a kind of fatalism. Its structure is more complicate than appears at first sight. The background is an old Arabic fatalism, which can hardly be reconstructed though it permeates some pre-Muslim poems. Mohammad rejected this belief in fate. He put man's lot into the hands of Allah, who sovereignly decrees on man's weal and woe, whose will is inscrutable, but whose wisdom and mercy cannot be questioned. The pious Muslim draws from this conviction the strength to resign himself in adverse times. Later on, the average Muslim fell back into a somewhat fatalistic attitude, partly under the influence of the concept of a heavenly book in which man's lot is definitely written down. However, protests against this version of predestination have never

been lacking. Notably the Muᶜtazilites have defended man's free will
and God's mercy. It is also interesting that in certain Persian epics
Muslim "fatalism" is mitigated by the idea that man can make a choice,
an idea which originated from Zoroastrianism. Thus it is clear that
religious Muslims have wrestled with the question, how they should
combine the idea of an almighty God with the reality of chance and
fate on the one side and man's undeniable ability to make a free choice
on the other. [14]

The Muslim doctrine of predestination mainly has a bearing on
man's wordly lot. Calvinism in its classic form deals with man's salvation or damnation. The Calvinist of the old style was firmly convinced that man's eternal bliss or everlasting perdition were predestined.
The so-called "tenets of Dordt" by which the Remonstrants, who
defended man's free will and God's mercy for the sinner, were condemned emphatically maintain: "This election is an unchangeable
decree of God by which, before the foundation of the world, a certain
number of persons, not better or more worthy than the others...
according to the free pleasure of His will, purely by grace, have been
elected to bliss in Christ." [15] This pronouncement sounds fatalistic,
especially when one thinks of the counterpart, i.e. the eternal damnation of the non-elect who may be virtuous and pious men and women.
In order to do justice to this doctrine one should not forget that it
originated from the sense of the overpowering holiness of God who
cannot tolerate sin, that horrible corruption of mankind. Therefore it
was taken as sheer grace when man nevertheless was saved. Curiously
enough, this belief in God's predestination has not killed the activity of
the Calvinists. On the contrary, they have become the most active
Christians. For a life spent in the imitation of Christ was the only
guarantee of gaining certainty that one actually was one of the elect.

These eight attempts to find a right attitude toward chance, fate and
providence, and possibly to harmonize them, are all both significant
and instructive. They demonstrate that the problem has many different
aspects, and they prove that the life of mankind has many different
dimensions, i.e. different levels on which religious truth may be understood. These levels illuminate, as a result of the various religious
experiences, man's fascinating, and yet often mysterious life on earth.

---

[14] H. Ringgren, *Studies in Arabian Fatalism*, 1955; *Fatalism in Persian Epics*,
U. U. Å. 1952.
[15] *De Drie Formulieren van Enigheid*, uitgegeven door Dr. A. Kuyper, 1900, p. 75.

SOME REMARKS ON THE RELIGIOUS
SIGNIFICANCE OF LIGHT *

In *Thespis: Ritual, Myth, and Drama in the Ancient Near East,*
T. H. Gaster offers an interesting and clarifying explanation of a
difficult sentence in "The Poem of Aqhat." This sentence occurs in
the passage in which Daniel expresses his joy over the decision of El—
communicated to him by Baal—that a son will be born to him. Thereby
his family will be prevented from dying out. Moreover, Daniel will
have a descendant who can fulfil the filial duties. This son, so says
Daniel, will be the man, "Who may make my smoke to go forth from
the ground."

What is the meaning of this utterance which sounds both poetical
and mysterious? Gaster proposes to consider the saying of Daniel
as the equivalent to the well-known adage: "keep the home fires burning." By means of a number of quotations from the Old Testament
he makes clear how much value the ancient peoples attached to the
fact that the fire, that is, the light, continued to burn in their homes.
In their opinion "the extinction of a light" was "a synonym for
disaster," as Gaster formulates it. [1]

There is no point in inquiring whether Gaster's exegesis of the
quoted sentence from "The Poem of Aqhat" is right or not. I have
drawn attention to the quoted passage in Gaster's famous work,
because it testifies to the vital importance of light for mankind. The
disappearance of light would mean calamity for humanity, causing
its sure ruin. From the remotest antiquity man has been conscious of
this fact. He has always regarded light as a great treasure, as an
indispensable condition of life. Therefore, light has become equivalent
to life. No wonder that light has a religious significance. It functions
as the bearer and the symbol of a series of moral and religious values.
This is evident, for instance, from the fact that *phōs* amongst other
terms, signifies salvation. [2]

Light shines in different shades. Poets praise the warm glow of
the sun and the silver rays of the moon. In the northern countries
one can enjoy the wonderful reddish evening-light which lends a

---

*Published in the *Festschrift for Th. H. Gaster* (1974).
[1] *Thespis: Ritual, Myth and Drama in the Ancient Near East* (1950), 274-76.
[2] Liddell and Scott, *Greek-English Lexicon* (1961), s.v. *phōs*.

nearly unearthly beauty to the landscape. In Greece, light is super-abundant, sparkling, graceful, the true element of the spirit of beauty and freedom. The eastern countries know a light which is excessive, overwhelming, dazzling, and sometimes demoniac. No wonder that light is variously appreciated, also, in a religious respect.

Thus, light presents itself as an appropiate subject for a religio-phenomenological research. Naturally the question arises: what does this term mean and what does such a treatment of the religious phenomena in question include? It is here not the place to digress on the aim and the method of the phenomenology of religion. We can even skip a reference to the relevant literature, because it is within everybody's reach. Suffice it to state that the aim of the said discpline can be formulated as an attempt to order a number of facts, taken from different religions in such a way that the religious significance of the phenomenon, to which these facts refer, clearly appears. Secondly it should be mentioned that the phenomenology of religion, after having won its victories, mainly owing to the work of scholars like G. van der Leeuw, Fr. Heiler, M. Eliade and G. Widengren, at the moment has become the subject of critical discussions. [3] Its method is newly subjected to a sharp inquiry, and in some quarters even its right to exist is questioned—exactly as happened when this branch of learning first entered the circle of the sister disciplines. In my opinion the phenomenology of religion has by its achievements once and for all obtained its right to exist. The only question is to state more precisely both its aim and its method. As to its aim, the definition presented above may be said to be generally acceptable. In regard to its method I strongly doubt whether there is any use in speculating about the manner in which the essence of the phenomenon can be grasped in a deeper sense than is done in the ordinary religio-phenom-enological research. For by these speculations one would enter the domain of philosophy in regard to which the student of the history of religions is a layman, so that he unavoidably draws conclusions which are not wholly correct. We had better make an inquiry into the function and value of the factual phenomena, primarily of those which occur in different religions. One such phenomenon is the religious appreciation of light.

In order to tackle this problem one should investigate which part light plays in the different components of the structure of religion.

---

[3] See, e.g., *Numen* 19, fascicles 2-3.

The term structure is used here, because it cannot be denied that all religions are founded on a certain pattern, which consists of: (1) an idea of God or a notion of the Holy; (2) a conception of man's nature and of his path of salvation; (3) a certain cult; and (4) a religious evaluation of the world. In my opinion, the religons significance of a certain phenomenon, in this case of light, can clearly appear only when one examines its function in the context of the different components of the said structure. It has already been indicated that light possesses different shades. This commonplace remark points in the direction of a more comprehensive religio-phenomenological research. This research differs, on the one hand, from a religio-historical monograph. There exists an excellent study by G. P. Wetter on the matter, entitled "Phōs, Eine Untersuchung über hellenistische Frömmigkeit; zugleich ein Beitrag zum Verständnis des Manichäismus." [4] On the other hand, the approach to the problem in question, which is made in this article, keeps a distance from the older religio-phenomenological studies in which a mass of interesting facts concerning a certain religious phenomenon are assembled by the author and are ordered by him as systematically as possible, but without any leading principle. Here the attempt is made to demonstrate, with regard to light, not only how it is evaluated by the differing religions, but primarily how its different qualities function within the fourfold scheme which has been sketched.

First, it is a striking feature that light is generally considered as an independent entity, though people have always known that light actually is the radiation of certain sources of heat and light, primarily the sun and the moon and, in a lesser degree, the stars. Nevertheless, light has made such a stark impression that it has been evaluated as a separate element. This idea is, for example, clearly expressed in the creation story in the book of Genesis. It is told that on the first day God called the light into existence by His creative word. The sun and the moon were created no sooner than on the fourth day.

Light is such a radiant element that nobody wonders that the deity is often conceived of as a light-figure, both in the literal and in the figurative sense. Examples of this concept can easily be given. The Indian word *deva* 'deity', can be derived from the verb *div* 'to beam'. The term *vasu* springs from *vas* 'to shine'. The old name *brighu* designates the gods as beings which spread *bhargas* 'brilliance'. [5] The

---

[4] *Skrifter utgifna af Kungl. Humanistiska Vetenskaps-Samfundet,* 17:1 f.
[5] R. Otto, *Das Gefühl des Überweltlichen (sensus numinis)* (1932), 95.

same idea is the basis of *aścarya,* an Indian designation of the divinity, that is, a being whose appearance calls forth the *aś* of awe. [6] This religious experience is expressed in the following poetical words:

> This is his (of Brahman) illustration:
> When it has lightened lightning—ah!
> When this has caused to close the eyes—ah!
> So far with regard to the divinity (*devatā*).

Other examples of this conception of the deity could easily be presented. I leave it at that, but I may add that in another context I have suggested that the different notions of the godhead, used in various religions, should be scrutinized in order to detect the original significance of terms for "the divine" worshipped in these religions. [7] In my opinion, this would be an important way to find out the key word of the religions in question and to solve the difficult problem of formulating a satisfactory definition of the phenomenon "religion" as such. Therewith, one arrives at interesting insights. One of them is the conception of the deity as a light-figure.

In the preceding argument, light is taken partly in a literal and partly in a figurative sense. Before tackling the question of the light as a symbol of a certain conception of God, we shall pay attention to the gods of light in the literal sense of the term. These gods belong to three categories: sky-gods, sun-gods, and moon-gods.

The sky shows itself in two appearances: in a mysterious, dark nightly garment and in the clear, shining attire of the day. It is the latter aspect that is of interest for the present argument. A striking instance of a sky-god who is conceived of as a luminous figure is the ancient Indian Dyaus, who is often called *pitar* 'father'. [8] In Greece, Zeus is the corresponding figure. The name of the latter god is supposed to signify the illuminator, the god of the heavenly light. [9] If this line of thought is extended to the Roman religion one meets Jupiter, who is primarily the god of the clear sky, though he also manifests himself as Jupiter Fulgurator and Jupiter Tonans. [10] No matter how many-sided the character of the latter two gods may be, they originally represent the heaven, which shows a shining face.

---

[6] Ibid., 204-5.

[7] C. J. Bleeker, *The Key Word of Religion* (*The Sacred Bridge,* 1963).

[8] Chantepie, *Lehrbuch der Religionsgeschichte* (1925), 2:36.

[9] K. Kerényi, *Zeus und Hera: Urbild des Vaters, des Gatten und der Frau* (1972), 12.

[10] *Lehrbuch,* 2:438; G. Widengren, *Religionsphänomenologie* (1969), 70 f.

Therewith, the idea that the sun actually is the source of light is absent. The sky-god himself is thought to be able to put on a bright dress.

The light-god par excellence is the sun-god. Considering the paramount importance which the light of the sun has for mankind, it is not surprising that the sun-god was hightly honoured in various religions. Famous representatives of this category of gods are Re in Egypt, Shamash in Mesopotamia, Helios in Greece, Amaterasu in Japan, and in certain sense, also, the Indian Mithra and the Hellenistic Mithras. They are so well known that it is superfluous to describe their nature and appearance. In the context of this religio-phenomenological study it is primarily Re who deserves the attention, as he is a typical representative of this category of gods. The best way of getting acquainted with him is in reading the many hymns which are written in his honour. [11] It is not mere chance that these songs are often directed to the sun-god at his rise and at his setting. For the rising sun-god demonstrates a capacity for conquering the forces of the netherworld, and the setting sun-god has reached the moment at which he enters the realm of the dead, where he will spread his light for the inhabitants of this chthonic abode. In both cases the sun-god manifests his highest light-force. Therefore, the sun-god is praised in these hymns, either by means of profound mythological terms or in easily understandable poetical images, by reason of his beauty, his might, and his goodness. As example the beginning of the famous sun-hymn of Pharaoh Amenophis IV-Echnaton may serve:

> Thou shinest gloriously in the horizon of heaven,
> Thou living Aton, who lives from remote times.
> When Thou risest in the eastern horizon,
> Thou filleth all countries with Thy beauty.
> Thou art beautiful and splendid, highly beaming over all countries.
> Thy rays embrace the countries
> To the borders of all that Thou hast created.

The third light-god, the moon, is likewise praised as the giver of light. With regard to the Babylonian moon-god Sin, for example, it is said that his light leads the nations. [12] This phrase possesses even a deeper meaning. Nomads often moved during the night in ancient times, guided by the light of the moon, in order to evade the heat of the day. In Mesopotamian mythology, the moon-god is con-

---

[11] A. Scharff, *Aegyptische Sonnenlieder* (1922).
[12] K. Tallqvist, *Månen* (1947), 329.

sidered to be older than the sun-god. Generally, the moon-calendar prcedes the sun-calendar. Also, in later ages, the moon was hightly estimated as a source of light, as appears, for example, from the poetical images used for the moon as giver of light, such as the torch, the lamp, the lantern. [13] In the case of the moon-god it is evident that such gods of nature should not be identified with their cosmic substratum. Gods like the Babylonian Sin and the Egyptian Thoth are no deifications of the moon, but show features which are only indirectly connected with the moon as celestial body. Thus the moon-god is always considered as the god of wisdom. [14] On account of the great wisdom ascribed to Thoth, this god could exercise an important function in the cosmos: he reconciled the fighting gods Horus and Seth with each other; he rendered judgment for Osiris against Seth, and he rendered judgment for the deceased. [15] The moon has always fascinated people by its changing phases, by its two sickles, by its darkening and by its reappearance as full moon. Stronger than the sun which rises and sets, which seems to die and to revive, the moon roused the idea that it is a being with a double nature.

The latter considerations naturally lead to a following remark on the character of the light-gods, especially the sun-god. Light is the indispensable condition for the existence and growth of life, in whatever form it may occur. Thus light has become equivalent to life. A further step is taken: to the light, also, moral values are connected. Light is the element of truth, purity, and righteousness, whereas darkness is thought to be the domain of falsehood, impurity, and crime. The character of the sun-god is mostly of a highly ethical quality. He functions as the creator of the world, as the institutor of the world order, as the lawgiver, as the guarantor of justice, as the judge who condemns the criminals. Did not the Babylonian king Hammurabi receive his famous law from Shamash? The children of Shamash are Kettu and Mesharu, that is, right and justice. [16] At the creation of the world Re instituted Ma-a-t. This is a polyvalent notion. It means truth, justice, order in society. Ma-a-t is also a goddess who personifies the world order. The relation between Ma-a-t and Re is twofold: she holds the rank of daughter, because Re called her into existence, but she is also his mother, because Re lives by Ma-a-t. In the hymns, the

---

[13] Ibid., 138.

[14] Chantepie, *Lehrbuch,* 1:546.

[15] C. J. Bleeker, *Hathor and Thoth: Two Key Figures of the Ancient Egyptian Religion,* (1973).

[16] Chantepie, *Lehrbuch,* 1:549.

latter idea is expressed in the following way: Ma-a-t is called the food, the beverage, the clothing of the sun-god. [17] It primarily has been the Pharaoh Amenophis IV-Echnaton, who in his solar theology has laid the stress on truth as the life-element of the sun-god. [18]

Because the sun-god maintains order and justice, people turn to him in case of injustice or oppression which they have suffered. In the Egyptian sun-hymns there is the prayer of a man who has been wrongfully persecuted and who now expects redress and rehabilitation from Re. [19] Shamash fulfils the same function. The poet of an Assyrian hymn invokes the god in this way:

> O Shamash, king of heaven and earth, lord of that, what is above and beneath,
> Without Thee no right is spoken for the oppressed and no judgement is passed on the oppressed.
> Thou has still taken pity on him, who is worn, dismayed, trembling, oppressed and till treated,
> At whom his god is enraged, and Thou hast spared him. [20]

In another long hymn Shamash is circumstantially lauded as the protector of the destitute. Significant are the following lines:

> Thou support the innocent man,
> Thou inquire into his crime and acquit him of guilt. [21]

This appreciation of the activity of the sun-god is also found outside Egypt and Mesopotamia. An analogus conception occurs in the Vedic literature, in which the Ādityas, the gods of heaven and light, act as the guardians Ṛta, the cosmic order. Their function is described as follows: "For neither at home nor abroad can the rogue, who speaks evil words, control them, when the sons of Āditi (the Ādityas) bestow their eternal light on a mortal man as a gift of life." [22] Sunlight is supposed to release people from every need. A morning song, directed to the sun-god Sūrya, contains the prayer: "By the light, by which Thou expel the darkness, by the ray, by which Thou awaken the whole world, may Thou thereby banish from us all famine, all scarcity of offerings, all illness and all evil dreams." [23]

---

[17] C. J. Bleeker, *De beteekenis van de Egyptische godin Ma-a-t* (1929).
[18] H. Schäfer, *Religion und Kunst von El-Amarna* (1923).
[19] Scharff, *Sonnenlieder*, 77 f.
[20] *JEOL* 7 (1940), 405.
[21] *JEOL* 8 (1942), 674 f.
[22] K. F. Geldner, "Vedismus und Brahmanismus," *Religionsgeschichtliches Lesebuch* (1928), 9:46.
[23] Ibid., 24.

These ethical qualities of the sun-god should not let us forget that the light is ambivalent. It is equivalent to life, but it belongs also to the realm of death. It creates life and blesses man, but it also is a scorching and destructive force. A myth of the Geb-Zé phratry in South New Guinea relates that the cave which the sun—in the shape of a red boy—inhabited, spread a terrible heat. Because this deity kidnapped children, the people decided to catch him. They first managed to carry out the plan after they had extinguished the fire in the abode of the sun. [24] Here the sun-god is a devastating force. In the background of the myth apparently lies the experience of the blistering radiation of the sun. Also, the Babylonian god Ninurta shows a similar demoniac nature. He is the god of the glowing summer heat. Correspondingly he is pictured as a redoutable warrior. [25] Though the Egyptians ascribed to Re many favorable qualities, his wrath is nevertheless not unknown. In the so-called wisdom of Anchcheshong, a passage is to be found in which the effects of this wrath are described. This is done in thirteen lines which all start with the words: "When the sun-god is angry at a country..." [26] Not only can the visible light be demoniac, but this also holds true for the invisible, spiritual light. The Quakers who took the Inward Light as their guide knew that this light could be numinous. [27]

The sun-god shows also chthonic features insofar as he is connected with death and with the netherworld. A curious light-myth was linked up with the mountain Lykaion in Arcadia, where Zeus, the light-god, possessed an altar. Men and animals who set foot within this forbidden domain lost their shadow. Whosoever transgressed the border of this holy region would at best prolong his life one year. He belonged to the other world. [28] Here the cult place of the light-god is the realm of death. W. B. Kristensen drew the attention to the chthonic traits in the character of the Greek sun-god Helios. [29] He is not the only sun-god who has a relationship with the netherworld. From the history of religions, many testimonies can be drawn which make it clear that religious people have conceived of the sun-god, who during the night passes through the netherworld, as a deity who

---

[24] J. van Baal, *Dema, Description, and Analysis of the Marind-Anim Culture* (*South New Guinea*) (1966), 225.

[25] Chantepie, *Lehrbuch*, 1:562.

[26] *JEOL* 15 (1957-58), 15.

[27] G. L. van Dalfsen, *Het Inwaartse Licht bij de Quakers* (1940), 148.

[28] Kerényi, *Zeus*, 301.

[29] W. B. Kristensen, *Het leven uit de dood* (1949), 184 f.

dies and revives—who, so to say, draws his force of resurrection from the realm of death. It is, therefore, not astonishing that the cult of the deceased is often linked up with the worship of the sun-god. [30]

Nobody has ever worshiped the light merely as rays of the sun or the moon, but always as the bearer of moral and religious values. Thus there is an imperceptible transition from the worship of visible light to the use of light as a symbol of the nature of the divinity. The symbolism is usually employed in order to denote the nature of gods, of whom one—for whatever reason—is not allowed to make an image. Thus the Vājaseneyi-Samhitā says, "The Brahman is the light that is like the sun." [31] Aša, the most important entity of the "Holy or Benificent Immortal Ones" (Ameša Spentas), which play an important part in the religion of Zarathustra, materializes itself in light and is situated in the uppermost heaven, the region of pure light. [32] This light which accompanies Aša is the so called Xvarenah. That Xvarenah possesses great importance in the ancient Persian religion, appears sufficiently from the fact that the nineteenth Yašt of the Avesta is dedicated to this entity. H. Lommel derives Xvarenah from the Arian notion *suvar, 'sun', so that in his opinion the original significance of this notion can be described as "etwas sonnenhaftes." The best translation would be: "Glückglanz." [33] It is the luck which, according to the ancient Persian idea, accompanies the good kings (thus the princely superiority which characterizes them). Further peculiarities of the relation of Xvarenah to the king will be discussed later on, when the connection between the light and man is dealt with. In the theology of Zarathustra, Xvarenah is a creation of Ahura Mazda. [34] In the Fravarāne, a credo which is to found in Yasna 12, Ahura Mazda is called "Eigner des Himmelsglanz, Eigner des Machtglanz (Xvarenah)." [35]

In this sense Jahveh is also a "light-god." Ps. 104:2 says that God covers Himself with the light as with a garment. Isa. 60:1 contains the admonition "Arise, shine: for thy light is come, and the glory of the Lord is risen upon thee." One meets the same idea in the New Testament. I Tim. 6:15-16, describes God as "the Kings of kings, and

---

[30] M. Eliade, *Traité d'histoire des religions* (1949), 125 f.

[31] Geldner, *Vedismus*, 104.

[32] J. Duchesne Guillemin, "The Religion of Ancient Iran," *Historia Religionum* (1969), 1:337.

[33] H. Lommel, *Die Yäšt's des Awesta* (1927), 169, 171.

[34] Ibid., 176.

[35] H. Nyberg, *Die Religionen des alten Iran* (1938), 273.

Lord of lords who has immortality, dwelling in the light which no man can approach unto." The latter idea has apparently inspired the great Dutch poet Joost van den Vondel to his beautiful and profound hymn of the angles in his tragedy "Lucifer." The first three lines of this song, in which the angels interrogatively describe God's being, in the German translation of R. Otto, go like this:

> Wer ist es der so hoch gesessen
> so tief im gründelosen Licht
> von Ewigkeiten ungemessen! 36

Also Allah belongs in a figurative sense to the catagory of the light-gods. *Sūra* 24:35 says: "Allah is the light of the heaven and of the earth; the likeness of his light is as a niche in which there is a lamp." In *Sūra* 33:43 it is testified that Allah leads the faithful from the darkness to the light. As-Suhrawardi praises Allah as "The Light of lights" 37 and Abū Bakr al-Wāsiṭī declares: "When you, in order to get to know God, look at the wonders of the creation... you can see the Light of his beauty in the leafs of the roses... and in the faces of beautiful men." 38 In the later Muslim theology the idea of "the light of Mohammed" occurs. This is a notion which will subsequently be explained. With regard to this item Sahl at-Tustari declares: "Allah has created 'the Light of Mohammed' from his Light and has formed it with his own hand." 39

In the preceding argument the significance of the light in its various qualities for the idea of God has been sufficiently explained. Therefore we can turn to answering the question of the function of the light in religious anthropology. In order to acquire a satisfactory answer one should consider that religious anthropology contains a number of themes. In this connection three subjects deserve to be treated, namely the nature of man, his path of salvation, and his future life. 40

As to the nature of man, one ought to distinguish two conceptions: the anthropology which teaches that man is akin to God and another one which contends that there is a big gulf yawning between God and

---

36 R. Otto, *Das Heilige*, 23rd-25th ed., 207.
37 J. Schacht, "Der Islam, mit Ausschluss des Qorʾān," *Religionsgeschichtliches Lesebuch* (1931), 16:118.
38 Ibid., 108.
39 Ibid., 97.
40 C. J. Bleeker, *The Nature and Destiny of Man in the Light of the Phenomenology of Religion* (The Sacred Bridge, 1963).

man. It is evident that people who adhere to the latter type of anthropology deny that man by his nature can participate in the divine light,
whilst the followers of the former anthropology assent to the thesis
in question. Examples of trust in man's capacity to take part in the
divine light can be met in Brahmanism, in Gnosticism, and in the
Hellenistic mystery religions. In the Vājasaneyi Samhitā, the *manas*,
the divine thinking of which man has part, is called "the only Light
of Lights." [41] In the famous conversation in which Yājñavalkya
teaches King Jamaka the nature of *ātman*, the sage says that after all
other lights have disappeared, man lives by the light of the *ātman*. [42]
One of the basic ideas of all gnostic systems is the thought that man
is the bearer of a spark of the divine light which has fallen into the
darkness, a spark which should return to the great "Treasure of Light,"
to "the Land of Light." [43] This idea that the soul has descended from
the kingdom of Light to the world of Darkness, matter, and sin, has
been elaborated by the gnostics in various ways. In the Mithras
mysteries, it is taught that man, who originates from the sphere of
heavenly light, during his descent to the earth passes seven spheres
and thereby receives from each planet a certain quality. [44] This is again
a modification of the theme of "die Himmelsreise der Seele" which
has fascinated the people of the later antiquity to such a high degree.

Thereby the subject of the path of salvation is introduced. Whatever
the view on the nature of man to which one may adhere, it is generally
accepted than man may acquire knowledge of the divine truth which
liberates. This knowledge of God is often appreciated as a spiritual
light. Sometimes man is deemed capable of receiving the light directly
in his heart. Mostly it must be conferred on him by a mediator, a
person who in the broader sense of the word fulfils the function of
a saviour. This first attitude is represented by all "spiritualists" (in the
sense of people whose sole guidance is the spirit), by many mystics,
and partly also by the Quakers insofar as they are guided by the Inward Light. As mediators of the spreading of the light of truth, first
the founders of well known religions can be mentioned. Thus the
Buddhists follow the path of Buddha. The decisive event in the life
of Buddha happened in the night when he got insight into the liberating truth, an event which is called an awakening or, more specifically,

---

[41] Geldner, *Vedismus*, 87.
[42] Ibid., 122-123.
[43] H. Leisegang, *Die Gnosis* (1955), 361 f.
[44] *Historia Religionum*, 1:514.

an enlightenment. In the Vinayapiṭṭaka-Mahāvagga, Buddha describes the middle path—between wordliness and ascetism—as the path "that opens the eye and clarifies the mind, and that leads to Rest, to Knowledge, to Enlightenment, to Nirvāna." [45] The so-called "light of Mohammed" has already been referred to. [46] Al-Hallāǧ deduces all prophecy from this light, namely in the utterance: "The Lights of Prophecy have come forth from his Light [of Mohammed]." [47] Under the *Shiᶜites* the idea circulates that since Adam, the divine Light was inherited by the prophets and subsequently by the descendants of Ali, an idea which caused some Ismāᶜīlīya-groups to consider the *imans* as the incarnations of the divinity and consequently as the bearers of the heavenly light. [48] Well known is the word of Jesus in the Gospel according to John 8:12: "I am the Light of the world: he that followeth me shall not walk in darkness, but shall have the light of life." The gnostics have placed this word in the frame of their doctrine of the descent of the light into the darkness. The Pistis Sophia teaches that, when Jesus left the first heavenly mystery in order to descend into the cosmos, he took out of the twelve saviours who dwelled in the Treasure of Light twelve forces which he put into the womb of earthly women. So the twelve apostles were born. [49] He himself left his garment of light behind during his descent, at the twenty-fourth mystery. He received it back on his return to the world of the aeons. Then he could say: "There is no measure for the Light which was upon me." [50] Elsewhere it is told that Jesus, after his resurrection, taught his disciples the deepest mysteries, namely, those regarding "the Treasure of Light." [51]

There are still other light-figures. To this category firstly belong the old Persian kings who possessed the said Xvarenah. [52] In ancient Iran these kings were sun-figures who spread so much brillance that ordinary mortals could not behold them. [53] According to the Zoroastrian belief, Xvarenah was bestowed upon them because they confessed the true religion, as was told of king Vištāspa. [54] But they

---

[45] M. Winternitz, "Der ältere Buddhismus," *Religionsgeschichtliches Lesebuch* (1929), 11:39.

[46] Chantepie, *Lehrbuch*, 2:674; *Historia Religionum*, 2:177.

[47] Schacht, *Der Islam*, 99.

[48] *Historia Religionum*, 2:138.

[49] Leisegang, *Die Gnosis*, 372.

[50] Ibid., 373 f.

[51] J. Doresse, *The Secret Books of the Egyptian Gnostics* (1960), 67.

[52] Lommel, *Die Yäšt's des Awesta*, 179.

[53] G. Widengren, *The Sacral Kingship of Iran* (*The Sacral Kingship* 1959), 247.

[54] Nyberg, *Die Religionen des alten Iran*, 273.

could also lose this gift, as happened to Jama, who by lying forfeited Xvarenah. [55] Also the saints are light-figures. The nimbus which on many pictures crowns their heads is a clumsy representation of the light of goodness and holiness which shone from them. Rembrandt possessed the wonderful capacity of painting the supernatural light which accompanied the holy persons from the Bible. The imagination of the faitful sees persons who dedicate themselves fully to God being set aglow with the fire and the light of piety. This is reported, for example, of the monks of the Eastern Orthodox Church. It is told about Abbas Joseph, that, when he raised his hands in prayer to heaven, his fingers became ten candle sticks. [56]

It is evident that chosing the path of salvation means that man wholeheartedly accepts and follows the light of truth. "He that followeth me shall not walk in darkness, but shall have the light of life," Jesus said. Both in the Old Testament and in the New Testament, primarily in the Psalms and in John, the idea recurs that God has granted His light to man and that the faitful should walk as "children of light." [57] It would be strange if this idea was confined to the Bible. Actually it is also to be found elsewhere. The gnostics, for example, did interpret the idea in their way. Two manuscripts in the collection of the Dead Sea Scrolls testify to it. The Manual of Discipline is addressed to "the children of light." Another book deals with the "War of the Sons of Light and the Sons of Darkness." [58] The Koran also voices the conviction that he that believes is led from the darkness into the light. [59]

As to the future of man, that is, his life after death, it is clear that the pious imagination has created different images of the land which lies beyond human knowledge. In this connection we shall pay attention only to those conceptions in which the light plays a part. They are easily to be found. Frequently the deceased is conceived of as a glorious being. In ancient Egypt one of the designations of the deceased was *achu* 'light-being'. [60] In the religion of Zarathustra the paradise

---

[55] Lommel, *Die Yäšt's des Awesta*, 179.

[56] N. von Arsenieuw, *Die Kirche des Morgenlandes* (1926), 71.

[57] See, e.g., Ps. 27:1; 43:3; 119:105; Prov. 6:23; 13:9; Isa. 9:1; 51:4; Mic. 7:8; Matt. 5:14; Luke 16:8; John 1:4; 3:19-20; 8:12; 12:46; Rom. 13:12; 2 Cor. 4:6; 1 Thes. 5:5; Rev. 22:5.

[58] T. H. Gaster, *The Dead Sea Scriptures in English Translation* (1956).

[59] *Sūra* 5:44, 46; 24:40; 33:43; 39:22; 42:52; 57:28; 65:11.

[60] Kristensen, *Het leven uit de dood*, 137; C. J. Bleeker, *Egyptian Festivals* (1967), 139 f.

of the faithful is the land of "the Lights that have no beginning." [61]
It was primarily the gnostics who implanted in the pious people,
fettered in the earthly world as they were, the longing for the realm
of light, to which they would return after death.

The third point in this argument that calls for attention is the cult.
Needless to say, the light played a big part in all kinds of cultic
performances. The cult is always a festive act. One can hardly think
of religious ceremonies at which no lights are kindled. These lights
are symbols of the truth to which religious people adhere and of the
joy which faith in God evokes. "The eternal light" which burns as
a token of God's presence both in the synagogue and in the Eastern
Orthodox and the Roman Catholic Churches deserves special attention. [62] Furthermore, it is interesting to know that Justinus Martyr
called baptism *phōtismos*. [63] As G. P. Wetter has shown, this term
should be understood in the context of the terminology and rites of
initiation of the mystery religions. At the ceremony of initiation into
these societies, which promised esoteric wisdom to their adepts, a play
of lights as a dramatization of the religious truth was likely resorted
to. [64] Well known is this element in the story of the initiation of
Lucius into the mysteries of Isis. After the initiation, Lucius is presented
to the Isis congregation arrayed as a sun-figure. [65]

Lastly, the question arises as to what function the light has in the
religious conception of the world. Two conceptions ought to be
distinguished. On the one hand, there is the idea that God has created
both the light and the darkness. In Isa. 45:7 God speaks: "I form
the light and create darkness." In the religion of Zarathustra it is also
taught that Ahura Mazda created both the light and the darkness. [66]
This means that God stands as a sovereign above light and darkness,
and also above good and evil. Notwithstanding the fear for the dark
and the loathing of sin which are a great puzzle, there sounds an optimistic tone in this conviction. On the other hand, one finds religious
people who are so impressed by the darkness in this world, so over-
whelmed by the evil, that they believe that there existed from the

---

[61] K. F. Geldner, "Die Zoroastitische Religion," *Religionsgeschichtliches Lesebuch*
(1926), 1:23, 43, 48.

[62] Fr. Heiler, *Erscheinungsformen und Wesen der Religion* (1961), 46.

[63] Wetter, *Skrifter utgifna af Kungl*, 1.

[64] K. H. E. de Jong, *De Oosters-Hellenistiscne Mysterien* (1949).

[65] *Historia Religionum*, 2:492; A. Harnack, *Lehrbuch der Dogmengeschichte*
(1909), 1:230.

[66] Geldner, *Die Zoroastische Religion*, 2.

beginning two kingdoms, one of Light and Good, and one of Darkness and Evil. The elements of these two realms have been mixed by a tragical event. Man bears the mark thereof. But the intention is that all particles of light shall be sifted from the darkness and be brought back to the kingdom of Light. This is the common conviction of the gnostics, [67] of the Mandaeans, [68] and of the Manichaeans. [69] No wonder that this world-conception strikes a pessimistic tone.

In conclusion it can be stated that light has a polyvalent religious significance.

---

[67] Doresse, *Secret Books*, 66 f.

[68] K. Rudolph, *Die Mandäer*, vol. 1; *Das Mandäerproblem* (1960); vol. 2; *Der Kult* (1961); *Theogonie, Kosmogonie und Anthropologie in den mandäischen Schriften* (1965).

[69] H. Puech, *Le Manichéisme, son fondateur, sa doctrine* (1949); G. Widengren, *Mani und der Manichäismus* (1961); L. J. R. Ort, *Mani: A Religio-Historical Description of His Personality* (1967).

SEXUALITY AND RELIGION
Some Reflections of a Student of the History of Religions

Love for a member of the other sex and belief in God undoubtedly
are the two forces which can recreate a miserable, selfish creature into
a happy and spiritually minded man or woman. They have much in
common. Love for the beloved and faith in God can fill the human
heart with estatic joy and raise the desire to be united with the object
of love or belief. This is the language which all love songs and all
religious hymns speak in an endless variety of flowery words. No
wonder that love and religion often go together. This means that not
only erotic feelings, but also sexuality (the basis of the relation between
man and woman who love each other and a prime driving force in
human life) is frequently associated with religion. This relationship
dates from the dark ages of prehistory.

Sexuality is a slippery subject for every author who does not possess expert knowledge on this field of research. Thanks to the prevailing so called "sex culture" everybody is informed nowadays about
the secrets of sexual intercourse between men and women. In former
times this was kept cautiously hidden. This general knowledge of
sexual affairs, often assembled out of sensual motives can be passed
over here in silence. Serious attention those works deserve which treat
the subject from a purely scientific angle, that is as a topic of biological,
anthropological, psychological, psychiatrical, sociological, ethical or
theological studies. It is evident that no scholar can boast of being
able to comprehend this endless literature. At any rate the student
of the history of religions does not need to possess an intimate knowledge of these aspects of the subject, because he is fully entitled to
tackle the question from his own point of view. His studies lead him
continually to religious concepts and acts which are utterances of types
of religion which make use of sexual-erotic symbolism. These facts
invite an inquiry into the relation of sexuality and religion and into
the significance of this connection. As we shall see the relationship
is both synthetic and antithetic. This is an entirely legitimate approach
to the subject.

In order to state the present case quite clearly it should be empha-
sized, that ordinary sexuality, both vulgar and secularized, is left out
of the picture. Only sexual evidence with a religious import deserves

attention. Neither are abnormal or perverse forms of sexuality of any value for this reseach. Obviously it is not easy to draw a clear distinction between people who enjoy sexuality for sheer lust or on immoral motives and others who express their religious conviction in sexual-erotic symbols and celebrate sexual rites. This latter variety is prompted by a type of religiosity which may look strange and unsanctionable but which none the less is genuine. Theoretically there is a great difference between the two attitudes. It is worthwhile to attempt to clarify this matter.

Before we can deal with the subject itself, we need make a few introductory remarks on the methods to be used in order to get the right grip on this extensive and complicate topic. These are listed as follows:

(1) In an article of a limited size one cannot claim to present an exhaustive treatment of this many-sided theme. The author must be brief in sketching the most characteristic festures. Nor can he offer a wealth of examples. This study will get the form of a torso, a figure whose beauty and significance I have pointed out previously. [1]

(2) The best method of treating the relevant facts is the so called phenomenological one. This method prescribes that the phenomena are ordered systematically and unbiasedly-without passing a judgment on the truth or the value of these facts-, so that the underlying motives and significance become manifest. In this case it means that the scholar puts aside his moral judgment and tries to understand the religious meaning even of unattractive phenomena. The guiding principle could be the approach which Ch. Wentinck made, in a study on "The Human Figure," to certain African figures when he said: "The African representation of the human figure is seldom sensual. If, as is often the case, the male or female genitals are exaggerated, the deformation is not with erotic intent but is solely a means of expressing vital force, creative power, or fertility."

(3) Much confusion in scientific reasoning is caused by the absence of a sharp definition of the notions which are used. Therefore it is useful to make a distinction between sexuality and eros, which are often linked together but also can be independent of each other and which have their own character and value. Sexuality comprises the processes of the sexual life of men and women. Erotic feelings blossom in the intercourse of the sexes even where no sexual union is desired or possible. Both the sexual urge and the erotic desire are paramount

<hr>

[1] C. J. Bleeker, *The Sacred Bridge*, 1963, p. VII, VIII.

important forces in human life. Throughout the world all people have known this. Apparently the Greek had a fine sense for this motive power which they attributed to Eros, a god who according to Hesiod was the first after Gaia to rise from the chaos. Eros is described in the translation of P. Mazon as "le plus beau parmi les dieux immortels, celui qui rompt les membres et qui, dans la poitrine de tout dieux comme de tout homme, dompte la cœur et le sage vouloir." [2] The Greeks also knew that Eros had his earthly, vulgar and his heavenly, spiritual features. In this last respect Eros is a prime incentive for human life, even having cosmic demensions. It is well-known that Plato has testified to this conception of Eros. A. Nygren's penetrating research makes clear how deep that eros-idea has influenced the Christian Gospel of agape. [3] In treating the problem of the relation of sexuality and religion it should never be forgotten, that it is eros that has come into play. And eros is akin to pietas.

(4) The present "sex culture" gives one the impression that all people are fully dominated by sexual desires. This is a fallacy. There are other passions, not to mention motivational norms and ideals, which take possession of persons. In the life of certain men and women, and at a certain age sex is only a peripheral affair. It might help then to define the function of sexuality and erotic feeling in man's spiritual life, especially as this relates to religion. In my opinion H. Scholz can lead the way here through his book "Religionsphilosophie" (1921). In the fourth paragraph of the first chapter he deals with "Die Religion in ihrem Verhältnis zu den übrigen Erscheinungen des menschlichen Geistesleben", i.e. metaphysics, ethics, the aesthetic evaluation and the erotic emotion. In regard to its category religion is related to metaphysics and ethics, because within these three domains the category of the absolute is normative. Yet the difference is more striking than the similarity. The experiences from which religion is born are of an "acosmistic" nature, while metaphysics is based on cosmic observations. In ethics the absolute is an idea, in religion it indicates a higher reality. The aesthetic emotions and the erotic feelings have their grade of emotionality in common with religious experiences. However the aesthetic evaluation takes no interest in its object. Religious claim is extremely interested in the reality of its object, namely the question that God exists. In this context it is of special interest that religious and erotic emotions are both characterized in that they

---

[2] Hésiode, *Théogonie*, texte établi et traduit par P. Mazon, 1951, p. 36.

[3] A. Nygren, *Den kristna kärlekstanken genom tiderna (Eros och Agape)* 1947.

overwhelm man by mysterious and boundless experiences. But the difference is that the erotic emotion is unique in the sence that it cannot be compared to anything else in the world, while the feelings roused by the encounter with the divine are absolutely incomparable. This penetrating analysis clarifies the problem in question in the following respects: a) it shows that sexuality and erotic feelings have a certain function, which is merely of relative importance, in human life, b) it makes clear that under certain circumstances a fusion of sexual-erotic and religious factors is the most natural arrangement in the world, c) and yet the two partners are fully different because religion always refers to a superhuman reality, outside the sphere within which eros plays its game.

(5) It is feasible to formulate the trend of the argument in a proleptic way. In the relation of religion and sexuality a number of "phases" can be distinguished. (Phase is not a chronological, but a typological notion; it indicates a certain structure, a type. [4]) Ideologically and partially also historically, the series starts with a phase in which sexuality and religion are closely connected. This is due to the fact that sexual symbolism is the natural expression of religious consciousness. In this sphere several types of erotic religiosity flourish. On the other hand, there have always been types of religion which indignantly rejected the alliance of sexuality and religion. Attention should be paid to these marked forms of anti-erotic religion. In our age sexuality has been secularized to such a degree that nobody seems to be shocked when what was once the most intimate part of human life is exposed to the eyes of a lustful or indifferent public. The student of the history of religion is no moralist. But he has no difficulty in quoting some striking examples of a harmonious combination of eros and pietas.

(6) From the above statement it follows that the following items should be dealt with subsequently: a) mythological concepts, b) sexual rites, c) erotic religiosity, d) anti-erotic religion, e) secularisation of sexuality, f) eros and pietas.

MYTHOLOGICAL CONCEPTS

A. Phallus and Vulva

In the first letter to the Corinthians St. Paul writes: "And those members of the body which we think to be less honourable, upon these we bestow more abundant honour, and our uncomely parts have

---

[4] H. Frick, *Vergleichende Religionswissenschaft*, 1928.

more abundant comeliness" (12:23). This rule has been followed by
all people of the world. Even the nations who go scantily dressed cover
their private parts. This custom has partly tended to surround the
genitals with a sphere of mysteriousness. But this is not the main
cause that from ancient times the phallus and the vulva have fascinated
religious imagination. People have sensed intuitively that sexual life
is a mystery, both alluring and dangerous [5] and that the genitals were
organs of creative life.

Furthermore it should be realized that the archaic people first met
the divine, the numinous, in cosmic occurrences and in the processes
of the physical, bodily life. Therefore only symbols, taken from natural
life could serve to express their knowledge of the deity. It is no wonder
that the phallus and the vulva were primeval signs of the divine,
generative life. G. van der Leeuw has rightly remarked: "Es ist
keineswegs eine seltsame Verirrung, sondern eigenste Menschlichkeit,
dass, fast überall in der Welt, eine der ältesten Formen unter denen
man Gott verehrt, der Phallus ist". Elsewhere he writes: "Das Heil
hat lange keine Gestalt. Der erste Heiland ist der Phallus, der die
Fruchtbarkeit bringt oder sein weibliches Gegenstück". [6] In the light
of these words one understands the mythological significance of the
phallus and the vulva.

Examples of the worship of the genitals can easily be selected:
from the religions of the illiterate people, of the nations of antiquity,
and of the Oriental world. In regard to the religious attention paid
to the vulva, one can think of the prehistoric figures of women with
a marked vulva or signs of pregnancy. [7] But the phallus prevails. In
ancient Egypt phalli are f.i. found in a chapel of Hathor, the goddess
of fertility and love at Deir el-Bahri. [8] Also well known is the Greek
herme, the emblem of Hermes, a raised stone, sometimes with a phallus, as the symbol of the god of resurrection. [9] Lucian reports that
two very great phalli, were standing in the entrance-hall of the temple
of the Syrian goddess. These phalli bore the following inscription:
"these phalli have I, Dionysos, devoted to my stepmother Hera". [10]

---

[5] Fr. Heiler, *Erscheinungsformen und Wesen der Religion*, 1961, p. 102.

[6] G. van der Leeuw, *Der Mensch und die Religion*, 1939, p. 157; *Phänomenologie
der Religion*, 1933, p. 84. See also: Marie Delcourt, *Hermaphrodite, Myths and Rites
of the bisexual Figure in classical Antiquity*, 1956, p. 52.

[7] C. J. Bleeker, *De moedergodin in de oudheid*, 1960, p. 9 sq.

[8] H. Bonnet, *Reallexikon der ägyptischen Religionsgeschichte*, 1952, p. 590.

[9] W. B. Kristensen, *Het leven uit de dood*, 1947, p. 247.

[10] C. Clemen, *Lukians Schrift über die Syrische Göttin*, 1938, p. 12.

In India even now one can still see examples of the *liṅga,* placed in the *yoni,* the sign of the womb. This emblem of the penis dates from remote times and is connected with Śiva, the god of fertility, creative life and also of destruction. [11] This is a curious instance of the worship of the phallus, because people have forgotten its original meaning and take it as a symbol of the *unio mystica* of mortal man with the deity or the Infinite.

Phallic gods occur in the religions of many peoples of antiquity. The image of Freyr in Uppsala had a great phallus. [12] The Shintoists in Japan worshipped a number of phallic gods. [13] Before the doors of the adyton of the temple of the Kabeiroi on Samothrace two phallic figures were standing. [14] Lucian reports that at the right side of the temple of the Syrian goddess a little man with a great phallus was placed. [15] In a hymn Osiris is addressed: "thou mummy with the long limb". [16] The dead Osiris is often represented ithyphallic. This picture expresses the paradoxical idea that divine life rises from death.

The best information about the significance of the symbol of the phallus can be drawn from the worship of the ancient Egyptian god Min. [17] The Egyptians have quite unhesitatingly portrayed Min as an ithyphallic god. In this shape he dominates the beautiful procession, to be admired in the temple of Medinet Habu. These pictures are a representation of his so called *pr.t,* his exodus, his appearance, namely as a god of creative, divine life. Min is not ashamed of his outward appearance. On the contrary, his phallus is called "his beauty" and the text states that "he is proud of his beauty". Diodorus Siculus gives a further explanation of the religious significance of the phallus by saying that it was worshipped as a holy limb because it ceated living beings: it is an organ of new life. [18]

B. *Androgynic Beings*

A number of gods are told to have an androgynic nature, for example the cow of heaven Aditi and Śiva in India, the Teutonic god Njord, the ancient Persian Zervan, the Australian Ungud-snake. The

[11] L. Renou et Jean Filliozat, *L'Inde Classique,* 1944, § 1061/2.

[12] Chantepie de la Saussaye, *Lehrbuch der Religionsgeschichte,* II, 1925, p. 588.

[13] Ibidem, I, p. 294, 337.

[14] B. Hemberg, *Die Kabyren,* 1950, p. 112.

[15] Clemen, *op. cit.,* p. 13.

[16] A. Erman, *Die Literatur der Aegypter,* 1923, p. 375.

[17] C. J. Bleeker, *Die Geburt eines Gottes, Eine Studie über den ägyptischen Gott Min und sein Fest,* 1956.

[18] Ibidem, p. 47.

moon too, which appears primarily in two shapes, is considered to be
bisexual. Ištar provides the most famous instance, because she, the
prototype of feminity, sometimes bears a beard. Her functions also
indicate this androgynic nature: she is the patrones both of love and
war.

Old myths tell that the primeval man was androgynic, obviously as
a replica of the gods. In this connection we may also mention the
wide-spread conception of the hermaprodite that is the human being
who combines the two sexes. Furthermore attention should also be
paid to transvestism, that is the custom (practised all over the world,
from ancient times till the present day) by which the sexes change
their clothes. It expresses the conviction that both sexes are incomplete
and therefore need to supplement each other. Moreover there is the
feeling that the border-line between the sexes cannot be sharply defined
and can flutuate. There are cases when men behave and dress like
women, and women like men. A famous instance of the last practice
are the Amazones. [19]

The religious significance of androgyny is the idea of the *coinci-
dentia oppositorum*, i.e. the conviction that both divine and human
beings can only reach fullness when they combine their respective
natures. Gods possess perfection by definition. No wonder that this
idea is often expressed by presenting them as being androgynic. Moreover this image includes the conception that a divine being does not
need a partner in order to create life, because it can fecundate itself
and cause a spontaneous birth. In addition man first becomes perfect
when he combines male and female natures. It is curious that three
modern Russian writers, i.e. Soloviev, Merezkowsky and Berdayev,
defend the thesis that the essence of the love between man and woman
is not the sexual act, but in stead the erotic feelings which liberate
each other from onesidedness and raise them to true androgyny. [20]

C. *The Virgin-Mother*

The prehistoric figures of women occur in two forms, i.e. as a
pregnant woman and as a slim young girl, a virgin. [21] It is likely that
they are amulets, but they can also be considered as forerunners of the

---

[19] J. Halley des Fontaines, *La notion d'androgynie dans quelques mythes et
quelques rites*, 1938; M. Eliade, *Traité d'histoire des religions*, 1949, p. 353 sq.;
Delcourt, *op. cit.*

[20] Ph. Sherrard, *The Meaning of Sexual Love in the Works of Three Russian
Writers* (Sobornost, Series 6, Number 8, Winter 1973).

[21] Bleeker, *De Moedergodin*, p. 9 sq.

Great Mother-Goddess who was so popular in antiquity. Sometimes this goddess is the virgin-mother: she is mother, because she bears new life, but she does not lose her virginity. She needs no partner to give birth. She creates by her own force and proves thereby that she is a divine being.

The Greek goddess Athene belongs to this category. Both her second name Pallas and her title Parthenos remove all doubt about her virginity. Though she is often in the company of men, as the advicer of warriors, she is not compelled by love for the other sex. Yet she was worshipped as mother in Elis. Erichthonios, usually called a son of Ge, was also alloted to her. [22] Though the accent falls on Athene's virginity, she was also conceived of as a motherly figure.

The same can be said of Anāhitā, the Persian goddess. In Yasjt 5 she is described as a beautiful young lady, with a tall, handsome figure and a noble, distinguished appearance. She is clothed in a expensive and richly embellished dress. Her full name Ardvī Sūrā Anāhitā means "the moist, strong, unstained." This name indicates that she is a river goddess, actually the patroness of the river which to day is called Syr-Darja. In this capacity she grants fertility. Later on prostitution was practised in her temples, which proves that she, though being a virgin, patronized sexual intercourse and procreation. But she has no partner. [23]

In my opinion, the Egyptian Hathor can also be mentioned in this connection. She is known as the goddess of fertility and love. Ihy and Harsomtus are ascribed to her as being her sons. It is generally thought that Horus of Edfu is her husband, with whom she celebrates the ἱερος γαμος during her visit to his city. In a painstaking argument I have been able to prove that this conception rests on very feeble points of support, to be euphemistic. Hathor is a too impressive, dynamic and independent a figure to be fettered in any mythological system or to be bound to a husband. In a way she is a virgin-mother. [24]

D. The lonely Creator-god

Apparently the people of antiquity have pondered over the question about how life could be created when the creator-god had no feminine partner and was lonely. In Egypt this was the lot of Atum after he

22 Kristensen, *op. cit.*, p. 188, 197 sq.; Bleeker, *De Medergodin*, p. 83 sq.
23 Bleeker, *De Moedergodin*, p. 75 sq.
24 C. J. Bleeker, *Hathor and Thoth, Two Key Figures of the Ancient Egyptian Religion*, 1973.

had climbed the hill which in the beginning arose from the primeval ocean according to a well known story of creation. In their pithy and unvarnished language the pyramid texts tell that he laid his phallus into his fist and impregnated himself. A later text explains this act in the following way: "He married with his fist, because there was not (yet) a female genetal." In this manner the air god Shu and his sister Tefnet were born, i.e. by masturbation, a sexual practise which to modern ethical standards is an immoral, or at least an unnatural habit. [25] The Indian creator god Prajapati and the Teutonic primeval giant Ymir are told to have fertilized themselves with their thumb. Apparently the thumb is an euphemism for the phallus. [26]

SEXUAL RITES

This is a very extensive subject. Sexuality and erotic feelings play such an important part in the life of humanity that it is no wonder, that they gave rise to the celebration of all kinds of sexual rites. Many games which men and women perform have an erotic vein and end in orgiastic festivals. In antiquity the so called phallophories, the phallic processions were a common phenomenon. Curious too is the custom of aischrology, the use of obscene language, during ritual performances. This is not a sign of perversity, but a means of finding a free attitude towards the fascinating and dangerous mystery of sex. [27] These examples may suffice to remind us that there is a pluriformity of sexual rites which is too numerous to be treated in this modest article. Let us limit ourselves to a few characteristic rituals.

A. ἱερος γαμος

Men and women who enjoy the bliss of sexual union have a remarkable experience: they reach the border of death and take part in a creative act. From this sensation one can understand that some people have thought that cosmic life was born from the union of huge, divine forces. Imagination prompted the idea, that heaven and earth were the actors in this process: heaven moistened and impregnated the earth and all of life came about. In Greece this divine couple bore the

---

[25] Pyr. 1248; A. de Buck, *Plaats en betekenis van Sjoe in de Egyptische theologie*, 1947; J. Zandee, *Sargtexte, Spruch 75* (Z. A. Z., 97. Band, erstes und zweites Heft, 1971).

[26] H. Baumann, *Das doppelte Geschlecht*, 1955, p. 224.

[27] B. Malinowski, *The Sexual Life of Savages*, 1929, p. 236 sq.; Chantepie, *op. cit.*, II, p. 440; Her. II: 48; K. Kerényi, *Eleusis, de heiligste mysterien van Griekenland*, 1960, p. 66 (42).

names of Zeus and Hera. Their wedding was the famous mythological prototype. [28] Less known, but at least as interesting is the story
of the union of the first Japanese divine couple, i.e. Izanagi (the
inviting man) and Izanmi (the inviting woman). After they have
created the first island of the Japanese archipelago, they married there.
The consumation of their wedlock is described in veiled language as
a coitus in which, after having discovered their incompleteness they
find their fulfilment by combining their genetals. The other islands of
the archipelago, the goddess Amaterasu, the storm god Susanowo and
the fire-god are born from this union of love. [29]

As myth and rite often go together, it goes without saying that
religious people have enacted a cultic ἱερος γαμος in order to actualize
the benefical results of the mythological prototype. Outside the cult
this act took place where people lived from agriculture and particularly
in times of sowing and harvesting. This telling symbolism compared
the phallus to the plough and the woman to the fertile field. [30] The
most famous example of the celebration of the cultic ἱερος γαμος
can be fetched from ancient Mesopotamia. The partners are Inanna
or Ištar and Tammuz or a kindred god. Apparently the partners could
change: they could be the god and the goddess, the goddess and the
priest king, or the god and the priestess. In all these cases the king and
the priestess or the queen or another lady were the real actors. The
drama went on as follows: at the fixed time the bridegroom came to the
temple where the bride awaited him in her festival dress. After a
series of ceremonies the couple retired to the bride chamber where the
rite was fulfilled. As soon as it was known that the holy rite had taken
place, joy ran high and people celebrated exuberantly. This was necessary to safeguard prosperity. [31]

B. Ritual Prostitution

Prostitution has been called the world's oldest occupation. However
this may be, the practise seems to be ineradicable. An analysis of the
factors which keep prostitution alive is neither feasible nor necessary
within the scope of this article. We can merely focus attention on
ritual prostitution.

---

[28] M. P. Nilsson, *Die Religion der Griechen* (Religionsgeschichtliches Lesebuch,
4, 1927), p. 24/5.

[29] E. Lehmann und H. Haas, *Textbuch der Religionsgeschichte*, 1922, p. 44.

[30] Chantepie, *op. cit.*, I, p. 41; Eliade, *op. cit.*, p. 224/5, 303.

[31] S. N. Kramer, *The Sacred Marriage Rite in Ancient Sumer*, 1969; Bleeker, *De
Moedergodin*, p. 41 sq.

In antiquity women served in the temples in a double function: some were chaste priestesses—the Vestals are the famous examples—, and others earned their living as sacral prostitutes (called hierodoules or hetaeres). [32] Reliable historians such as Strabo, Herodotus and Lucian relate that women gave themselves to strangers who visited the temple as a sacrifice of their virginity in the service of the goddess of love. In this case these women lent themselves to this practice only once, and it was not considered as something shameful, but as a heavy tribute to the goddess. [33] Neither were hierodoules and hetaeres despised. In the society of the Barbelo gnostici men and women celebrated sexual union not to impregnate the women, but in order to acquire salvation: they made an offering of sperma and menstruation blood. [34]

These few instances may suffice in drawing up a picture of this strange ritual. Naturally, a modern man has the suspicion that sexual desires have their fling in this practice under a religious cover. Yet undeniable evidence makes clear that the people of antiquity—and also of the Orient—conceived of this custom as a sacrifice to the goddess of fertility and love, and therefore kept it in honour. [35]

C. Sacral Nudity

Sacral nudity should be sharply distinguished from the nude which the artist portrays, and from the nudity which people nowadys propagate, from a variety of motivations. Sacral nudity is situated in another dimension.

Let me start by giving a few examples. The first is the so called *ritus paganus*, which means that people, primarily women, circumambulate the fields in order to avert evil forces, destroy the weed and further fertility. [36] The meaning of this rite is clear: the nude body radiates force, which is exerted for the benefit of agricultural work. It therefore happens that people sow and harvest in the nude. [37] The ancient Germans took the oath in a nude state in order to enforce this solemn act. [38] Furthermore priests and prophets often go naked when

---

[32] W. B. Kristensen, *The Meaning of Religion*, 1960, p. 323; Heiler, *op. cit.*, p. 412 sq.

[33] Chantepie, *op. cit.*, II, p. 225; Her. I; 199; Clemen, *op. cit.*, p. 8.

[34] H. Leisegang, *Die Gnosis*, 1955, p. 187 sq.

[35] Van der Leeuw, *Phänomenologie*, p. 212 sq; Heiler, *op. cit.,* p. 243 sq.; W. Schubart, *Erotiek en godsdienst*, 1941.

[36] Van der Leeuw, *op. cit.*, p. 309; Nilsson, *op. cit.*, p. 7.

[37] Eliade, *op. cit.*, p. 287 sq.

[38] Van der Leeuw, *op. cit.*, p. 387.

serving the deity or when preaching. [39] Obviously they take off their clothes because they have left the human sphere and have come into contact with the numinous. There is also an ascetic motive for nudity. The ascetic wants to subdue his passions and to liberate himself from slavery to earthly goods. He wishes to be absolutely free and to draw his value not from what he possesses but from the strength of his personality. Under some circumstances this may demand that he go nude. Thus Mahāvira, the founder of Jainism took off his clothes at the moment when he decided to tread the path of absolute asceticism. His example was followed by the group of his followers who are called Digambaras = "they who are clothed by the air," a custom which seems to have dropped in disuse.

There are various motives for sacral nudity. However this is never a sign of exhibitionism, but a rite which will enhance the spiritual force of those who put off their garment.

EROTIC RELIGIOSITY

There are various forms of erotic religiosity of which only a few types can be treated.

In ancient China the art of making love was practised to perfection. It is evident that considerate prostitution occurred, though mostly with a certain elegance, and that there was no lack of pornographic books. In this connection only the form of love making is interesting, which was consummated within the framework of the typical Chinese conception that the interplay of Yang and Yin dominates all cosmic processes and that man can only be virtuous and happy by being in tune with Tau the worldorder. In the present case this means that coitus should increase the vitality of both men and women. The man should not lose his sperma, but this should rise to his head and strengthen his vital force. Thus the sexual union became a ritual act. Consequently the thirty main positions for consumating the sexual union—which also have become known in the West, however without their spiritual background—had to function in the religious context and bore poetical names which express this sense. [40]

In India analogous practices are to be found, especially among the adherents of Tantrism and Śāktism. Also here the *ars amandi* was practised on different levels and even taught by refined prescriptions. It really was an art, and the women who devoted themselves to this

---

[39] Ibidem; H. Ringgren, *Religions of the Ancient Near East*, 1973, p. 25.
[40] R. H. van Gulik, *Sexual Life in Ancient China*, 1961.

business had to be cultured. [41] Leaving these secular customs aside we can concentrate our attention on the secret ritual of Śāktism, which was based on the conviction that the sexual union was the main road to salvation. [42] In order to understand this idea one should take notice of the religious presuppositions: first the followers of Śāktism were convinced that body and mind were manifestations of the Power (Śakti) and that nothing in natural functions is low or impure; second they held a kind of Antinomianism—also well known in the Christian West—which gave them the assurance that no enlightened soul could sin. So they worshipped the divinity with five elements: wine, meat, fish, grain and women, unusual elements for a sacrifice in India. The ritual sexual union could be performed with different partners: preferably with one's own wife. But also with another woman (especially if one was unmarried or his wife was incompetent) "as a wife in religion," under the guidance of the guru. It also happened that a partner was chosen by lot from a group of fifty women. At any rate the union was realized as an imitation of the mythological protype: the eternal embrace of the god and his Śakti, an act which has been many times represented by artists, because it was the symbol of the *unio mystica* which one can reach by the liberating insight. [43] It should be added that some adherents of Śāktism deemed that the coitus was superfluous, as it could be enacted spiritually, i.e. by meditation. In a Tantra it is said: "What need do I have of any woman. I have an Inner Woman within myself." [44]

A word should also be said about the so called bride mysticism of some mysticae, primarily from the Middle Ages. [45] These women had acquired the status of brides of Christ. They therefore described the ecstatic experiences of their love for the Lord in symbols taken from the intercourse between loving men and women. Sometimes the utterances of the love for Christ and God have an openly sexual tinge. Mechtild from Magdeburg declares: "Je mehr seine Lust wächst, je enger er sie umschliesst, um so grösser wird das Glück der Braut. Je inniger die Umhalsung, um so süsser schmeckt das Mundküssen". Christine Ebner dreamed that she became pregnant from the Lord and

[41] S. K. De, *Ancient Indian Erotics and erotic Literature*, 1959.

[42] Sir John Woodroffe, *Śakti and Śākta, Essays and Addresses on the Śākta Tantraśāstra*, 1959, p. 565 sq.; J. Gonda, *Die Religionen Indiens*, II, 1963, p. 26 sq.

[43] F. Sierksma, *Tibet's Terrifying Deities*, 1966; H. Hoffmann, *Die Religionen Tibets*, 1956.

[44] Van Gulik, *op. cit.*, p. 344/5.

[45] M. Buber, *Ekstatische Konfessionen*, 1909.

that she gave birth to a child. In other cases the language is clearly symbolic. Sofia from Klingnau dreamt that her soul was a beautiful light which became one with the supreme light of God: "Und in dieser Liebeseinung bekam meine Seele von Gott die Gewissheit, das mir alle meine Sünden vollkommen vergeben worden seien." No justice can be done to the religious value of this bride mysticism by explaining it as an outcome of subdued sexual and erotic passions. Let us not forget that for centuries both Jewish and Christian theologians have given a spiritual exgesis to the Song of Solomon, a collection of love songs, treating it as an expression of love between the soul and God. It is quite natural that religious people should chose metaphors from the intercourse between loving men and women, to give utterance to their ardent love for God, under the condition that the symbolic value of such expressions is apparent.

ANTI-EROTIC RELIGION

Treatises on sex and also on sexuality and religion can make one believe that people are secretly obsessed by sexual desires. This surely is a wrong image of mankind. For some types of men and women sex means very little. But it is even more important that throughout the ages religious people have strongly rejected blending sexuality and erotic feelings with religion. When treating the subject in question one should be faitful to the norm of scholarly objectivity by underlining the significance of anti-erotic religion. This phenomenon occurs in different shades.

In antiquity sexual intercourse was forbidden in some temples and could not be enjoyed before initiation into the mysteries. [46] Everybody who wanted to meet the deity was obliged to abstain from sexual passions. Priestesses and prophetesses who lived in the neighbourhood of the deity had to guard their virginity. [47] Celibacy has always been considered as a high ideal, even as a condition for those people who wanted to devote themselves fully to God. It is well known that one of the three vows which those Christian monks and nuns who leave the world have to make is that of chastity.

There are types of religion which for various motives are decidedly anti-erotic. Classical Hinduism preached a salvation which freed one from the chain of rebirths, and thereby recommended control of carnal desire. This excluded sexual relations. Sanskrit literature states again

---

[46] Nilsson, *op. cit.*, p. 4/5; Heiler, *op. cit.*, p. 198.
[47] Heiler, *op. cit.*, p. 413 sq.

and again that suppression of sexual desire is a *condition sine qua non* for reaching salvation. [48] Religions with an ascetic strain like Jainism and Buddhism have taken this principle as one of the principal tenets of their doctrine. It is explicitly stated that Mahāvira, the founder of Jainism, did not enjoy sexual relations. The fourth great vow which a monk had to make runs as follows: "I abstain from all sexual acts, in regard to heavenly, human and animal beings." [49] On the question asked by Ānanda about how the monks should behave towards women Buddha answered that they should neither look at them nor speak to them. Only reluctantly Buddha gave his permisson for the founding of an order of nuns to whom he gave an instruction in eight strict points. [50] The attitude of Judaism, Christianity and Islam in this matter is more complicated. On the one hand these religions fully allow sexual intercourse within a legitimate marriage, meanwhile condemning all kinds of sexual transgressions. The Old Testament is very explicite, both in the Law, the Thorah and in the preaching of the prophets in branding various types of objectionable sexual behaviour. [51] It should be added that modern sexual ethics has made this attitude problematic, to say the least. However this may be there is a danger to which these religions are highly sensitive, i.e. the eroticisation of the conception of God. They do not tolerate the least sexual stain on the purely spiritual image of God. This is quite understandable, for these religions are founded on a knowledge of God which is not derived from cosmic phenomena, to which also sexuality belongs, but from the revelation of a God who transcends the world.

SECULARISATION OF SEXUALITY

In another context it would be worthwhile to inquire into the cause of this process. Here we can only make a few remarks. We have to state the fact that the veil of mystery which has covered the sexual life for a long time is now removed. In books, illustrations, films and the theatre different forms of sexual relationship are openly exposed. There is no longer any secret. And the connection between this and religion lies outside the mental horizon of the general public. What are the causes of this profanisation of sexuality? In my opinion the

---

[48] Van Gulik, *op. cit.*, p. 348/9.

[49] W. Schubring, *Die Jainas* (Religionsgeschichtliches Lesebuch, 7, 1927), p. 4, 22.

[50] M. Winternitz, *Der ältere Buddhismus* (Religionsgeschichtliches Lesebuch, 11, 1929), p. 142-5.

[51] J. Pedersen, *Israel, its Life and Culture*, I-II, 1946, p. 415, 485, 549, III-IV, 1947, p. 166, 173, 468, 471, 537, 592, 607, 640.

sexual enlightenment of young and older people, useful in itself, is not the main cause. The real driving factor is a dominant anthropology, i.e. a conception of the nature of man in which he is considered to be a creature which obeys and should obey his passions, under pain of becoming frustated and fostering psychopathological neuroses. Man must indulge his sexual desires in the same way as he must quench his thirst and still his hunger. This is a radically different conception than the conviction of so many people in previous centuries that the sexual union is a holy act.

EROS AND PIETAS

The student of the history of religions passes no judgement on the moral or metaphysical quality of the religious phenomena. He tries to describe and to order them unbiasedly and to understand their significance. Concerning a subject that has been discussed in the previous pages he can try to sketch the different "phases", when this notion is taken in the meaning, stated in the beginning of this argument. However there is one "phase" left. It is evident that the combination of sexuality and religion which the people of antiquity and of the Orient performed possesses historic value only. Is there an enduring relation between Eros and Pietas? The history of religions is able to produce evidence which solves the question. Let me quote three instances.

In ancient Egypt people in love turned to Hathor the goddess of fertility and love to get the fulfilment of their dearest wish. Lovers who found each other were convinced that Hathor had granted them this happiness. In a hymn devoted to Hathor the poet exclaims:

"I prayed to her (Hathor) and she heard my prayer
She destined my mistress (beloved) for me" [52]

The dutch poet J. H. Eekhout sings:

"Love, I have told my beloved about you,
how death and life in you, Love, are one,
and that no death, no life can quench
the fire, in which, Love, we are united with you." [53]

Finally the resemblance of God's love and the love between husband and wife is beautifully formulated in one of the chorusses of the dutch poet Vondel in his drama "Gysbrecht van Aemstel":

[52] C. J. Bleeker, *Der religiöse Gehalt einiger Hathor-Lieder* (Z. Ä. S., 99. Band, zweites Heft, 1973, p. 82 sq.).
[53] J. H. Eekhout, *Het andere Koningschap.*

"Where can more sincere fidelity
than between husband and wife
on earth ever be found. ...
No love resembles more God's love
nor is so great." [54]

---

[54] *Vondel, volledige dichtwerken en oorspronkelijk proza,* verzorgd en ingeleid
door A. Verwey, 1937, p. 200.

EGIL SKALLAGRIMSSON: EIN ISLÄNDISCHER HIOB

Die isländischen Geschlechter-Sagas bilden eine fesselnde Lektüre. Sie beschreiben das Leben der ersten Kolonisten auf dieser Insel, die berühmt ist wegen ihrer Geysire, ihrer Lavafelder und ihrer Eiskappen.

Irische Mönche, die in ihrer Weltflucht die Einsamkeit des Meeres suchten, entdeckten Island am Ende des achten Jahrhunderts. Im neunten Jahrhundert, der Wikingerzeit, besuchten einzelne Wikinger die Insel für kürzere oder längere Zeit. Der erste Kolonist war Ingolfr Arnarsson, der sich 870 an der Stelle ansiedelte, wo heute die Hauptstad Reykjavik liegt. In der darauf folgenden Kolonisationsperiode (870-1030) trafen in kurzer Zeit viele tausend Wikinger ein, meistens Norweger, die "Land-nahmen", wie der term.techn. lautet, ein Prozess, der im "Landnámabók" beschrieben wird. Die Geschehnisse, von denen die Familiensagas erzähhlen, spielen in dieser Periode.

Im Hinblick auf die Knappheit des biographischen Materials in den Quellen zur Kenntnis der Religionen der Welt und nicht zuletzt der Religion der Germanen, sind diese Sagas merkwürdige Schriften. Sie enthalten keine Geschichten in der Art von Märchen und sind auch keine Chroniken, die trockene Tatsachen berichten, sondern geben einen Schatz an Information über die Geographie, Kultur und das Rechtswesen aus diesen Tagen. Ihre Anziehungskraft besteht besonders in der Schilderung von einer Anzahl Männer und Frauen besonderen Formats, Persönlichkeiten, behaftet mit Tugenden und Untugenden, die mit Besessenheit leben, sich von Leidenschaft oder Ehrgefühl leiten lassen zu Taten von beispielloser Grausamkeit oder eigenartigem Heldenmut, Menschen, die sich vor keiner Gefahr fürchten und die in trotziger Verteidigung untergehen, wenn das Schicksal es so beschlossen hat. Nicht nur Männer, sondern auch Frauen treten vor die Rampe. In der Saga von den Laxdalingers spielt Gudrun, die Tochter Osvivrs, eine bedeutende Rolle: eine faszinierende Frau, gekennzeichnet durch starken "sex-appeal". Sie war hübsch, intelligent und geistreich und wusste sich stilvoll und vornehm zu kleiden, so dass die Gewänder anderer Frauen neben ihren als "kindlicher Flitter" erschienen. Sie hatte vier seltsame Träume, die von Gest Oddleivsson ausgelegt wurden als Prophezeiungen über vier Männer, die sie hintereinander besitzen und wieder verlieren sollte. Eine Frau also, die ein bewegtes Eheleben hatte. Ein ganz anderer Typ ist Aud, Gisle Surssons treue, starke Frau, die seine Verbannung als Ausgestossene und wie ein gehetztes Tier vierzehn Jahre teilte, bis Gisle in einem letzten Verteidigungskampf gegen einen übermächtigen Feind den Heldentod erlitt.

Die Gestalt, die den grössten Eindruck erweckt, aber auch die komplizierteste in dieser Gesellschaft von kraftstrotzenden Männern und Frauen ist, ist Egil Skallagrimsson. Er war hässlich wie die Nacht, ein Umstand, dessen er sich, wie man erzählt, voll bewusst war. Er war aber ausgestattet mit einer besonderen Geisteskraft. Eine angenehme Persönlichkeit war er indess nicht. G. Turville-Petre charakterisiert ihn folgendermassen: "Egil is not a pleasing person, but no poet is described so realistically as he. He was avaricious, often unscrupulous and ill mannered, although capable of deep affection. Poetry had been the strongest of his interests even since his childhood, and in times of adversity it was his solace." [1]

In dieser Charakteristik fallen zwei Züge direkt ins Auge. Egil war einerseits ein unverfälschter Wiking, ein Mann, der nie längere Zeit Ruhe auf seinem Hof fand, sondern der immer wieder auszog nach Norwegen, Russland, Schweden, Dänemark und England, manchnal auf Abenteuer um zu plündern, manchmal auch, um sich zu rächen oder um einen Prozess auszufechten. Andererseits war er ein virtuoser Dichter. Die Saga erzählt, dass er schon im Alter von drei Jahren sein erstes kurzes Gedicht verfasste, mit dem er viel Ehre einlegte. In seinem späteren Leben besiegelte er so manches wichtige Ereignis mit einem kernigen Gedicht, bisweilen auch in der Form eines Spottverses oder einer magischen Beschwörung. Als Dichter stand er nicht allein. Island wies verschiedene Skalden auf, die oft in Verbindung standen mit dem Hof eines Königs. Berühmt waren Hallfred und Sighvat. Aber Egil übertraf alle. Seine Poesie ist das schönste Spezimen der altisländischen Dichtkunst, die meistens kurzzeilige Verse anwendet mit einer komplizierten Satzkonstruktion und "kenningar", das heisst poetischen Umschreibungen, die die Aussagekraft erhöhen. Die Isländer haben von altersher bis heute eine ausgesprochen literarische Begabung an den Tag gelegt. Noch immer blühen auf Island die Beredsamkeit und die Kunst der Poesie. Das isländische Volk hält seine literarische Vergangenheit in Ehren. Während meines Aufenthaltes in Reykjavik im Jahr 1949 konnte

---

[1] G. Turville-Petre, *Origins of Icelandic Literature*, 1933, 230.

ich ein Exemplar der Edda in der Ursprache in einem Strassenkiosk kaufen. Es wird wenig Länder geben, in denen die Klassiker des jeweiligen Volkes zwischen der Tageslektüre so zum Verkauf angeboten werden.

Die Saga von Egil Skallagrimsson lässt begreifen, warum sein Geschlecht sich auf dem unwirtlichen Island niederliess. Beinahe ein Drittel der Saga ist der Vorgeschichte in Norwegen gewidmet und führt die Vorfahren Egils auf. Sie bildeten ein stolzes und freiheitsliebendes Geschlecht, das sich in seiner Mehrheit gegen den Versuch König Harald Hårfagre (Schönhaar), Norwegen zu einem Einheitsreich, zu machen, wehrte. Der älteste Sohn des alten Kvällulv, Thorolf, trat in des Königs Dienst. Aber Skallagrim, Egils Vater, beugte sich nicht, und er wich nach Island aus.

Als Mann in vorgerücktem Alter wurde Egil von einem Schlag getroffen, der ihn tief verletzte: sein geliebter Sohn Bodvar ertrank bei seiner Rückkehr vom Marktflecken. Dieser Verlust brachte Egil völlig aus dem Gleichgewicht und machte ihn zu einem beklagenswerten Menschen, der ähnlich dem biblischen Hiob wird.

Bevor ich nun den Verlauf der Dinge beschreibe und eine Antwort suchen will auf die Frage, in welcher Hinsicht Egil mit Hiob verglichen werden kann, muss erst das Problem der Zuverlässigkeit der isländischen Sagas, vor allem der in ihnen enthaltenen Mitteilungen über die Religion der alten Isländer geprüft werden. Das Christentum wurde im Jahr 1000 auf Beschluss des Althings, des isländischen Parlamentes, eingeführt. Die Sagas sind literarisch fixiert im 13. Jahrhundert. So erhebt sich also die Frage: in wie weit sind sie historisch zuverlässig, besonders in Bezug auf das Bild des religiösen Lebens der Isländer im 9. Jahrhundert? Im Hinblick darauf gibt es zwei Auffassungen: Nach der ersten Theorie sind die Sagas im 10., 11. Jahrhundert durch "Sagnamenn" geschaffen, mündlich überliefert und im 13. Jahrhundert aufgezeichnet worden. Nach der zweiten Ansicht sind sie literarische Produkte von Schriftstellern aus dem 12.-14. Jahrhundert. Wie dem auch sei, die Sagas weisen sich deutlich als mündliche Familientraditionen aus und müssen daher eine bestimmte Zuverlässigkeit besitzen. [2] In religiöser Hinsicht aber enttäuschen sie etwas. Es fällt auf, dass wohl Kultplätze genannt und Opfer berichtet werden, dass der Schicksalsglaube eine grosse Rolle spielt, dass viele übernatürliche Geschehnisse erzählt werden, dass ferner von Spuk,

---

[2] H. Ljungberg, *Die nordische Religion und das Christentum*, 1940, S. 35 ff.

Zauberei, Visionen, Prophezeiungen und Träumen die Rede ist, aber dass die bekannten grossen Götter der Germanen kaum eine Rolle zu spielen scheinen. Diese Tatsache lässt sich daraus erklären, dass man nach der Einführung des Christentums die grossen Götter als Konkurrenten des Christus nicht in den Sagas dulden konnte, aber keine Schwierigkeit darin sah, die Beschreibungen von Äusserungen des niederen Volksglaubens in diesen Erzählungen unangetastet zu lassen. [3] Das Bild der vorchristlichen isländischen Religion würde also richtig, aber unvollständig sein. Es ist noch eine andere Erklärung denkbar. In einem bemerkenswerten Artikel hat M. Draak darauf hingewiesen, dass Auswanderung über das Meer stets grosse Veränderung im Glauben der Auswanderer hervorruft. [4] Sie sind ja religiös entwurzelt. In diesem Fall wären die Vorstellungen von den Göttergestalten der Vorfahren im Bewusstsein der isländischen Kolonisten verwischt worden, wodurch der Akzent sich verlagerte auf das Bewusstsein von etwas Übernatürlichem: das unentrinnbare Schicksal, Visionen, Geistererscheinungen. Es scheint in der Tat so zu sein, dass die Isländer noch heutzutage empfänglich sind für mystische Erlebnisse und Botschaften aus einer anderen Sphäre.

Was nun Egil angeht, der von 901-983 gelebt haben soll, so befinden wir uns in einer günstigen Lage. Obwohl er in England mit dem Zeichen des Kreuzes geweiht war (prímsignaðr), so dass er das Recht besass, gottesdienstlichen Handlungen beizuwohnen, und insofern mit dem Christentum vertraut gewesen sein muss, ist er doch in seinem Herzen ganz und gar Heide. Ausserdem kann man sein religiöse Einstellung kennenlernen aus dem grossen Gedicht, das er nach Bodvars Tod schuf. Dies geschah im Still der alten Skaldenpoesie, an der naturgemäss nichts verändert werden konnte. Weil Odin in diesem Lied eine grosse Rolle spielt, ist es ein einzigartiges Zeugnis von der Bedeutung, die dieser Gott für einen Mann wie Egil besass. Interessant ist ferner, dass sowohl dieses Lied, als auch die einleitende Erzählung dazu, die Gemütsbewegungen Egils ganz aufdecken, sodass hier ein Mensch in seiner seelischen Not lebensgross vor uns steht. Die Frage, ob der hier gezeichnete Egil historisch echt genannt werden darf, ist völlig irrelevant. Sie ist ebenso unwichtig wie die Frage, ob der Held des babylonischen Gilgamesch-Epos wirklich so gewesen ist, wie er beschrieben wird. Was uns religionswissenschaftlich interessiert, ist diese Hiobsgestalt.

---

[3] *Op. cit.*, S. 47 ff.
[4] Maartje Draak, "Migration over Sea" (*Numen*, Vol. IX, 1962, Seite 81-98).

Bodvar und fünf Knechte Egils ertranken in einem schweren Sturm auf ihrer Heimkehr vom Marktflecken. Am folgenden Tag wurden ihre Leichen angespült. Sobald Egil die Hiobsnachricht erhalten hatte, ging er aus, um Bodvars Leiche zu suchen. Als er sie gefunden hatte, legte er sie vor sich auf sein Pferd und ritt mit ihr zum Grab von Skallagrim, das er öffnen liess und worin er Bodvar beisetzte. Danach kehrte er nach Borg, seinem Wohnsitz, zurück, legte sich völlig angekleidet auf seine Schlafstätte, verschloss die Türe und weigerte sich, mit jemandem zu sprechen und Nahrung zu sich zu nehmen. Am dritten Tag sandte seine besorgte Frau Asgerd einen Eilboten zu ihrer Tochter Torgerd. Als diese hörte, was zuhause los war, machte sie sich unverzüglich auf und gelangte nach Borg, nachdem sie die ganze Nacht durchgeritten war. Auf die Frage ihrer Mutter, ob sie denn zu Abend gegessen habe, antwortete sie mit lauter Stimme: "Ich habe keine Mahlzeit genossen, und ich will auch keine haben, bevor ich bei Freyja (hier die Göttin der Toten) bin. Nach meinem Vater und nach meinem Bruder will ich nicht länger leben." Sie ging zum Schlafgemach und rief: "Vater, öffne die Türe, ich will, dass wir zusammen denselben Weg gehen." Egil schob den Riegel zurück, und Torgerd legte sich in das andere Bett, das im Raum stand. Egil war hocherfreut, dass sie ihm folgen wollte. Nach einem Augenblick fragte er: "Worauf kaust Du?" Sie antwortete, es sei Tang, und sie wolle dadurch den Tod beschleunigen. Auf seine Bitte hin gab sie auch ihm davon. Danach wurde sie durstig und bat um Wasser zum Trinken. Auch Egil nahm einen grossen Schluck. Dann sagte Torgerd: "Nun haben sie uns betrogen, dies war Milch." Egil wurde so zornig, dass er ein Stück vom Rand des Trinkbechers abbiss. Beide erkannten nun, dass ihre Absicht missglückt war. Torgerd überredete ihren Vater, am Leben zu bleiben und einen Totengesang auf Bodvar zu dichten. [5] So entstand einer der schönsten altisländischen Gesänge, dem Egil den Namen Sonatorrek gab, durch A. G. van Hamel übertragen unter dem Titel: "De zware zonenwraak" (Die schwere Rache für den Sohn) und durch Turville mit der Überschrift: "The irreparable Loss of his Sons".

Das Gedicht besteht aus 25 Strophen, von denen eine in unordnung geraten ist. Alles spricht dafür, dass man van Hamel folgen sollte

---

[5] Egils Saga Skalla Grimssonar, *Sigurdur Nordal*, Izlenzk Fornit II Bind, 1933; *Isländska Sagor, översatta och utgivna av Hjalmar Alving* 1938; *Die Geschichte vom Skalden Egil*, übertragen von Felix Nieder, Thule, Band 3, 1963.

bei seiner Auffassung von der Struktur des Sonatorrek. [6] Der Gang
des Gedichtes wird durchsichtig, wenn man es in drei Gruppen von
zweimal zehn und einmal fünf Strophen aufteilt. Die beiden Gruppen
von je zehn Strophen sind demselben Thema geweiht, d. h. Egils
ausweglosem Kummer. Die letzten fünf Strophen bringen den Um-
schwung: Egil erfasst, dass Odin ihn beschenkt hat mit der hohen
Gabe der Dichtkunst, die ihn fähig macht, seine Not zu besingen,
sodass er danach ruhig dem Tod entgegen sehen kann.

Um zu begreifen, aus welcher Stimmung heraus Egil dieses Gedicht schuf, muss man sich in seine religiöse Gedankenwelt vertiefen.
Wie bei allen Germanen, so bestand auch bei den Isländern eine
starke Familienbindung. Ein Mord an einem Familienglied bedeutete einen Einbruch in das Leben, in das Glück und die Ehre des
Clans, Werte die nur dann wieder hergestellt werden konnten, indem
man der Familie des Mörders eine ähnliche Schade erleiden liess. In
Egils Tagen bestanden recht primitive rechtliche Gesetze, nach denen
Genugtuung nach einem Mord geleistet werden musste. Bisweilen
ergab sich eine Möglichkeit, durch Vergütung in Geld zu einem
Vergleich zu kommen. Primär aber war in einem solchen Fall, in
dem Egil sich befand, Rache Pflicht und Recht des Isländers. Egil
stand jedoch machtlos da: kein Mensch, sondern der Meeresgott
Aegir und seine Gemahlin Ran hatten ihn seines Sohnes beraubt. An
diesen übermenschlichen Wesen konnte er keine Rache üben. Wohl
aber konnte er sie in seinem Lied anklagen. Dazu fasste er Mut, weil
er Odin, der ihm sein Dichtertalent verliehen hatte, an seiner Seite
wusste, wenn er auch anfänglich einen Augenblick an der Treue und
Hilfe dieses unergründlichen Gottes gezweifelt hatte. Nun muss man
bedenken, dass seine Anklage nicht nur eine rührende Klage über
menschliches Leid war, sondern dass sie auch nach den religiösen
Auffassungen dieser Zeit beschwörende Kraft hatte. Dieses Gedicht
übte eine magische Wirkung aus. Durch sie wurde Egils Ehre gerettet, und konnte er gelassen der Zukunft entgegengehen.

In der ersten Strophe spricht Egil es aus, wieviel Mühe es ihn
kostet, dieses Lied über Bodvar zu dichten.

"Schwer fällt's mir,
Die Zunge zu rühren,
Nicht vermag ich
Worte zu erwägen,

---

[6] A. G. van Hamel, *IJslands Odingeloof* (Mededeelingen der Kon. Ak. van
Wetenschappen, Afd. Letterkunde, Deel 82, serie B., 1936).

Leicht ist es nicht,
Um Odins Gabe
Tief aus der Seele
Verborgenen Falten zu holen."

Denn er fühlt sich beraubt und einsam. Sein Geschlecht neigt sich dem Ende zu, sagt er in der vierten Strophe. In diesem Zusammenhang berichtet er den Heimgang seines Vaters und seiner Mutter derer "Andenken aus der Erinnerung kommt, geschmückt mit der Blätterkrone schöner Worte." In der dreizehnten Strophe kommt es ihm zum Bewusstsein, dass er auch keinen Bruder mehr hat, der ihm im Kampfgetümmel zu Seite stehen könnte. Schon früher hatte er ausserdem einen vortrefflichen Sohn durch Krankheit verloren, wie aus der zwanzigsten Strophe zu ersehen ist. Jetzt wurde ihm der Lieblingssohn Bodvar geraubt.

"In ihm war
Was ich genau wusste,
Anlage zu
Einem Edelen Mann..."
Immer folgte er
Seines Vaters Rat,
Wenn auch alle Menschen
Etwas anderes sagten..."

Glühender Hass gegen die Meeresgottheiten flammt auf in seinem Gemüt:

"Vieles hat
Ran mir geraubt,
Ausgeplündert bin ich
Von dem, was ich liebte.
Das Meer hat zerbrochen
Das Band meines Geschlechts,
Nahm mir weg
Die starke Stütze."

Den Meeresgöttern fühlt er sich nicht gewachsen:

"Könnte ich mit dem Schwert
Meinen Sohn rächen
Weiss, dass es
Mit Aegir aus wäre,
Gegen Aegir würde ich
Zum Kampf ziehen
Und gegen Aegirs
Hartherzige Gemahlin."

Aber nun steht er machtlos da. "Vor aller Augen liegt offen die
Machtlosigkeit des alten Mannes." Merkwürdig ist, dass Egil den
Eindruck erweckt, als habe er gar keinen Sohn mehr. Er schweigt über
seinen Sohn Torstein, der in einem nachfolgenden Kapitel der Saga
als ein besonders hübscher blonder Jüngling beschrieben wird mit
klugen und friedfertigen Anlagen. Es wird aber hinzugefügt, dass
Egil wenig Zuneigung zu Torstein hegte, und dass Torstein nicht
an seinem Vater, aber umso mehr an seiner Mutter hing. Das war
sicher der Grund dafür, weshalb Torstein in dem Gedicht nicht
vorkommt.

Um die Einsamkeit, in die sich Egil nach dem Tod seines Sohnes
Bodvar gestossen fühlte, ganz empfinden zu können, muss man bedenken, dass diese Wikinger in einer Männergemeinschaft ihres Clans
oder von Freunden lebten und sich darin stark fühlten. Egil klagt, dass
nun niemand mehr da ist, auf den er sich verlassen kann. Unter Menschen fühlt er sich nicht mehr zuhause, und seine Einstellung zu
ihrer Zuverlässigkeit ist ziemlich pessimistisch. In der achtzehnten
Strophe sagt er:

"Unter Menschen
Bin ich nicht mehr zuhause,
Selbst, wenn Eintracht
Zu herrschen scheint..."

Und in der fünfzehnten Strophe erklärt er:

"Zu finden ist schwer
Unter den Zweigen
Des Odinbaumes
Ein Mann, dem man vertrauen kann..."

Mitten in seinem Leid und in seiner Verlassenheit erinnert er sich
aber Odins, des Gottes, mit dem er sich stets stark verbunden gefühlt
hat:

"Ich stand mich gut
Mit der Gere Fürsten, 7
Und ich vertraute
In Treue ihm,
Bis der Freund
Des frohen Sieges
Mich trog und mir
Die Treue brach.

---

7 "Kenning" für Odin.

Nicht huldige ich
Der Götter Herrn
Viles Bruder 8
Mit willigem Gemüt..."

Diese Strophen verlangen einige Erklärungen. Um die Worte Egils zu begreifen, muss man wissen, dass die Beziehung des Germanen zu seinen Göttern gekennzeichnet werden kann als das Verhältnis eines Freundes zum Freund. Die Germanen schauten die Gottheit, die sie unter vielen Göttern besonders verehrten, als einen Freund an, dem sie voll vertrauen konnten. Vor allem Thor und Freyr tragen das Epitheton "fulltrúi" = "dem man vollständig vertraut". Doch vergass man nicht, dass der geliebte Gott auch zürnen konnte. 9 Auch Egil erklärt, dass er gut mit Odin stand, bis der Gott ihm untreu wurde. Nun ist ja Odin nicht nur eine komplizierte Göttergestalt, man weiss auch, dass er sich der Untreue schuldig machen konnte und seine Verehrer bisweilen im Stich liess. 10 Darum geht es Egil bei seiner Klage in den zitierten Strophen. Er hat keine Lust mehr, Odin zu huldigen. Es ist nicht klar, in welcher Hinsicht sich Odin gegenüber Egil als treulos erwiesen hat. Vielleicht wirft Egil ihm vor, dass er Bodvars Tod durch Ertrinken nicht verhindert hat. Wie dem auch sei, Egil hat Odins Unergründlichkeit kennengelernt und erfahren, dass ein Gott anders handelt als menschliche ethische Normen es vorschreiben.

Egil will sich aber nicht als undankbar erweisen. Odin, der Zauberer, der Besitzer des Metes, des kostbaren Trankes, der die Inspiration verleiht zur Dichtkunst und darum unter allen Göttern derjenige, mit dem Egil sich ganz besonders verbunden fühlt, er hat ihm eine wunderbare Gabe verliehen:

"...Dennoch hat Mims Freund 11
Mir gegeben
Einen Schadenersatz,
Den hoch ich schätze.

Eine edele Gabe
Schenkte mir Odin:
Den lauteren Antrieb
Zur schönen Dichtkunst..."

---

8 Idem.
9 J. de Vries, *Altgermanische Religionsgeschichte*, II, § 568.
10 *Op. cit.*, II, § 379, 404, 410.
11 Mim oder Mimir ist ein weiser Riese, dessen Rat Odin in schwierigen Fallen einholte.

Dank seiner poetischen Begabung ist Egil imstande, ein Gedicht zu verfassen, das nicht nur seinen Kummer darstellt, sondern das auch die Anklage enthält gegen die Götter, die ihn seines Sohnes beraubten. Seine Ehre ist gerettet, nachdem er seinen ertrunkenen Sohn besungen und die Meeresgötter für schuldig erklärt hat. Das mächtige, beschwörende Dichterwort hat Egil gesunden lassen von seinem Schmerz, seinem Gefühl der Machtlosigkeit und seinem Zweifel am Sinn seines Lebens. Darum kann er gelassen seinem Lebensende entgegensehen.

> "Mein Ende ist nahe.
> Draussen auf der Landzunge
> Steht die blasse Schwester
> Des Wolfen. [12]
> Dennoch werde ich froh
> Mit gutem Willen
> Und sorgenfreiem Gemüt
> Hel [12] erwarten."

Egil, der sich nach dem Tode Bodvars in sein Schlafgemach zurückzieht und sterben will, erweckt den Eindruck, eine Hiobsfigur zu sein. Ein Vergleich mit dem biblischen Hiob kann neues Licht werfen sowohl auf Egil, als auch auf Hiob, seinen alttestamentlichen Vorläufer. Da die Leser, wie ich annehmen kann, völlig vertraut sind mit dem Inhalt des Buches Hiob, kann die Gegenüberstellung der beiden Gestalten sofort beginnen.

Literarisch gesehen lassen sich die Erzählung von Bodvars Tod, von Egils Reaktion darauf und sein Gedicht von 25 kurzzeiligen Strophen kaum mit dem umfangreichen Buch Hiob vergleichen. Dieses besteht, abgesehen von der Einleitung in Prosa, in der berichtet wird, wie Gott dem Teufel die Erlaubnis gab, die Frömmigkeit Hiobs auf die Probe zu stellen und ihn mit einem Unheil nach dem anderen zu treffen, und der Schluss, ebenfalls in Prosa, der das glückliche Lebensende des Hiob beschreibt, hauptsächlich aus langen Streitgesprächen in poetischer Form der Freunde Hiobs, Elifaz, Bildad, Zofar und schliesslich Elihu und aus den Antworten, die Hiob darauf gibt. Das Buch Hiob zeigt deutlich eine komplizierte Struktur: es behandelt nicht nur den Sinn des Leides eines Frommen, in diesem Fall Hiobs, sondern es enthält auch einen Schatz von religiöser Weisheit, die nicht direkt eine Lösung erteilt für das Problem in der Streitfrage.

---

12 Hel, die Schwester des Wolfes Fenris, ist die Göttin der Unterwelt.

Diese Strukturunterschiede zwischen den beiden literarischen Produkten können wir weiterhin unbesprochen lassen. Es geht um die Gestalten von Hiob und Egil.

Es ist evident, das sie in einem unterschiedlichen religiösen Klima stehen. Hiob bekennt den Glauben Israels, der auf der Offenbarung an Gottesmänner beruht. Egil hat sein Vertrauen in Odin, den mächtigsten der germanischen Götter, gesetzt, Götter, die Personifikationen sind von kosmischen, numinosen Erscheinungen. Man ist geneigt, hier die Gegenüberstellung von Monotheismus und Polytheismus herauszufinden. Doch ist diese Antithese irreführend. Denn im Buch Hiob kommen verschiedene Namen für Gott und deshalb verschiedene Gottesvorstellungen vor, z.B. ausser Jahwe auch noch El, Eloach und Sjaddai. [13] Das sind unverkennbare Aspekte der göttlichen Gestalt. Es bleibt eine offene Frage, wie sie zusammenhängen. Andererseits hat Egil ein Verhältnis zu Odin, das man mit einem term. techn. Monolatrie nennt, d. h. unter allen Göttern, deren Bestehen Egil nominal anerkennt, hat er sein Vertrauen ganz und gar auf Odin gesetzt.

Es besteht auch ein deutlicher Unterschied in der Problemstellung. Nach der Auffassung der Freunde Hiobs beweist sein Unglück eine verborgene Sünde. Gott ist nämlich gerecht. Er bestraft die Bösen und belohnt die Guten. Hiob dagegen bezeugt hartnäckig seine Unschuld und verlangt von Gott leidenschaftlich einen Aufschluss für den Sinn seines Leidens. Egil ringt um den Sinn seines Leides und ist niedergedrückt von der Schmach, dass er sich nicht rächen kann. Seine seelische Not ist nicht weniger tragisch und ergreifend als die Hiobs.

Beide müssen sie erfahren, dass Gottes Walten über menschlich-sittliche Normen erhaben ist, und dass der Mensch nicht eingeweiht ist in Gottes Weisheit, eine Einsicht die bündig ausgedrückt wird in den Schlusssätzen des Lobgesanges auf die Weisheit (Hiob 28), wo Gott zum Menschen sagt: "Siehe, die Furcht des Herrn, das ist Weisheit; und meiden das Böse, das ist Verstand". [14]

Sowohl Hiob als auch Egil führen "das Streitgespräch des Menschen mit seinem Gott", von dem M. A. Beek eine Anzahl merkwür-

---

[13] B. D. Eerdmans, *The Religion of Israel*, 1947, S. 285; Martin Buber, *Het Geloof van Israel* (G. van der Leeuw en C. J. Bleeker, *De Godsdiensten der Wereld*, II, 1956, S. 269 ff.).

[14] W. B. Kristensen, *Het boven-ethische in de godsdienst* (Symbool en werkelijkheid, 1962, S. 36 ff.); Rudolf Otto, *Das Heilige*, 1936, S. 97.

diger alttestamentlicher Beispiele behandelt hat. [15] Zwar antworten Aegir, Ran und Odin nicht auf die Anklage und Klage Egils, aber der Tendenz nach ist sein Gedicht doch ein Streitgespräch mit den angeführten Göttern. Und was Hiob betrifft, so möge er als ein sehr frommer Mann dargestellt werden, es fehlt ihm aber nicht an Offenheit, Gott zur Verantwortung zu rufen. Und er schweigt erst dann, als der Herr Seine Majestät und Schöpferweisheit beschrieben hat und Hiob hat fühlen lassen, dass er als sterbliche Kreatur Gottes Absichten nicht durchschauen kann. In jedem Fall zeigt die anfängliche Haltung sowohl die des Egil als die des Hiob, dass Glaube an Gott nicht identisch ist mit Demut und Unterwerfung, sondern dass der religiöse Mensch sich ab und zu die Freiheit nimmt, seinen Protest gegen Gottes Handeln laut werden zu lassen.

Zum Schluss schicken sich beide in ihr Los. Hiob nimmt sein nicht verstandenes Leid auf sich. Egil gewinnt das Vertrauen zu Odin wieder in dem Bewusstsein, dass seine durch Odin ihm geschenkte Dichtergabe ein Pflaster auf die brennende Wunde ist.

Hiob, der seines Besitzes und seiner Kinder beraubt sich in die Asche setzt, bedeckt mit argen Schwären und sich mit einer Tonscherbe kratzt, hat immer stark die Phantasie bewegt. Es ist das Bild des Menschen, der auf dem Tiefpunkt seines Elends seine menschliche Nichtigkeit erfährt. Egil ist aber tatsächlich menschlicher in seinem Schmerz. Denn Hiob lässt keine einzige Klage hören über die sieben Söhne und drei Töchter, die er in einem einzigen Augenblick verloren hatte, als das Haus, in dem sie eine festliche Mahlzeit hielten, einstürzte. Seine Antworten auf die Ausführungen seiner Freunde kreisen immer um das Problem seiner eigenen Unschuld. Von einem frommen und liebenden Vater hätte man ein Wort der Trauer über den Verlust seiner Kinder erwartet. Egils Gedicht ist verschiedenen Motiven entsprossen. Tonangebend aber ist bei ihm der Schmerz über den Verlust des Sohnes, den er von ganzem Herzen geliebt hatte.

In der tiefsten Not des Lebens ist Hiob frömmer, Egil aber menschlicher.

---

[15] M. A. Beek, *Het twistgesprek van de mens met zijn God. Een paragraaf uit de godsdienst van Israel*, 1946.

HUGO GROTIUS IM RAHMEN DER RELIGION SEINER ZEIT *

"De Dordtsche Zegepraal"! (Der Triumph von Dordrecht). So betitelt Professor dr. L. Knappert das Kapitel seiner "Geschiedenis der Nederlandsche Hervormde Kerk gedurende de 16e en 17e eeuw" (Geschichte der Niederländischen Reformierten Kirche im 16. und 17. Jahrhundert), in dem er ein anschauliches Bild entwirft von der berühmten "Dordrechter Synode der Niederländischen Reformierten Kirche", die in den Jahren 1618 und 1619 stattfand. In der Tat triumphierten die Calvinisten, die Gegner der Arminianer (Remonstranten), über ihre Widersacher, sowohl in der Kirche, als auch in der Staatsverwaltung. Aber man darf nicht fragen, wie teuer dieser Sieg erkauft wurde. Von einem theologischen Gespräch auf wissenschaftlichem Niveau war in Dordrecht keine Rede. Ja selbst ein ordentlicher Prozess fand nicht statt. Es stand eben von vornherein fest, dass die angeklagten Remonstranten verurteilt werden mussten. Zum Schluss machte Bogerman, der Vorsitzende, dem anstrengenden Wortwechsel mit den halsstarrigen Remonstranten ein Ende mit den Worten: "dimittimini, exite, exite!" Will man auf den Ton des leidenschaftlichen Zornes hören, in dem Bogerman sprach, so muss man das anscheinend so feierliche Latein wiedergeben mit einem Ausruf wie etwa dem folgenden in der Sprache unserer Zeit: "Schert euch weg, raus mit euch, verschwindet!" In einem unbeherrschten Moment hatte Bogerman die Entscheidung, die alle wollten, vorangetrieben. Während der Nachsynode wurden etwa 200 Pfarrer abgesetzt und 80 verbannt. Dieser Kirchenkampf fand zugleich seinen Widerhall im Staatsleben. Am 29. August 1618 wurden Oldenbarneveldt, Grotius und Hogerbeets verhaftet. Am 13. Mai 1619 folgte Oldenbarnevelts Enthauptung. Die Calvinisten verstanden, sich durchzusetzen. Aber es war ein Pyrrhussieg! Die calvinistisch-reformierte Kirche, die zur offiziellen Kirche ernannt wurde, bekam trotzdem das Joch der Obrigkeit weiter zu spüren. Sie war keineswegs frei in ihrer Beweglichkeit. Politische Kommissare wohnten kirchlichen Versammlungen bei. Die Obrigkeit behielt weitgehend ein Mitbestimmungsrecht bei den Ernennungen der Pfarrer. In unseren Ohren hat die Bezeichnung "Sieg

---

* Veröffentlicht in *Theologie en Praktijk*, 32, jrg., nummer 3, Herfst 1972.

von Dordrecht" einen ironischen Klang. Man sollte eher von einer Dordrechter Tragödie sprechen! Vondel nannte die Verurteilung Oldenbarnevelts "des Landes Trauerspiel". Es gab recht viele Opfer dieses tragischen Geschehens. Das am meisten bekannte ist zweifellos Hugo Grotius (de Groot). Zwar befand er sich nicht bei den zu Dordrecht verurteilten Remonstranten, doch hatte er die Folgen dieses Umbruchs in Staat und Kirche in einer lebenslänglichen Verbannung zu tragen. Ein hartes Los für einen Mann, der Holland liebhatte, und der mit seinen genialen Gaben seinem Land unschätzbare Dienste hätte erweisen können.

Eine Tragödie! Die klassische Darstellung von dem tragischen Schicksal eines Menschen haben die griechischen Tragödiendichter gegeben. Sie führen Personen auf die Bühne, die, obwohl von besten Vorhaben durchdrungen, unschuldig-schuldig werden, weil sie in einen unauflöslichen Konflikt verwickelt werden. Nur in einem heldischen Untergang können sie ihren Seelenadel bewahren. Ödipus, berühmt und geehrt, weil er Theben von einem Monstrum, der Sphinx befreite, musste zu der bestürzenden Einsicht kommen, dass er eine untilgbare Schuld auf sich geladen hatte: ohne sein Wissen hatte er seinen Vater getötet und seine Mutter geheiratet. Gebrochen durch Wahnsinn, stach er sich die Augen aus. In einem tiefsinnigen Artikel "Der Reflex des Antik-Tragischen in dem Modern-Tragischen" hat Sören Kierkegaard nachgewiesen, dass die moderne Tragödie sich dadurch von der antiken unterscheidet, dass in dem modernen Trauerspiel der Held durch eigene ethische Schuld fällt, während in der antiken Tragödie "die Handlung zwischen Handeln und Leiden hin und her schwebt".

Hugo Grotius ist zweifelsohne eine tragische Figur. Bis zu einem gewissen Mass hat er sein trauriges Los sich selbst zu verdanken, d. h. bestimmten, für ihn bezeichnenden Charaktereigenschaften, und der Tatsache, dass in gewissen Punkten seine Einsicht getrübt war. Tatsächlich aber ist er gegen seine Absicht hineingezogen worden in das wirbelnde Ringen von Elementen und Mächten, die sogar völlig lautere Menschen zu gefährlichen Ketzern und Staatsfeinden machen können und sie manchmal gänzlich zermalmen.

Um Hugo Grotius als religiösen Denker im Rahmen seiner Zeit den richtigen Platz zu weisen und ihn verstehen zu können, muss man sein Augenmerk einen Augenblick richten auf die verschiedenen Momente, die dieses Trauerspiel beherrschen. Absichtlich halte ich diesen Exkurs kurz. Wie verlockend es auch sein möge, allerhand Nebenwege zu betreten, die zu interessanten Nebenaspekten unseres Themas führen, so verlangen es jedoch der verfügbare Raum und die Beschränkung auf eine bestimmte Erörterung, dass wir dem königlichen Weg folgen, der uns zu einer tieferen Einsicht in das Problem führt, das in dem Titel dieser Einführung enthalten ist.

Es trifft zu, dass in dem verwickelten Spiel der Kräfte, in das Grotius hineingezogen wurde, die politischen Faktoren leicht herausgefunden werden können. Grotius hatte sich auf die Seite von Oldenbarnevelt gestellt, des Landesadvokaten, der glaubte, das gute Recht der Stände von Holland gegen das der Generalstände der Republik verteidigen zu müssen. Aus "de verhoren en andere bescheiden betreffende het rechtsgeding van Hugo de Groot" ("den Verhören und Urkunden, die den Prozess des Hugo Grotius betreffen"), die R. Fruin im Jahr 1871 zur Wiederherstellung der Ehre von Grotius gesammelt und herausgegeben hat, geht denn auch hervor, dass Grotius bei den fünf Verhören (examinaties), denen man ihn unterworfen hat, vor allem über sein politisches Verhalten ausgefragt worden ist. In den "verklaringen van de sententien" (Erläuterungen zu den Sentenzen) gegen Oldenbarnevelt und die Seinen wurde ihnen sogar das *crimen laesae maiestatis*, die Majstätsbeleidigung, vorgeworfen. Doch legte offenbar die "Irrgläubigkeit" von Grotius bei seiner Verurteilung ein nicht unbedeutendes Gewicht in die Wagschale. Denn in den Sentenzen (sententien) steht zu lesen, dass er "sich unterstanden habe, zu der Verwirrung der religiösen Lage beizutragen und die Kirche Gottes stark zu belasten und zu betrüben". (hij hem onderstaen heeft den stant van de religie te helpen perturberen ende de kercke Godes grootelycx te beswaren ende bedroeven)

An zweiter Stelle sollte man sich klar darüber sein, dass auf der Synode von Dordrecht die Entscheidung über zwei gewichtige Streitpunkte erkämpft wurde, nämlich die Frage nach der Kirchenordnung und die Frage nach dem bindenden Charakter des Bekenntnisses. Bei dem ersten Punkt ging es um das Verhältnis von Kirche und Staat. Wir sagten schon, dass die Reformierte (Hervormde) Kirche wohl eine privilegierte Stellung im Hinblick auf die "Dissenters" zu erobern wusste, im übrigen aber die Einmischung der Obrigkeit ertragen musste. Was nun den zweiten Punkt angeht: die calvinistischen Eiferer wollten die Unterzeichnung der sogenannten "dreifachen Formulierung der Einigkeit" (Drie Formulieren van Enigheit) d. h. das Niederländischen Glaubensbekenntnisses, des Heidelberger Katechismus und der Dordrechter Lehrsätze gegen die Remonstranten für

Pfarrer und Angehörige der Obrigkeit zur Pflicht machen. Sie haben dieses Verlangen nicht durchsetzen können, zumindest nicht, was die "Regenten" betrifft. Trotzdem wurde de Groot von beiden Fragen betroffen. Er musste dazu Stellung beziehen, wobei seine freieren Auffassungen rasch auffallen mussten.

Als dritter Punkt muss man auch auf die Art und den Charakter de Groot's selbst Rücksicht nehmen, wenn man diese Tragödie verstehen will. Leider gibt es über die Struktur seiner Persönlichkeit keine einzige Abhandlung. Eine solche würde eine spannende Untersuchung ergeben. Niemand darf sich einbilden, dass er die Tiefe eines solch einmaligen Geistes, wie Grotius einer war, ergründen könnte. Doch bekommt man aus der Literatur wohl ein Bild seiner Persönlichkeit: ein genial begabtes Kind, ein sehr frühreifer Knabe, ein Mann mit einem glänzenden Intellekt ,dadurch selbstbewusst und auch ein wenig eitel — trotz seiner christlichen Demut —; eine Eitelkeit, die ihn leider bewog, sich in die Politik zu begeben, während er doch an der Universität eine glänzende Karrière hätte durchlaufen können — aber dann hat er sich vermutlich keinen sehr grossen Ruhm erworben —; ein Mann, der während des Prozesses einen unsicheren, ängstlichen Eindruck macht, sodass Prinz Maurits ihn einen wetterwendischen Menschen nennen konnte, der andererseits charakterfest und stolz ist, so dass er sich nach der Flucht aus Loevestein weigert, um Gnade zu bitten, sondern erhobenen Hauptes nach Holland zurückkehren will, unterstützt von seiner beherzten Frau Maria von Reigersberch, die felsenfest an die Integrität Oldenbarnevelts und ihres Hugo glaubt; ein eigensinniger Mann, der sich nicht davon abbringen lässt, seine Schrift "Verantwoording van de wettelijke Regering van Hollandt en Westvrieslandt" (162) (Verantwoording der gesetzlichen Regierung von Holland und Westfriesland) zu publizieren, wodurch er sich die Rückkehr in die Republik für immer versperrte; ein Mensch, der die Kunst "human relations" auszunutzen, nicht verstand und die Einstellung "Paris ist eine Messe wert" ("Paris vaut bien une messe") ablehnte, ein etwas naiver Idealist, unverstanden von seinen Zeitgenossen, nicht passend in seine Zeit, aber doch ein grosser Mann mit weitschauendem Blick, der Ideen in Umlauf brachte, von denen spätere Generationen kaum die Reichweite begriffen.

Diese drei Faktoren: der politische Machtkampf, die kirchlichen Auseinandersetzungen über die Kirchenordnungen und das Glaubensbekenntnis, dazu die Eigenart von de Groot's Charakter haben weitgehend sein Leben und sein Schicksal bestimmt und es zu einer Tragödie gemacht. Sie bilden auch den Hintergrund zu dem Bild von Grotius als religiösem Denker, das, so hoffe ich, allmählich sprechende Farben bekommen wird.

Um es aber richtig zu sehen, muss man wissen, dass Grotius keinesfalls ein Einzelgänger in seiner Zeit war. Abgesehen von den Remonstranten (Arminianern), mit denen er sympathisierte, doch denen er sich nicht anschloss, hatte er eine ganze Reihe von ihm geistig Nahestehenden. Die Calvinisten hatten zwar durch ihren Dordrechter Sieg allen in ihren Augen Irrgläubigen den Mund verboten — wenn auch nur für begrenzte Zeit —, aber sie konnten nicht verhindern, dass das Bild der religiösen Niederlande zu diesen Zeiten viel farbenprächtiger war, als man aus ihrer starren Theologie entnehmen konnte. Da waren vor allem die Täufer, die nicht in den Staatsdienst treten konnten, weil sie sich weigerten, Waffen zu tragen und den Eid zu leisten. Sie bildeten die "Stillen im Lande", die das Ideal von makellosen Gemeinden anstrebten. Ferner fand man in den Niederlanden dieser Zeit Spiritualisten von allerlei Schlag, Männer und Frauen des "Inneren Wortes" und des "Freien Geistes", die das innerliche Geistzeugnis höher stellten als das Wort der Heiligen Schrift. Man darf auch die Jünger des grossen Erasmus nicht vergessen, die an ein humanistisches Christentum glaubten. Unter den "Regenten" traf man viele Freigeister an, die es mit der Lehre nicht so genau nahmen. Ja, im Wesentlichen ging der Streit, von dem die Dordrechter Synode den Höhepunkt bildete, zwischen zwei Parteien vor sich, die man die "Geschmeidigen" (rekkelijken) und die "Präzisen" (preciesen) genannt hat. Die Erstgenannten, die "rekkelijken", gehörten zu dem typisch niederländischen nationalen reformierten Protestantismus, dessen Kennzeichen Knappert in wenigen theologischen Ausdrucksformen folgendermassen beschreibt: dieser Protestantismus war erasmianisch-sakramental, biblisch-evangelisch, soteriologisch, tolerant und antikonfessionell. Was den zuletzt genannten Charakterzug betrifft, nämlich den Antikonfessionalismus, ist es interessant zu wissen, dass die ältesten Reformierten in Holland kein Glaubensbekenntnis besassen und es auch nicht haben wollten. Ihre Gefühle wurden wiedergegeben durch Jan van Marnix, der 1556 sagte, dass "die Calvinisten sich an kein Glaubensbekenntnis halten wollten, sondern nur an die Lehre der Evangelien". Für alle streitenden Parteien aber galt die Bibel als Erkenntnisquelle der Wahrheit, auch für die Remonstranten, und im Prinzip auch für Grotius. Nur auf die Auslegung kam es an. In dieser Hinsicht setzt Grotius die Gedankengänge der genannten ersten Reformierten in unserem Land fort mit seinem sehr oft wiederholten Ausspruch, dass Dogmen überflüssig und schädlich seien. Grotius fühlte sich von Calvin abgestossen. Er hegte auch keine übermässige Sympathie für Luther, wusste sich aber geistesverwandt mit dem gelehrten und milden Melanchthon. Es sollte mich nicht verwundern, wenn er auch unter dem Einfluss Heinrich Bullingers (1504-1575) gestanden hätte. Dieser Schweizer Theologe legte den Nachdruck auf die Bedeutung des Bundes, den Gott mit seinem Volk geschlossen hat. In diesen Bund, der durch die Taufe bestätigt wird, sind alle Menschen eingeschlossen, sodass keine Prädestination ihnen Gottes Gnade rauben kann. Grotius hat ein Glaubensbekenntnis im Dialog mit seiner Tochter Cornelia verfasst, das ausgeht und zum Schluss zurückkehrt zum Sinn der Taufe, und das deshalb auf dem unausgesprochenen Gedanken von dem Bund zwischen Gott und den Menschen beruht.

Diese letzte Bemerkung führt direkt zu einer Charakterisierung des theologischen Standpunkts der scharfen Gegner von Grotius, der "Präzisen", der Calvinisten. Überall bekannt ist der Streit zwischen Arminianern und Gomaristen um das Dogma von der Prädestination. Durch einige Zitate kann man sofort deutlich machen, wie die Calvinisten dieser Zeit die Auserwählung oder Vorherbestimmung verstanden. Die Dordrechter Lehrsätze sagen: "Diese Wahl ist ein unabänderlicher Entschluss Gottes, durch den Er vor der Erschaffung der Welt eine bestimmte Anzahl Menschen, nicht besser oder würdiger als andere, wohl aber im gemeinsamen Elend mit anderen sich befindend, aus dem ganzen Menschengeschlecht, aus der ursprünglichen Sündlosigkeit durch eigene Schuld der Sünde und dem Verderben verfallen, nach dem freien Wohlgefallen Seines Willens zur Seligkeit, allein aus Gnade, auserkoren hat in Christus usw." Diese Formulierung geht zurück auf die Conzeption Calvins, der in Kapitel 21 seines dritten Buches der "Institutie of onderwijzing in den Christelijken godsdienst" (Lehrplan zum Unterricht im christlichen Glauben) mit grosser Bestimmtheit, aber mit der nötigen Zurückhaltung diesen schwierigen Gegenstand behandelt. Calvin war davon überzeugt, dass Gott durch die endgültige Erwählung einige zur Seligkeit, andere zur Verdamnis führt. Die Vorherbestimmung zum Heil fliesst aus Gottes unverdiente Barmherzigkeit. Im übrigen ist es ein Geheimnis aus Gottes Weisheit, das man nicht leichtfertig und verwegen, sondern nur im Licht Seines Wortes in der Bibel forschen soll. Calvin weist weiter darauf hin, dass die Auserkorenen auf Grund von zwei Zeichen Sicherheit über ihre Auserwählung erlangen können, einmal durch ihre Berufung, zum anderen durch ihre Rechtfertigung dank Gottes Gnade. Bei Calvin ist trotz seines Hanges, alles zu dogmatisieren, hier noch deutlich spürbar, dass die Prädestination ein religiöses Ideogramm ist, d. h. ein verkürztes Begriffszeichen oder Symbol für ein bestimmtes Verhältnis von Gott und Mensch. Wie Rudolf Otto in seinem berühmten Buch "Das Heilige" dargelegt hat, kann man die religiöse Bedeutung der Prädestination nur dann verstehen, wenn man begreift, dass dieses Dogma sich ableitet aus dem überwältigendem Eindruck, den Gottes Heiligkeit auf den gläubigen Menschen macht. Wenn der Mensch trotz seiner Schuld und Verworfenheit doch noch die Sicherheit gerettet zu werden erlangt, so ist das ausschliesslich Gottes gnädiger Auserwählung zu danken. Die Prädestination braucht den freien Willen gar nicht auszuschliessen. Kraft ihrer empfangenen Berufung sind Calvinisten oft sehr tatkräftige Menschen gewesen. Den Stein des Anstosses bildete immer wieder die sogenannte *praedestinatio ambigua*, die doppelte Auserwählung zum Heil und zum Verderben, das *decretum horribile*, der "entsetzliche Beschluss" Gottes. Auch die Remonstranten waren, wie in der "Remonstratie" zu lesen steht, überzeugt von Gottes gnädiger Auserwählung. Doch legten sie den Nachdruck darauf, dass Christus für alle gestorben ist, und dass deshalb niemand in Prinzip für vom Heil ausgeschlossen gehalten werden darf.

Damit konnte Grotius völlig übereinstimmen. Diese Auffassung passte ganz zu dem Geist, in dem erzogen war, und mit der Struktur seines Denkens. Sein Vater war ein liberal eingestellter Mann, dem die Einheit der Christen sehr am Herzen lag. Seine Mutter stammte aus katholischem Haus. In ihrem bekannten historischen Roman "Vaderland in de verte" (Vaterland in der Ferne) beschreibt Annie Romein-Verschoor ,dass sie das Weihwasserbecken und das Kruzifix in ihrem Schlafzimmer behielt. Grotius ist niemals Protestant in dem engen Sinn des Wortes gewesen, eher Anhänger eines allgemeinen Christentums. Er fühlte sich als Glied einer echten Katholischen, das heisst allumfassenden Kiche.

Welches sind nun die Quellen für unsere Kenntnis von de Groots religiösem und theologischem Standpunkt? Wer das hervorragende Buch von Dr. A. H. Haentjens über "Hugo de Groot als religiöser Denker" ("Hugo de Groot als godsdienstig denker" 1946) gelesen hat, spürt, dass man, wenn man so will, seinen Stoff aus einer Vielheit von grösseren und kleineren Schriften herausholen kann. Wir beschränken uns hier auf die Angabe von drei Werken, die direkt auf den Gegenstand unserer Untersuchung Bezug haben:

(1) "Beweijs van de ware godsdienst" (Beweis für die echte Religion), auf Loevestein in Reimform für Seeleute geschrieben, um sie fähig zu machen, in fernen Ländern vom Christentum zu zeugen, ein Werk, das de Groot später in lateinischer Sprache in Prosa niederschrieb unter dem Titel *De veritate religionis Christianae* (1640), versehen mit einem mächtigen Apparat von Anmerkungen.

(2) das bereits erwähnte Glaubensbekenntnis im Dialog mit Cornelia, und

(3) die Reihe *Annotationes* (Scholien), Anmerkungen zu den Büchern des Alten und Neuen Testamentes. Diese drei Schriften sind nur ein kleines Bruchstück aus seinem mächtigen Werk, doch weisen sie stellvertretend für die anderen Schriften seine Haltung und seinen Standpunkt klar nach.

Jeder, der sich in die Schriften von Grotius vertieft, ist betroffen von seiner ungeheuren Belesenheit. Das gilt auch für die theologische Literatur. Mit grösser Sicherheit zitiert er nicht nur aus den klassischen Autoren, aus den Kirchenvätern, aus dem Talmud sondern auch aus den Werken ganz verschiedener jüdischer Schriftsteller. Auf mich als Religionswissenschaftler hat es Eindruck gemacht, dass Grotius in seiner Arbeit *De veritate religionis christianae* die besten Kenntnisse besitzt von den zu seiner Zeit erreichbaren Quellen über antike Religion. Doch darf man andererseits diesen Aufwand an Gelehrsamkeit nicht allzu hoch veranschlagen. Dr. J. Meyer hat in einer Studie über die "Remonstrantie nopende de ordre dye in de landen van Hollandt en Westvrieslandt dyent gestelt op de Joden" (Remonstrantion in Bezug auf die Disziplin, die in den Gebieten von Holland und Westfriesland den Juden auferlegt werden muss) angedeutet, dass seine Kenntnis der rabbinischen Literatur weniger tief geht, als seine sehr zahlreichen Zitate es vermuten lassen. Doch besass Grotius für seine Zeit und als Nichttheologe von Beruf eine so grosse Kenntnis von allen Fragen und eine solch originelle Einsicht in alle Probleme des Christlichen Glaubens, dass er eine ganz spezielle Position einnahm im religiösen Denken seiner Zeit. Ich kann hier nicht die Struktur seiner Glaubensposition ausführlich darlegen, sondern muss mich darauf beschränken, die Hauptsachen anzudeuten.

Mit einem terminus technicus kann man Grotius kennzeichnen als rationalistischen Supranaturalisten, d. h. er akzeptierte die supranaturale Gotteserkenntnis, die in der Bibel gegeben ist, aber schrieb der Vernunft gleiche Bedeutung zu. So fand er einerseits die Kriterien für den Wahrheitsgehalt des Christentums in der Person Jesu Christi, in seinen Wundern und in seiner Auferstehung. Andererseits macht er in seinen *Annotationes*, die kein durchgehender Kommentar, sondern Anmerkungen zu den biblischen Büchern sind, allerhand kritische Bemerkungen zum Text. So zweifelte er an der Echtheit bestimmter Schriften, reihte die biblischen Bücher in die Liste der antiken und klassischen Literatur ein, sodass er mit vollem Recht als Vorläufer für das spätere historisch-kritische Bibelstudium gelten kann. Er nahm auch an, dass alle Völker das Bewusstsein, dass es etwas Göttliches gibt, besitzen. Obwohl er doch den christlichen Glauben in der reformierten Verkündigung (Hervormde Kerk) als die seligmachende Wahrheit bejahte, ist er zu seine Zeit einer der Wenigen, die die Werte anderer Religionen und Konfessionen anerkannten, d. h. der Heidnischen Religion mit grosser Zurückhaltung, des Islam bis zu einem gewissen Grad, des Judentums unbedingt und auch der römisch-katholischen Kirche, die er nicht mit dem päpstlichen System gleichsetzte. Im Hinblick auf die beiden letztgenannten Punkte musste er es sich gefallen lassen, Juden-freund und Papist gescholten zu werden. Mit Recht zeigt Dr. W. Roldanus in ihrer kritischen Studie über "Hugo de Groot's Bewijs van de ware Godsdienst" (Hugo de Groots Beweis für die echte Religion), dass die Hl. Schrift für ihn als Norm galt und der Consensus der Kirche als Richtschnur. Diese Übereinstimmung der Kirche mit der Schrift fand er in der Kirche der ersten Christenheit. Daher kommen seine vielen Zitate aus den Kirchenvätern. Von da aus ist auch seine Achtung vor der kirchlichen Tradition zu begreifen. Sein Streben richtete sich darauf, die Einheit der Urchristlichen Kirche, die er idealisierte wiederherzustellen. Er glaubte in der Tat, dass die verschiedenen Konfessionen, zwar mit einiger Mühe, aber doch zu einer Übereinstimmung gelangen könnten. Solange diese Einheit noch nicht erreicht sei, wie sie in der Urchristlichen Kirche nach seiner Meinung geherrscht habe, sieht er sein Ideal am besten verkörpert in der Anglikanischen Kirche. Man begreift, dass sein Eintreten für kirchliche Einheit und seine Arbeit für den Frieden unter den Völkern in eine Richtung gingen. In mancher Hinsicht stritt er mehr als Jurist, denn als Theologe. In dieses Gedankenklima passt auch seine schon erwähnte Abkehr von jeder Dogmatik, die er für schädlich hielt für Frömmigkeit und Gemeindeleben. In seinen Werken befasst er sich nicht besonders mit der Trinität und der Zwei-Naturen-Lehre Christi, doch stritt er ab, dass sie selbstverständliche Wahrheiten seien. Ein scharfer Gegner aber war er von der Prädestination.

Bei einer so komplizierten Gestalt wie de Groot überrascht es nicht, dass er auch als Autor widerstreitende Züge aufweist. Durchweg ist seine Beweisführung ernst zu nehmen und erfüllt von Achtung gegenüber der tiefen Wahrheit, die er verkünden will. Bisweilen aber ertappt man ihn auf einer platten Ausdrucksweise über erhabene religiöse Dinge. Manchmal macht er den Eindruck eines echten Intellectualisten. Eins aber steht fest: an seiner tiefen und aufrechten Frömmigkeit darf nicht gezweifelt werden. Sie spricht zum Beispiel aus dem Brief vom 21. September 1618 an seine Frau, in dem er schreibt: "Gott, der Allmächtige, der uns bisher und noch immer so gnadenvoll beigestanden hat, wird nicht aufhören, uns zu helfen und uns zu trösten".

Am reinsten klingt dieser Ton an in seinem herrlichen Abendgebet:

O Schöpfer, Du, von Tag und Nacht!
Die Dunkelheit, durch Dich gebracht,
bedeckt das All mit ihrem Schatten.
Verdecke nun zu dieser Stund'
durch deine Gnade ohne Grund
auch unser Aller schlimme Taten.

Der Feind auf uns gerichtet ist
mit viel Gewalt und schlauer List;
O Hirte, bleib bei Deinen Schafen!
Von böser Lust befrei uns Du,
Damit getrost wir voller Ruh
In Deiner Hut nun dürfen schlafen.

Wir legen an Dein Vaterherz
Gefangene, Kranke voller Schmerz,
jetzt lindere Du ihr bittres Leid.
Wenn unser Lauf vollendet ist,
Durch Deinen Frieden nach der Frist
Erfreu uns dann in Ewigkeit!

GUSTAF FRÖDING: EIN SCHWEDISCHER DICHTER ZWISCHEN DEN ZEITEN

In einer kurzen Erzählung, mit dem Titel "En saga om en saga" (Eine Sage über eine Sage) hat Selma Lagerlöf enthüllt, wie sie dazu kam ihr berühmtes Buch "Gösta Berlings Saga" zu schreiben. Wie der Titel dieser Erzählung vermuten lässt, hat sie ihren Mitteilungen die Form der Sage gegeben. Sie erzählt: es gab in Värmland — wo ihr Elternhaus Mårbacka stand — eine Sage, die erzählt werden wollte. Aber nirgends fand sie Gehör, weil die Leute mit wichtigeren Sachen beschäftigt waren. Nur ein kränkliches Mädchen auf Mårbacka, das nicht mit den anderen Kindern spielen konnte und deshalb viel las, lauschte begierig auf das, was die Sage zu erzählen hatte. Dennoch dauerte es viele Jahre, bevor Selma Lagerlöf sich entschloss der Sage eine literarische Form zu geben. Zwei Ereignisse gaben dazu Veranlassung. Erstens eine Erfahrung in Stockholm, wo sie zu Lehrerin ausgebildet werden sollte. Nachdem sie einige Monate in dem grauen Häusermeer gewohnt hatte, überfiel sie plötzlich auf dem Heimweg von einer Vorlesung über schwedische Literaturgeschichte wie eine Offenbarung der Gedanke, dass die Figuren in der Sage aus Värmland, die in einem so schroffen Gegensatz zu ihrer prosaischen Umgebung standen, sich ebenso gut zu einer literarischen Behandlung eigneten wie die Personen in den Werken von Bellman und Runeberg, die das Thema der Vorlesung gebildet hatten. Den eigentlichen Anstoss zum Schreiben ihres Buches gab ein Ereignis, das sie tief traf, nämlich die Auktion von Mårbacka. Sie bekam auf einmal das Gefühl, dass die Sagenwelt, die sie so liebte, auf immer verschwand. Da entschloss sie sich diese alte, schöne Welt der Kavaliere zu retten.

Selma Lagerlöf steht nicht allein in diesem Bestreben, Kulturwerte, die mit Vernichtung bedroht werden, literarisch zu erhalten. Es gibt eine Anzahl von schwedischen Verfassern und Dichtern aus dieser Zeit, die von demselben Verlangen, eine schöne, sterbende Kultur literarisch auferstehen zu lassen, bewogen wurden, weil die Sachlichkeit des aufsteigenden Industrialismus die Oberhand über den von ihnen geliebten poetischen und gemütlichen Lebensstil bekam.

In gewissem Sinn gehört auch Gustaf Fröding zu dieser Gruppe. Auch er stammt aus Värmland, aus der Provinz, die so viele grosse Geister hervorgebracht hat. Er war der geniale Repräsentant einer ver-

schwindenden Aristokratie, und zu gleicher Zeit ist er einer von
Schwedens grössten Lyrikern. Ausserhalb Schweden ist er kaum bekannt, weil seine Gedichte nicht übersetzt sind und sich wegen ihrer
originellen Ausdrucksweise schwer übertragen lassen. In Schweden
ist er aufs Neue entdeckt worden und geniesst, besonders bei dem
jüngeren Geschlecht, eine erhöhte Popularität. Davon zeugt zum Beispiel ein Buch von Stellan Ahlström und Göran Algård, mit dem Titel
"Frödings Värmland" (1967), in dem schöne Bilder, begleitet von
Zitaten aus Frödings Dichtwerk, den ganzen Reiz der Umgebung des
Dichters heraufbeschwören. Weiter hat H. Olssen in zwei Studien die
Persönlichkeit, das Leben und die Dichtung Frödings in tiefschürfen-
der Weise behandelt. [1] Ausserdem hat er die Erinnerungen von Cecilia,
der Schwester des Dichters, herausgegeben und mit Erläuterungen
versehen. [2]

Selbstredend erhebt dieser Artikel nicht den Anspruch, den sehr
eingehenden Untersuchungen von Olsson noch irgend welche literarischen oder literaturhistorischen Besonderkeiten beizufügen. Mein
Gesichtspunkt ist ein anderer. Fröding, den ich als Dichter sehr be-
wundere, hat mich als Religionshistoriker fassiniert, weil er meiner
Ansicht nach ein Dichter zwischen den Zeiten ist. Es sei mir erlaubt
diese Vorstellung näher auszuführen.

Der Ausdruck "zwischen den Zeiten", der in der theologischen
Terminologie Bürgerrecht erworben hat, besitzt eine polyvalente Bedeutung. Man kann dabei sowohl an ein Leben auf der Bruchlinie von
Vergangenheit und Gegenwart als auch an ein Stehen auf der Grenze
von einer verschwindenden alten Periode und der hereinbrechenden
neuen Zeit denken. In beiden Fällen lebt man in der Spannung zwischen Ideal und Wirklichkeit. Man blickt mit Heimweh zurück in
die goldene Zeit der Vergangenheit, oder man schaut mit Verlangen
aus nach dem Heilsstaat der Zukunft. Dies bedeutet, dass der Mensch
der zwischen den Zeiten lebt, Gefühle und Erwartungen hegt, die eine
religiöse Spannkraft besitzen. Die Religionsgeschichte kennt deswegen
viele Beispiele von den genannten zwei Arten von Verhaltensweisen.
Einerseits gibt es religiöse Menschen, die sich an einer mythischen Vergangenheit, die massgebend für sie ist, orientieren; andererseits leben
Gläubige aus eschatologischen Erwartungen, mit denen sie das kom-
mende Reich Gottes erwarten. Dabei ist es merkwürdig, dass die

---

[1] H. Olsson, *Fröding, Ett diktarporträtt*, 1967; *Vinlövsranka och hagtornkrans, En bok om Fröding*, 1970.
[2] Cecilia Fröding, ... *Och minns du Ali Baba? Cecilia berättar om sin bror*, 1960, med inledning och kommentarer av H. Olsson.

mythische Urzeit und die eschatologische Endzeit auf einander bezogen sind und den Platz mit einander wechseln können.

Gustaf Fröding stand meiner Ansicht nach in diesem Gedanken-klima. Hinter seinem tragischen Lebenslauf und seinen Gedichten, wie verschieden von Tonart sie auch sein mögen, liegt das Gefühl des Dichters, dass er in seiner Zeit, in seiner Umgebung nicht zu Hause war, liegt ein Sehnen nach einer vergangenen, idealisierten, schönen Lebensart.

In sozialer Hinsicht gehörte Fröding zur Kategorie der Versager. Seine Lebensführung war nicht-bürgerlich, was deutlich aus der Tatsache hervorgeht, dass er mit Geld nicht umgehen konnte und verschwenderisch lebte. Er litt an psychischen Defekten und war heftigen Leidenschaften unterworfen. Dennoch besatz er das Vermögen der scharfen Selbstkritik, die er sowohl an sich selbst, als auch an seinem Dichtwerk übte. Trotz seiner Verirrungen hatte er ein klares sittliches Bewustsein, und seine religiöse Überzeugung hat er niemals ganz verloren. In gewisser Hinsicht war er skrupulös. Auf Grund seiner Herkunft lebte er wie ein "grand seigneur", aber durch seine Lebenserfahrungen hatte er Mitgefühl mit den "underdog", und er lehnte sich gegen seinen eigenen Stand auf. Seine unvergängliche Bedeutung steckt in seiner genialen dichterischen Begabung, die immer wieder durch sein Ängste und durch Zustände geistiger Finsternis durchbrach. Er war ein Mann, der schwer gelitten hat und der sich manchmal erniedrigt fühlte. Dennoch wusste er seine Würde als Mensch und als Dichter zu behaupten. Eine kurze Skizze seines Milieus und seines Werdeganges möge dienen zur Erhärtung der gegebenen Charakteristik. Zur gleicher Zeit können die kurzen biographischen Notizen den Hintergrund bilden zu einigen Zitaten aus seinem Dichtwerk.

Gustafs Grossvater, Jan Fröding, ein Fabrikant und erfolgreicher Geschäftsmann, scheint eine kräftige und harmonische Persönlichkeit gewesen zu sein. Er war verheiratet mit Gustava Branzell, die aus einem Geschlecht mit pathologischen Einschlag stammte. Diese Grossmutter wohnte auf Gunnerud, wo Gustaf öfters zu Gast war. Sie hatte eine sonderbare Tageseinteilung, forderte von ihrer Umgebung vollkommene Ruhe und war herzlos gegen ihre Schwiegertochter, Gustafs Mutter. Gustafs Vater Ferdinand hatte keine Veranlagung für Geschäfte, war viel auf Reisen und vernachlässigte seine geschäftlichen Interessen. Er war musikalisch begabt und zeigte anfänglich keine abnormalen Geisteszüge. 1865 erkältete er sich, bekam eine Gehirnhautentzündung, geriet in eine geistige Krisis und suchte sein Heil in

einer überspannten Religiosität. Die Mitglieder seiner Familie sahen
dies mit missliebigen Augen an. Es gelang ihnen schliesslich, ihn zur
Seite zu schieben.

Es ist schwierig, sich ein genaues Bild von Gustafs Verhältnis zu
seinem Vater zu bilden. Zweifellos hegte er Respekt für ihn. Andererseits gab es eine Kluft zwischen Vater und Sohn, so dass sie einander
nicht verstanden. Das geht hervor aus dem Gedicht "En främmande
man" (Ein fremder Mensch), das sich offensichtlich auf den Vater
bezieht und in dem der Dichter sagt: [3]

> „Er war nicht jung, denn das Haar war ergraut,
> Sein Rücken war gekrummt von etwas Schwerem, das er getragen
>   hatte ...
> Seine Lippen waren fest zusammengeschlossen
> wie wegen eines Kummers, eines Vergehens in der Vergangenheit ...
> Ich wollte ihm näher treten, ich wollte tragen
> das schwere Gewicht, das sein Leben elend gemacht hatte,
> aber er wich aus, wenn ich ihm näher kam,
> und zwischen uns lag die Kluft, weit wie immer."

Seine Mutter Emilia war die Tochter des Bischofs Agard. Dieser
Mann war eine sehr begabte Persönlichkeit, hübsch, intelligent, zu
vielen Ämtern fähig, zuerst ein gefeierter Professor, später ein aktiver
Bischof, ein Mann mit abenteuerlichen Neigungen, der sich auch in
finanzielle Schwierigkeiten verwickeln konnte. Emilia war bei Gustafs
Geburt nervenkrank, blieb lange Zeit in Dänemark zur Erholung und
duldete Gustaf nach ihrer Heimkehr schwer in ihrer Nähe. Dennoch
bewunderte der Dichter seine Mutter sehr, hielt später mit ihr Wettkämpfe in der Dichtkunst und schrieb ihr in seinem Gedicht "Dolores
di Colibrados" eine Herkunft aus südlichen Ländern zu. In diesem
Gedicht sagt er, dass er sie nicht in ihrer Jugendblüte gekannt habe,
sondern erst in der Herbstzeit ihres Lebens:

> „Aber die Augen sah ich, die nicht verlieren konnten
> ihren letzten erbitterten liebenden Funken
> des Feuers, das früher so herrisch war;
> und der Stolz lag wie eine säumende Erinnerung
> an der Sonne, welche die Zinne ihres Stammschlosses beleuchtet hatte
> auf der gelbbleichen, gerunzelten Stirn"

Die wichtigsten Daten von Frödings Lebensgeschichte mögen kurz
erwähnt werden. Er wuchs auf als ein lieber und scheinbar etwas

---

[3] Um das schwedische Original so gut wie möglich wiederzugeben ist hier und in
den folgenden Zitaten von einer Versform in Reimen abgesehen worden und wird
nur eine genaue Übersetzung geboten.

indolenter Junge neben vier tatkräftigen Schwestern, von denen Cecilia ihm am nächsten stand. Er hat ihr gehuldigt in dem Gedicht "Sagoförtäljerskan" (Die Sagenerzählerin), das so anfängt:

„Und erinnerst du dich an Ali Baba
und erinnerst du dich an unsere grüne
Syringegrotte, schattenreich und kühl,
wo schwarz wie die schöne
Sultanin von Saba
und mit braunen Augen und schlank und schmal
du sassest und erzähltest
eine Sage, die du wähltest
aus der Anzahl der Tausend und Einer Nacht"

Dieses Gedicht lässt verstehen in welcher Sphäre die Kinder Fröding lebten. Sie wohnten auf dem einsamen Herrenhaus Byn neben dem lieblichen See Alster. Sie waren nicht wie andere Kinder, das heisst, sie trieben keine wilden Spiele. In den lichten Nächten konnten sie Wölfe herumschleichen sehen. Auf einer Landzunge hauste eine Familie von Landstreichern, deren Männer Raufbolde und Pferdediebe waren, während den Weibern Zauberkunst zugeschrieben wurde. Diese romantische Umgebung befruchtete die Phantasie dieser Kinder, besonders Gustafs, so dass er immer etwas Weltfremdes behielt und sich seiner Umgebung nie ganz ampassen konnte.

Nach der Mittelschule ging Gustaf nach Uppsala, wo er Geschichte studieren wollte mit dem Ehrgeiz, ein Gelehrter zu werden. Aber er lebte als "bohémien" und verschwendete einen Teil des Familiekapitals. Im Jahr 1881 starb sein Vater. Darauf zog die Familie Fröding einige Zeit mehrmals um. Gustaf trat als Journalist in den Dienst einer radikalen Zeitung in Karlstad, in welcher er zusammen mit Gesinnungsgenossen Aufsehen erregende Artikel schrieb. 1887 verschied seine Mutter. Gustaf, der wie aus dem Vorhergehenden klar wurde, erblich belastet war, erkrankte seelisch. 1889/90 weilte er zur Erholung in Görlitz in Deutschland und nachher in einem Sanatorium in Norwegen. Später wohnte er längerer Zeit zusammen mit Cecilia.

Diese Schwester verdient Aufmerksamkeit. Sie war eine hochstehende Frau, das normalste der Kinder Fröding. Obgleich sie aristokratisch erzogen war, zeigte sie später eine demokratische Gesinnung. Sie besass Malerbegabung, aber sie gab ihre Kunst auf, da sie meinte, nicht genügend Gestaltungskraft zu besitzen. In Paris verlobte sie sich in 1880/1 mit einem deutschen Juristen, aber sie löste die Verlobung, weil sie fand, dass ihre Familie erblich zu stark belastet war. Sie war die erste, die die Genialität ihres Bruders erkannte. Sie schützte ihn,

GUSTAF FRÖDING

half ihm hochherzig mit Geld und versuchte, ihn aus allen seinen
Verirrungen zu lotsen, in einer liebenvollen Weise, aber mit einem
nüchtern Blick: sie kannte seine Schwächen: Alkoholismus und ero-
tische Veranlagung. Ihr Schlussurteil über ihn lautete: seine seelische
Krankheit hat seinen Charakter nicht verletzt, ihn nur ohnmächtig
gemacht im Kampfe gegen das Böse und hat sein Leben zerstört. So
verhielt sie sich kritisch, aber auch verstehend und seine Poesie wür-
digend.

Am Ende seines Lebens wurde Fröding von Schwester Signe Trotzig
gepflegt. Sie widmete ihm grosse Fürsorge, führte ihn mit Takt und
hat ihn zu seinem letzten dichterischen Werk aufgemuntert. Sie war
seine Pflegerin, sein Freundin, seine Geliebte. Im Jahr 1911 ist er
gestorben.

Das Auftreten von Gustaf unter seinen Kameraden wird verschieden beschrieben. Einige Zeugen nennen ihn fröhlich, unterhaltend und
sehr intelligent. Andere Leute sagen, dass er unbeholfen war und gern
die Rolle eines "Dummen August" spielte. Als solcher hat er sich
auch später öfters aufgeführt, besonders in der Liebe. Davon zeugt
gewiss ein Gedicht über den Clown Clopopisky, der in einem Nacht-
café bei einem Whisky die Tragödie seines Lebens erzählt: er war
verliebt in die schöne Kunstreiterin Teresa, die einen stürmischen
Beifall erntete, der besiegelt wurde durch ein Bukett des russischen
Botschafters. Der Clown, der danach auftreten musste, war wild vor
Neid. Seine Clownskunststücke wollten nicht gelingen. Das Publikum
wurde ungeduldig. Der Clown, der wütend wurde, schimpfte auf das
Publikum, das ihn darauf mit allerhand Gegenständen beschoss und
ihn bewusstlos schlug. Mit einem blutenden Kopf kam er auf einem
Haufen Stroh in dem Stall wieder zum Bewusstsein. Da hörte er leichte
Schritte. Gewiss war es Teresa: sie würde ihn versorgen und trösten.
Aber da hörte er auf einmal die Stimme des Botschafters, der für den
nächsten Freitag eine Verabredung mit Teresa fest machte. Darauf
verbarg er sein Gesicht ins Stroh: er schrie, er lachte, er weinte und
er stand auf seinem Kopf, und er krähte, denn das war die "pièce de
résistance" seines Zirkusauftritts. Nachdem der Clown dieses erzählt
hatte, nahm er einen Schluck und zeigte seine beste Kapriole: er stand
auf seinem Kopf, er weinte und er krähte. Dieses Gedicht offenbart
Frödings grandiose Gabe, sein Missgeschick poetisch zu verarbeiten, in
völliger Ehrlichkeit, mit Humor und dabei dennoch seine Würde be-
haltend.

Dabei soll man bedenken, dass der Gang der Ereignisse, die Fröding miterlebte, sein persönliches Gefühl von Frustration verschärfte. Er lebte in einer Zeit, in der die leicht lebende Aristokratie im Verschwinden war, um einer nüchteren Industriegesellschaft Platz zu machen. Er erlebte den Konflikt zwischen dem neuen sachlichen Ethos und dem Lebensstil seiner Familie in dem er gewisse Untergangstendenzen spürte. Denn er war sich seiner erblichen Belastung bewusst und hat oft darüber nachgedacht. So lebte er zwischen den Zeiten. Dieses Los erzeugte ein tragisches Lebensgefühl. Das äusserte sich in den Begriff der vergeudeten Erbschaft: seine Familie war beschenkt mit reichen Gaben, aber hatte ihre Talente verdorben. Aus diesem tragischen Bewusstsein und aus dem Heimweh nach einer verschwindenden Kultur sind die schönsten Gedichte geboren.

Man würde sich irren, wenn man dächte, dass Fröding die Figur des verkannten Genies spielte. Er hatte eine feine Nase für das Komische im Leben und hat gewisse Typen mit köstlichem Humor geschildert. So gibt es ein kurzes Gedicht über die Überlegungen eines neuvermählten Paares. Beide sind Hungerleider, aber das verhindert nicht dass sie plantasieren, wie sie er haben werden: sie wollen Land für Gemüse, ein Schwein, Hühner, Wurst aufs Brot, weiche Betten und schönes Geschirr haben. Schliesslich sagt der Mann: "Maja, wo kriegen wir das alles her; ich bin zu arm, und du bist zu faul; ich zehre von der Armenverwaltung und du von der Staatsunterstützung". Amüsant ist auch das Dilemma eines Mädchens, das wählen muss zwischen dem jungen Menschen, dem sie das Heiratsversprechen gegeben hat, aber der an der anderen Seite des atlantischen Ozeans ist, und einem alten, kahlköpfigen Witwer. Sie weiss, dass der Witwer geizig ist und hart zu seinen Untergebenen, und dass er viele Kinder hat. Sie fühlt, dass es Sünde ist, das Heiratsversprechen zu brechen. Aber als sie an den reichen Besitz des Witwers denkt, kommt sie schnell zu ihrem Entschluss: "... ich glaube, ich nehme ihn, wenn er auch achtzehn Kinder hätte". Als Beispiel dieses Genres nehme ich das folgende Gedicht über "Lelle Karl-Johan" (der kleine Karl-Johan):

„Der kleine Karl-Johan
er, sollt Ihr glauben, er
artet sicher mir nach und ist sanfmütig wie ein Lamm,
vernünftig ist er auch,
er schneuzt sich in die Faust
schon wie sein Vater, Karl-Johan, komm näher!

Sieh, wie er sich verbeugt,
sieh, wie es sich kräuselt
reizend auf dem Scheitel bei dem kleinen Karl-Johan,

ja freilich mögt Ihr glauben,
er weiss sich schon in Gesellschaft zu benehmen,
die Bibelgeschichten kennt er
so gut wie irgend ein
Propst oder Pfarrer oder Küster sie kennt.
Sage mir, Karl-Johan, was versprach Moses
-trockne die Nase ab-
Israels Kindern, die er aus Gosen führte,
wenn man seinen Vater und seine Mutter ehren will?
Nun werdet Ihr hören, dass der kleine Karl-Johan
sicher Pfarrer wird, wenn Karl-Johan gross ist"
— sprach die Mutter zu Karl-Johan
und liebkoste ihren Karl-Johan,
aber denkt Euch, könnt Ihr glauben, er
fluchte
unverschämt und böshaft: „ich schere mich zum Teufel nicht um die
    Mutter!"

Neben seinem Dichtwerk verfasste Fröding als Journalist viele
Artikel, in denen er die grossen Probleme der Gesellschaft kritisch
behandelte. Er hatte tiefes Mitleid mit den Leuten der unteren Klasse.
In gewissem Sinn hatte er sich mit dem "establishment" entzweit.
Diese Haltung äusserte sich zum Beispiel deutlich in seiner Weigerung,
dem "landshövding" Malmborg zu begegnen. Dieser hatte den Wunsch
zu verstehen gegeben, dass er den berühmten Dichter auf einem Ball
in 1891 kennen lernen möchte. Fröding lehnte dies ab. Er wollte
solidarisch mit seinen Kameraden von der Zeitung bleiben. In dieser
Zeitung hatte man Karlstad oft beschimpft als Brackstad oder
Brackopolis (bracka = Philister) und man bekämpfte den Brackiotis-
mus. Diese Stimmung ist auch spürbar in einigen Gedichten, am deutlichsten, wenn er in beissend sarkastischem Ton "die gute alte Zeit"
verhöhnt. Das Gedicht schildert die Arbeit in einer Eisengiesserei, wo
die Hammer dröhnen, die Funken sprühen, eine erstickende Hitze
herrscht, die Männer in Staub und Hitze arbeiten müssen und deshalb
klagen:

„Sie geben uns Schlacken für Erz
und einen Fusstritt für unsere Schinderei und Quälerei,
sie dreschen uns wie Stroh
und löschen uns danach mit Alkohol.

Der Hunger hat meine Alte geknickt,
meine Tochter ist die Hure der Fabrik,
der Verwalter selber ist verwandt
mit dem ersten Kinde der Ärmsten."

Das ist eine aufrührerische Sprache, ein Beweis dass Fröding bei all seiner Liebe zu den alten Zeiten, dennoch ein offenes Auge hatte für deren Schattenseiten. Trotzdem war er keine entwurzelte Persönlichkeit. Obgleich er oft zwischen Glauben und Unglauben hin und herschwankte, ist er niemals Atheist geworden, sondern er hat seine religiöse Überzeugung behalten. Die religiöse Sphäre des Elternhauses wirkte offensichtlich nach. Sein Interesse für die Bibel zeigt sich in einer Reihe schöner Lieder, in denen er biblische Gedanken poetisch gestaltet hat.

Der grosse Echec seines Lebens war, dass er keine ebenbürtige Lebensgefährtin hat finden können. Die Freuden und Enttäuschungen der Liebe spiegeln sich in seinen Gedichten wider. Seine Erfahrungen mit Frauen haben ihn inspiriert zu wunderschönen Gedichten in verschiedener Tonart: humoristisch, spielerisch, tiefsinnig, bitter, wehmüttig. Bitter klingt "en kärleksvisa" (ein Liebeslied):

„Ich kaufte meine Liebe mit Geld,
für mich gab es nichts anderes zu haben,
singet schön, ihr verstimmten Saiten,
singet trotzdem schön von der Liebe.

Der Traum, der niemals Wahrheit wurde,
als Traum war er schön zu bekommen,
für denjenigen, der aus Eden verbannt ist,
ist Eden dennoch ein Eden.''

und eine poetisch-zarte Saite schlägt er an in dem Gedicht über Ingalill:

„Inga lilla, Ingalill, sing ein Lied für mich
Meine Seele ist so einsam auf dem Lebensweg...''

und in dem Gedicht "En vårfästmö" (om jag hade haft någon) (eine Frühlingsverlobte (wenn ich eine gehabt hätte)), in dem das unstillbare Verlangen nach der unerreichbaren reinen Liebe widerhallt.

In seinen jungen Jahren verliebte Fröding sich in Hildegard Alstermark, ein Mädchen von Stande, die Tochter eines Gutsbesitzers, eine verlegene, träumerische Person. Der Gegensatz zwischen ihnen war zu gross, denn er war ein radikaler Journalist ohne Position in der Gesellschaft, der nichts zu bieten hatte. Seine Liebe fand keine Erwiderung. Das Mädchen beantwortete schliesslich seine Liebesbriefe nicht mehr. Für Gustaf war das ein grosser Schlag. Er hatte gehofft sich durch diese Liebschaft zu rehabilitieren. Jetzt fühlte er sich ausgeschlossen.

Nachdem dieser Kontakt abgebrochen war, fing er eine Korrespondenz mit Ida Cederroth, der Witwe eines verstorbenen Neffen, an. Sie hatte ihm ihre Sympathie und ihr Mitleid gezeigt. Auch diese Freundschaft endete nicht mit einer Heirat.

Merkwürdig ist, dass Fröding in März 1891 eine Heiratsannonze beantwortete und ein Jahr lang einen Briefwechsel unterhielt mit einem achtzehnjährigen Mädchen aus Göteborg, das sich Astrid Carlesohn nannte. Er ist ihm nie begegnet und es hat seine Identität nie enthüllt. Was Fröding nie gewusst hat, ist, dass sich hinter Astrid eine Gruppe von Mädchen verbarg, die diesen Briefaustausch zum Spass gemacht hatten. Sie waren jedenfalls kulturell so hoch gebildet, dass sie flott und geistreich mit dem Dichter korrespondieren konnten. Spätere literaturhistorischen Forschungen haben herausgebracht, dass die Hauptperson Ellen Bjerre war, die sich 1892 mit einem Leutnant der Marine verheiratete.

Ein besonderes Kapitel bildet seine Liebe für Vivi, eine Servierin in der Freimaurerloge, die er regelmässig besuchte. Sie war ein nettes Mädchen, etwas schwermüttig, mit einem gewissen Charme, obgleich sie keine "beauty" war. Vor ihr machte er seinem Herzen Luft. Sie wusste seine Lust zum Trinken taktvoll zu beschränken. Sie war die einzige, für die er reine Zuneigung fühlte, so dass er sie heiraten wollte, was sie vorsichtig ablehnte. Der Verkehr mit diesem Mädchen hat ihn inspiriert zu einigen von seinen schönsten Gedichten. Von Vivi ist nur ein Brief erhalten. Was einen darin trifft, ist der reservierte, schwesterlich-herzliche Ton und ihre aufrichtige Bekümmernis um seine Gesundheit.

Zusammenfassend kann man sagen, dass Fröding ein merkwürdiger Mensch war, der ein eigenartiges Leben geführt hat. In gesellschaftlicher Hinsicht war er ein Versager, ein fremdartiger "bohémien", ein Mann, der sein Leben nicht in seiner Gewalt hatte, psychisch labil und seinen Leidenschaften unterlegen. Dennoch war er ein Mensch, der kämpfte, um die Würde eines Menschen zu behalten, ein Mann mit einem reinen Verständnis für den Wert ethischer und religiöser Normen, ein Mensch mit einem Mitgefühl für das Leiden der Bedrückten. Als Dichter war er ein Genie und ein Zeuge von der Macht des schöpferischen Geistes, der auf eine unerklärliche Weise durch allerhand Hindernisse und menschliche Schwächen hindurchbrechen kann. Er lebte zwischen den Zeiten, auf der Grenze von zwei Welten. Deshalb ist er unser Zeitgenosse, weil auch wir auf der Bruchlinie der Zeiten stehen. Und zur gleichen Zeit ist er, obgleich er sich dessen nie bewusst gewesen ist, ein Beispiel des "homo religiosus".

DEMCO 38-297